THREE CENTRAL ISSUES IN
CONTEMPORARY
DISPENSATIONALISM

THREE CENTRAL ISSUES IN
CONTEMPORARY
DISPENSATIONALISM

*A Comparison of Traditional
and Progressive Views*

Herbert W. Bateman IV
GENERAL EDITOR

Grand Rapids, MI 49501

Three Central Issues in Contemporary Dispensationalism: A Comparison of Traditional and Progressive Views

© 1999 by Herbert W. Bateman IV

Published by Kregel Publications, a division of Kregel, Inc., P.O. Box 2607, Grand Rapids, MI 49501.

For more information about Kregel Publications, visit our web site: www.kregel.com

Library of Congress Cataloging-in-Publication Data
Bateman, Herbert W. IV
  Three central issues in contemporary dispensationalism: a comparison of traditional and progressive views / by Herbert W. Bateman IV.
    p.   cm.
  Includes bibliographical references and indexes.
  1. Dispensationalism. I. Bateman, Herbert W.
BT157.T47   1999   230'.0463—dc21   99-43085
                                               CIP
ISBN 0-8254-2062-8

Printed in the United States of America

1 2 3 4 5 / 03 02 01 00 99

To my wife,
Cindy Ann Bateman,
my devoted partner and faithful supporter of my various
ambitions in ministry for Jesus Christ.

Linda KERR - 310-575-9803

Contents

Part Three: Israel and the Church

Conclusion

Foreword

Three Central Issues in Contemporary Dispensationalism contains a series of essays written by faculty members of Dallas Theological Seminary. These men represent varying perspectives within the dispensational heritage. The introductory and concluding chapters are written by a Dallas Theological Seminary graduate as well. Navigating through three dispensational institutions—Philadelphia College of Bible, Dallas Theological Seminary, and Grace Theological Seminary—Herb Bateman is conscious of the continuing discussions both within dispensationalism and the dialogue of dispensationalists with nondispensationalists in the larger evangelical community. All the contributors to this book would affirm a pretribulational and premillennial perspective on eschatology as well as the more fundamental commitment to the inspiration and inerrancy of the Scriptures. The three central issues in contemporary dispensationalism discussed in this volume include hermeneutics, the biblical covenants, and the relationship between Israel and the church.

   The *hermeneutical* dialogue between Elliott Johnson and Darrell Bock focuses on the use of the Old Testament by the New Testament writers. Darrell Bock asserts that the New Testament writers expanded the meaning of the Old Testament promises as they applied its fulfillment to a wider audience than just Israel. Elliott Johnson would argue that a much tighter correspondence of meaning exists between the words used in the Old Testament and

9

the words used in the New Testament. While there may be a fuller realization, it will not be in a different sense than what was intended by the Old Testament author.

The dialogue between Johnson and Bock, as it relates to *biblical covenants*, centers on whether or not all of the unilateral (unconditional) covenants find an initial fulfillment in the ministry of Jesus and His dealings in the church before they find their consummation in the earthly millennial kingdom. Questions that are debated between Johnson and Bock include: How much fulfillment took place with these promises as a result of the First Coming? How much is reserved for the Second Coming? Is there a partial fulfillment to any of the covenants? Do all covenants work the same way, with initial fulfillment at the First Coming and with consummated fulfillment at the Second? How is the nature of fulfillment tied to the central role that Jesus, as the Messiah, plays in each of the covenants? Was Jesus born as the Davidic King or has His regal role not yet commenced? If there are initial fulfillments of the Abrahamic Covenant and the New Covenant that the church experiences, is there initial fulfillment with the Davidic Covenant as well? And if so, how much?

Both Bock and Burns, as representatives of progressive dispensationalism, affirm a future for the nation of Israel in which the Old Testament promises will be ultimately fulfilled. Whatever initial fulfillments take place as a result of the First Coming, they do so because they are linked to Jesus Christ who, as the Messiah, has a ministry in the church before He rules on planet earth in the earthly kingdom. Neither advocates a replacement theology in which the church takes the place of Israel, though each sees an initial fulfillment, with varying provisions, of all three unilateral covenants being extended to the church prior to the consummate fulfillment with the nation of Israel and the rest of the world in the future kingdom.

In the discussion of *the relationship between Israel and the church*, Lanier Burns argues that "The Jewish Christian remnant in the church is God's assurance of the future fulfillment of His promises to Israel, and that the present age of the church is vitally connected to God's past promises and His future fulfillments." His argument is derived from an exposition of Romans 11 with its olive tree metaphor. The natural and the unnatural branches show diversity, while the single root and tree support the continuity of God's soteriological and eschatological plan.

Stanley Toussaint follows Alva McClain in advocating an "intercalation" view of the kingdom. Such a view would not see either a mystery form in the present age or an inaugurated fulfillment in the church prior to a consummating fulfillment with Israel and the earthly kingdom. The present age between the two advents of Christ is a parenthesis, or an "intercalation," prior to the establishment of the messianic kingdom. For Toussaint, all references to kingdom in the New Testament have the earthly millennial kingdom in view.

Questions in the dynamic dialogue between Lanier Burns and Stan Toussaint include the following: Does the kingdom refer to the millennium in each of its New Testament uses? Is the kingdom only to be defined in terms of realm, ruler, and governmental authority, or is it more complex? Does the first advent fulfill the father/son expectation in Davidic promises passages from the Old Testament? Does contingency undermine divine certainty, or is the offer of the kingdom a legitimate offer and its postponement a legitimate consequence of rejection? How does one distinguish between analogical and typological fulfillment as the Old Testament is used in New Testament epistles? Does initial fulfillment in promises relating to Jesus necessarily assume initial fulfillment in promises relating to the kingdom over which He will rule?

There are variations among different authors of traditional dispensationalism and the same among authors who would classify themselves as progressive dispensationalists. While all of these presentations represent a sample, they are by no means representative of the entirety of either school of thought within the broader movement of dispensational theology. One of the greatest benefits of this book is that it demonstrates that these issues do not result in a dogmatic monolith but rather leave room for a dynamic discussion among biblical students and scholars who seek to handle the Word of God carefully and continue to evaluate their findings under its authority. The dialogue represented here is straightforward yet congenial—a good model for any healthy theological debate.

I commend this volume to all who are seeking a deeper understanding of the debatable issues related to dispensational theology.

The mutual respect these theologians have for one another is a reminder of Philipp Melanchthon's wise and balanced advice, "In essentials, unity. In non-essentials, liberty. In all things, charity."

CHARLES R. SWINDOLL
President, Dallas Theological Seminary

Preface

This book is a collection of frank but congenial presentations and responses between traditional and progressive dispensationalists concerning three central issues frequently discussed among today's dispensationalists: (1) hermeneutics; (2) the Abrahamic, Davidic, and new covenants; and (3) Israel and the church. Many works by traditional and progressive dispensationalists exist on these issues, but *Three Central Issues in Contemporary Dispensationalism* is the first of its kind, in that it brings together such discussions in a single volume. The presenters are longstanding dispensationalists who have made meaningful contributions to dispensational discussions.

The work begins with an introduction highlighting what I refer to as transitional stages in dispensationalism. Although the discussions at times echo previous presentations by Robert Saucy and Craig Blaising, they are based primarily upon my observations while a student at Philadelphia College of Bible (1978–1982) and then Dallas Theological Seminary (1983–1993). Part one presents issues in hermeneutical methods characteristic of both traditional and progressive dispensationalists' approaches to Scripture. Part two exemplifies the outworking of those hermeneutics as applied to the Abrahamic, Davidic, and new covenants. The benefit of parts one and two is that Elliott Johnson and Darrell Bock bring a working knowledge to the discussion. For several years now, they have amicably team-taught their respective hermeneutical approaches to students at DTS, exemplified those approaches in Scripture, and

13

discussed the contrasts in their methods. Part three examines the issue concerning Israel and the church from both traditional and progressive perspectives. Although they approach the issue from different perspectives, Stanley Toussaint and Lanier Burns demonstrate that one's beliefs about the uniqueness of the church and the future for national Israel continue to be foundational for distinguishing a dispensationalist from a nondispensationalist.

I would like to thank Darrell Bock, Elliott Johnson, Lanier Burns, and Stanley Toussaint for their willingness to participate in this project, for their sacrifice of time to help make this project become a reality, and for the spirit in which they interact with one another as fellow dispensationalists. Absent are acrimonious and uncharitable comments that question commitment to a common dispensational heritage. I also would like to thank Paulette Sauders and Dan O'Hare, who carefully read through completed portions of the manuscript. Finally, I would like to thank my former teachers (John Cawood, John McGahey, Renald Showers, Darrell Bock, Craig Blaising, and Elliott Johnson), who stirred me to pursue, investigate, and expand my understanding of dispensationalism.

The book, however, would never exist were it not for my wife, who has been my faithful partner for twenty years. Dispensational discussions, such as those in this work, have been the focus of many breakfast and dinner conversations in our home. I am grateful for a wife who is grounded in God's Word.

HERBERT W. BATEMAN IV

Contributors

All contributors are longstanding dispensationalists and significant scholars within their respective disciplines.

HERBERT W. BATEMAN IV is professor of New Testament Studies at Grace Theological Seminary. He holds a B.S. degree from Philadelphia College of Bible and Th.M. and Ph.D. degrees in New Testament Studies from Dallas Theological Seminary. He is the author of *Early Jewish Hermeneutics and Hebrews 1:5–13: The Impact of Early Jewish Exegesis on the Interpretation of a Significant New Testament Passage.*

DARRELL L. BOCK is research professor of New Testament studies at Dallas Theological Seminary and corresponding editor for *Christianity Today.* He holds a Th.M. degree in Old Testament Studies from Dallas Theological Seminary and a Ph.D. degree in New Testament from the University of Aberdeen. He has written a two-volume commentary on Luke, *Luke 1:1–9:50* and *Luke 9:51–24:53,* as well as *Proclamation from Prophecy and Pattern: Lucan Old Testament Christology.* He is coeditor of *Dispensationalism, Israel, and the Church* and coauthor of *Progressive Dispensationalism.* Bock received the German government's prestigious Alexander von Humboldt Scholarship to research and write *Blasphemy and Exaltation in Judaism and the Final Examination of Jesus,* published in the WUNT Series.

J. LANIER BURNS is chairman and professor of Systematic Theology at Dallas Theological Seminary. He holds a B.A. degree from Davidson College, Th.M. and Th.D. degrees from Dallas Theological Seminary, and a Ph.D. degree from the University of Texas at Dallas. He contributed to *Dispensationalism, Israel, and the Church: The Search for Definition.*

15

ELLIOTT E. JOHNSON is professor of Bible Exposition at Dallas Theological Seminary. He holds a B.S. degree from Northwestern University and Th.M. and Th.D. degrees from Dallas Theological Seminary. He is the author of *Expository Hermeneutics: An Introduction* and contributed three significant pieces on hermeneutics in *Hermeneutics, Inerrancy, and the Bible [papers from ICBI Summit II]*, *Walvoord: A Tribute*, and *Issues in Dispensationalism*.

STANLEY D. TOUSSAINT is senior professor emeritus of Bible Exposition at Dallas Theological Seminary. He holds Th.M. and Th.D. degrees in New Testament Studies from Dallas Theological Seminary. He has written *Behold the King: A Study of Matthew*, contributed to and coedited *Essays in Honor of J. Dwight Pentecost*, and contributed to *Integrity of Heart, Skillfulness of Hands*. His latter two contributions were insightful pieces concerning the coming kingdom.

Bateman, Bock, Burns, and Johnson are also members of the Dispensational Study Group that meets during the annual meeting of the Evangelical Theological Society.

Abbreviations

AB	The Anchor Bible
BAGD	W. Bauer, W. F. Arndt, F. W. Gingrich, and F. Danker, *A Greek-English Lexicon of the New Testament and Other Early Christian Literature*
BETS	*Bulletin of the Evangelical Theological Society*
BKC	*Bible Knowledge Commentary*
BSac	*Bibliotheca Sacra*
CBQ	*Catholic Biblical Quarterly*
ChrTo	*Christianity Today*
CTJ	*The Conservative Theological Journal*
CTR	*Criswell Theological Review*
DTS	Dallas Theological Seminary
ETS	Evangelical Theological Society
ExpBC	*Expositor's Bible Commentary*
GTJ	*Grace Theological Journal*
GTS	Grace Theological Seminary
ICC	The International Critical Commentary
Int	*Interpretation*
JETS	*Journal of the Evangelical Theological Society*
JMT	*The Journal of Ministry & Theology*
JSNT	*Journal for the Study of the New Testament*
JSNTSup	JSNT Supplement Series
JTS	*Journal of Theological Studies*
MSJ	*Master's Seminary Journal*

18   *Abbreviations*

NASB	New American Standard Bible
NICNT	New International Commentary on the New Testament
NIGC	New International Greek Commentary
NIV	New International Version
NKJV	New King James Version
NTC	New Testament Commentary
NTS	*New Testament Studies*
PCB	Philadelphia College of Bible
TDNT	*Theological Dictionary of the New Testament*
TDOT	*Theological Dictionary of the Old Testament*
TrinJ	*Trinity Journal*
TSFBull	*Theological Students' Fellowship Bulletin*
WTJ	*Wesleyan Theological Journal*

INTRODUCTION

CHAPTER ONE

Dispensationalism
Yesterday and Today

Herbert W. Bateman IV

For more than one hundred years (1878 to the present),[1] men and women who adhere to what became known as dispensationalism have greatly impacted the world for Jesus Christ through their writings,[2] their schools,[3] and their various parachurch organizations.[4] Beginning with the nineteenth-century Plymouth Brethren movement in Britain, and particularly John Darby (1800–1882),[5] dispensationalism transcended doctrinal boundaries that separated denominations both in Britain and here in North America. Throughout the United States, premillennialism and dispensationalism infiltrated the large subculture of evangelical Protestantism through Bible and prophecy conferences (1870s–early 1900s),[6] Lewis Sperry Chafer's *Systematic Theology* (1948), and particularly the *Scofield Reference Bible* (1909, reprinted in 1917, and revised in 1967).

Despite its widespread impact, dispensationalism is not always well received.[7] For instance, Canfield presents an *ad hominem* argument against C. I. Scofield (1843–1921) in his book *The Incredible Scofield and His Book* to discredit dispensational premillennialism and the *Scofield Reference Bible*.[8] Nevertheless, Hannah rightly argues that "the truth of this system of theology (dispensationalism) is determined not by the life of an individual but by its biblical

21

moorings."[9] "True," he says, "the *Scofield Reference Bible* has had great
impact, but it should be remembered that *dispensationalists believe
their view is derived from the Bible,* not from Darby, Brookes, Scofield,
or anyone else."[10] In fact, dispensationalism is marked not only by
its exposition and high regard for God's Word but also by its emphasis on biblical prophecy, by its divisions of salvation-history events
into dispensations,[11] by its stress on the uniqueness of the church,
by its anticipation of Jesus Christ's premillennial return, and by its
confidence in a future for national Israel. Many of these "mark-
ings," however, are not unique to dispensationalism.

For instance, dispensationalists are not alone concerning their
high regard for Scripture as God's Word. In 1949, evangelical
scholars established the Evangelical Theological Society as a forum for evangelicals "to foster Biblical scholarship by providing
a medium for oral exchange and written expression of thought
and research in the general field of the theological disciplines
as centered in the Scriptures."[12] Members of the Evangelical
Theological Society acknowledge annually that "The Bible alone
and the Bible in its entirety is the Word of God written, and
therefore inerrant in the autographs."[13] A quick glance at the
Evangelical Theological Society's membership roster (totaling
2,562)[14] reflects the large number of dispensationalists and
nondispensationalists alike who have a similar high regard for
God's Word.

Nor is the idea of dividing salvation-historical events into dispensations unique to dispensationalism. Although Ehlert appeals to
John Edwards's (1637–1716) "three great 'Catholic and Grand
Oeceonomies'" as "the beginnings of dispensationalism in its larger
sense,"[15] Poythress correctly argues that an individual who evidences
a "sensitivity to the topic of redemptive epochs" (dispensations) is
not necessarily a dispensationalist.[16] Like Edwards, Poythress—a
modified amillennial covenant theologian—acknowledges the existence of dispensations and yet neither he nor Edwards—an
amillennial covenant theologian—are dispensationalists. What
marks a dispensationalist is the person's stress on the uniqueness
of the church and confidence that a future millennial period exists in human history—when God will consummate His Abrahamic,
Davidic, and new covenants with national Israel through the physical, earthly reign of Jesus Christ here on earth—that are the linch-

pins for distinguishing a dispensationalist from a nondispensationalist. These linchpins will be discussed in more detail in chapters six and seven.

Since its early beginnings, however, distinguishing characteristics of dispensationalism have undergone clarification, modification, and change. Although Blaising describes three periods within dispensationalism when distinguishing characteristics were developed or changed (classical, 1878–1940s; revised, 1950s–1970s; and progressive, 1980s–present),[17] people take issue with his historical descriptions. For instance, some who maintain the views of the revised period prefer the use of "normative dispensationalism" and thereby insinuate that recent developments in dispensationalism by Saucy, Bock, and Blaising are abnormal or aberrations from "normative dispensationalism."[18] As a result of this particular turn of events, I will refer to those who have been described as revised and progressive dispensationalists as "today's dispensationalists."[19] Although I generally use Blaising's descriptive terms, my intention here is not to label a dispensationalist but to focus attention on the developments, changes, and variety of perspectives within dispensational thinking that have impacted contemporary dispensational discussions. These developments, changes, and perspectives seem to have occurred during the 1900s in two transitional stages of the dispensational movement.

First Transitional Stage

During the 1950s, 1960s, and 1970s, the offspring of previous dispensationalists made clarifications and, when necessary, changed their predecessors' dispensational interpretations of the text. As a student at Philadelphia College of Bible (1978–1982), I remember several changes in dispensational thinking that were emphasized. Two significant changes, in my mind, concern (1) the lack of distinction between the kingdom of God and the kingdom of heaven, and (2) the emphasis of one new covenant. Thus, by way of introduction, I will describe these changes based upon first-hand experience.

Kingdom Distinctions

During my early years at Philadelphia College of Bible, I remember that Dr. Clarence Mason quite frankly disagreed with Scofield's notes on Matthew 3:2 and specifically 6:33 in which C. I. Scofield clearly distinguishes between the kingdom of heaven and the kingdom of God. The following notes are from the *Scofield Reference Bible* (1917).

Matthew 3:2 Note	Matthew 6:33 Note
The phrase, kingdom of heaven (lit. of the heavens), is peculiar to Matthew and signifies the Messianic earthly rule of Jesus Christ, the Son of David. It is called the kingdom of the heavens because it is the rule of the heavens over the earth (Mt. 6. 10). The phrase is derived from Daniel, where it is defined (Dan. 2. 34–36, 44; 7. 23–27) as the kingdom which "the God of heaven" will set up after the destruction by "the stone cut out without hands" of the Gentile world-system. It is the kingdom covenanted to David's seed (2 Sam. 7. 7–10, *refs.*); described in the prophets (Zech. 12. 8, note); and confirmed to Jesus the Christ, the Son of Mary, through the angel Gabriel (Lk. 1. 32, 33).	The kingdom of God is to be distinguished from the kingdom of heaven (Mt. 3.2 *note*) in five respects: (1) the kingdom of God is universal, including all moral intelligences willingly subject to the will of God, whether angels, the Church, or saints of past or future dispensations (Lk. 13. 28, 29; Heb. 12. 22, 23); while the kingdom of heaven is messianic, mediatorial, and Davidic, and has for its object the establishment of the kingdom of God in the earth (Mt. 3.2 *note;* 1 Cor. 15. 24, 25). (2) The kingdom of God is entered only by the new birth (John 3. 3, 5–7); the kingdom of heaven, during this age, is the sphere of a profession which may be real or false (Mt. 13. 3, *note;* 25. 1, 11, 12). (3) Since the kingdom of heaven is the earthly sphere of the universal kingdom of God, the two have almost all things in common. (4) The kingdom of God "comes not with outward show" (Lk. 17. 20), but is chiefly that which is inward and spiritual (Rom. 14. 17); while the kingdom of heaven is organic, and is to be manifested in glory in the earth. (See "Kingdom (OT)," Zech. 12. 8 *note;* (NT), Lk. 1. 31–33; 1 Cor. 15. 24, *note;* Mt. 17. 2, *note.*) (5) The kingdom of heaven merges into the kingdom of God when Christ, having "put all enemies under His feet," "shall have delivered up the kingdom to God, even the Father" (1 Cor. 15. 24–28).

Several distinctions are worth highlighting. First, the kingdom of God is *spiritual,* hence a heavenly kingdom (6:33 n. 4); whereas the kingdom of heaven is located on earth, hence a *physical* kingdom (3:2 n., 6:33 n. 4). Second, the beings of the kingdom of God include angels and all saints—past (OT saints), present (Church saints), and future (millennial saints) (6:33 n. 1); whereas in the kingdom of heaven true believers are intermingled with people who merely profess (6:33 n. 2). Third, the kingdom of God is theocentric, subject to God (6:33 n. 1), whereas the kingdom of heaven is Davidic, subject to the Messiah, as "described by the prophets and confirmed to Jesus the Christ (3:2 n.). Fourth, though the kingdom of God is a spiritual entity, it encompasses the kingdom of heaven and hence is universal in scope (3:2 n., 6:33 nn. 1, 3); whereas the kingdom of heaven clearly comprises two parts, a kingdom in mystery (the church age, 6:33 n. 2; cp. Matt. 13:3 n., 13:47 n.) and a kingdom in manifestation (the anticipated earthly millennial rule of the Davidic Messiah, 3:2 n.). Finally, the kingdom of God is eternal whereas the kingdom of heaven is temporal but will eventually become eternal when Christ, the Messiah, delivers it to God at the end of His one-thousand-year millennial reign and it merges into the kingdom of God (6:33 n. 5, cp. Matt. 13:43 n.). The following diagram attempts to capture not only Scofield's kingdom distinctions but also the fact that the kingdom of God, though separate, encompasses the kingdom of heaven.[20]

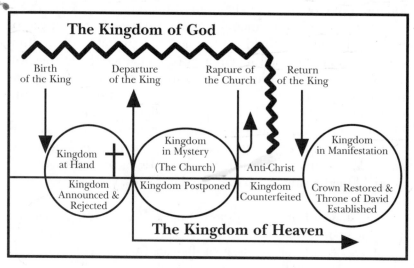

Confounded by Scofield's dichotomy between the kingdom of heaven and the kingdom of God, Mason writes:

> The net result of this attempt to distinguish the two phrases is that it baffles even Scofield's friends and gives enormous comfort to

his enemies. One writer (George Ladd, *Crucial Questions Concerning the Kingdom of God*) feels he has completely shattered the whole argument for our view (that the Kingdom Christ offered Israel was rejected and postponed) by the simple expediency of showing that by all natural language laws the two terms are synonymous. Dr. Ladd is both right and wrong—right in asserting that the two phrases are properly equated, but very, very wrong in saying that the argument for the postponed kingdom rests on the distinction some early premillennial writers made between the kingdom of heaven and the kingdom of God. (The New Scofield helps very little here.)[21]

Mason continues and unequivocally contends that Scofield's arguments are "invalid."[22] Then, based upon his reexamination of the text, he establishes his contention that the kingdom of God and the kingdom of heaven are synonymous terms. Thus, Mason is not confined to Scofield's predisposed theological categories. Since the text seems to deem it necessary, he changed or revised an aspect of Scofield's dispensational way of thinking about the kingdom of God and the kingdom of heaven.

Two points are to be made here. First, Mason is a successor of both Chafer and Scofield in that he was a member of the first class at Dallas Theological Seminary (then named the Evangelical Theological College), founded by Lewis Sperry Chafer, and he was the academic dean of the school C. I. Scofield played a significant role in founding, Philadelphia College of Bible.[23] Second, Mason exemplifies Hannah's statement, quoted earlier in this chapter, ". . . that *dispensationalists believe their view is derived from the Bible,* not from Darby, Brookes, Scofield, or anyone else."[24] Scofield held a similar perspective. He writes,

The student is earnestly exhorted not to receive a single doctrine upon the authority of this Tract (i.e., *Rightly Dividing the Word of Truth*), but, like the noble Bereans (Acts 17:11), to search the SCRIPTURES daily whether these things are so.[25]

Scofield is not necessarily excluding the community element involved in such discussions, but he seems to imply that community discussions about such matters are to be driven by the text and not the conclusions drawn by an individual per se. Thus, after wrestling with the text of Scripture, Mason identifies and changes what he considers a discrepancy within Scofield's theological way of thinking. And although Mason does not consider the notes concerning the kingdom of God and kingdom of heaven in the *New Scofield Reference Bible* as very helpful, they too evidence a shift away from Scofield's distinct dichotomy between the two kingdoms.

The *New Scofield Reference Bible* was published in 1967. A committee of scholars, namely, Frank E. Gaebelein (then headmaster of the Stony Brook School), William Culbertson (then president of Moody Bible Institute), Charles L. Feinberg (then dean of Talbot Theological Seminary), Allan A. MacRae (then president of Faith Theological Seminary), Clarence E. Mason (then dean of Philadelphia College of Bible), Alva J. McClain (then president emeritus of Grace Theological Seminary), and John F. Walvoord (then president of Dallas Theological Seminary) took part in this major undertaking. They worked hard *not* to call it a revision, yet they made numerous changes. In fact, the term "revised" used by Blaising to describe this period of dispensationalism (1950s–1970s) is due primarily to this 1967 revision of the *Scofield Reference Bible.*[26] The 807 notes in the *Scofield Reference Bible* of 1917 were edited, revised, and nearly doubled in number (1528 notes).[27] Many of the notes echo Scofield's notes. The additional notes enhance Scofield's work. Other notes, however, are revised and at times present different dispensational perspectives. Such is the case concerning Scofield's notes about his explicit dichotomy between the kingdom of God and the kingdom of heaven. When compared with Scofield's note above, the committee presents a changed perspective.

Whereas the kingdom of God and the kingdom of heaven were distinct in the *Scofield Reference Bible,* they are in many cases interchangeable phrases in the *New Scofield Reference Bible* (3:2 n., 6:33 n. 3) and thus reinterpreted. First, the scope of the kingdom of God continues to be perceived as a universal kingdom, but it no longer is relegated to the heavenly (spiritual) realm—it now more specifically includes the kingdom of heaven (3:2 n., 6:33 n. 1). The kingdom of heaven, however, remains located on earth, hence a physical kingdom (3:2 n., 6:33 n. 3).

Second, the beings of the kingdom of God are spiritual, but

Matthew 3:2 Note	Matthew 6:33 Note
The expression "kingdom of heaven" (lit. "of the heavens"), one that is peculiar to Matthew, refers to the rule of the heavens, i.e., the rule of the God of heaven over the earth (cp. Dan. 2:44; 4:25, 32). The kingdom of heaven is similar in many respects to the kingdom of God and is often used synonymously with it, though emphasizing certain features of divine government. When contrasted with the universal kingdom of God, the kingdom of heaven includes only men on earth, excluding angels and other creatures. The kingdom of heaven is the earthly sphere of profession as shown by the inclusion of those designated as wheat and tares, the latter of which are cast out of the kingdom (Mt. 13:47), and is compared to a net containing both the good and bad fish which are later separated (Mt. 13:47).	The expression "kingdom of God," although used in many cases as synonymous with the kingdom of heaven is to be distinguished from it in some instances (see Mt. 3:2, *note*); (1) The kingdom of God is at times viewed as everlasting and universal, i.e., the rule of the sovereign God over all creatures and things (Ps. 103:19; Dan. 4:3). In this sense the kingdom of God includes the kingdom of heaven. (2) The kingdom of God is also used to designate the sphere of salvation entered only by the new birth (Jn. 3:5–7) in contrast with the kingdom of heaven as the sphere of profession which may be real or false (see Mt. 13:3, *note;* 25:1,11–12). And (3) since the kingdom of heaven is in the earthly sphere of the universal kingdom of God, the two have many things in common and in some contexts the terms are interchangeable. Like the kingdom of heaven, the kingdom of God is realized in the rule of God in the present age and will also be fulfilled in the future millennial kingdom. It continues forever in the eternal state (cp. Dan. 4:3).

physical beings are also included ("all creatures and things," 6:33 n. 1). In the kingdom of heaven, however, the kingdom continues to consist of earth-bound people where true believers and mere professors are intermingled (3:2 n., 6:33 n. 2).

Third, and most interestingly, though the kingdom of God remains a theocentric kingdom, the kingdom of heaven is also subject to God's rule (3:2 n., 6:33 n. 1). Retracted is Scofield's clear articulation that the kingdom of heaven speaks of the future messianic rule of Jesus in fulfillment of God's covenant with David as prophetically foretold and "confirmed to Jesus the Christ" (see

Scofield's note for Matt. 3:2 above). Thus, the emphasis is upon the scope or the universality of God's rule (the kingdom of God), an aspect of which includes the kingdom of heaven.

Fourth, and closely related to the third point, the committee contends that the kingdom of God now consists of two parts, a spiritual kingdom ("the kingdom of God") and an earthly kingdom ("the kingdom of heaven") (3:2 n., 6:33 n. 1). Although the kingdom of heaven continues to comprise two parts, namely a kingdom in mystery (the church age: 3:2 n., 6:33 n. 2; cp. Matt. 13:3 n., 13:45 n., 13:47 n.) and a kingdom in manifestation (the anticipated earthly millennial rule of the Davidic Messiah), the latter is presented in a veiled statement, a statement that seems uncharacteristic of Scofield. The committee makes an ambiguous allusion to the future Davidic kingdom: "*Like* the kingdom of heaven, the kingdom of God is *realized* in the present age and *will* also *be fulfilled* in the future millennial kingdom" (conclusion of the 6:33 n.). Thus, one aspect of these kingdoms is presently realized, namely the kingdom in mystery (the church age) and God's present rule. Another aspect of the kingdom is yet to be fulfilled, namely the messianic kingdom, thus fulfilling the Davidic covenant and the future amalgamation of the messianic kingdom into the kingdom of God, at which time God will rule for all eternity.

The fifth and final point is that the kingdom of God is eternal and the kingdom of heaven continues into the eternal state (6:33 n).

Thus, like Mason, who disagreed with the explicit dichotomy Scofield made between the kingdom of God and the kingdom of heaven, the committee also found it necessary to make theological changes to Scofield's dispensational way of thinking. Unlike Mason, however, not everyone was willing to say that absolutely no distinction existed between the two kingdom phases. A former professor of Philadelphia School of the Bible (1919–1923; renamed Philadelphia College of Bible), founder and first president of Grace Theological Seminary, and fellow committee member of the *New Scofield Reference Bible*, Alva J. McClain muses,

> In one sense it would not be wholly wrong to speak of *two kingdoms* revealed in the Bible. But we must at the same time guard carefully against the notion that these two kingdoms are absolutely distinct, one from the other. There is value and instruction

in thinking of them as *two aspects* or phases of the one rule of our sovereign God.[28]

Thus, dispensationalists not only changed a dispensational perspective of Scofield's but also were divided concerning the extent to which his view should be changed.[29] The following chart represents how the offspring of yesterday's dispensational thinkers differed in their interpretation of the kingdom of God and the kingdom of heaven.[30]

"The Kingdom of Heaven" and "The Kingdom of God"		
Yesterday's Dispensationalists	Today's Dispensationalists (1950s–1970s)	
Distinct	Interchangeable, Yet Distinct	Synonymous, No Distinction
John N. Darby Clarence Larkin C. I. Scofield Lewis S. Chafer Charles C. Ryrie (1950s)	*New Scofield Reference Bible* Alva J. McClain J. Dwight Pentecost John F. Walvoord	Eric Sauer (Contemporary of Chafer) Clarence E. Mason Charles C. Ryrie (1970s) Stanley D. Toussaint

Although I agree with Ryrie and Saucy that the dichotomy between the kingdom of heaven and the kingdom of God is not *now* a determinative feature of dispensationalism, the point is that the distinction was *at one time* a distinguishing feature which marked early dispensationalism.[31] Future earthly Davidic/messianic kingdom discussions were not sustained *entirely* upon distinguishing between these phrases, but the clearly defined distinctions had been used as a biblical support for a future Davidic/messianic kingdom, which in turn would fulfill God's covenantal promise to David (2 Sam. 7:14). In Bailey's survey of dispensational definitions of the kingdom, he also considers "the clearly defined bifurcation of the kingdom of heaven and the kingdom of God" to be "a basic distinction within dispensationalism."[32] Thus, a distinguishing feature of dispensationalism voiced by yesterday's dispensationalists was reexamined, changed, and aspects retracted by several of today's more prominent dispensationalists.

As a result, kingdom discussions were diverted away from the strict dichotomy between a spiritual kingdom and an earthly kingdom, an earthly kingdom which spoke more pointedly of the future fulfillment of the Davidic covenant. Emphasis was placed upon the *universal or eternal* kingdom of God. Discussions about the kingdom of heaven were redirected to stress (1) the postponement of the Davidic/messianic kingdom[33] but with some aspect of the kingdom present today (alternatively described as a kingdom in mystery form or a present theocratic kingdom); and (2) the future fulfillment of the Davidic kingdom (either a messianic kingdom,[34] a mediatorial kingdom,[35] or a future theocratic kingdom[36]). In fact, kingdom discussions, especially as they pertain to the future messianic kingdom, continue to be the focal point among today's dispensationalists. Although this shift affects other areas of dispensational thinking such as the relevance of the Sermon on the Mount for the church age, that discussion is beyond the scope of this essay and was not an issue at Philadelphia College of Bible while I was a student. On the other hand, the new covenant and its promises were discussed.

New Covenant Promises

Not only did Philadelphia College of Bible emphasize that the kingdom of God and the kingdom of heaven are synonymous (which differed from both Scofield and Chafer), emphasis also was placed on there being *only one* new covenant. Thus, the second transition in dispensational thinking concerns the new covenant. Early dispensationalists espoused at least three perspectives concerning the new covenant promises. (1) On the one hand, the new covenant promises were considered to be for future Israel and for Israel alone. The church had no part in any of the new covenant promises. For instance, Larkin argued that

> The new covenant has not yet been made. It is to be made with Israel after they get back to their own land. It is promised in Jer. 31:31–37. It is unconditional and will cover the Millennium and the New Heaven and New Earth. It is based on the finished work of Christ, Matt. 26:28. It has nothing to do with the Church and does not belong to this Dispensation.[37]

(2) Chafer, on the other hand, argued that two new covenants existed, one for the church (Luke 22:20) and one for national Israel (Jer. 31:31–34; Heb. 8:7–12).[38] "Upon entering their kingdom," says Chafer, "He (God) will make a new covenant with the nation

which will govern their life in the kingdom (Jer. 31:3–34)."[39] Elsewhere Chafer argues, "To suppose that these two covenants—one for Israel and one for the Church—are the same is to assume that there is a latitude of common interest between God's purpose for Israel and His purpose for the Church."[40]

(3) Scofield, however, argued for one new covenant with an "already-not yet" fulfillment and a heavy emphasis on the "not yet." He explained that "chapters 30–36 in Jeremiah constitute a kind of summary of prophecy concerning Israel as a nation, *looking on* *especially to the last days,* the day of the LORD, and the kingdom age to follow" (Jer. 30:1 n.).[41] Although the new covenant looked especially to the kingdom age, it "rests upon the sacrifice of Christ, and secures the eternal blessedness, under the Abrahamic Covenant (Gal. 3:13–29), of all who believe" (Heb. 8:8 n.).[42] Thus, those who presently believe (i.e., the church) experience some of the spiritual blessings of the new covenant based upon, and in much the same way as they presently experience, aspects of the Abrahamic covenant promises. As observed below, the *New Scofield Reference Bible* adds a note for Jeremiah 31:31 in which Scofield's original note for Jeremiah 30:1 is made clearer and more pointed about the inauguration of the new covenant for the church.

Jeremiah 30:1 Note	Jeremiah 31:31 Note
Scofield Reference Bible (1917)	*New Scofield Reference Bible* (1967)
The writings of Jeremiah in Chapters 30–36 cannot with certainty be arranged in consecutive order. Certain dates are mentioned (e.g. 32. 1; 33. 1; 34. 1, 8; 35. 1), but retrospectively. The narrative, so far as Jeremiah gives a narrative, is resumed at 37. 1. These chapters constitute a kind of summary of prophecy concerning Israel as a nation, looking on especially to the last days, the day of the LORD, and the kingdom age to follow.	The New Covenant of 31:31–40 and 32:40ff is one of the significant covenants of Scripture, and is remarkably full, stating: (1) the time of the covenant (vv. 31, 33); (2) the parties to the covenant (v. 31); (3) the contrast in covenants—Mosaic and New (v. 32); (4) the terms of the covenant (v. 33); (5) the comprehensiveness of the covenant (v. 34); (6) the basic features of the covenant: (a) knowledge of God and (b) forgiveness of sin; (7) the perpetuity of the people of the covenant (vv. 35–37); and (8) the guarantee of the covenant (the rebuilt city) (vv. 38–40). See Heb. 8:8, *note.* Although certain features of this covenant have been fulfilled for believers in the present Church Age (e.g., number 6 above), the covenant remains to be realized for Israel according to the explicit statement of v. 31.

The *New Scofield Reference Bible* quite clearly concludes that the church shares in the inauguration of the new covenant with a future consummation yet to come for national and ethnic Israel. But when did the New Testament writers make the connection with Jeremiah? John McGahey, former professor of Biblical Studies at Philadelphia College of Bible, unequivocally contended that when Christ instituted the Lord's Supper with His disciples, ". . . there is no doubt that their minds went back to the prophecy of the New Covenant in Jeremiah thirty-one."[43] "It should be observed," says McGahey, "that there is no indication in the context that the Lord's pronouncement concerned a different New Covenant which was being established with the church, as some have suggested."[44] Thus, in keeping with the *Scofield Reference Bible* and particularly the *New Scofield Reference Bible,* Philadelphia College of Bible professors such as McGahey (DTS graduate), Cawood (DTS graduate), Showers (GTS graduate), and others took issue with the two-new-covenant view and emphasized an "already-not yet" fulfillment of the new covenant.

Two points are to be made here. First, McGahey is another offspring of Chafer in the sense that he was a student of Chafer and in that he received both his master of theology and doctor of theology degrees from Dallas Theological Seminary.[45] However, as he studied and examined the text, he differed with his predecessor's dispensational perspectives about the New Covenant and argued for a single new covenant in his 1957 doctoral dissertation. Second, McGahey further clarifies Scofield's position by demonstrating that "Christ's reference to the New Covenant was not only for the purpose of confirming Israel's hope, but also for the purpose of giving additional revelation concerning the New Covenant—information which was not mentioned in the prophecy of Jeremiah."[46] The additional revelation includes: (1) the basis for God's initiating the new covenant, which is the blood of Christ Jesus and the benefits of His sacrifice that extend beyond Israel, and (2) a provision not stated in Jeremiah, which is the *forgiveness of sins for the many* (Jew and Gentile alike) who believe.[47] Thus, in the progress of God's revelation, the new covenant is based upon the sacrifice of Jesus Christ which secures eternal blessings such as the forgiveness of sins for *anyone* who might believe.

Although today's dispensationalists generally maintain an

"already-not yet" fulfillment of the new covenant, many nuance and support their respective positions differently. Nevertheless, dispensationalists continue to differ in their interpretation and application of the new covenant.[48]

	"The New Covenant"		
	Only for Israel	One for Israel, One for the Church	One New Covenant "Already" – "Not Yet"
Yesterday's Dispensationalists	John N. Darby Clarence Larkin	Lewis S. Chafer	Eric Sauer C. I. Scofield (emphasis on "not yet")
Today's Dispensationalists (1950s–1970s)		John Walvoord (see n. 46) Charles C. Ryrie (1950s)	*New Scofield Reference Bible* Alva J. McClain John McGahey Charles C. Ryrie (1970s)
Today's Dispensationalists (1980s–1990s)	John Master	Charles C. Ryrie (1990s)	Robert Saucy Darrell Bock

Philadelphia College of Bible graduates and graduates from other dispensational schools like Philadelphia during the 1960s and 1970s will probably recall the rearticulation and softening of former dispensational discussions such as the overstated dichotomy between law and grace which had been misconstrued as two different ways of salvation.[49] Perhaps other issues come to mind. The two I mention strike me as significant in light of the discussions among dispensationalists of the 1990s. However, other meaningful clarifications and changes in dispensationalism occurred during a second transitional stage of development by some of today's dispensationalists.

Second Transitional Stage

During the 1980s and the 1990s, another generation of dispensationalists arose who knew not Scofield or Chafer but who grappled with the text and their dispensational tradition. While a student at Dallas Theological Seminary (1983–1993), I was exposed to another form of questioning of dispensationalism. Foremost was the rethinking and questioning of Ryrie's definition of dispensationalism.

In 1965, Ryrie published *Dispensationalism Today*, in which he not only addressed various forms of opposition but also presented a systematization and development of dispensationalism simply and succinctly. Frank E. Gaebelein praised the work: "As a reasonable and scholarly apologetic for dispensationalism it cannot be ignored."[50] Even today, thirty-four years later, the work cannot be ignored. Ryrie's work has been revised and retitled *Dispensationalism*. The most notable contribution was Ryrie's description of the *sine qua non* of dispensationalism—one that I memorized on more than one occasion for Dr. John Cawood while a student at Philadelphia College of Bible. Ryrie's *sine qua non* of dispensationalism is threefold.

1. Dispensationalism keeps Israel and the Church distinct.
2. The distinction between Israel and the Church emerges from a hermeneutical system that is usually called literal interpretation, namely the employment of a normal or plain interpretation.
3. Dispensationalism understands that the basic purpose of God in all of His dealings with people is to bring glory to Himself through salvation and other purposes.[51]

This landmark definition for dispensationalism clearly reflects a systematizing and even a development in dispensational thinking. "Like all doctrines," Ryrie concedes, "dispensational teaching has undergone systematization and development."[52] However, the new generation of dispensationalists of the 1980s and 1990s questioned Ryrie's definition. Their point in raising questions was not to reject the categories but to nuance them, as well as to show that they were not "historically" conscious distinctives in the movement or its adherents. The *sine qua non* was merely an attempt by Ryrie to state an essential core to dispensationalism. Thus, the focus of their questioning was the accuracy of Ryrie's *sine qua non* as it pertained to two issues: (1) the historicity of Ryrie's statement that all dispensationalists believed the unifying principle of Scripture to be the self-glorification of God and whether this goal was a unifying principle for dispensationalists (#3 above), and (2) Ryrie's articulation of the consistent practice of a literal interpretation of Scripture as unique to and a defining hermeneutic of dispensationalism, especially in light of recent developments in hermeneutical discussions among dispensationalists and non-dispensationalists alike (#2 above).

The Unifying Principle

The unifying principle of dispensationalism is questioned on two levels. First, do all dispensationalists agree that the self-glorification of God is the unifying theme of Scripture (#3 above)? Not really! According to those raising the questions, this was not a "historically" *conscious distinctive* in the movement or its adherents. While taking issue with this doxological principle, Blaising points out differences between Ryrie, Chafer, and other contemporary dispensationalists of the 1950s and 1960s. On the one hand, Chafer's defining feature of dispensationalism was twofold: one that involved a heavenly people (Christians) and one that involved an earthly people (Israel), which is supported by the dichotomy between the kingdom of God and the kingdom of heaven.[53] Since Chafer never clearly identifies a unifying feature in Scripture, Ryrie seems to reorient Chafer's thinking and thereby develop a unifying theme of Scripture for dispensationalism. On the other hand, 1950 and 1960 contemporaries of Ryrie have argued that the unifying feature of Scripture is the kingdom. While McClain maintained that the unifying theme is a mediatorial kingdom, Pentecost argues for a theocratic kingdom.[54] Thus, Ryrie's doxological principle is not, and never was, universally held by all dispensationalists, though Walvoord maintains a similar perspective.

The second question concerns whether the doxological principle is a unique or distinguishing feature of dispensationalism. It is not. Once again, Blaising points out that the Westminster Confession clearly states that "God . . . [works] *all things* according to the counsel of His own immutable and most righteous will, *for His own glory*."[55] Thus, in much the same way that other evangelicals maintain a high regard for God's Word and many divide salvation-historical events into dispensations, the doxological theme of Scripture does not distinguish a dispensationalist from a non-dispensationalist. Consequently, it was argued that the doxological principle was not a historically accurate consensus among all dispensationalists nor was it a principle unique to dispensational thinking.

Literal Interpretation

The "consistently literal or plain interpretation" of Scripture (#2 above) is another aspect of Ryrie's definition that is questioned.

Although Ryrie's 1965 use of *consistently literal interpretation* was sufficient for 1965 discussions, it was deemed inadequate to define the essence of dispensationalism in the 1980s and 1990s. Here, according to those raising the questions, the need to nuance Ryrie's statement was required for the following reasons.

First, debates between evangelical dispensationalists and nondispensationalists in the 1960s and 1970s were confined to "literal" versus "spiritual."[56] Each condemned the other for either offering an overly literal interpretation or an overly spiritualized (allegorical) interpretation of the text, especially when it concerned prophecy. (Blaising even questions whether the *consistently literal or plain interpretation* accurately characterized the interpretive practices of yesterday's dispensationalist [Scofield, Gaebelein, Chafer] and Ryrie himself.[57]) Recent debates, however, are more complex due to developments in hermeneutics, especially *how to interpret* a New Testament author's use of the Old Testament and *how to integrate* teachings in the Old and New Testament concerning similar themes. Poythress and most dispensationalists agree that dispensationalists and nondispensationalists alike employ a literal hermeneutic in their respective application of the historical-grammatical hermeneutic.[58] Thus, it can no longer be said that the practice of a consistently literal or plain interpretation of Scripture distinguishes a dispensationalist from a nondispensationalist *without qualification*.

Stallard, a theology professor at Baptist Bible College and Seminary, more specifically contends that "to prove that the definition of dispensationalism is tied to literal hermeneutics in some way requires the dispensationalist to prove either that the nondispensationalist is incorrect in asserting his use of the method or that there is some particular way in which the literal hermeneutic is *used* that is unique to dispensationalism."[59] As a result of these sorts of hermeneutical realities, Johnson and others attempt to retain and thereby more clearly define what a dispensationalist means by a *consistently literal interpretation*. Bock, however, moves beyond the discussion by simply acknowledging that dispensationalists and nondispensationalists alike attempt to interpret Scripture literally when exercising a historical-grammatical hermeneutic. The primary difference comes in how one relates the results of canonical integration. The nondispensationalist argues that Israel becomes subsumed in the church. The dispensationalist argues that Israel retains an identity in God's plan.

Second, the use of the phrase *"consistent literal interpretation"* to define the essence of dispensationalism ignores the existence of a more central issue of disagreement between dispensationalists and most nondispensationalists. The more central issue is "testament priority." Testament priority is a presuppositional preference of one testament over the other that determines a person's literal historical-grammatical hermeneutical starting point. This is especially significant concerning a New Testament author's use of the Old Testament.

For the evangelical nondispensationalist such as Waltke, his literal historical-grammatical hermeneutic begins in the New Testament.[60] The New Testament "unpacks" the literal historical-grammatical meaning of the Old Testament. The Old Testament is reread by the New Testament because Old Testament authors presented their subjects in ideal forms and thereby never fully understood what they wrote. The human author's intended meaning is clouded. However, the divine author's intended meaning—the ultimate meaning—is more clearly discernible due to the coming of Jesus Christ and the close of the New Testament canon. Thus, the New Testament brings into focus the divine author's intent of an Old Testament text and thereby *clarifies* the human author's meaning. Consequently, the New Testament is the starting point for nondispensationalists such as Waltke. Bock refers to this literal historical-grammatical approach as the Canonical Approach and New Testament Priority School[61] and it may be diagrammed in the following manner.[62]

Canonical Approach and New Testament Priority School

Starting Point

Old Testament   New Testament

Human Intent   ←   *Clarifies*   Divine Author's Intended Referent   ✝   Jesus Christ

For dispensationalists, however, their historical-grammatical hermeneutic keeps a reference point in the Old Testament. In an attempt to describe more clearly the employment of a consistently literal hermeneutic, Elliott Johnson argues that the interpreter must realize the human hagiographer's sense of meaning through his specific choice of words. What the individual Old Testament author wrote is a "type" of the fuller sense of meaning that corresponds to the divine author's sense of meaning communicated in the New Testament. Johnson argues that an extremely tight correspondence of meaning exists between the words used in the Old Testament and the words used in the New Testament. The Old Testament hagiographers' choice of words or their types of meaning anticipate subsequent revelation, specifically as it involves the historical referent Jesus Christ. Words are thereby circumscribed, and thus Johnson's approach limits what words can ultimately mean canonically. Thus, Johnson argues for a modified *expansion of meaning* of words between the testaments and, thereby, emphasizes a stable meaning approach to Scripture.[63]

Johnson refers to these words or their types of meaning in an Old Testament text as a bud of a flower which eventually manifests itself as a flower in full bloom in the New Testament. The flower is the intended referent, Jesus Christ. The present-day interpreter *identifies* the bud of the flower in the Old Testament because of the blooming flower in the New Testament. Thus, unlike Waltke, the key reference point for Johnson's historical-grammatical hermeneutic begins with a *more* literal historical understanding of an Old Testament author's choice of words and their original sense of meaning.

Although the New Testament plays a significant role in his interpretations of the Old Testament, there are significant preunderstood theological limitations (i.e., Israel is not the church) in Johnson's approach. Bock refers to this and other *expansion of meaning* approaches as the Divine Intent-Human Words School (see n. 63). Although Johnson will speak in more detail about his view (chap. 2) and illustrate his view in relation to the Abrahamic, Davidic, and new covenants (chap. 4), his approach is graphically reflected in the following diagram.[64]

Divine Intent-Human Words School

Starting Point

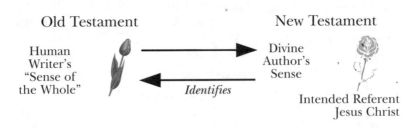

Old Testament   New Testament

Human   Divine
Writer's   Author's
"Sense of   Sense
the Whole"   *Identifies*

Intended Referent
Jesus Christ

Darrell Bock also begins in the Old Testament but practices a complementary historical-grammatical hermeneutic.[65] His approach differs from Johnson's in at least two ways. First, Bock more willingly moves from the Old Testament to extrabiblical material such as the Septuagint (LXX), Targums, Pesher, Midrash, and other first-century literature of the intertestamental period. Like Richard Longenecker,[66] Bock considers the historical progress of Jewish theological understandings and the use of the Old Testament in second temple literature important in understanding a New Testament author's use of the Old Testament. New Testament authors use and adopt concepts and ideas that were part of first-century religious thinking. They also adapt such thinking in their teaching. Even as basic a term as *Messiah* emerges as a technical term in this period and is seen in a variety of ways within Judaism.[67] The New Testament presents a coherent portrait of Messiah that addresses Jewish background and yet goes its own way. Thus, in addition to the development of first-century Jewish exegesis and theological concepts from the Old Testament, Bock also recognizes the progress of revelation due to Jesus' use of the Old Testament and the direction of the Holy Spirit. Consequently, Bock tends to take into consideration the New Testament author's historical milieu as a backdrop to New Testament meaning *more so* than Johnson.

A second distinguishing feature from Johnson's consistent literal hermeneutic is Bock's emphasis on "promise-fulfillment." God's promises are initially presented in general terms, but as God works in history He progressively reveals and provides the specifics of His promises. Words, then, may take on an extended sense of meaning when an Old Testament text is recontextualized in the New Testament by an author who was influenced by his historical milieu and the progress of revelation. The New Testament can tell us more about God's promise but does not say less than the Old Testament did. Bock's *expansion of meaning* perspective is not as tight as Johnson's approach in that while the teaching of the Old Testament is retained, Bock's approach allows the New Testament to develop Old Testament promises via intertestamental works, Jesus, and the Holy Spirit. Thus, Bock's approach affirms the discontinuities as well as continuities of Scripture more so than Johnson's. Although he will speak in more detail about his view (chap. 3) and illustrate his view in relation to the Abrahamic, Davidic, and new covenants (chap. 5), Bock has described his approach as the Jewish Background and Apostolic School and is visually presented below.[68]

Jewish Background and Apostolic School

Starting Point

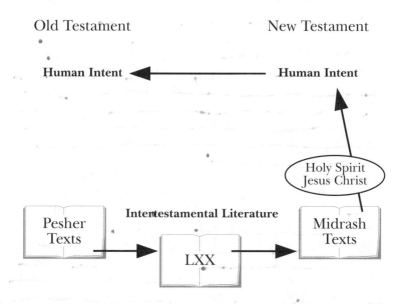

Unlike Waltke and other nondispensationalists, Bock and Johnson view the New Testament as an illuminating factor in understanding Old Testament "types" (Johnson) or "patterns" (Bock) with the same preunderstood dispensational recognition: Israel is not the church. This recognition comes from the Old Testament's point that promises to Israel are everlasting for Israel in perpetuity (even if others later benefit from those promises). Thus, their shared starting point and preunderstood recognition distinguish Bock and Johnson from nondispensationalists.

Obviously, Ryrie's work greatly impacted dispensationalism, yet the questions raised in the 1980s and 1990s are not without justification. The self-glorification of God as the unifying principle of Scripture is not a conscious distinctive of all dispensationalists nor is it unique to dispensationalism. In addition, hermeneutical discussions are far more complicated than those Ryrie addressed years ago. In fact, the hermeneutical approaches mentioned above and the application of those approaches to God's covenants that affect one's canonical understanding of the kingdom of heaven are central issues for today's dispensationalists.

Conclusion

Dispensational discussions obviously have advanced since the days of Scofield and Chafer. Distinguishing characteristics of the dispensationalism of yesterday's dispensationalists are different from today's dispensationalists. In fact, today's dispensationalists maintain many divergent positions, and their perspectives tend to interact more directly with criticisms of their approach. Nevertheless, reflection on the interpretive clarifications, modifications, and changes in dispensational thinking causes me to wonder what yesterday's dispensationalists like Scofield and Chafer would say in light of current discussions.

Unfortunately, no one will ever know for sure because most of the transitions articulated above and many others occurred after they died. We will never know how Scofield would have responded to the *New Scofield Reference Bible* or how Chafer would have responded to Walvoord's edited version of his *Systematic Theology*. Perhaps a recontextualized *cliché* may serve to transition our discussion into the present: "While yesterday's dispensationalism is dispensational history, today's dispensationalism is history in the making." We have before us an opportunity to interact with today's dispensationalists—dispensationalists who represent two transitional stages in dispensational thinking. Here is the reason for this book. The following pages will focus attention on three central issues that exist among today's dispensationalists: (1) hermeneutics; (2) the application of a literal historical-grammatical hermeneutic with regard to the Abrahamic, Davidic, and new covenants; and finally (3) Israel and the Church. I trust that these discussions will provide not only an understanding of the contemporary scene within today's dispensational movement but also an appreciation for each dispensationalist's sincere attempt to wrestle with the text. One thing all dispensationalists share is a sincere desire to present clearly and biblically the depth of God's promises for those who call Jesus both their Lord and Christ.

Chapter Notes

1. The year 1878 marked the beginning of the Niagara Bible and Prophecy Conference, which was the catalyst for the spread of premillennial and dispensational thinking in North America. In 1869, George C. Needham (1840–1902), James Inglis (1813–1872), and several others began conducting "believers' meetings" in various places throughout the United States and Canada. Beginning in 1878, the group became more organized. First, they chose James H. Brookes to preside over the conference. Second, they adopted a premillennial fourteen-point creed. Finally, in 1883 they settled in one location, Niagara, Ontario. The conference remained in Niagara until 1897 (the year Brookes died). The Niagara conference not only attracted the leading premillennial and dispensational thinkers of the day—men such as A. J. Gordon, W. G. Moorehead, A. T. Pierson, C. I. Scofield, and J. Wilbur Chapman—the periodical, *The Truth,* became the unofficial organ of the conference (1875–1897). "Niagara," according to Sidwell, "became the exemplar of prophetic conferences and influenced nearly every American conference on prophecy." Mark E. Sidwell, "The History of the Winona Lake Bible Conference" (Ph.D. diss., Bob Jones University, 1988), 25–29. George C. Needham, "Preface," in *The Prophecy Conference Movement,* vol. 2, ed. Joel A. Carpenter (New York: Garland, 1988). Craig A. Blaising, "Dispensationalism: The Search for Definitions," in *Dispensationalism, Israel, and the Church:*

The Search for Definition (Grand Rapids: Zondervan, 1992), 13–34, esp. 16–20. The premillennial and dispensational influence over large cross sections of evangelical Protestants seems to begin with the Niagara Bible and Prophecy Conference.

2. Although dispensational works are numerous, the *Scofield Reference Bible* is by far the most significant. The 1909 edition represents some thirty years of study (2d ed., 1917). It was the first significant work to become famous throughout the United States and around the world. Half a century later (1967), the *New Scofield Reference Bible* was published. For a summary of C. I. Scofield's life, see the *Dictionary of Premillennial Theology*, 1996 ed., s.v. "Scofield, Cyrus Ingerson." Another significant work is Lewis Sperry Chafer's *Systematic Theology* in seven volumes. Chafer appears to be the only dispensationalist to construct a full system of biblical theology based upon dispensational and premillennial distinctions. For summaries of Chafer's life, see George G. Houghton, "Lewis Sperry Chafer, 1871–1952," *BSac* 128 (October–December 1971): 291–99. John D. Hannah, "The Early Years of Lewis Sperry Chafer," *BSac* 144 (January–March 1987): 3–23; *Dictionary of Premillennial Theology*, 1996 ed., s.v. "Chafer, Lewis Sperry."

3. In chronological order, the following are some of the more widely known dispensational colleges and seminaries that blanket the United States: Moody Bible Institute, founded in 1886; Philadelphia College of Bible, which initially began as two schools, the National Bible Institute of Philadelphia (1913 by W. W. Rugh) and Philadelphia School of the Bible (1914 by C. I. Scofield and William L. Pettingill), which joined in 1951; Dallas Theological Seminary founded in 1924 (though officially in 1936); Western Conservative Baptist Seminary (now Western Seminary), founded in 1927; Baptist Bible College and Seminary, founded in 1932; Multnomah School of the Bible, founded in 1936; Lancaster Bible College and Graduate School, founded in 1933; Grace College and Seminary founded in 1937 (Grace College was founded in 1948); Grand Rapids Baptist College and Seminary, founded in 1941 (though officially in 1949); Talbot Theological Seminary, founded in 1952; Central Baptist Theological Seminary, founded in 1956; Capital Bible Seminary, founded in 1958; and Master's Seminary, founded in 1986.

4. Central American Mission (CAM, now CAM International), founded in 1890 by C. I. Scofield; *Bibliotheca Sacra* (Latin for "sacred library") was begun at Union Theological Seminary in 1843, moved to Oberlin College in 1884, purchased by Xenia Theological Seminary in 1922, and finally purchased by Dallas Theological Seminary in 1934, and thus became a major publication for dispensationalism (see Roy B. Zuck, *"Bibliotheca Sacra's* Sesquicentennial Anniversary," *BSac* 150 [January–March 1993]: 3–8); Young Life, founded in the 1930s by James Rayburn; Friends of Israel, founded in 1938 by Philadelphia Evangelical Christians during the time of Hitler's atrocities against the Jews; Word of Life Ministries, founded in 1940 by Jack Wyrtzen; "Grace to You," founded in 1969 by John MacArthur; Walk Thru the Bible, founded in 1975 by Bruce Wilkinson; "Insight for Living," founded in 1979 by Chuck Swindoll; Zion's Fire, founded in 1989 by Marv Rosenthal; and many others.

5. John Nelson Darby (1800–1882) was a leading force behind the Plymouth Brethren movement in England and is described by Blaising and Elmore as the "father of modern dispensationalism." Craig Blaising, "Developing Dispensationalism, Part 1: Doctrinal Development in Orthodoxy" *BSac 145* (April–June 1988): 133–40. *Dictionary of Premillennial Theology*, 1996 ed., s.v. "Darby, John Nelson." Darby advanced the idea that there are distinct stages in history administrated and ordered by God that place people in a specific relation of responsibility to Him. These divinely administrated stages or periods in history are dispensations. MacLeod demonstrates that Walter Scott is a direct link between Scofield and Darby. David J. MacLeod, "Walter Scott, A Link in Dispensationalism Between Darby and Scofield?" *BSac* 153 (April–June 1996): 155–78. For a historical discussion of Darby see Larry V. Crutchfield, *The Origins of Dispensationalism: The Darby Factor* (New York: University Press of America, 1985). Although Ryrie at one time argued that dispensationalism was a pre-Darby phenomenon, he more recently acknowledges that Darby "had much to do with the systematizing and promoting of dispensationalism." Compare *Dispensationalism Today* (pp. 74–76) with *Dispensationalism* (Chicago: Moody, 1996), 67–69; "Update on Dispensationalism," in *Issues in Dispensationalism*, ed. Wesley R. Willis and John R. Master (Chicago: Moody, 1994), 16–17.

6. Not all Bible conferences of the late 1800s were necessarily premillennial and dispensational. The Northfield Conferences (1880–1899) tended to be more tolerant of speakers of differing persuasions. Although sympathetic to Keswick holiness and premillennialism, D. L. Moody, founder and long-time director of the Northfield Bible Conference, invited promoters of the Social Gospel (i.e., Josiah Strong and Washington Gladden) to speak, as well as Henry Drummond, who made attempts to reconcile Christianity with Darwinian evolution. Like Northfield, the Winona Lake Bible Conference (1895–1968) was also tolerant, at least for the first twenty-five years of its existence. As time went on, however, Sidwell observed through *Winona Echoes* (its publication of selected conference speakers) that "Winona took an increasingly rigorous stand for orthodoxy." Nevertheless, he also observed that, "by the 1940's premillennialism in its dispensationalist form had come to dominate the major Bible conferences." Others, such as Northfield, were swept away by modernism. Sidwell, "The History of the Winona Lake Bible Conference," 29–47.

7. The following are a few examples of books and articles that were written in an attempt to show that dispensationalism was wrong. Oswald T. Allis, *Prophecy and the Church* (Philadelphia: Presbyterian & Reformed Publishing, 1945). John Wick Bowman, "The Bible and Modern Religions II: Dispensationalism," *Int* 10 (April 1956): 170–87. Loraine Boettner, *The Millennium* (Philadelphia: Presbyterian and Reformed, 1958). William E. Cox, *Examination of Dispensationalism* (Philadelphia: Presbyterian & Reformed Publishing, 1963); idem, *Biblical Studies in Final Things* (Philadelphia: Presbyterian & Reformed Publishing, 1966). Daniel P. Fuller, *Gospel and Law* (Grand Rapids: Eerdmans, 1980). C. Crenshaw and G. Gunn, *Dispensationalism Today, Yesterday, and Tomorrow* (Memphis, Tenn.: Footstool, 1985). Joseph M. Canfield, *The Incredible Scofield and His Book* (Vallecito, Calif.: Ross House, 1988). John H. Gerstner, *Wrongly Dividing the Word of Truth* (Brentwood, Tenn.: Wolgemuth & Hyatt, 1991).

8. Joseph M. Canfield, *The Incredible Scofield and His Book* (Vallecito, Calif.: Ross House, 1988).

9. John D. Hannah, "A Review of *The Incredible Scofield and His Book*," *BSac* 287 (July–September 1990): 351–64, esp. 364.

10. Ibid., 363 (emphasis mine). For Hannah's excellent summary of

C. I. Scofield's life, see the *Dictionary of Premillennial Theology,* 1996 ed., s.v. "Scofield, Cyrus Ingerson."

11. The word *dispensation* is the anglicized form of *dispensatio,* the Latin Vulgate rendering of οἰκονομία. The term, οἰκονομία, "relates primarily to household administration and applies generally to 'direction,' 'administration,' 'provision.'" *TDNT,* 1967 ed., s.v. "οἰκονομία," by Otto Michel. See also BAGD, 559c 1. Thus, the English translation of the Greek word *oikonomia* (οἰκονομία) primarily speaks of "household administration" (cf. Luke 16:2-4). Theologically, the word is used to speak of (1) how God sovereignly and progressively reveals His salvation-history program in stages throughout human history (Hebrews 1:1-2), and (2) how human beings are to relate to God as He administers His program in various dispensations (John 1:17). For instance, the New Testament clearly speaks of a previous dispensation (Eph. 3:8-9; Col. 1:25-26), a present dispensation (Eph. 3:2-3), and an anticipated or future dispensation (Eph. 1:9-10).

12. ETS Constitution, Article II. The Society's purpose has always been acknowledged on the inside cover of the journal. *BETS* 1-3 (1958-1960) to *JETS* 41 (1998).

13. The commitment to Scripture has been readily acknowledged inside the journal jacket from *BETS* 1-3 (1958-1960) to *JETS* 41 (1998). In 1991, the society added to its doctrinal basis the following statement: "God is a Trinity, Father, Son, and Holy Spirit, each an uncreated person, one in essence, equal in power and glory."

14. James A. Borland, Secretary-Treasurer of the Evangelical Society, informed me by telephone in June 1998 that the membership breakdown was 1,494 full members, 602 associate members, and 466 student members. Thus, ETS's total membership was 2,562 pending the removal of a few members due to their lapse in paying dues.

15. Arnold D. Ehlert, *A Bibliographic History of Dispensationalism* (Grand Rapids: Baker, 1965), 36-38. Other dispensationalists have perpetuated Ehlert's mistaken conclusion: Clarence E. Mason, "A Review of *Dispensationalism* by John Wick Bowman: Part I," *BSac* 114 (January-March 1957): 11-23; Charles C. Ryrie, *Dispensationalism Today,* 65-85; Renald E. Showers, *There Really Is a Difference!* (Bellmawr: The Friends of Israel Gospel Ministry, 1990), 27. Although Ehlert cites 1639-1716 as the dates for Edwards's life, *The*

Dictionary of National Biography correctly cites 1637–1716. *The Dictionary of National Biography*, 1917 ed., s.v. "Edwards, John" (1637–1716).

16. Vern S. Poythress, *Understanding Dispensationalists* (Grand Rapids: Zondervan Publishing House, 1987), 10–13. See also "Response to Paul S. Karleen's Paper 'Understanding Covenant Theologians,'" *GTJ* 10 (fall 1989): 147–155.

17. Craig A. Blaising, "The Extent and Varieties of Dispensationalism," in *Progressive Dispensationalism*, ed. Craig A. Blaising and Darrell L. Bock (Wheaton: Victor, 1993), 9–56; idem, "Changing Patterns in American Dispensational Theology," *WTJ* 29 (spring–fall 1994): 149–64. Unlike Blaising, who refers to the time of Chafer and Scofield as the classical period, Saucy refers to it as "the traditional dispensational system." Robert Saucy, "The Crucial Issue Between Dispensational and Nondispensational Systems," *CTR* 1 (fall 1986): 149–65. Regardless of how one refers to the time period or the system, a transition occurred in dispensational thinking during the 1950s, 1960s, and 1970s.

18. Ryrie, "Update on Dispensationalism," 20. Nichols echoes Ryrie and adds that Crutchfield uses the term "normative" to speak of "the entire dispensational tradition (classical and revised), excluding the progressives." He concludes that "the legitimacy of calling *progressive dispensationalism* part of the dispensational tradition is questionable." Stephen J. Nichols, "The Dispensational View of the Davidic Kingdom: A Response to Progressive Dispensationalism" *MSJ* 7 (fall 1996): 213–39. More recently, Robert Lightner has used the expression in *The Last Days Handbook: Revised and Updated* (Nashville: Nelson, 1997), 209–11. However, at a recent meeting of the Evangelical Theological Society (19 November 1998), Nichols expressed to Bock and me that he "overstated himself" in his above mentioned article. In fact, many dispensationalists (i.e., Walvoord, Campbell, Swindoll, and Toussaint, to name a few) regard progressive dispensationalism as part of the dispensational tradition.

19. The use of "today's dispensationalists" is merely a descriptive term chosen for this essay and is in no way intended to suggest that classical dispensationalism ("yesterday's dispensationalism") no longer exists.

20. For other charts that distinguish between the kingdom of God

and the kingdom of heaven, see Clarence Larkin, *Dispensational Truth* (Philadelphia: Rev. Clarence Larkin Est., 1918), 85–86. Craig A. Blaising, *Progressive Dispensationalism: An Up-to-Date Handbook of Contemporary Dispensational Thought* (Wheaton: Bridgepoint Books, 1993), 31. For another discussion concerning Scofield's perspective, see "The Doctrine of the Last Things as Found in the Prophets," "The Doctrine of the Last Things as Found in the Gospels," and "The Doctrine of the Last Things as Found in the Epistles and Revelation," in *The Coming and Kingdom of Christ* (Chicago: The Bible Institute Colportage Association, 1914), 89, 110–19, 175–82.

21. Clarence E. Mason Jr., "Matthew and Outlines of Mark, Luke, John," (n.p. class notes: Philadelphia College of Bible, 1971), 43. Although I never had Dr. Mason for a course, he spoke frequently in chapel, and his notes and the *New Scofield Reference Bible* with notes were required reading in the Bible courses I took while at PCB. Although Mason's notes are no longer required, reading the *New Scofield Reference Bible* with notes is still required reading.

22. Mason unequivocally says in his notes that "*Scofield's arguments are invalid:* The arguments for supposed distinctions between 'kingdom of *God*' and 'kingdom of *heaven*' given in the old Scofield at Mt. 6:33 are not valid." Elsewhere he says, "I came to the conclusion that this distinction . . . is not a valid distinction." Clarence E. Mason Jr., "Matthew and Outlines of Mark, Luke, John," (n.p.: Philadelphia College of Bible, 1971), 44; idem, *Prophetic Problems with Alternate Solutions* (Chicago: Moody, 1973), 101–109.

23. Carole Wenger, secretary to the president of PCB, W. Sherrill Babb, informed me by telephone on 10 June 1998 that Dr. Clarence E. Mason graduated from Wheaton College in 1924 and from the Evangelical Theological College (renamed Dallas Theological Seminary) in 1927. When he left Dallas, he assumed a pastorate at Weston Memorial Baptist Church in Philadelphia (1927–1934). He later pastored the Chelsea Baptist Church in Atlantic City (1935–1946). In 1928, he took a part-time teaching position at Philadelphia School of the Bible. In 1933, he assumed the position of academic dean. In 1946, he left the pastorate to devote his full attention to the school. He played a significant role in the 1951 merger of Philadelphia School of the Bible and Bible Institute of Pennsylvania. Although he retired from the office of academic

dean in 1969, he continued teaching at PCB. His teaching career spanned 46 years, from 1928–1974. He was not only a key player at PCB but played a significant role in the editing of the *New Scofield Reference Bible*.

24. Hannah, "A Review of *The Incredible Scofield and His Book*," 363.

25. C. I. Scofield, *Rightly Dividing the Word of Truth (2 Tim. 2:15)* (Findlay, Ohio: Fundamental Truth Publishers, 1936), 6. Although the work was initially published sometime during the 1890s, the edition I used is as Scofield wrote it.

26. Blaising, "Changing Patterns in American Dispensational Theology," 156. In fact, not only do the transcribed notes of the committee meetings state that it was a "Revision Committee," but also the notes reveal explicit references to conscious changes to Scofield's interpretations. I'll limit my citations to two documents: Scofield Revision Committee, *Transcription of Scofield Revision Committee Meeting* (Chicago, November 6–8, 1958). Scofield Revision Committee, *Transcription of Scofield Revision Committee Meeting* (Chicago, April 23–25, 1959).

27. Notes in the Pentateuch increased from 199 to 337 (138 were added), notes in the Historical Books increased from 41 to 138 (97 were added), notes in the Poetical Books increased from 55 to 76 (21 were added), notes in the Prophetical Books increased from 179 to 380 (201 were added), notes in the Four Gospels and Acts increased from 167 to 345 (178 were added), notes in the Epistles of Paul increased from 99 to 148 (49 were added), and notes in the Jewish Christian Epistles increased from 67 to 104 (37 were added).

28. Alva J. McClain, *The Greatness of the Kingdom* (Grand Rapids: Zondervan, 1959), 21; idem, "Greatness of Kingdom—Part IV: Mediatorial Kingdom from Acts to Eternal," *BSac* 112 (October 1955): 308. For a historical sketch of Alva J. McClain, see Norman B. Rohrer, *A Saint in Glory Stands: The Story of Alva J. McClain, Founder of Grace Theological Seminary* (Winona Lake: BMH Books, 1986).

29. The division is evident in the transcribed committee notes of the Scofield Revision Committee, *Transcription of Scofield Revision Committee Meeting* (Chicago, November 6–8, 1958), 78–86. Culbertson concludes a somewhat lengthy debate with "May I suggest that I agree with what Dr. Walvoord said to this extent, that whatever we do ought to be in keeping with what Scofield

has done. I think you have made a wise decision. Let's take it from there." Six months later, disagreement continued to exist among the committee members. At the conclusion of what may have been quite a lively discussion, English says, "I think this is one of the places where we have to stay with the Scofield position. It is not our Bible, it is the Scofield Bible." Gaebelein's response: "But we have the right to change it if there is a truth involved." Scofield Revision Committee, *Transcription of Scofield Revision Committee Meeting* (Chicago, April 23–25, 1959), 170–81, esp. 174. Debate continued until the notes we have in the *New Scofield Reference Bible* were approved with some resistance from Mason ("Oh, I'll accept them") and disappointment from Gaeblelein ("I think he [Walvoord's reworking of McClain's work] has done the very best he can do. But I would be much happier if there was mention made of the other view"). The "other view" is the one that says no distinction exists between the kingdom of God and the kingdom of heaven. Scofield Revision Committee, *Transcription of Scofield Revision Committee Meeting* (Chicago, April 23–25, 1959), 244–53.

30. *Distinct:* John N. Darby, "The Dispensation of the Kingdom of Heaven," in *The Collected Writings of J. N. Darby*, ed. William Kelly, 34 vols. (reprint, Sunbury, Pa.: Believer's Bookshelf, 1972) 2:54–55. For a discussion of Darby's view, see Mark. L. Bailey, "Dispensational Definition of the Kingdom" in *Integrity of Heart, Skillfulness of Hands: Biblical and Leadership Studies in Honor of Donald K. Campbell*, ed. C. H. Dyer and R. B. Zuck (Grand Rapids: Baker, 1994), 201–21. Clarence Larkin, *Dispensational Truth*, 85–86. Chafer, *Systematic Theology*, 4:26; V, 316; idem, "Dispensationalism," *BSac* 93 (October–December 1936): 390–449, esp., 424–26. Charles C. Ryrie, *The Passion of the Premillennial Faith* (Neptune, N.J.: Loizeaux Brothers, 1953), 98–104. *Synonymous Yet Distinct:* McClain, *The Greatness of the Kingdom*, 16–21. J. Dwight Pentecost, *Things to Come* (Grand Rapids: Zondervan, 1958), 142–44. John F. Walvoord, "The New Testament Doctrine of the Kingdom," *BSac* 139 (July–September 1982): 208–13, 302–303; idem, *Matthew: Thy Kingdom Come* (Chicago: Moody, 1974), 30–31. *Synonymous:* Erich Sauer, *The Triumph of the Crucified* (Grand Rapids: Eerdmans, 1951), 23. Clarence E. Mason, see discussion above. *The Ryrie Study Bible*, Matt. 3:2 n.; Mark 1:15 n.; "The Doctrine of Future Things," 1953. Stanley

D. Toussaint, *Behold the King: A Study of Matthew* (Portland: Multnomah, 1980), 65–68; idem, "The Kingdom in Matthew's Gospel" in *Essays in Honor of J. Dwight Pentecost,* ed. C. H. Dyer (Chicago: Moody, 1986), 23.

31. Mason (above), Ryrie, Blaising, and Saucy all point to Ladd as one who viewed the distinction between the kingdom of God and the kingdom of heaven as a significant feature in dispensational thinking. George E. Ladd, *Crucial Questions About the Kingdom of God* (Grand Rapids: Eerdmans, 1952), 212. Saucy adds Millard Erickson, *Contemporary Options in Eschatology* (Grand Rapids: Baker, 1977), 212. We might also add to the list Clarence B. Bass in *Backgrounds to Dispensationalism: Its Historical Genesis and Ecclesiastical Implications* (Grand Rapids: Baker, 1960), 31; and Cox in *Biblical Studies in Final Things,* 39. See Ryrie, *Dispensationalism Today,* 170–73; idem, *Dispensationalism,* 154–55. Blaising, "Developing Dispensationalism Part 1," 260. Saucy, "The Crucial Issue Between Dispensational and Nondispensational Systems," 19 n.18.

32. Mark L. Bailey, "Dispensational Definitions of the Kingdom," in *Integrity of Heart, Skillfulness of Hands: Biblical Leadership Studies in Honor of Donald K. Campbell,* ed. C. H. Dyer and R. B. Zuck (Grand Rapids: Baker, 1994), 201–21, esp. 213. For a similar perspective, see Charles L. Feinberg, *Premillennialism or Amillennialism* (Wheaton: VanKampen, 1954), 123–28; and idem, *Millennialism: The Two Major Views* (Chicago: Moody, 1936; repr. Winona Lake: BMH Books, 1985), 253–54.

33. Chafer, *Systematic Theology,* 5:347. PCB places particular emphasis on the postponement of the kingdom. A portion of their creed reads: "We believe in the actual offering of a kingdom to Israel by Christ as His first coming, and His postponement thereof as a result of their rejection." *Philadelphia College of Bible 1997–98 Catalog* (Philadelphia: Philadelphia College of Bible, 1997), 8.

34. Charles Ryrie, *The Basics of the Premillennial Faith,* 130–35; *Basic Theology* (Wheaton: Victor Books, 1986), 397–99. John Walvoord, *Matthew: Thy Kingdom Come* (Chicago: Moody, 1974), 95–108; *Major Bible Prophecies* (Grand Rapids: Zondervan, 1991), 212–18, 361–62. For a brief discussion and chart of Ryrie's and Walvoord's view, see Blaising's discussion in *Progressive Dispensationalism,* 40–44.

35. Rather than use the phrases the "kingdom of God" and "kingdom of heaven," McClain prefers the phrases "the universal king-

dom" of God and "the mediatorial kingdom." The universal kingdom speaks of God's eternal kingdom whereas the mediatorial kingdom speaks of God's reign on earth: (1) the past mediatorial kingdom is the period during which time God's promises were made with Israel beginning with Abraham, (2) the interregnum age is the period during which time no mediatorial reign of Israel exists—it is the period between the reigns—and (3) the future mediatorial kingdom is the period during which time Israel's promises are consummated. Hoyt (the second president of Grace College and Seminary) echoed McClain's teachings, and Toussaint from Dallas Seminary adopted McClain's view of the present age as an "interregnum." "Dispensationalists owe much to McClain," says Bailey, "for one of the first comprehensive treatments of the kingdom as it is developed throughout history." For a brief discussion and chart of McClain's view, see Blaising's discussion in *Progressive Dispensationalism,* 39–40. McClain, *The Greatness of the Kingdom.* H. Hoyt, *The End Times* (Chicago: Moody, 1969); idem, "Dispensational Premillennialism," in *The Meaning of the Millennium,* ed. Robert G. Clouse (Downers Grove, Ill.: InterVarsity, 1977), 63–92. Stanley D. Toussaint, *Behold the King* (Portland: Multnomah, 1980), 172–76. Bailey, "Dispensational Definitions of the Kingdom," 210.

36. Rather than use the phrases the "kingdom of God" and "kingdom of heaven," Pentecost prefers the phrases "the eternal kingdom of God" and "the theocratic kingdom on earth." For a brief discussion and chart of Pentecost's view, see Blaising's discussion in *Progressive Dispensationalism,* 44–46. Pentecost's book, *Thy Kingdom Come* (Wheaton: Victor, 1990), excludes any mention of the kingdom of heaven.

37. Larkin, *Dispensational Truth,* 151.

38. Lewis Sperry Chafer, "Bibliology," *Systematic Theology,* 8 vols. (Dallas: Dallas Seminary Press, 1948), 1:43.

39. Chafer, *Systematic Theology,* 4:314–15. A contemporary dispensationalist from Philadelphia College of Bible, John R. Master, nuances a similar view ("The New Covenant," in *Issues in Dispensationalism,* ed. Wesley R. Willis and John R. Master [Grand Rapids: Moody, 1994], 93–110).

40. Chafer, *Systematic Theology,* 7:98–99. Ryrie at one time argued that two new covenants were possible, but later shifted back to his

previous position. Compare Ryrie, *The Basis of the Premillennial Faith,* 106–25, with *Ryrie's Study Bible,* Hebrews 8:6 note.

41. *Scofield Reference Bible,* 804 n. 1 (emphasis mine).

42. *Scofield Reference Bible,* 1297–98 n. 2. In his previous note (same verse), Scofield says, "the New Covenant secures the personal revelation of the Lord to every believer (v. 11); the complete oblivion of sins (v. 12; Heb. 10. 17; cf. Heb. 10. 3); rests upon an accomplished redemption (Mt. 26. 27, 28; 1 Cor. 11. 25; Heb. 9. 11, 12, 18–23); and secures the perpetuity, and future conversion, and blessing of Israel (Jer. 31. 31–40). . . ."

43. John F. McGahey, "An Exposition of the New Covenant" (Th.D. diss., Dallas Theological Seminary, 1957), 184. McGahey makes a similar connection when he discusses Paul's use of the new covenant in 1 Corinthians 11:23–24. Ibid., 200–207.

44. Ibid., 185. McGahey previously points out that "Literature on the theory of the two New Covenants is scarce, and that which is available does not dwell particularly on the point of time when the New Covenant with the church was established." Such a position, says McGahey "is tantamount to saying that there are two covenant peoples, Israel and the Church." Ibid., 57–58.

45. James R. McGahey, son of John F. McGahey, informed me by telephone on 14 July 1998 that his father graduated in 1950 from Upsala College in Newark, N.J., and from DTS in 1954 (Th.M.) and 1957 (Th.D.). When he left DTS in 1957, he took his one and only teaching position at PCB (1957–1986). He served as interim pastor in various churches throughout his teaching career. He was a devoted teacher of God's Word, and his students will always remember him for his favorite theological discussion, which began with "Israel is not the church."

46. McGahey, "An Exposition of the New Covenant," 186.

47. Ibid., 186–94; cf. McGahey's discussion of "Ministers of the New Covenant" (2 Cor. 3:5–6), 209–15; "Identity of the New Covenant (Heb. 8:6–13)," 230–36. In a similar view, Scofield says "the New Covenant rests upon the sacrifice of Christ, and secures the eternal blessedness, under the Abrahamic Covenant (Gal. 3. 13–29), of all who believe" (*Scofield Reference Bible,* 1298; cp. *New Scofield Reference Bible,* 1318).

48. *Only for Israel:* John N. Darby, "The Dispensation of the Kingdom of Heaven," in *The Collected Writings of J. N. Darby,* ed. William

Kelly, 34 vols. (reprint, Sunbury, Pa.: Believer's Bookshelf, 1972), 27:565–66. John R. Master, "The New Covenant," in *Issues in Dispensationalism* (Chicago: Moody, 1994), 93–110. *Two New Covenants:* Chafer (see above); idem, "Dispensationalism," 437–38. Walvoord, "The New Covenant with Israel," *BSac* 110 (1953), 193–205. In a more recent publication, Walvoord seems to argue for one new covenant as it is mediated through a doctrine of grace. See Walvoord, "The New Covenant," in *Integrity of Heart, Skillfulness of Hands: Biblical and Leadership Studies in Honor of Donald K. Campbell,* ed. C. H. Dyer and R. B. Zuck (Grand Rapids: Baker, 1994), 186–200. Charles C. Ryrie, *Dispensationalism* (Chicago: Moody, 1996), 170–74. *Inaugurated New Covenant:* Homer Kent Jr., McClain's former student and colleague, informed me by telephone on 16 June 1998 that McClain agreed with the *New Scofield Reference Bible's* presentation of the new covenant and disagreed with the two new covenants theory. Ryrie appears to maintain an "already-not yet" view of the covenant in his Hebrews 8:6 note. See *Ryrie Study Bible,* 1846. Bock, see chapter 5 of this book.

49. Ryrie refers to such statements as "unguarded." Ryrie, *Dispensationalism,* 107. Alva J. McClain addresses the issue in his book, *Law and Grace* (Winona Lake: BMH Books, 1954).

50. Charles C. Ryrie, *Dispensationalism Today* (Chicago: Moody, 1965), 7.

51. Ibid., 44–47. Ryrie restates this definition in *Dispensationalism,* 38–41. The three points of Ryrie's definition as well as Scofield's seven dispensations are still maintained by some contemporaries of the 1960s. See, for instance, Thomas's definition and dispensational divisions in the *Dictionary of Premillennial Theology,* 1996 ed., s.v. "Dispensationalism."

52. Ibid., 9. Ryrie expands this statement in his new book to include ". . . though the basic tenets have not changed." *Dispensationalism,* 11.

53. "The dispensationalist believes," according to Chafer, "that throughout the ages God is pursuing two distinct purposes: one related to the earth with earthly people and earthly objectives involved, while the other is related to heaven with heavenly people and heavenly objectives involved." This twofold purpose of God is based upon Chafer's plain and natural understanding of the phrases "kingdom of God" and "kingdom of heaven." Chafer, "Dispensationalism," cp. 448 w/446–47, 424–25. For Blaising's discussion, see "Doctrinal Development in Orthodoxy," 267–69.

54. "The Kingdom of God is," says McClain, "in a certain and important sense, the grand central theme of all Holy Scripture." McClain, *Greatness of the Kingdom,* 4–5. Thus, to understand the kingdom of God, for McClain, is to understand God's mediatorial kingdom, which began in the Old Testament and will eventually be consummated in the future with the second advent of Jesus Christ. "The great theme of God's kingdom program," says Pentecost, "can be found throughout the Bible, from Genesis to Revelation. It is a theme that unifies all of Scripture." Pentecost, *Thy Kingdom Come,* 11. For a similar statement, see Pentecost's *Things to Come,* 433. See Saucy's discussion in "The Crucial Issue," 24–27.

55. Blaising, "Development of Dispensationalism," 267–69; "Dispensationalism, the Search for Definition," 23–30, esp. 27.

56. Ryrie at one time argued, "If one interprets literally, he arrives at the premillennial system. If one employs the spiritualizing or allegorizing method of interpretation in the field of eschatology, he arrives at amillennialism." Ryrie, *The Basics of the Premillennial Faith,* 47. Chafer likewise contended that "it should be observed that the liberal theologian spiritualizes both the virgin birth and the Davidic throne; the partial dispensationalist (amillennialist) 'shares the fundamental error' of the liberal theologian to the extent of spiritualizing the Davidic throne; while the dispensationalist, believing that no justification of interpretation within the bounds of an utterance confined almost to one sentence, spiritualizes neither the birth nor the throne." Chafer, "Dispensationalism," *BSac* 93 (October–December 1936), 400. Such statements are over-simplifications of the issue and unfortunately reflect a guilt-by-association argument.

57. Blaising contends that the consistently literal hermeneutic never was the practice of earlier dispensationalists. Nor was it ever a conscious objective until Ryrie. He also argues that the consistently historical-literary hermeneutic is more completely realized in progressive dispensationalism than in any of the earlier varieties of dispensationalism. However, it is also being pursued by other evangelicals. See n. 58 below. Thus, consistently literal or historical-literary hermeneutics never was and could not be said to be the hermeneutic that is practiced only by dispensationalists. Craig Blaising, review of "Dispensationalism Yesterday and Today," 8 Sep-

tember 1998; "Dispensationalism, the Search for Definition," 23–30, esp. 26.

58. Poythress, *Understanding Dispensationalists,* 82–86. When the Dispensational Study Group convened in 1989, dispensationalists and nondispensationalists alike came together to interact with Poythress and his book. A significant amount of time was spent discussing the literal hermeneutic of the dispensationalist and nondispensationalist. In his paper, Karleen (former professor at PCB) admitted that "it is not simply the case that the dispensationalist holds to literal interpretation of the prophets and the covenant theologian does not. That is not the distinguishing feature" (p. 131). "We have to get at," says Karleen, "the roots of the system" (p. 133). The "roots" are the presuppositions that dominate both the dispensational and nondispensational traditions. In fact, during the Dispensational Study Group's interaction time, the question was posed, "Do [dispensationalists] have a different hermeneutic? Virtually all agree that they do not. The point is a different outcome because of different assumptions in thinking rather than a different hermeneutical approach" (p. 162). For Paul S. Karleen's paper, "Understanding Covenant Theologians: A Study in Presuppositions"; Robert L. Saucy's paper, "Response to *Understanding Dispensationalists* by Vern S. Poythress"; and "Dispensational Study Group Discussion," see *GTJ* 10:2 (1989): 123–64.

59. Mike Stallard, "Literal Interpretation, Theological Method, and the Essence of Dispensationalism," *JMT* 1 (spring 1997), 5–36. Blaising more pointedly contends, "Today, for many scholars to say the difference (between a dispensationalist and a nondispensationalist) is simply between literal and spiritual exegesis is not accurate and is in fact misleading." Blaising, "Doctrinal Development in Orthodoxy," 270–71.

60. In fairness to Waltke, he is not to be confused with precritical or noncritical amillennial expositors who cite OT texts (specifically the Psalms) to be direct prophecy because of a NT author's selective usage of OT texts. In Waltke's opinion, "the noncritical approach tends to discredit the messianic claims of Christ by its neglect of history." He clearly argues for a canonical approach to the Psalms by interpreting them in light of their historical significance(s) and their messianic significance. B. K. Waltke, "A

Canonical Process Approach to the Psalms," in *Tradition and Testament*, ed. J. S. Feinberg and P. D. Feinberg (Chicago: Moody, 1981), 3–18. See also "Is It Right to Read the New Testament into the Old?" *ChrTo* 27 (September 2, 1983): 77.

61. In his article "Evangelicals and the Use of the Old Testament in the New," Bock astutely identifies four divergent "schools" in evangelicalism and artfully labels them according to their "distinctive qualities." Bock qualifies his use of the term "schools" when he says, "None of these groups has consciously attempted to form a 'school'; but the term is used simply for convenience." For Bock's discussion of the Canonical Approach and New Testament School see D. L. Bock, "Evangelicals and the Use of the Old Testament in the New: Part 1," *BSac* 142 (1985): 219–20.

62. For my more complete discussion and evaluation of Waltke's perspective, see "Jewish and Apostolic Hermeneutics: How the Old Testament is Used in Hebrews 1:5–13" (Ph.D. diss., Dallas Theological Seminary, 1993), 26–38.

63. The use of *expansion of meaning* reflects a more recent choice of terminology. In the past, *sensus plenior* was the way to describe what was happening between the testaments. In his article, "The History and Development of the Theory of a *Sensus Plenior*," *CBQ* 15 (1953): 141–62, Raymond Brown traces the historical development of the theory of *sensus plenior* in Roman Catholicism and notes that the first use of the term *sensus plenior* was a contribution of Fr. Andrea Fernández in the late 1920s. The *sensus plenior* concept emerged as early as 1885 by R. Cornely. Cornely referred to the concept as "consequent sense" in his book *Introductio Generalis*, in Cursus Sacra Scripture (Paris: Lethielleux, 1885), 1:527–30. For a Catholic, however, *sensus plenior* may entail more than Scripture (i.e., Deutero-Canonical Books, Church Councils, and Ministeriums). Bock prefers to discuss *expansion of meaning* without connecting it to *sensus plenior* approaches, given that *sensus plenior* is held in so many different ways that it is no longer considered a helpful term. This example shows the increasing complexity that has entered into current hermeneutic discussion. Old boxes no longer help us discuss current phenomena. For Bock's broader discussion, see "Evangelicals and the Use of the Old Testament in the New," 212–15. The divine intent-human author school is also referred to as the *sensus plenior* theory in that article.

64. E. E. Johnson, "Author's Intention and Biblical Interpretation," in *Hermeneutics, Inerrancy, and the Bible: [papers from ICBI Summit II]*, ed. E. D. Radmacher and R. D. Preus (Grand Rapids: Zondervan, 1984), 409–29; "Hermeneutics and Dispensationalism," in *Walvoord: A Tribute*, ed. Donald K. Campbell (Chicago: Moody, 1982), 239–56; "Dual Authorship and the Single Intended Meaning of Scripture," *BSac* 143 (1986): 218–27; *Expository Hermeneutics: An Introduction* (Grand Rapids: Zondervan, 1990); "What I Mean by Historical-Grammatical Interpretation and How That Differs from Spiritual Interpretation" *GTJ* 11 (fall 1990): 157–69; "Prophetic Fulfillment: The Already and Not Yet" in *Issues in Dispensationalism*, ed. W. R. Willis and J. R. Master (Chicago: Moody, 1994), 183–202. For my more complete discussion and evaluation of Elliott Johnson's perspective, see "Jewish and Apostolic Hermeneutics," 39–61.

65. Darrell L. Bock, "Interpreting the Bible—How Texts Speak to Us," in *Progressive Dispensationalism*, ed. C. A. Blaising and D. L. Bock (Wheaton: Bridgepoint, 1993), 76–105.

66. Richard N. Longenecker, *Biblical Exegesis in the Apostolic Period*, 2d ed. (1975; Grand Rapids: Eerdmans, 1999).

67. Jacob Neusner, William S. Green, and Ernest Frerichs, eds., *Judaisms and Their Messiahs* (New York: Cambridge University Press, 1987). James H. Charlesworth, ed. *The Messiah: Developments in Earliest Judaism and Christianity* (Minneapolis: Fortress, 1992). James VanderKam, "Messianism in the Scrolls," in *The Community of the Renewed Covenant*, ed. Eugene Ulrich and James VanderKam (Notre Dame: University Press, 1994), 211–34. Craig C. Broyles, "The Redeeming King: Psalm 72's Contribution to the Messianic Ideal" in *Eschatology, Messianism, and the Dead Sea Scrolls*, ed. Craig A. Evans and Peter W. Flint (Grand Rapids: Eerdmans, 1997), 23–40. William Horbury, "Messianism in the Old Testament Apocrypha and Pseudepigrapha," in *King and Messiah in Israel and The Ancient Near East*, ed. John Day (Sheffield, England: Sheffield Academic Press, 1998): 402–33. George J. Brooke, "Kingship and Messianism in the Dead Sea Scrolls," in *King and Messiah in Israel and The Ancient Near East*, ed. John Day (Sheffield, England: Sheffield Academic Press, 1998): 434–55.

68. Although he at one time referred to this school of thought as the Historical Progressive Revelation & Jewish Hermeneutic School,

today he prefers to speak of it as a Jewish Background and Apostolic School because there is more involved than a Jewish reading of Scripture. It also includes how they tried to integrate Scripture, recontextualize Scripture, and apply Scripture to their time. For Bock's broader discussion of the Historical Progressive Revelation & Jewish Hermeneutic School, see "Evangelicals and the Use of the Old Testament in the New," 216–18. For my more complete discussion and evaluation, see "Jewish and Apostolic Hermeneutics," 62–71.

PART ONE
HERMENEUTICS

CHAPTER TWO

A Traditional Dispensational Hermeneutic

Elliott E. Johnson
with a response by Darrell L. Bock

Dispensationalists agree that the Bible must be at the center of discussions in theology. The book jacket of *Progressive Dispensationalism* describes the "tradition's ongoing commitment to examine itself in light of Scripture and engage in a biblically focused dialogue. . . ." This recognized emphasis naturally raises the questions about the interpretation of the Bible. These questions take on a featured prominence in a dispensational theology, and account for Charles Ryrie's consideration of literal interpretation of a *sine qua non* of the system. Thus, this chapter will focus our attention on literal interpretation. The point of the chapter will be to clarify what a dispensationalist means when speaking of a consistent literal interpretation and *then* to defend this rule in principle as one *sine qua non* of a dispensational system of theology.[1]

Evangelical interpreters since the Reformation have recognized the importance of literal interpretation.[2] The Council on Biblical Inerrancy repeatedly returned to discussions that reinforced a literal interpretation as being a foundation from which to fashion hermeneutics. Until recent years, there has been little consensus about what in particular is meant by "literal." Dispensationalists have further debated how consistently that rule ought to be used or whether it is merely a desirable goal. Ryrie speaks of it as "an absolutely indispensable part," or as a *sine qua non* of the system. He writes, "To be sure, literal/historical/grammatical interpretation is not the sole possession or practice of dispensationalists, but *the consistent use* in all areas of biblical interpretation is. . . ."[3]

It is precisely this claim of consistent use of literal interpretation with which Blaising and Bock raise issues. Blaising contends that at times in the history of the tradition, spiritual interpretations of classical dispensationalists have controlled interpretation in the traditional system rather than historical or grammatical factors in the text.[4] Thus, Blaising summarizes that "a clear-plain-normal" principle is "at best oversimplified and at worst false" as a claim to represent dispensationalists' use of the Bible in history.[5]

Bock's critique features the oversimplification of consistently literal interpretation in his book *Progressive Dispensationalism*, in which he introduces a more sophisticated consideration of what is "clear or plain or normal."[6] "Interpretation is not," according to Bock, "a matter of seeing one rule or approach applied to every text. . . ."[7] Thus, Ryrie's claim is questioned both historically and hermeneutically. In spite of these criticisms, this chapter will advance Ryrie's claim again and seek to establish its validity.

What Is Literal Interpretation?

Today, dispensationalists would agree that literal interpretation is a grammatical, historical interpretation.[8] The question of definition that remains concerns what aspects of grammar and what factors in history are necessary to the interpretation of biblical texts. Early in dispensational hermeneutics, Rollin Chafer cast the discussion in the context of axioms of general hermeneutics. Axiom five states: "The true object of interpretation is to apprehend the exact thought of the author."[9] The International Council on Biblical Inerrancy recognized the relationship between these necessary factors in Article XV: "WE AFFIRM the *necessity* of interpreting the Bible according to its literal, or normal, sense. The literal sense is the grammatical-historical sense, that is, *the meaning which the writer expressed.*"[10]

What these statements specify is that an author communicates through a text to an audience in a specific historical period of time. Thus, the grammar that is necessary is that related to what an author has written—including lexicography, syntax, and literary genre. The history that is necessary involves the author and his worldview, the occasion for the original communication and the original readers and their worldview. Thus, *literal* interpretation entails those meanings which the author intended to communicate in the expressions of the text (grammar) in the original setting (historical). *Literal* thus works with a text within the frame of an author and his communication.

Such a definition of literal provides an answer to a problem Ryrie originally posed. "Hermeneutics is that science which furnishes the principles of interpretation. These principles guide and govern anybody's system of theology. They ought to be determined *before* one's theology is systematized, but in practice the reverse is usually true."[11] While in practice, simple reading of texts comes first, from which doctrines are formed, it is also evident that this reading is based on a common-sense belief, that is, when we read, we seek to grasp what the author has said.[12] Thus, while no formal hermeneutic may be in place, yet the core maxim from which all other principles are framed is present and is informally guiding the reading of texts and, thus, the forming of a theology. This belief gave direction to early dispensationalists in their study of the Bible, even though it was not in a self-conscious awareness.

While Bock might accept this definition, he certainly would criticize the proposal as overly simplistic. In principle, "interpretation is not a matter of seeing one rule or approach" because of the variety of ways meaning operates and texts are reused whether they are reused within Scripture or extrabiblical material.[13] In spite of his objection, the divine author/human author who intends to communicate through a text is a genuinely normative fact of every biblical text. That fact makes the principle necessary to recognize the meaning of any text as written or as reused, based on meaning.

This response, however, should not be taken to suggest that the task is simple. It is clearly not. And that reality is the basis for Bock's second criticism. He describes that complexity in that often the Bible contains a "mediated message."[14] That mediation occurs in the consideration of authorship, message, and history. First, related to authorship is inspiration, which introduces multiple authors (the human and the divine). He then asks, "Whose intent is to be pursued? Are they always the same?"[15] If they are different, how different may they be and still have shared authorship?

Second, related to message, is the condition of gospel literature or the presence of Psalms ascribed to possible multiple authorship (Pss. 84–85) presenting two messages? Is the message of the text Jesus' historical message? Or, is it the gospel writer's message? Are these messages ever different or may they be disparate?

Third, related to history, does a stated meaning about a historical event change or expand when that event is again interpreted with the benefit of a perspective of time? Bock uses the illustration of the election of President Clinton. On the evening of the election, a journalist ventures an interpretation of what that event meant. The meaning of that same election is revisited after the President has entered his second term. The question is, has the meaning of his original interpretation changed or expanded? It is important that that question be distinguished from another. Does the meaning of that event, now seen in light of subsequent events, change or expand? The answer to the second question is likely to be yes. With the benefit of the perspective of time, his understanding, now viewed more as a historian, may well change. But that change does not alter or expand the meaning of his originally stated interpretation. That is the first question. And in fact, he may even judge that original interpretation to be wrong, or inadequate, or even right on target. But to make such a judgment depends upon the stability in meaning of the original statement. In other words, there is in the judgment another common-sense belief that an expressed meaning is stable, based on the statement made.

Similarly, the Bible contains numerous statements and interpretations about historical events and the meaning of those events. In the progress of revelation, does the meaning of these statements change or expand due to the perspective of added revelation? As an example, does the meaning of Moses' historical record interpreting the exodus from Egypt change or expand soon after Israel had been deposed from the land again? Or does the meaning of Isaiah's sign given to Ahaz in his unbelief change or expand in light of Matthew's use of that sign to interpret the

Virgin Birth? Our principle is that the meaning of these statements is stable in spite of the perspective gained by further revelation. And the truth of these statements made by prophets is also stable in spite of subsequent revelation.

So the meaning of Moses' historical record of the Exodus is stable even though a reader's understanding may be enriched and deepened by subsequent revelation. It now is clear that Israel's redemption at the Exodus is not complete. Yet in speaking of what God would do in the future as redemption, this further revelation reflects that the original record of the experience was a true model of what God does. Thus, our understanding has matured in time, but the type of meaning originally expressed has not expanded. It still means "redemption from Egypt."

Similarly, Isaiah's statement, which provided a sign for Ahaz, is stable in meaning. That stability is undermined if the sign in the original set of circumstances meant a natural conception, the timing of which is a sign, and if in the later set of circumstances the sign means a supernatural conception, which is the sign. The original sign may be followed by a second sign, but the original sign does not change to become a second sign.

While the questions of history and the benefits gained in the progress of revelation may introduce added complexity to interpretation, it does not invalidate the principle that literal is what an author intends to communicate through a text. Of primary importance is the relation between the intended meaning of the divine author and the human author. Bock helps as he points out that "Author(s) and text go together."[16] The words of the text are both the words of God and the words of the human author. In some sense, then, the meaning of God and the human author is the same. In another sense, the meaning intended by God may well be richer than the meaning of which the human author was aware (1 Peter 1:10–11). The shared meaning must be based on the words of the text. This meaning expressed may be conceived as a comprehensive or generic message. At the same time, the divine author knows all the implications entailed in that message of the text, expressed or unexpressed. So the principle of dual authorship can be included in a workable definition of literal interpretation. Ultimately, it is the meaning of the divine author that the Christian seeks. Yet it is the human author's writing that is the doorway that frames our access to what God means.

Of subsequent importance is the mediated message in history which creates a significant conflict in the view of the dispensational system of theology. This conflict appears as the New Testament is seen to reuse Old Testament texts and expand upon the meaning expressed in the Old Testament. One such opinion, shared by both Blaising and Bock, is the use of the Abrahamic covenant to refer to Gentile believers. That reference is said to involve a spiritual fulfillment. Blaising writes: "In spite of revised dispensationalism's insistence on consistent literal interpretation, they believed that the church was the 'spiritual' seed of Abraham, that is, the Abrahamic covenant was fulfilled 'spiritually' in the church."[17] To describe this as "spiritual fulfillment" and not simply as "spiritual application"[18] carries with it certain entailments. At the core, fulfillment answers a previous commitment to act toward a particular people that has now been realized. But in reference to a spiritual seed, where does such a commitment appear? Statements in Genesis (13:16; 15:5; 22:17) commit God to multiply Abraham's descendants. Such descendants would be "spiritual" in the sense that God provided them, but the focus is that the descendants are "physical or natural." So the statements of Genesis do not include references to Gentiles as descendants.

Thus, the question must be asked: in what sense are the Gentiles' spiritual seed in fulfillment of Abraham's promises? If it would be determined from the perspective of Christ, then the original meaning of Genesis is *expanded* based on this new perspective. This *sensus plenior* must then be attributed to what God meant in some fashion. Bock follows a similar argument for expanded meaning in fulfillment.[19]

Such an argument for a spiritual fulfillment is neither necessary nor warranted from the texts involved nor from a dispensational system. Rather, Gentiles, as blessed, are a literal fulfillment of Genesis 12:3, and the blessing of becoming the seed of Abraham is received as the theological result of the work of Christ (Gal. 3:26–29).

A literal reading of Genesis 12:3 promises that "*through* Abraham, *all nations* of the earth shall be blessed." In Abraham's life, that promise experienced some initial fulfillments, as in the case of Eliezer of Damascus who was blessed through association with Abraham. In the lives of the faithful heirs of Abraham in the Old Testament, an unspecified number of Gentiles were blessed, as in David's fighting men (2 Sam. 23). Now that the heir of Abraham has appeared in Jesus Christ, Gentiles are blessed *through* Him (Gal. 3:26–29).

Paul does not argue that Gentiles are blessed because the promise in reference to multiplied seed has been spiritually fulfilled in Gentiles. No quote nor allusion to these promises in Genesis appears in the text of Galatians. Rather, Paul argues on the basis of Gentile identification with Christ *through* whom they are blessed. Paul identifies that blessing because they are now heirs of the promise given to Abraham. This is true because the promise to Abraham is now given to Christ (Gal. 3:16). He is heir of all that was promised to Abraham, and since we as Gentile believers are identified with Him (baptized into Him), we now share as fellow heirs with Him in His inheritance (Rom. 8:16–17). The New Testament specifies what was simply promised as "blessing" in the Old Testament. And this specification came as new revelation, and that new revelation is a surprise as Gentiles become joint heirs with Christ. It is a surprise because no clue of equal blessing for Gentiles appears in the Old Testament. That is *not* a spiritual fulfillment but a literal fulfillment of Genesis 12:3.

The warrant claimed by Bock for his interpretation is the broader considerations of the system of progressive dispensationalism rather than the texts involved. After sketching an outline of his proposed "already-not yet" fulfillment of the covenants of promise—Abrahamic, Davidic, and new covenants—he advances his reasoning. "The entire discussion *assumes* a context of promise and fulfillment (system of theology), so it is the realization of one fundamental promise to Abraham that is being realized. Even then, with Jesus as the turning point (system of theology), we are not done. For those who are 'in Christ' also become 'the seed,' as Galatians 3:29 shows."[20] This is a departure from consistent literal interpretation to introduce spiritual meanings based on a construed "already-not yet" model of fulfillment. Such conclusions are neither necessary because of a lack of textual evidence nor warranted by the texts that are used and reused. Rather, the assumed context of promise and fulfillment becomes the basis for arguing spiritual fulfillment of promises of Abraham. This is a similar argument that Blaising posits for the "revised dispensationalists," who inconsistently and unconsciously see the church as a spiritual fulfillment of the Abrahamic covenant.

This first section has defined literal interpretation based on a belief in the testimony of Scriptures. This definition is that the meaning of a text is what the divine author intends to communicate as expressed by the Spirit-empowered human author. In addition, the consistent use of this principle was presented in distinction to advocating a theological system to expand or alter the meaning that was expressed in a text. In principle, if not always in practice, traditional dispensationalism would strongly contend this point with progressive dispensationalism.[21]

What Is Consistent Literal Interpretation?

An absolutely indispensable part of dispensationalism is an appropriate approach to the reading of the Bible. That is the *sine qua non* of literal interpretation. As defined, one reads to recognize what the divine author intends to communicate based on what he expressed in the text. This final section seeks to defend the consistent application of the principle in response to four questions.

1. *Is consistent literal interpretation possible?* It is possible because the literal principle as defined is genuinely normative. Every text has an author. Whether that author is unknown—as in the epistle of Hebrews—or that traditional testimony of authorship is questioned—as in critical studies—there still remains an implied textual author. Our limited historical knowledge does not alter the nature of biblical writings.

In the Bible, every text is meant to communicate a meaningful message. The doctrine of inspiration of an author or an editor (such as Ezra) provides the theological warrant to apply literal interpretation consistently.

2. *Is consistent literal interpretation determinative of a dispensational system of theology?* Blaising misrepresents Ryrie's proposal that consistent literal interpretation is a *sine qua non*. Blaising seems to mislead readers to believe that Ryrie "claimed that only dispensationalists practiced consistently literal interpretation. If a person practiced consistently literal interpretation (as defined

by the equation), then he or she would be a dispensationalist."[22] All that Ryrie claims is that it is "an absolutely indispensable part of dispensationalism" and not that it is in and of itself sufficient to determine that system of theology. E. D. Hirsch[23] has demonstrated that no general principle, like the principle of literal interpretation, is capable of determining particular conclusions about the meaning of the text. Thus, to reject the "consistent literal interpretation" as a *sine qua non* of dispensationalism based on Blaising's misrepresentation of the role of the principle is invalid.

3. *Is consistent literal interpretation necessary?* Ryrie argues that three reasons exist that explain why a consistent literal interpretation is "absolutely indispensable." First, a consistent literal interpretation is a necessary principle of interpretation because the Bible claims to be God's communication to men through human writers. If communication is to exist, the interpreter must first listen to what the divine author intends to communicate. As New Testament authors recognize the fulfillment of Old Testament promises, they are simply acknowledging what God has done to keep the commitment He made in these Old Testament promises.

Second, a consistent literal interpretation is indispensable because it provides a normative definition of verbal meaning.[24] Only such a common definition, when consistently applied, can provide a basis for validation of interpretation. Then, the relative strengths of competing interpretations may be weighed and a "biblically focused dialogue" of the merit of each be pursued.

Finally, a consistent literal interpretation is indispensable because only a principle that forces the interpreter to consistently consider the text as the basis of the meaning can satisfy the priority of the Bible in formulating doctrine. While the consistency of the system of theology may have an influence on interpretation, it ought never supersede the commitment to biblicism in forming our beliefs from what is revealed to be true.

4. *Is consistent literal interpretation workable?* Some may agree in general with literal interpretation as a goal, as even Blaising does,[25] but the thrust of what he says suggests that it is not always based on the text because of the diversity of ways meaning operates. In particular, this seems to be demonstrated in texts reused in the

New Testament. It is claimed that the New Testament does not always interpret literally. While this question can never be answered conclusively, since someone may always raise another example of proposed nonliteral interpretation, yet there are a number of well-known test cases. So the argument presented in this final section of the chapter is that a consistent use of literal interpretation is workable because a literal approach clarifies difficult cases where the New Testament interprets the Old Testament. These interpretations are thus consistent with literal interpretation.

The test case that we will propose is Paul's use of the promise to Abraham and to his seed as reflected in Galatians 3:16. This notoriously difficult example raises the question of whether God clarified in Genesis that the promise was to be given to one seed in distinction to many seed, and also, what text or texts make(s) that promise? These two questions will be answered in reverse order.

What text or texts make(s) a promise to Abraham's seed? The first distinction concerns promises *made about* Abraham's seed (Gen. 13:16; 15:5; 22:17)[26] and are promises *made to* Abraham's seed (Gen. 12:7; 13:15; 15:18; 17:8).[27] Based on this first distinction, only those statements of promise made to Abraham's seed are relevant. It would not be difficult to narrow the candidates further since all restate, with some qualification, the first promise (12:7) that "I will give this land to your seed."

Does the promise in Genesis make clear that the reference is to Christ? At first glance, it would seem impossible that Genesis meant Christ. But further consideration may override what seems obvious on the surface. First, God's initial words to Abraham (12:1–3) had featured what God would do for Abraham. The climax of those first promises features a work that would "use Abraham (through you) to bless all nations of the earth" (12:3). The scope of such a promise would create an expectation for Abraham himself that God would use him far beyond anything he had experienced. That expectation would naturally imply that Abraham's descendants must be included with Abraham himself in reaching a worldwide scope to bless all nations.

Added to that expectation was a further clarification when God promised that the land would be given to his seed (12:7). That clarification is masked in the use of the collective noun "seed," which may be one descendant or many descendants to whom the land would be given. So God's plan was being formed in the promises being communicated to Abraham. It included specific promises, although the completed plan was neither fully revealed nor capable of being fully understood at this time.

Each of these pieces was forming part of Abraham's expectation. What God promised to do would not be completed with Abraham alone. The seed to whom the "land between the nations" would be given would be involved in blessing all nations. In addition, this seed would be given the land forever (13:15).

This developing promise is what G. B. Caird calls "a Situation Vacant advertisement: it describes in some detail a person whose identity is not yet known to the writer."[28] He uses Isaiah 42–53 and the character of the "servant" as an example. He further describes the kind of reference. "It is as though he had published an advertisement, 'wanted, a servant of the Lord,' accompanied by a job description. He was undoubtedly aware that many famous men, such as Moses and Jeremiah, had sat for the composite portrait he was drawing. What he could not know was that in the end there would be only one applicant for the post."[29] While Caird's imagined experience of Isaiah is too speculative,[30] the concept of an advertisement is helpful. Moses' record of God's promise to Abraham of a seed also takes the form of a "situation vacant advertisement." His identity is a promised, physical descendant or descendants of Abraham. The job description specifies that the seed is the means through whom all nations will be blessed and the recipient to whom the land would be given to possess forever. Thus, based on this advertisement, Abraham could ask himself if Isaac was that seed. In identity, he matched the promised descendant from God but he hardly met the job description as he was the one who attempted to thwart God's blessing Jacob. The advertisement also had that same function for the reader of the text. Was the seed Jacob? Was the seed Joseph or Joseph's generation? In each case, aspects of the job description went unmet. In addition, further descriptions were revealed in each subsequent statement of the promise.

As each generation passed, no individual or generation of individuals met the job description. And in each generation, based on a literal interpretation, enough is known to identify what to expect from God but not enough to know how in fact it must happen. It was clear who must appear and what must be accomplished. That had not happened in history. When Christ came, it then became clear what they expected had come. Paul concluded that Christ alone was intended by God as the seed (Galatians 3:16). Thus, literal interpretation is demonstrated on the basis of understanding texts in Genesis, and the workable use of its consistent application is defended.

Conclusion

Ryrie featured "consistent literal interpretation" as a *sine qua non* of the dispensationalist's theological system. This is not to say, however, that any individual or any generation consistently applied that principle. It is to say that the very premise of a biblically based theology of progressive revelation provided warrant for that hermeneutical procedure.

One influence that challenged the consistent application of literal interpretation within the immediate context was the framing influence of the whole context of the system. So among early dispensationalists, attempts to establish distinct dispensations lured some writers to represent salvation as different in each dispensation. Ryrie was clear in pointing out that this emphasis had no basis in texts.[31] Nevertheless, in considering this *sine qua non*, the influence of the whole system must be weighed. The whole system is greater than the mere sum of the parts. And each part coheres with other parts in forming a unified whole. So when the meaning of a particular passage is understood in the framework of the whole, the meaning understood will be in some sense clearer than the meaning understood in the immediate context alone. But that greater meaning need be only a deepening and enriching of the meaning and not a determining and altering of an original type of meaning. Thus, Genesis 12:3, "through you all nations of the earth will be blessed," is deepened to mean "through your ultimate descendant all nations are now blessed as His co-heirs." This is the case as texts are reused in progress of revelation. In particular, this is the case in many, if not most, of the early prophetic texts of the Bible.

On the other hand, Blaising and Bock have proposed a role for the system to determine and even to alter the interpretation of some particular passages. So a feature like the "already-not yet" model of fulfillment has become the basis to inform passages like the Davidic and new covenants. Such a move is compatible with similar moves made by other evangelical models of progressive revelation (i.e., historic premillennialism or even amillennialism). Questions remain to be answered about the consequences of these moves. Four answers are proposed in conclusion about such consequences.

1. The "already-not yet" model of fulfillment introduces *instability* into the interpretation of texts. When the meaning of a text may be altered in type of meaning because of a broadened context, the determination of the meaning by the author as originally expressed in a text is lost. That loss now, for theological and historical reasons, resembles the loss of meaning in historic documents as read by postmodern reconstructionists.

2. The "already-not yet" model of fulfillment relies upon an *expansion* of an original meaning to satisfy the reframing of a text in a new context. When the original promise of a seed (physical) as provided by God (spiritual) is expanded to include spiritual seed (Gentiles), then the original meaning is altered. That expansion is not the result of anything found in the original text but is determined by the "already" context of progressive fulfillment. Formerly this expansion was called *sensus plenior* or even "spiritualized" interpretation. Because an "already-not yet" framework assures a future—completed fulfillment—it is not a spiritualized interpretation. But both promote in common an altered meaning based on a broadened context. As a result, an Old Testament text means one thing for now and a textually literal thing for the future.

3. The "already-not yet" model of fulfillment advocates *unique interpretations* for New Testament apostles. Interpretation of an author's meaning is constrained by the author's textual expressions. To argue that an apostle has the right to interpret expanded meanings is to confuse revelation and interpretation. An apostle reveals new truths in addition to truth revealed originally in the Old Testament. Such new revelation is often identified as "mysteries" (Matt. 13; Eph. 3) when spoken of in the New Testament. To introduce a new freedom for apostles reusing Old Testament texts is to confuse categories of what is interpreted and of what is revealed.

4. The "already-not yet" model of fulfillment *oversimplifies* the variety of promises in progressive revelation. The "already-not yet" fulfillment pattern relies upon partial fulfillment to determine what is already fulfilled. The concept of "partial fulfillment" often equivocates on what is meant by "partial." There are some Old Testament promises that are partially fulfilled now (such as redemption or salvation) in light of Christ's first advent. However, there are other promises (such as the Davidic and new covenants) that are fulfilled only in part (the Davidic king has come but was not established as king, Deut. 17:14–15).[32] Yet both are described as partial fulfillment and, thus, the equivocation. The result is that the first advent of Christ is oversimplified in what is accomplished rather than considering the accomplishment reached for each individual promise.

The bottom line is this: To adopt literal interpretation as a *sine qua non* is to affirm that the context of the theological system provides no valid warrant to expand or alter the meaning understood in the immediate context.

RESPONSE

Elements of Agreement
(and the nuance of difference within this agreement)

1. We are agreed that it is important to pursue an original meaning, authorial intent, a literal sense, and a stable meaning. Anyone reading my essay will see that I share these concerns. I am even content, contrary to the argument of Johnson's essay, to pursue such a meaning *consistently* (see the opening quotation in my essay). This agreement renders much of part two of his essay irrelevant. What we disagree about is how this consistency works across the canon. These are issues of correlation, hermeneutical reading, and how texts work *across time* as part of the canon. For Johnson, there is a claim that stable meaning requires a certain kind of canonical reading *as a matter of interpretive principle* (reinforcing another point I made in my essay about traditionalist method as principial).

I reject the contention that a stable meaning requires a certain kind of canonical reading as a matter of interpretation. One example (Genesis in Galatians 3) cannot prove the sweeping claims Johnson makes (as he rightly notes). Nonetheless, he makes them, even though there are dozens of texts read differently by *others who also claim to be reading the Bible consistently and literally* (and here I am not just speaking of progressives). It is this principial dismissal by understating or ignoring the problematic factors in a traditional dispensational reading that have caused many to be dissuaded that dispensationalism has anything biblical to say. Even though this principle is advocated out of an important and sincere concern for the integrity of the text and out of respect for the meaning and inspiration of Scripture, it does not adequately explain what is happening in Scripture. I am arguing that a consistent, literal reading of each context surfaces the distinctions and expansions of meaning *in the text and that this kind of a reading makes sense of both the Scripture and dispensationalism.* This is something that texts, not prestated principles, must show if we wish to be textually biblical.

2) We are agreed that Gentiles are a part of Abraham's seed in line with Genesis 12:3 and its declaration that through Abraham's seed all the nations will be blessed (though reading Johnson's essay, the reader might not know that [see my essay in chapter 5]). This view is a normal reading of this text. What we disagree about is how to label the resulting category where Gentiles are called seed of Abraham. As a hermeneutical category, how does the New Testament call Gentiles seed? Is this claim unrelated to the Genesis portrait of the Abrahamic promise? Hardly! That connection is the very point of Paul's invocation of promise in Romans 4 and Galatians 3. Gentiles as Abraham's seed are clearly not so identified on the basis of a natural meaning of the term seed, for Gentiles are not naturally, physically descended from Abraham. We agree that it comes through Christ as evidenced by the presence of the Spirit.

But what then is the result for an understanding of seed? That is where we disagree. Paul sees Gentiles as *part of the fulfillment of this category and promise,* even as it comes through Christ. There is no presumption on my part of a promise-fulfillment context in Galatians 3. Rather, that is precisely the context that is invoked by Paul (vv. 7–8, 14, 16–18, 24–29). (If it is not this theological underpinning, then what is invoked in such a way that law is now done away?) When I said the Galatians text *assumes* this structure, I am not importing "already-not yet" or my "theological system" in this context. I am arguing that Paul was invoking the presence of the covenant promise of Abraham, which Paul did not specify in detail because all of his readers knew its contents. This is the knowledge he presumed in making his argument. By the way, outline points # 6 and # 9 in Galatians 3 from the original *Scofield Reference Bible* agree with me about the Abrahamic covenantal contents of this context.

I would argue that since Gentiles receive the benefits *through Christ* and the *spiritual* presence of blessing in the *Spirit,* this seed is intended by Scripture to be seen in a *spiritual* sense, distinct from the natural meaning in Genesis 12. It is this sense that Paul introduces in Romans 4 and Galatians 3. In both contexts Paul is invoking the "promise to Abraham" as realized. If I am wrong, then to what category of meaning does this sense belong, since natural and physical are clearly not intended? The fact is that most evangelicals, including many *traditional* dispensationalists of the past, see this as the original *Scofield Reference Bible* note on Genesis 15:8 argues that the promise "I will make of thee a great nation" includes a reference to "a spiritual posterity" with Romans 4:16–17 and Galatians 3:6–7, 29 cited as realization (*Scofield Reference Bible,* 25). So numerous questions need attention. Has Johnson defined consistent literal interpretation so narrowly that even traditionalists cannot fit within the *sine qua non?* If so, does it not show that the definition he argues is so central to the dispensational system that it is not as central historically as he suggests? Might not the failure of the example to work even in a traditionalist context show that it is not adequately stated as a standard and that another standard, such as a complementary reading, might do a better job of describing the history and the exegesis?

3. It may surprise the reader to note that, according to point four in Johnson's conclusion, we are agreed that the Abrahamic, Davidic and new covenants are all "fulfilled in part" (though I do not see how this is different than "partially fulfilled"). To some, this might make Johnson a progressive, since they, as traditionalists, see no such fulfillment at all, when it comes to David (and some with respect to the New), whether partial or in part. The

distinction he attempts to make in point four between partial fulfillment and fulfilled in part does not work. He places salvation
under the example of partially fulfilled and yet we are not yet glorified in part (I am still longing for my sinless, glorified body, as
is the creation [Rom. 8]). If that observation about salvation is
right, salvation is no different in how it works than how the covenants work. Some elements are fulfilled now and others come
later. In fact, Johnson's distinction possesses no real material difference when applied to specific examples. It really concedes that
an "already-not yet" structure is a part of New Testament teaching in all of these areas, *regardless of the semantic tags we attempt to
make in differentiating how we see these issues.* We discuss only which
elements are already and which are not yet.

4. I agree with the claim of G. B. Caird and Johnson that some
texts have a "situation vacant" character, a kind of blank advertisement extending into the future and looking for fulfillment.
The example Johnson picks is a good one at one level. The category warns us how seed can be narrowed as revelation proceeds
to cause us to realize that an individual can be a part of the realization of that promise.

What produces this narrowing, however, is not the seed promise
in Genesis alone but how that promise ends up being tied to the
promise to David of an everlasting kingship. That promise itself gets
narrowed to look for one who will do this. In fact, Johnson's illustration makes my point. Let me explain. He argues that history
showed that no one qualified to be the seed until Christ came. But
one of the qualifying promises that is the test of the presence of
promise, according to Johnson, is that to the seed will be given the
land (and he appears to mean the singular seed here). Now Jesus
did not take possession of the land in His first coming. (By the way,
what does saying that Jesus as seed receives the land according to
Abrahamic promise do for the claim that Israel gets it as Abraham's
seed *if seed is only singular?* Johnson's narrowing may be problematic for dispensational concerns about Israel unless it is properly
qualified. See disagreement "3" below.) So what "had come" that
allowed Jesus to be identified as the singular seed? Only an aspect
of the promise, the distribution of the Spirit to Gentiles according
to the promise of Abraham (Gal. 3:14). So does Jesus fail to qualify
as seed because He does not yet fulfill one element of the promise

(the promise of possessing the land)? Of course not. My point is that Johnson's very example of "situation vacant" makes my point about "already-not yet" and shows how *fulfillment takes place in a process across time.*

Elements of Disagreement

1. The comparison of our approach with postmodernism in part one of the conclusion is regrettable. It reflects a serious misunderstanding about our approach. It is the one place in the essay where I sense being seriously misrepresented in a way I noted of others in my hermeneutics essay. Two reasons exist for my claim. First, postmodernism is not concerned at all about original reading and original setting. Reading through any of the varieties of postmodern interpretation (Continental or Anglo-American), one can see how unconcerned they are for original setting and meaning. Through both of my essays there is a constant reaffirmation of the importance and *abiding value* of the original sense of the author. Second, the claim that our approach resembles a "loss" of meaning baffles me as a description of our view. No meaning is lost. Our only claim is that such meaning is realized later. *Meaning that comes one day in the future is not lost.*

2. I reject Johnson's claim that I read my theological system into my exegesis of New Testament texts. The theological structures for which I argue are present in the text, as even some traditional dispensationalists have argued. I would appeal to the textual details I am raising in both my essays and the textual details of Galatians 3 as noted in agreement point "2" above. I would also note that the structure of our salvation (justified—yes; sanctified—in process; glorified—yet to come) and Christology (first coming—already fulfilled; current work—also part of fulfillment; return and beyond—yet to come; see covenants essay for details) also support the point that elements of the promises as they relate to these areas are acknowledged by virtually all to possess "already-not yet" elements. That eschatology should also fit this pattern is not surprising. This is not a reading into texts. It is the recognition that what is present is a fundamental structure of New Testament teaching on the plan of God as read in a consistently literal way.

3. Perhaps the nature of our hermeneutical difference can be seen in my reaction to Johnson's citation in the Genesis 12 ex-

ample. He states in discussing a clarification of promise that came in Genesis 12:7, "That clarification is masked in the use of the collective noun 'seed,' which may be one descendant or many descendants to whom the land is given." My question here is, why make this choice either-or? It seems to me that the biblical text argues both-and with regard to the seed. It has both collective and singular force *depending on the context*. This is even the case in Galatians 3:16, 29.

My fundamental contention with Johnson's essay is that the principal narrowing of hermeneutical choices before we engage the text leads to readings within the traditional view that shortchange the consistent literal reading of the New Testament text and its connections to Old Testament promise. This shortcoming is precisely why progressives argue for a complementary reading of the text, where both-and, "already-not yet" fulfillments and typological-prophetic readings are not ruled out by principial fiat before the texts are carefully considered. Rather than going through distinctions that do not sound so different or through explanations that seem to understate connections to promise the New Testament makes, progressives prefer a consistent, stable reading that lets each context speak.

Such complementary readings do not introduce instability into interpretation because meaning is never lost; it is only deepened and enhanced. Expansion when God is elaborating His promise is not a violation of basic rules of communication; it represents the right of the divine author to explain Himself. When the apostles explain the promise and connect it to current activity in the early church, they are not uniquely interpreting but both revealing *and* explaining. Romans 16:25–27 mentions mystery *and* the prophetic writings (which must be the Old Testament here [no New Testament exists yet]) side by side, relating them. This is evident in Paul's argument for the Gentiles in Romans 15:7–13, where he simply cited texts for proof of their inclusion. Granted, such a complementary reading does result in an aspect of meaning now and another as present later, but never in a way where a contradiction or loss of meaning results. For both the "already" and the "not yet" share fundamental characteristics that allow the meanings to be consistently and literally related to each other. The one principle I wish to affirm in all of this is that it is the biblical text that counts most.

Chapter Notes

1. Charles Ryrie, *Dispensationalism Today* (Chicago: Moody, 1965), 86–109.
2. Earl D. Radmacher and Robert D. Preus, *Hermeneutics, Inerrancy, and the Bible* (Grand Rapids: Zondervan, 1984).
3. Charles Ryrie, *Dispensationalism* (Chicago: Moody, 1995), 38–41.
4. Craig A. Blaising, "The Extent and Varieties of Dispensationalism" in *Progressive Dispensationalism*, coauthors Craig Blaising and Darrell L. Bock (Wheaton: Bridgepoint, 1993), 9–56, esp. 35–37. Using Blaising's categories, classical dispensationalists adopted spiritual interpretations due to "the dualistic idea of redemption" (pp. 23, 24) and due to typological interpretation of the Old Testament to disclose God's spiritual purpose for a spiritual people (pp. 27, 28). Further, revised dispensationalists also allowed the system to dictate spiritual interpretation of "everlasting" promises to be limited for national Israel. The Abrahamic covenant was fulfilled spiritually in the church based on Galatians 3:26–29.
5. Blaising argues that some things that earlier interpreters thought they "clearly" saw in Scripture are not "clearly" seen today at all. Blaising, "The Extent and Varieties of Dispensationalism," 36.
6. In general terms, Bock considers what is clear or plain in a chapter on "Interpreting the Bible—How We Read Texts" (pp. 57–75) and what is normal in a second chapter on "Interpreting the Bible—How Texts Speak to Us" (pp. 76–105) in *Progressive Dispensationalism*, Craig A. Blaising and Darrell L. Bock (Wheaton, Ill: Bridgepoint, 1993), 57–105.
7. Bock, "Interpreting the Bible—How We Read Texts," 68.
8. Ryrie, *Dispensationalism*, 40. Blaising, "The Extent and Varieties of Dispensationalism," 35–37.
9. Rollin Chafer, *The Science of Biblical Hermeneutics* (Dallas: Bibliotheca Sacra, 1939), 30.
10. Radmacher and Preus, 884–85.
11. Ryrie, *Dispensationalism Today*, 86.
12. E. D. Hirsch, *Validity in Interpretation* (New Haven and London: Yale University Press, 1967), 1.
13. Bock, "Interpreting the Bible—How We Read Texts," 62–68.
14. Ibid., 62.
15. Ibid., 63.
16. Ibid.

17. Blaising, "The Extent and Varieties of Dispensationalism," 37. In Blaising's description of the inevitable flaw of revised dispensationalism, Blaising seems to be expressing his own resolution of the difficult use of the Abrahamic covenant.
18. Application would argue that the meanings expressed *relate* in some sense to another audience rather than fulfillment would argue that the meanings expressed *refer* to the audience in an intended sense.
19. Bock, "Interpreting the Bible—How Texts Speak to Us," 101.
20. Ibid., emphasis and explanation added.
21. By traditional, I am including what progressive dispensationalists view as a classical and a revised dispensationalism. Note, however, that within the use of the "traditional hermeneutic" differences of interpretation occur concerning the unity of the people of God, fulfillment of the new covenant, the nature of kingdom fulfillment, and the nature of the kingdom of God and the kingdom of heaven.
22. Blaising, "The Extent and Varieties of Dispensationalism," 36.
23. E. D. Hirsch, *Validity in Interpretation,* 164–207.
24. If the meaning of one interpretation is what the author intends to communicate and the meaning of another is what the reader hears or perceives, then a common ground for validation and discussion is lost.
25. Blaising, "The Extent and Varieties of Dispensationalism," 35–37.
26. The promise made about Abraham's seed refers to the many who would make up Abraham's seed.
27. God says to Abram in Genesis that "to your seed, I will give this land" (12:7); "all the land which you see I give to you and your seed forever (13:15); "to your seed I have given this land (15:18); and "I give to you and your seed after you, the land in which you are a stranger, all the land of Canaan as an everlasting possession" (17:8).
28. G. B. Caird, *The Language and Imagery of the Bible* (Philadelphia: Westminster, 1980), 57–58.
29. Ibid., 58.
30. Isaiah writes before Jeremiah appeared in history. Any attempt to formulate what was in an author's mind at the time of writing, beyond what is written in the text, remains merely speculation.
31. Ryrie, *Dispensationalism Today,* 110–31.
32. The terms *partially* and *in part* are chosen to refer to distinct views of textual meaning. *Partially* refers to all elements of the promise

realized but not in the full scope, and *in part* refers to some elements of the promise realized and other elements not realized.

CHAPTER THREE

Hermeneutics of Progressive Dispensationalism

Darrell L. Bock
with response by Elliot E. Johnson

> It should be noted that progressive dispensationalism is not an abandonment of "literal" interpretation for "spiritual" interpretation. Progressive dispensationalism is a development of "literal" interpretation into a more consistent historical-literary interpretation.
>
> —Craig A. Blaising[1]

These two sentences, written by my colleague in introducing progressive dispensationalism, summarize the major point of this essay. Since progressive dispensationalism emerged, many more traditionally oriented dispensational interpreters have tried to claim that the differences within dispensationalism are hermeneutical and have suggested that this newly emerging approach is really a form of spiritualizing.[2] Others have suggested that the approach either reflects or is better associated with an "amillennial" hermeneutic or is a serious deviation from the historical-grammatical method leading to unstable and uncontrollable meaning.[3]

Such claims reflect a poor understanding of the hermeneutical claims of progressives and simply are misleading. Such a misunderstanding deserves correction. There are differences between progressives and earlier expressions of dispensationalism, but they

85

are not a dispute over spiritualizing, nor are they about serious deviations in the historical-grammatical method. They are debates over how to read the Bible in a normal literary-theological manner and as a canonical whole. The dispute is about the most appropriate way to synthesize vast amounts of biblical material. Both approaches respect the Scripture and seek to read it faithfully. They simply disagree on how this is best and most consistently done.

This essay proceeds in four steps. First, I shall try to identify the difference in hermeneutical method that exists between progressives and many of those more traditional dispensationalists who have tried to assess the progressive approach. Second, I shall explain what progressive dispensational hermeneutics is not. Third, I shall define what it is and what its interpretive concerns are. Finally, I will conclude with some observations about the current discussion and how it should proceed in the future.[4]

Two Types of Approach

As one looks at the discussion between progressives and other dispensationalists, a difference in method does surface. This difference involves methodological emphases.

A Principial-Traditional Approach. Whether one considers the work of Ice, Ryrie, Couch, or Thomas, the emphasis of nonprogressives involves a claim about the consistent literal approach. A reading of their articles will quickly show that the argument contains three factors: (1) setting forth definitions of method and key categories; (2) dealing with key, specific single terms in sequence; and (3) making arguments surrounding the history of tradition on certain views or where those views may one day lead. I call this a *principial-traditional* approach.

The argument sets forth certain fundamental rules that must be present for interpretation to be valid or consistent and then argues that passages must be read accordingly.[5] Though many of these articles also go on to consider specific texts, the rules of the game are determined principally before one reads the texts. In effect, competing readings are ruled out by definition before the passages are looked at in their exegetical and canonical contexts.[6] A particular reading of the history of dispensational tradition is also invoked.[7]

In many of the articles that do discuss texts, the key terms are handled as a singular entity, often without indicating any of the contextual, conceptual connections that are associated with their presence. For example, in one key article that does seek to engage the text, the phrase "throne of David" is treated in the only two places it appears in the New Testament (Luke 1:30–33; Acts 2:30) as if that is all one has to consider in considering the idea of fulfillment of Davidic promise and the meaning of Davidic throne.[8] The sweeping conclusion based on a quick examination of the two passages is, "There is not the slightest shred of evidence that the throne of David ever was conceived as anything other than the earthly seat of authority where David reigned and where only his physical descendants could legitimately reign. The term 'throne of David' simply refers to this—nothing else."[9]

Such nonprogressive treatments of single terms, isolated from the phrase's previous canonical associations and treated as if they exhaust the discussion, are inadequate. Absent are discussions of the Old Testament concept of the throne of David *and its connection to the Davidic covenant* as the backdrop for New Testament remarks.

First, no mention is made of the fact that the phrase appears *within* the discussion of the Davidic covenant in the Old Testament or that several of the images of the covenant are invoked in the space of Luke 1, indicating Luke's desire to present, explain, expound, and connect the category. Nonprogressives are interested only in raising the issue of the location of the chair on earth with the presence of national Israel. Such an Old Testament backdrop shows, however, that "the throne" conceptually invokes the presence of the Davidic covenant through one who sits on a throne that is everlasting (2 Sam. 7:16).

Second, nonprogressives present no development of Psalm 132:11 in its original context. Psalm 132:11, alluded to in Acts 2:30 and in its original context, refers to David's throne as an expression of the Davidic covenant of promise. In fact, that psalm includes a reference to the "horn of David," a concept that appeared previously in Luke's gospel (1:69) along with the image of a lamp, a regal image much like the light of 1:79. This means that Acts 2 is NOT discussing the Lord's throne in distinction from David's throne in invoking Psalm 110:1 but that it is interested in the throne of David *and* the Lord (1 Chron. 28:5–6; 29:23–24 show how the two are equated in the OT). At the least, such a case can credibly be made without invoking anything foreign to the meaning of the terms. These omissions of conceptual connections and meaning elements indicate that rather than discussing a "chair" and its location, the point is the evocation of a promise about a figure and the functions he performs from that position. These elements of textual meaning counter Couch's claim that "nowhere does the Bible say that Christ is presently on David's Throne, either in a spiritual or a physical sense."[10] One has to explain why Psalm 132:11 and its reference to promise, an oath, and to David's throne is evoked, if it is a reference to a different throne than the one Jesus is sitting upon as a result of resurrection. One could argue that to read the text with this distinction is to read *into* the Acts passage something that Acts 2 does not mention. All of the factors that I have noted are omitted in the critique of the progressive view, and yet those textual details are a crucial part of a normal contextual reading of the passage. There is no spiritualizing present. The example surfaces a potential inadequacy in the principial-traditional approach to historical-grammatical interpretation.

One other point about the example needs mention because no critic mentions it. It is that there is no denial by progressives that *the throne of David* looks one day to a period of Jesus' reign on the earth as Son of David (see Acts 3:19–22). In other words, a key aspect of the meaning of the term as seen by more traditional dispensationalists is retained in the way progressives ultimately use the phrase. A one-meaning principle is maintained. There is no substitution of meaning here, only the highlighting of an aspect of meaning. The New Testament itself indicates that the term is invoking a key context and function that is an aspect of its meaning, namely the rule of the Son of David. When Jesus acts from the side of God by dispensing the Spirit, he is acting in accordance with the promised ruling-blessing activity of the Messiah. It is a meaning for which the text itself within Luke through Acts has explicitly prepared the reader in discussing John the Baptist's ministry. John indicated when he presented the messianic hope (as the last of the line of Old Testament prophets) that the way to know the Christ *is present* is that he will baptize with Spirit and fire (Luke 3:15–17; 7:28; 16:16; 24:43–49; Acts 1:5–8; 11:15–17; 13:23–25).[11] This is precisely what Jesus does in Acts 2 and is what Peter preaches about him. The one thing Jesus is not doing is sitting and waiting, doing nothing, only having qualified through the resurrection for a future rule on the throne of David from Israel. Such a conclusion has to ignore the argument of this New Testament text *and* a major motif of Luke through Acts.

The detailed example about the throne of David attempts to illustrate the inadequacy of the hermeneutical argument made by more traditional expressions of dispensationalism on one of the more debated points between the two views. In that way, the differences in approach between the two views can be made clear first from the text before explaining the nature of the difference in methodological emphasis.

The Complementary Approach. When progressives speak of a complementary relationship between Old Testament and New Testament texts, they are claiming that a normal, contextually determined reading often brings concepts from the Hebrew Scripture together in the New Testament in a way that completes and expounds what was already present in the older portion of God's Word.[12] As revelation proceeds, the texts themselves, New and Old Testament, are brought together in a way that links concepts together, so that both old and fresh associations are made (Matt. 13:52). Such fresh associations, canonically determined and defined, have a stable meaning because they emerge from within a normal reading of the text. In sum, if there is a difference between progressives and more traditional dispensational readings, it is that progressives are asking dispensationalists to work more integratively with the biblical text, as the example above shows.[13]

The example and highlighting of a complementary way of reading Scripture gets us started in seeing a key emphasis in progressive dispensational hermeneutics. But a real definition must specify what something is and is not. I begin by making clear what we are not arguing.

What Progressive Dispensational Hermeneutics Is Not

As I have already suggested, most treatments of progressive dispensationalism by more traditional critics have either misunderstood or misrepresented the hermeneutical elements of the view. To clarify what the view does hold, it is important to make clear what it does not argue. Hopefully, by addressing such elements directly, we can clarify where the real debates are.

Not Anti-Authorial Intent. The progressive approach is not an attempt to argue that the original historical setting or the human author's meaning is irrelevant.[14] In fact, the progressive approach is just the opposite. Progressives have argued that what is originally said *remains* a relevant aspect of ultimate meaning.

Here is how we discussed the "complementary" concept originally and the point is still relevant: "According to this approach, the New Testament does introduce change and advance; it does not merely repeat Old Testament revelation. In making complementary *additions,* however, it *does not jettison* old promises. *The enhancement is not at the expense of the original promise.*"[15] Here is an attempt to respect original authorial meaning and yet allow the New Testament to speak in a progressive way about how to put the pieces of Old Testament hope together. A complementary emphasis does not remove meaning; it makes new, sometimes fresh, additional connections. It works canonically. It does so without removing what was originally affirmed, since those factors of meaning will come to play in the era to come. It is this maintenance of meaning that gives stability to the approach, a stability that resides within the canon. We posited this approach as an alternative to two other ways of integrating texts, namely substitution (e.g., church for Israel), which is what covenantal readings tend to do, and repetition (e.g., Israel must mean ultimately only millennial application), which is what other expressions of dispensationalism tend to do.[16] It is the difference in integrating texts that serves as our point of discussion.

One other point needs attention with the focus on original setting and utterance. It is the observation that in Scripture we are dealing with the unique circumstance of *dual* authorship. This means that although we are concerned with the meaning of the human author in his setting, we are also to be sensitive to the meaning of the divine Author, who knows the whole of the story and the entirety of canonical promise. The reality of dual authorship in Scripture is what permits and requires consideration of the development of meaning in three settings. Some critics have wished to censure us for holding to the relevance of the three settings, namely, the reading of the text in its original setting, in light of the biblical book, *and* in light of the canon.[17] It is dual authorship that opens up the canon for consideration as a factor in determining the ultimate scope of meaning. The view argues that ultimately the Bible is one book with one author.

Not Allegorizing, Spiritualizing, Sensus Plenior, *or Multiple Meaning.* What we are saying is that the categories with which progressives are working are generated internally within Scripture. When, for example, the throne of David takes on a heavenly dimension of function in its meaning,[18] it is because the Acts 2 text functions in a context where this heavenly authority, messianic activity, and messianic affirmation are the explicit backdrop for such an articulation of its meaning.[19]

There is no "fuller sense" here. All that has happened to the term "throne" is this: a functionally descriptive term has been brought into a new context in this era based on a meaning it already possessed that happens to include this authority exercised from above. There is no replacement of meaning, only the advance of a fresh setting to which it also applies.

Neither is there multiple meaning because the term has always denoted the presence of a shared authority between God and the Davidic descendant. This throne reflects the fact that He is a mediator of God's rule to His people and a bestower of His power and blessing. These are all regal (and ultimately messianic) prerogatives that show that it is the promise of God to David at work.[20] In fact, Jesus' resurrection helps to show his qualifications to be seated in this chair and remain there forever, one of the fundamental qualifications of the promise that Jesus now meets in a way that no previous Davidite could.

Fundamental to this hermeneutical approach, then, is the direct engagement of the biblical text starting with its near context. Terms are defined in terms of the settings in which they are functioning. However, attention is also given to any conceptual connections the term may possess based upon other canonical features. Such connections require that the context being read triggers the concepts where a link is claimed. This careful kind of associative reading is how meaning can remain stable, even as it is developed.

Not Amillenarian or Covenant Hermeneutics. What makes this

hermeneutic dispensational is the insistence that exegetical meaning be retained as it appears in each Testament in the currently
read context. Old Testament texts about the central role of national Israel in the kingdom program affirm that Israel will have
a decisive role at some time in the outworking of that plan. This
is why progressives will read a text such as Isaiah 2:2–4 or Micah
4:1–5 as ultimately about the future era of kingdom hope when
Israel again has a key role in the outworking of promise.[21] In this,
they agree with other dispensationalists. This is also why
progressives read Acts 3:19–22 or Romans 11 as still looking for a
day when Israel will again enter into the plan of God in a central
way. Everything about these textual readings is dispensational.[22]

On the other hand, New Testament texts that point to the current activity of God and even point to Old Testament promises to
explain that activity are also best honored contextually when they
are seen as relevant to the current activity of hope being described.
Thus, the appeal to Amos 9 in Acts 15 or to Jeremiah 31 in Hebrews 8–10 points to direct realizations of promises of old brought
into the fresh sphere of present activity. The key to fulfillment in
these near contexts is not a nation that receives the promise, it is
a figure, Jesus Christ. It is in and through Him that both the nation and the world receive the benefits of fulfillment. Here one
can see the point of a text like Galatians 3:6–14. Here fulfillment
resides in one unique seed, Jesus Christ, who brings the realization of covenant blessing in that He is the son of Abraham who
fulfills the promise as the Christ in line with Davidic hope (see
also 2 Cor. 6:18). He does so by bringing the promise of the Spirit.
That promise must be in line with new covenant hope, since it is
called "the promise" in a context where Old Testament hope is
the subject (see also 2 Cor. 3–4 and 6:14–7:1). In these few verses,
all of the covenant promises are invoked. It is the consistency with
which progressives attempt to articulate these current connections
that make progressive dispensationalism distinct from previous
expressions of dispensationalism. This element of emphasis also
gives progressive dispensationalism its points of contact with the
reading of Scripture of other evangelical traditions.

Our point has been that dispensationalism has something very
important to say to all evangelical traditions about the message
of Scripture. It argues that we should continue to read the Old

Testament as still telling us something about Israel in God's plan, while being sensitive to how the New Testament complements that hope by expressing fulfillment today in Christ.

Some on both sides have argued that there is something inherently "unstable" in reading the text this way.[23] But we would argue that it is decidedly biblical. Salvation itself has an "already-not yet" quality to it in that we are justified now but await glorification. There is nothing inherently problematic, then, that eschatology will reflect a parallel kind of structure. One can have a future for national Israel without being required to reinstitute all of the practices of the Mosaic Law, something Hebrews 8–10 is quite clear was altered by the coming of Christ. Progressives are saying to all evangelical traditions that we should be sensitive to reading both the Old and New Testaments in ways that honor each context *and* unify them canonically in ways that make sense of the original utterance. This consistent respect for the original context in the passage's ultimate application is a dispensational emphasis.

Not Insensitive to Distinctions. The previous point illustrates that progressives are not insensitive to distinctions, but that they wish to be careful in how those distinctions are defined. In fact, progressives are making a distinction that more traditional dispensationalists seem to want to avoid.

Progressives maintain a distinction between Israel and the church, something that nonprogressives say progressives blur. However, progressives define that distinction as applying to a specific aspect of the structure of God's plan. Progressives are stressing that the distinction remains when it comes to the structures through which God works in each period. It also applies when one thinks temporally about the plan of God (i.e., the church is not the same structurally as Israel was or what the millennium will be, and these structures belong to distinct periods in God's plan). However, Israel-church is not a distinction to be affirmed when one is thinking of the theological-redemptive makeup of the people of God. In other words, Abraham is the father of all believers—of every era—because all are saved on the basis of faith in the context of God's grace as grounded in Christ's redemptive work (Rom. 4). In addition, all ultimately are headed for a destiny of total reconciliation with the creation in a totally restored cosmos when heaven and earth shall be at one (Rom. 8; Rev. 21–22).

This means that Jews and Gentiles can be heirs according to the promise of Abraham, who became the ancestor and *type* of blessing *while still uncircumcised* (Rom. 4; Gal. 3, esp. vv. 28–29).[24] Thus, progressive hermeneutics seeks to honor both the discontinuities of Scripture and its continuities. Progressives work hard textually to define precisely where and how those continuities and discontinuities apply.

In our affirmation of greater continuity, we have a difference with more traditional expressions of dispensationalism. From this difference emerges a fresh theological emphasis, as progressives give more attention to how fulfillment takes place in the messianic work of the exalted Christ in the present, while also highlighting how God's ultimate reconciliation will one day bring together the creation into a restored and total fullness and wholeness. It is this coming fullness and wholeness of redemption that provides theological guidance for the mission and vision of the church today. The church is called to be a place where an authentic preview of what God will do is seen. This mission and testimony comes in terms of worship, encourages healthy relationship with God, genuinely transforms lives and community, and creates works of compassion and testimony to the needy, especially to the marginalized of our world.[25]

So progressive dispensational hermeneutics is not against the pursuit of original meaning or stable meaning. It is not engaged in allegorizing, spiritualizing, or pursuing *sensus plenior*. It is not "covenantal" in its approach because of how it handles a future for national Israel. It is an approach that believes the text calls us to make distinctions, but to define them structurally and temporally, not in terms of the inherent unity the saved people of God ultimately possess as part of a redemption that will unify the creation, removing divisions introduced by the effects of the Fall.

We are left, then, to summarize and briefly discuss what progressive dispensational hermeneutics affirms, though most of these emphases are already seen in what has just been said.

What Progressive Dispensational Hermeneutics Is

Affirms One Stable Meaning in Texts, Dual Authorship, Progress of Revelation, and the Dynamic Character of History and Promise. Progressive hermeneutics argues for stability of meaning while also honoring the dimensions that dual authorship brings to the gradual unfolding of promise. The literary-theological argument is that God reveals the outworking of His promise gradually as Scripture unfolds its meaning and introduces new promises and connections.

The promise starts out as a hope expressed in very general terms in the Abrahamic covenant. Here God promises to create a great nation (Israel) and bring blessing to all the world through Abraham. This promise is specified in the promise that the patriarch's seed is ultimately found in the Christ, something Paul makes clear in Galatians. By highlighting the Christ as the one through whom the realization of this promise comes, the general promise to Abraham gets specified as well in the Old Testament promise to David of a line of kings that ultimately culminates in One who will permanently sit on his throne and bring the promise. The Old Testament itself indicates that David's throne and the everlasting throne of the Lord are designed to be one.

The question of how this promise comes is found as well in the hope of a new covenant, where God will write His presence on His people's hearts and forgive their sins. Here the promise is made initially in Jeremiah 31, but Ezekiel 34–36 adds the note that this great era of the washing by the Spirit of God is associated with the presence of the great "David." That message is repeated by John the Baptist as a summary of Old Testament promises about the Christ and how one can know that the era is come (Luke 3:15).[26] Though this promise is made initially to Israel, it is made so that all the world can be blessed as the Abrahamic promise said and as Paul also emphasizes in his preaching of the gospel (Gal. 3; Rom. 15:7–13). How the promised Spirit came is a major burden of New Testament teaching and preaching with the door being opened by the sacrifice of the Lord on behalf of many, making the establishing of new covenant hope possible and active (Luke 22:17–22—another context where Old Testament imagery is invoked for what Jesus is about to experience as something decreed).[27]

This overview of scriptural promise shows its character as dynamic. Promises are made and then elaborated upon as more revelation comes. New Testament promise and gospel preaching are not to be severed from their Old Testament roots as if something completely distinct is present, when Scripture itself raises the links (Rom. 1:1–7; 16:25–27).[28] The biblical text and its presentation of promise encourage us to look for the connections that bring together the promise of God.

Let me illustrate briefly how Scripture develops promise. Imagine that I find a young, unmarried man whom I believe has great potential for ministry. I tell him in a general way, "I will support you and your descendants in ministry as long as they minister." I do not give details. This means that the "how" of this promise is left for later. Now let us suppose that he meets the woman of his dreams. Does my promise include supporting her as a part of his ministry, or was I referring only to those expenses incurred directly in gaining ministry (i.e., education) and executing it (i.e., church salary support)? We do not know the promiser's intent until he acts. And what about any children (descendants) who are "adopted" into the family? Will they get my support because of their connection to the one to whom the original promise was given? Often promises by their nature show their outworking by how God responds and directs as time passes. Intention becomes revealed through subsequent action and disclosure. So when I pay assistance to the married family and go on to support any adopted sons in ministry, I make clear what I mean by my promise. So God made a general promise to Abraham. He made clear that *the seed* was Jesus. Anyone connected to Him gets access to blessing, just as anyone connected to my promising young man obtains my support. Here is what biblical promise is like as it is disclosed across time. It is dynamic in its progress, being revealed in what God both does and says.

Affirms a Complementary Reading Involving Near Context, Book, and Canon as Well as a Connection of Concepts that Scripture Explicitly Ties to Its Own Previous Revelation. In sum, what we are saying is that the meaning of promise is defined by Scripture. Nonprogressives agree with this general affirmation about getting our view from Scripture, but they are more hesitant to make the kinds of synthetic connections progressives make. Here is where our differences lie. It is not in a radically different hermeneutical method, one being literal and the other, not. Rather, *we discuss how best to fit the various pieces of the scriptural puzzle together.*

Progressives assert that there is a unified meaning and a unified plan to be found in the Scripture that places continuity and discontinuity at various specified points. Nonprogressives insist on discontinuity as an abiding-defining-comprehensive principle in discussing the plan.

I have used the example of the Davidic throne throughout this essay to give one detailed example of how the approaches differ. This detail has been the topic of much discussion, and rightly so, since it so nicely shows the different ways progressives and nonprogressives handle the reading of the text. What progressives argue is that the forgiveness of sins and the distribution of the Spirit are parts of Jesus' current messianic activity that show his ruling-blessing authority as the promised One of God. More, much more on which dispensationalists agree is yet to come in that rule, when He returns and rules the nations from Jerusalem as God finishes completing the execution of His promise to Abraham, Israel, and the world.

What I am arguing is that this theme appears naturally in New Testament contexts where the Law, Psalms, and/or Prophets are being invoked. It also is found in contexts where near fulfillment is the topic as current activity is being discussed. The terminology itself comes from Old Testament contexts that are marked by the presence of promise themes, Scripture, and/or fulfillment. A more normal (literal) reading of such texts is to connect them to the events being alluded to in the New Testament context, rather than to insist that the Old Testament so limits the definition of the term that only an analogy to the future is present.

I am claiming that a nonprogressive hermeneutic operates at a principial-traditional level and shortchanges the canonical meaning, not because such a reading does not provide for a possible sense of the text or because it affirms a discontinuity I reject, but because the sense for which it argues is not the most normal way to read the New Testament context in which the Old Testament promise appears. A consistently normal and complementary reading of the New Testament context introduces a fresh note of continuity in the progress of revelation without resulting in an alteration of the ultimate meaning of the Old Testament passages. Thus, a progressive dispensational hermeneutic is committed to stable meaning as it is progressively revealed across the canon and across the dispensations, eras which in turn build on one another as an advancing sequence in the promise of God. This is the reason why the view is called progressive dispensationalism.

Final Appeal

This is not an easy chapter to write. It can be hard to discuss differences, especially within one's own tradition. Many of the views I have criticized come from people whose ministries I pray for, appreciate, and respect. Some of those criticized were my teachers. Some are colleagues. Some of the views criticized were views I once held.

I have tried to reflect on those who have criticized my reading of the text. Yet I often have found that I did not recognize myself in the view they were criticizing. I have tried to show why at times I have sensed being misunderstood or misrepresented.[29] Whether the fault lies with my clarity, or with another's failure to understand, or with both of us, this essay is an attempt to clarify what progressive dispensational hermeneutics is and to lower the level of misunderstanding, especially since some of the critics have said that we are unclear. I also have sought to explain why my reading of Scripture has caused me to advocate a progressive dispensational approach as well as why I think it is a dispensational reading of Scripture.

One of my critics has asked why progressives "still want to be a part of the dispensational family."[30] The answer is really rather simple. When I read Scripture I see a dispensational structure at work that the Bible affirms. It may not match the details of the structure my critic has, but it is a dispensational structure nonetheless. I do not identify with other traditions that have no place for a future for national Israel or see her totally swallowed up in the church. I have tried to show how my view is differentiated from other nondispensational evangelical traditions. That also answers this question in a concrete way.

So, honesty requires that I address not only our differences but also explain why I think this dispensational view is what Scripture teaches. I also have addressed in detailed notes the way in which our views have been addressed up to this point. Those notes are a crucial part of the essay.

I find one feature of the discussion particularly unfortunate, and

I would be remiss not to address it. It involves the use of names for the views of the types of dispensationalism. Many nonprogressives have adopted the name "normative" dispensationalism (or similar variations) for their own view.

This terminology is unfortunate for at least four reasons. First, unlike "progressive," it is not a name that attempts to describe the inner nature of the type of dispensationalism in view. The term "progressive" is solely intended to describe how this view highlights the progressive movement of God's plan from one dispensation to the next. The name says nothing about where or how other dispensational views stand. By contrast, "normative" is a seemingly blatant attempt to classify the view prescriptively.[31] I am not discussing whether one ought to have the right to chose a name, but the wisdom of picking a name that immediately marks another view as "in" or "out," especially when some representations of the positions being criticized are not accurate. I have referred to nonprogressives as more "traditional" expressions of dispensationalism, because this is how many in that approach see themselves. This is a good descriptive term to use to differentiate one from the progressive view, because it is descriptive and not prescriptive.

Second, such a prescriptive classification ignores the historical variation within the history of dispensationalism and almost pretends variation, even significant variation, did not exist in our tradition's history before the rise of progressive dispensationalism. More importantly, who gets to decide which variations count as deviations or departures from the tradition? Is that a decision that individuals should make? Does this really matter for a tradition that has argued it is biblically, not traditionally, oriented?

Third, the prescriptive move reflects a kind of creedalism that has never been a part of the dispensational tradition in its previous internal discussions. In the previous generation of dispensationalists, no fewer than four views of how the kingdom is related to promise have been defended without recourse to raising such prescriptive language. Our tradition has tried to engage in testing ourselves against Scripture, of being biblical. On the other hand, prescriptive labeling tries to cut off discussion in the very principial-prescriptive way I have criticized throughout the article.

Fourth, I think that the effort cuts off positive discussion, suggesting that everything is settled. It undercuts some of the very values of reflecting biblically on our theological formulations, which some of these critics have written about and still write about when they feel misrepresented by those who criticize their form of dispensationalism.[32]

Now I realize those who use this term are expressing the view— a view sincerely held—that they believe that the differences between traditionalists and progressives are so great that progressive dispensationalism should be called change and a species of a different kind, not development. I am content to let each of us make the case for this and let readers judge that issue for themselves. I think that a fair way to do this is not to use names that are prescriptive in character.

Perhaps a fifth reason I make this point is that I recognize that all of us are making interpretive, synthetic judgments about the whole of Scripture that involve many parts of the text. These discussions are exceedingly complex, as our students will attest. Yet when I look at my differences with those in the dispensational tradition, I do not sense that they are as great or as seemingly threatening as the critics sometimes suggest. I do sense differences of emphasis between us. I have tried to show what those are and why we have them. I hope that in the future we may have a healthy discussion about what Scripture teaches and avoid the prescriptive labeling of others, which often has the effect of duly politicizing the debate and cutting off discussion.

There are nonprogressives with whom I have such healthy discussions. We engage each other about the text and why we read it as we do, as the essays in this book attempt to do. These discussions revolve around the extent of *linkage* one can make between certain themes. Different views exist because progressives and nonprogressives relate texts to different, larger categories of relationship. We each try to make the case for the relationships we see based on textual details. They are textual-synthetic debates of detail, not principial debates. They reflect different views of judgments about the text and its scope. I believe that many of the differences you see and will read about in this book operate at this textual level. Some differences are impacted by the hermeneutical differences of method I have just described. The disagreements are sincere and yet held by many without trying to put anyone "in" or "out" of any tradition. This type of dialogue is what should be taking place in our communities, and it does already in many locales. Readers can decide which of the represented views better and more comprehensively explains the textual details.

I have tried to explain to you, the reader, what progressive dispensational hermeneutics is, why I affirm it textually, and why I believe it yields stable meaning for the students of Scripture. Other essays in the book will make the same case for a differing expression of dispensationalism. Perhaps we can all do it in a way that shows how we ought to have such a discussion. I think we can all do better than we have done. If that takes place, I am sure we will all learn a great deal from our interaction and our mutual attempt to be faithful to Scripture.

RESPONSE

Darrell Bock's discussion on hermeneutics and dispensationalism mirrors a continuing dialogue taking place in the classroom. It is a discussion in which we desire to pursue a contending for truth in a spirit of love. In reading the chapter, it is encouraging to read about a rejection in principle of allegorizing, spiritualizing, *sensus plenior,* or multiple meaning, and to read about an advocacy in principle of the author's intended meaning of one stable meaning in texts, dual authorship, and progress in revelation. Such encouragement, however, is tempered when these principles are compared with the exegesis among progressive dispensationalists where what is affirmed is cast into question by what is done with texts.

One such tempering arises when the different methods are distinguished as two types of approach. One approach is a "principial-traditional approach" in distinction to a "complementary approach." One distinction between these two approaches is clear—one considers the history of tradition as relevant while the other pays less attention to tradition. The other distinction is less clear—does one rely on principles while the other avoids principles?

If so, then how can the "major point of this essay" claim "a more consistent historical-literary interpretation" (p. 83)? Consistency presupposes some form of principle or norm of practice. In addition to references made to grammatical, historical, literary, and theological points, the chosen title of complementary hermeneutics focuses the reading of the New Testament as a complement or completion of the Old Testament revelation. That focus is itself a principle. The real difference is not between one that settles questions of interpretation by rules and definitions while the other settles them by the exegesis of texts. It is hoped that both study the text exegetically and that exegetical practice is based on principles. The actual difference is in the rules we follow and how those rules are used.

The one principle that will be the focus of this review concerns "theological." Bock describes the issue as a "dispute (that) is about the most appropriate way to synthesize vast amounts of biblical material" (p. 84). That theological synthesis comes from a view of the first and second advents of Christ as an "already-not yet" pattern of fulfillment. As a result, nonprogressives "are more hesitant to make the kinds of synthetic connections progressives make." I accept Bock's charge as guilty. I would, however, invite the reader to consider one claimed connection based on Peter's allusion to Psalm 132:11 in Acts 2:30. That connection concerns *when* Christ is seated on David's throne. Psalm 132:11 refers to David's throne as an expression of the Davidic covenant of promise. Peter alludes to the psalm to clarify the purpose of the resurrection, that being to be seated on David's throne. The allusion does not include *when* Christ will be seated on David's throne. Is it immediately or is it at some unspecified time in the future? Bock responds that it must be immediate, for this allusion to Psalm 132:11 is followed by the quote of Psalm 110:1 when Christ is ascended and seated next to the Father. Another question then must be answered. Are these the same seatings? Bock concedes that the seat *now* in heaven is not the same as the *future* seat when Jesus reigns on the earth as the Son of David (see Acts 3:19–22). In addition, it is not the same seat which Solomon took when he assumed David's throne (1 Kings 1–2). David pointedly directed Solomon to enforce his rule and authority while in heaven Christ awaits the Father, who will put

His enemies under His feet. Further, Luke clarified that while Christ departed, Israel, rather than ruling, still remained under Gentile rule (Luke 21:24) during the times of the Gentiles.

The connection that a complementary reading makes between the seating would be difficult unless the texts are read in the perspective of an "already" First Advent fulfillment and a "not yet" Second Advent fulfillment. Is it faithful to the text, however, to use such a general principle as "already-not yet" to specify an exegetical link between seatings even though the immediate exegetical evidence is far from decisive? Rather than make such a connection, a traditional exegesis sees the allusion to Psalm 132:11 as necessary to keep the final goal of a Davidic enthronement before the reader. With this final goal in mind, the reader would be guarded against concluding that the heavenly seating is Christ's ultimate goal. (This is in fact the way an amillennialist would read this text.) Thus, this complementary reading of Acts 2:30 only completes the Old Testament allusion when the canonical principle of "already fulfillment" determines the meaning of *when* Christ is seated on David's throne.

That exegetical conclusion leads to a concern over *semantic identification*. Is it sufficient to identify the seating of Christ in the heavenlies as a Davidic covenant seating? Making an identification based on two common elements—seating of Messiah—runs the risk of making an egregious error. A simple example reminds us of the problem. The identification of a piece of fruit based on a surface skin, a meaty flesh, and a core with seeds and stem that attaches it to a tree is not sufficient. The fruit could be either an apple or a pear. More defining traits are needed when the identification is not made directly in the text naming it as the Davidic throne. Even though we readily acknowledge that the throne of David and the throne of the Lord are related (1 Chron. 28:5–6; 29:23–24) in the sense of a delegated rule of God, such a relationship is not an identification of the two thrones. In addition, there is a distinction recognized between the heavenly throne and the throne in Jerusalem (Ps. 2:4, 6) and a difference in scope of reign between all of creation and the nations of the earth.

Some may propose that the identification is sufficient because "seat" is a metonymy. Thus, "seat" stands for kingship (cf. Col. 1:16).

Nevertheless, kingship and Davidic kingship are not identical. Even Messiah's kingship and the Davidic kingdom are not necessarily identical, as my next chapter will propose to demonstrate. This confusion in identification has an additional hermeneutical consequence. To press an identity in seatings forces one to conclude that "the throne of David" means different identities at different times in the history of revelation. First, in 1 Kings, the throne of David meant the rule which Solomon assumed in Jerusalem as he aggressively established his rule over his enemies. All would agree that this is the inaugural fulfillment of the Davidic covenant. Second, in Acts 2, the Davidic throne now means an enthronement determined by the Father alone and awaiting His enemies to be overcome. Third, in Revelation 19 and 20, Christ returns to Jerusalem (Matt. 24:15, 31) to judge the nations and His enemies and thereby to establish His reign *and will share His throne with those who had been given authority to judge along with Him.* All dispensationalists would identify Christ's throne as the throne of David. However, the identification of these three thrones as the Davidic throne results in two identical meanings and one altered meaning (Acts 2). This conclusion seems to challenge at least two claims of hermeneutics. Is the meaning of "the throne of David" actually stable throughout history when it is altered in Acts 2? Further, does the divine author's intended meaning, as circumscribed in the revelation of the Davidic covenant (2 Sam. 7:12–16), determine the meaning of "seated" in Acts 2:34–35? While Psalm 110 is generally recognized as referring to Messiah as Lord (Mark 12:35–37), as of yet the debate over the seat being the Davidic throne remains in discussion. It seems clear that the burden of proof rests with those who would *expand* the covenantal meaning of the seat (2 Sam. 7:12–16).

This enlarged meaning of the "throne of David" in Acts 2 is the result of a canonical *expansion* in meaning made by Peter. While Bock would *limit* the interpretive expansion to the apostle's interpretation of the Old Testament, it still is an interpretation of an Old Testament text. Such a move to expand the meaning of an old and classical text is an interpretive move commonly made in our postmodern age. So it is not surprising to read what Clark Pinnock proposes in his article "The Role of the Spirit in Interpretation." He contends that "Classical texts like the Bible or the

Declaration of Independence project an effective history of interpretation, in which intended meanings get enriched, sharpened and *enlarged*. The reader is not reading alone but participates in a community of readers over time" (my emphasis, *JETS* 36, no. 4 [December 1993], 495). While Bock does *not* share Pinnock's perspective, yet there is nothing in a text or in our cultural practice to resist such a move, if the task of interpretation is not limited to what the divine author intends to communicate as expressed in the original text. This concern seems to further challenge Bock's rejection of *sensus plenior* or multiple meaning. Further, is this not a natural move for one advocating "the Dynamic Character of History and Promise"? The only way to resist this is to restrict a "complementary reading" to a special hermeneutic operating in the Bible alone rather than a general hermeneutic suitable to any personal communication.

In a brief addendum, I would like to comment on terminology used to refer to different positions of dispensationalism. I agree with Bock's plea that we not choose terms that disadvantage those who disagree. While "normative" is a term that sits in judgment on any variation from it, the term "progressive" could be understood with judgmental connotations. The choice of the term to refer to "progressive" revelation is certainly appropriate. However, the writings of the progressive dispensationalist have not made a strong statement about their choice. Rather, the term could naturally be taken to connote the status of a progressive statement of dispensationalism. Thus, by connotation one might conclude that all previous statements and, in fact, all other statements, are regressive or outdated. Looking at the choice from the outside, the choice seemed masterful, but the connotations felt painful for all of us who are "nonprogressive." Our words often have the effect which James warns, "see how great a forest a little fire kindles" (3:5). *The ideals with which Bock speaks of his position fall short of what has been achieved.*

Chapter Notes

1. Craig A. Blaising and Darrell L. Bock, *Progressive Dispensationalism* (Wheaton: Bridgepoint, 1993), 52.
2. Mal Couch, "Progressive Dispensationalism: Is Christ Now on the Throne of David?—Part I," *CTJ*, 1988, 32–46. Couch uses the terms

spiritual, allegorizing, or *spiritualizing* several times in the first several pages of this article. He groups the progressive reading of Acts 2 with amillennialists on page 37. The entire argument is a caricature, a guilt-by-association move, ignoring how progressives read Acts 3 historically-grammatically to argue for a future for national Israel and a form of distinction between Israel and the church that stands in total contrast to amillenarians. A similar approach and impression appears initially in Charles C. Ryrie's *Dispensationalism* (Chicago: Moody, 1995), 166–68, though he does qualify it to some degree on page 175. His argument that progressives' view of the kingdom are those of Ladd also unfortunately ignores how we handle a future for national Israel in relationship to the future kingdom program [This argument also appears in Robert Lightner, *The Last Days Handbook: Revised and Updated* (Nashville: Nelson, 1997), 132]. Such omissions mean that assessments are being made without accurately describing the view. Ryrie then goes on to argue against the view by hypothesizing what progressives might argue based on their principles, even though he knows that they do not make this argument now. I believe that fairness would dictate that the view be assessed on what it does argue, while trying to appreciate why distinctions from other views are being made, rather than positing conclusions not actually made. Nonetheless, his question about stability of meaning and where the limits in the method are is a fair one that I shall address directly below. One more example of this charge is Thomas D. Ice, "Dispensational Hermeneutics," in *Issues in Dispensationalism,* ed. Wesley R. Willis and John R. Master (Chicago: Moody, 1994), 28–49.

3. Robert L. Thomas, "The Hermeneutics of Progressive Dispensationalism," *MSJ* 6 (1995): 79–95, attempts to argue that progressives deviate from the historical-grammatical method. Thomas does a guilt-by-association argument more subtly on page 91. Here, he equates *sensus plenior* with Roman Catholic readings and calls it allegorical (ignoring completely the role of the *magesterium* in this Catholic view). Then he claims progressives "clearly" argue for a *sensus plenior* and thus are guilty of the same error. Why do such arguments consistently resort to putting words in the position's mouth? Thomas even noted my denial of this connection on page 92, note 61, but treated it as irrelevant! He argued, in effect, that my view of typology is *sensus plenior,* even though I expressly ex-

plained it otherwise on the basis of only canonical factors within the biblical text. Those who understand pattern-typology know that it is not the same thing as *sensus plenior*. Thomas Ice explicitly acknowledged this point in *Issues in Dispensationalism,* 39–40, when he advocates the legitimate category of "literal plus typical." One should note, however, that Ice's claim that Scofield did not use the typological method on pages 37–38 contains not a single historical example of what Scofield did and did not do, unlike Blaising's historical work (Blaising/Bock, *Progressive Dispensationalism,* 28–30). One should also note that Ice's need to have four categories, three of which are "literal plus," shows that the term *literal* itself is inadequate as a summarizing category. In doing so, Ice, in effect, makes a point progressives have made about literal being a poor and fuzzy term in the hermeneutical discussion. My point is that perhaps even revised dispensationalists do not agree on method, indicating that the topic is open for discussion. Even more amazing is that Thomas himself, in an article he wrote later, holds to a similar multiple setting view for some prophetic texts in a way that parallels what I mean by typology. See his "The Mission of Israel and the Messiah in the Plan of God," *ISRAEL The Land and the People: An Evangelical Affirmation of God's Promises,* ed. H. Wayne House (Grand Rapids: Kregel, 1998), 272. Here, in critiquing the views of N. T. Wright, he says, "For instance, he overlooks the different direction God took in light of Israel's rejection of her Messiah at His first coming. That difference was well known in advance to God, but he did not see fit to reveal it to man in the pages of the Old Testament. *The new direction in his dealings with mankind resulted in additional meanings being assigned to Old Testament passages by authoritative New Testament writers.* For example, Paul's use of Isaiah 42:6 (cf. Isa. 49:6) in his speech in Acts 13:47 applies to his own ministry as he preached in Pisidian Antioch God's words to Isaiah's Messiah-Servant. In the Isaianic context, that promised salvation to the ends of the earth was to come in conjunction with repentant Israel's liberation from foreign oppressors. *No strict application of grammatical-historical hermeneutics to the Isaiah passage could have interpreted it to refer to a Jewish Christian preacher, himself a fugitive wanted by Israel's authorities, offering international peace and prosperity to a mixed audience of Jews and Gentiles.* Israel had not yet repented and still remained under foreign domination. *Paul's meaning, inspired by the Holy Spirit, went beyond anything intended for Isaiah's original readers.*" (The italics are ours to show the points that relate to this issue.) Now questions abound. How can Thomas argue this for Acts 13 and not allow the possibility that other texts ultimately display a similar double setting? If what Paul did was legitimate, then what does that say about how meaning operates in the context of the canon? Are there perhaps conceptual keys tied to the nature of the Servant and those connected to him that allow Paul to make such an interpretive move (i.e., Servant as a corporate entity in which the Messiah is contained as the representative of those associated with him; Isa. 49:6; 52:13–52:12)? Now that Paul has made this point, should we not include this understanding *as a part of the discussion of meaning for Isaiah when one considers its canonical force?* If not, on what basis is it to be excluded? (Are we not then rejecting Paul's reading or suggesting that it is illegitimate?) Might then our approach to the text be inadequate by not explaining hermeneutically how Paul could do this? Does the presence of "additional meaning" here suggest that meaning is now unstable in Scripture and that the Spirit is the cause of such instability? Thomas answers the final question by making it clear that the answer is no. Later on page 272 he says, "The new meaning of Old Testament prophecies applied to the church introduced by New Testament writers did not cancel out the original meaning and their promises to Israel. God will yet restore the nation of Abraham's physical descendants as He promised He would." This final statement is precisely what progressives say about how complementary meaning works! The New Testament sense comes in alongside what has already been affirmed in the Old Testament *without removing what the Old Testament affirms.* This example suggests that the disagreement may not really be so much about method as it is about certain textual conclusions, which are prejudged to be inadequate simply on the basis of principial-tradition grounds. If our critique here of Thomas is appropriate, then it also illustrates an example of preunderstanding in operation for him in a way he denies when he claims to be strictly objective.

4. Not everyone critical of progressives misrepresents us or engages in the polemics described in the above notes. Elliott Johnson and

I have amicably team-taught a class on hermeneutics at DTS for several years in which we openly discuss our views. We disagree about certain points, but our discussions are textual, methodological, and substantive. We have a mutual commitment to each other to represent one another fairly. Another example of an attempt to engage fairly in textual discussion is Zane Hodges, "A Dispensational Understanding of Acts 2," in *Issues in Dispensationalism,* 166–80.

5. Ice, "Dispensational Hermeneutics," 32; Ryrie, *Dispensationalism,* 80–85; Couch, "Is Christ Now on the Throne of David?—Part I," 33–34; *Dictionary of Premillennial Theology,* 1996 ed., s.v. "Dispensationalism, Progressive" by R. L. Thomas; and Thomas, "The Hermeneutics of Progressive Dispensationalism," 84–93.

6. The article on hermeneutics by Elliott Johnson in *A Case for Premillennialism* (Chicago: Moody, 1993), 15–34, is a hybrid of this pattern. He also goes about defining his principles before considering his texts, but he does so more carefully than others from a more traditional background because he interacts with biblical texts and competing views more honestly as he is discussing his principles. He acknowledges in spots where competing views do have a point that require dispensationalists to be more reflective.

7. I will not deal with the historical argument here because I do not have space. I will note, however, that the historical points made by my colleague in *Progressive Dispensationalism* still stand and support the claim that dispensationalism has undergone development in its history. For example, the important relationship between the kingdom and Old Testament promise has been variously expressed. We have said that some of what we have argued for is new to our tradition, but we also argue that what we retain concerning a future for national Israel shows that we are an expression of dispensationalism. We have also noted that critiques by the other side have either cited no historical detail in making their claims about the tradition's history or they have done so selectively. For example, Steve Nichols in "The Dispensational View of the Davidic Kingdom: A Response to Progressive Dispensationalism," *MSJ* 7 (1996): 213–39 manages to discuss the history and not even mention the views of Eric Sauer, who argued for elements of Davidic fulfillment today. A claim that he is a continental dispensationalist is no excuse for not covering this. This fact qualifies the absoluteness of his historical claim. To Nichols's

credit, he does acknowledge that progressives have raised real interpretive issues that more traditional views need to address (Eric Sauer, *From Eternity to Eternity: An Outline of the Divine Purposes*, trans. G. H. Lang [Grand Rapids: Eerdmans, 1954], 236–37). In the end, the historical argument is irrelevant, as the ultimate issue that counts is what the Bible teaches, not what a tradition has said it teaches. (For more on this article, see note 18 in the introductory essay of chapter 1.) At the height of dispensationalism's dispute with covenant theology, it claimed that it was not a creedal theology but a biblically grounded one. Lewis Chafer, a well-known classical dispensationalist, was reputed to have said that if something was in the Westminster Confession but not in the Bible, then so much for the Confession. Unlike other traditions, dispensationalism is not creedal in an ecclesiastical-denominational sense. It never had a church council-like meeting to formulate a historical creed. Progressives argue that a historical study of the tradition reveals its fundamental emphasis across its various subexpressions, at least within America, see Craig A. Blaising and Darrell L. Bock, eds., *Dispensationalism, Israel and the Church: The Search for Definition*, 378–79, as well as the points of debate with nondispensationalists noted on 388–93, and my "Why I am a dispensationalist with a Small 'd,'" *JETS* 41, no. 3 (September 1998): 383–96, in the sections entitled "Covenant Premillennialism?" and "The Value of Dispensationalism."

8. Hodges, "A Dispensational Understanding of Acts 2," 173–74. My latter essay on the covenants in chapter 5 treats this background in detail.
9. Ibid., 174.
10. Mal Couch, "Is Christ Now on the Throne of David?—Part 1," 33. The argument I make here does not even raise the confirming formal evidence of word linkage, so common in Jewish and early Christian exegesis to show that Old Testament ideas are being linked. For the most recent expression of this argument dealing with Hodges's objections to this claim, see my review of *Issues in Dispensationalism* in *BSac* 152 (1995): 98–101, esp. 99–100, where I point out that both the verb "to set" (κάθημαι) and the verb "to sit" (καθίζω), which are both used in Acts 2, are used to discuss Psalm 109:1 LXX in the New Testament (BAGD, 389–90). One more point: Couch appeals to Revelation 3:21 as if it answers the issue of a distinction

of thrones. Couch is arguing that Revelation teaches that the Father's throne and Christ's throne are distinct. But questions abound. Why select Revelation, which comes after the Acts speech and was not yet written at the time of the book of Acts, as a parallel and ignore the equation of thrones in 1 Chronicles, a text which already existed and that is the biblical base for the image? The objection also ignores the fact that progressives discussed Revelation 3:21 in their work, explaining that the Old Testament shows that what is rhetorically presented as distinct thrones in Revelation is actually affirmed as one throne (1 Chron. 17:13–14; Ps. 89:26, 29). It is Christ's shared authority with the Father and the oneness of the reward that is the point! The fact that God is the Davidite's Father by divine covenantal commitment and that the throne endures forever shows that David's throne and the Father's throne are seen as one. His claim also ignores the point that Revelation, up to this point, has named Jesus as functioning in Davidic covenantal language *through what he has already done* in several texts before this point of the book (Rev. 1:5–Jesus *Christ* . . . first born, ruler of the kings of the earth [Ps. 89:27]; 2:18–received authority from His Father to rule the nations; 2:26–27–"have received power from my Father"; 3:12–"has received the key of David"; see *Progressive Dispensationalism,* 183–84. Also, Revelations 5:5–6 says that the Lion of the tribe of Judah, the Root of David *has conquered* as it looks at Jesus' work as Lamb). The progressive's claim is that it is the Bible that explicitly links Messiah to these *Davidic* categories and *current* activities. This is our reply to the claim that progressives "are misunderstanding the obvious fact that Jesus as one person is carrying out many roles and offices in several dispensational settings." Our reply is that Jesus' many roles, which do exist, are unified in Scripture under the conceptual heading that the Messiah-Son combines all these roles as Romans 1:1–7 suggests. In fact, one of the burdens of the gospels is to show that all of the various eschatological functions of Jesus unite in Him and are rooted in His role as Messiah, a role that He performs both in this age *and* in the age to come. This idea is so pervasive that Jesus of Nazareth is called Jesus *Christ* in the New Testament. His fundamental office, the office of Davidic promise and activity, became a part of His name *and* points to the confession of Him as the anointed king both now and in the age to come (Eph. 1:18–23).

11. A check of the passages just noted shows how Luke is tracing *and emphasizing* a fundamental story line of fulfillment that directly ties *current* activity to Old Testament messianic hope. The way to know that the promised Messiah is present and that Davidic hope is being realized is when "the one to come" baptizes with the Holy Spirit. That is exactly what Peter argues in Acts 2:30–36. One other note here: this activity is *not* an exclusively priestly exercise by Jesus. Luke describes it as a Davidic messianic function (note the OT background of the voice's confession at Jesus' baptism in Luke 3:21–22). Appeals to a Melchizedekian, priestly (devoid of regal Davidic) connection ignore the fact that for the New Testament, Psalm 110 is a Davidic, messianic text (Luke 20:41–44) and that Luke's use of this imagery is exclusively Davidic. The point from Hebrews is a more complex matter. Nevertheless, I would argue that an appeal to Melchizedekian background from Hebrews actually makes our point, since that figure is introduced as a king-priest from texts that are introduced by the author of Hebrews in the context of Davidic promise (Heb. 1:5–13; see also chaps. 7–8). I make this point to counter the Melchizedekian claim of Elliott Johnson in *A Case for Premillennialism,* 28–34. Finally, against Thomas (*Revelation 8–22: An Exegetical Commentary* [Chicago: Moody, 1995], 551), the idea of Jesus exercising His rule from heaven is not a violation of the understanding of Psalm 110:1 when applied to Jesus' Davidic role as Messiah. Jesus Himself raised Psalm 110:1 as a Davidic, messianic text as was just noted above in the references to Luke 20:41–44. Even if one reads Psalm 110:1 as a directly prophetic text, it still puts a Davidic Messiah and the rule exercised as a Davidite from heaven. See also note 10 above, in which the Father's throne and Christ's throne are seen as one in the Old and New testaments.

12. The use of the term complementary, ironically enough, goes back to Charles Ryrie. See his *Dispensationalism Today* (Chicago: Moody, 1965), 101. It is retained in the revised book, *Dispensationalism* (Chicago: Moody, 1995), 92–93. On page 93 of the new edition he says, "Unity and distinction are not incompatible concepts. They may be quite complementary, as indeed they are in dispensationalism." This is exactly what progressives claim, though they do not define the complementary relationships as tightly as more traditional expressions of the view do. In the midst of this discus-

sion, Ryrie cites approvingly of the work of Eric Sauer, who made
the very points about Davidic promise in general that we are making specifically about the Davidic throne. See Sauer, *From Eternity
to Eternity,* 171–78.

13. Examples could be multiplied. What consistently emerges from
such a reading is the presence of more continuity in the biblical
promise. For other examples of such integrative readings, see Craig
Blaising and Darrell Bock, *Progressive Dispensationalism;* Darrell
Bock, "The Son of David and the Saints' Task: The Hermeneutics
of Initial Fulfillment," *BSac* 150 (1993): 440–57, and "Current
Messianic Activity and OT Davidic Promise: Dispensationalism,
Hermeneutics, and NT Fulfillment," *TrinJ* 15ns (1994): 55–87;
Mark Strauss, *The Davidic Messiah in Luke–Acts: The Promise and
Its Fulfillment in Luke–Acts.* JSNTSup 110 (Sheffield: Sheffield Aca-
demic Press, 1995).

14. This suggestion is made in the discussion of the historical dimension by Thomas, "The Hermeneutics of Progressive Dispensationalism," 86–88.

15. *Dispensationalism, Israel, and the Church: The Search for Definition*
(Grand Rapids: Zondervan, 1992), 392–93. I italicize the key portions of the citation that relate to the current discussion.

16. It is our refusal to substitute with regard to these ultimate meanings that makes our approach dispensational in orientation. There
is maintained here a distinction between Israel and the church,
even though it is less distinct than other dispensational expressions of the difference.

17. Thomas, "The Hermeneutics of Progressive Dispensationalism,"
87, complains about "multi-layered" readings that add to the original meaning of the text's original context. He does not like the
consideration of the canon as a factor in defining meaning. However, this is something *all dispensationalists do* as a fundamental
part of their system. When we call an Old Testament passage
millennial, are we not taking a term from the book of Revelation
(i.e., on the basis of a canonical consideration) and reading it back
(legitimately) into the Old Testament setting? Do we not do this
in multiple passages? Such a move is being sensitive to the theological nature and unity of the divinely inspired text. Another example of the same type of canonical reading is how we argue that
the angel of the Lord in the Old Testament is really the presence

of the preincarnate Christ. This is a move only we can make because we have read the text in light of the canon. See n. 23 below.

18. Note that this "heavenly" dimension is *not* spiritualizing or allegorizing. It is not reducing the text to a two-level symbol. It is arguing for a *real, concrete* connection between the authority Jesus
exercises as Messiah and what is happening on earth. My colleague
addressed the issue of spiritualization earlier, in *Progressive
Dispensationalism,* 186–87. No historical or hermeneutical critique
has interacted textually with these pages. Nichols, "The Dispensational View of the Davidic Kingdom," 233–34, mentioned these
pages only to note how the progressive view is historically distinct
from nonprogressive readings in their typical principial-traditional
manner. No direct textual discussion takes place. This leaves the
misimpression that we have said next to nothing about this issue
or that there is little we can say.

19. We could also point out the relevance of other texts such as the
use of Isaiah 55:3 in Acts 13:34, or the use of Davidic themes in
Ephesians 1:19–23; Hebrews 1:5–13; 1 Corinthians 15:25; and
Revelations 1:6–7. This brief list of texts is but a glimpse of a larger
list that shows how pervasive this theme is in texts discussing
Christ's current role and activity in *Davidic* terms. Here the image of the throne is not present, but the repeated invocation of
Davidic promise and covenant imagery is. When one works conceptually and not merely lexically, then these connections can be
seen. Here is another method we all use. The term *trinity* appears
nowhere in Scripture, yet we all affirm its presence conceptually
in the Bible. To interpret, one must work with more than words;
one must work with semantic fields that show the conceptual backdrop at work in the meaning of passages.

20. It is not to be disputed that originally in the Old Testament this
throne was to be applied to the nation of Israel, but Peter in Acts
2 is preaching to Jews and is making claims about their Christ as
he explicitly addresses Israel (Acts 2:36). The point of the story of
Acts is to show how this promised messianic blessing came despite Israelite rejection and how it came to include Gentiles (Luke
24:43–49; 3:24–26; 26:15–23). Note how the Acts 26 passage explicitly connects Paul's preaching to Gentiles to what Moses and
the prophets said would happen. If this preaching is totally de-
tached from the revelation of the Old Testament, then how can

Paul make this claim about his ministry to Gentiles in the church era? I will address the issue more when I discuss the term mystery later in this essay. See *Progressive Dispensationalism,* 184–86, where Blaising discusses the relationship between God's heavenly rule and Israelite kingship, as well as the divine-human connection of Jesus' person in His regal activity.

21. Note that I did not say a soteriologically favored role. Christ's coming has made it clear that those who share in messianic promise and blessing, whether Jew or Gentile, do so as equals in terms of access to the basic benefits of grace (Eph. 2:11–22; 3:5–6). That is something Christ has put in place that is true from the work of His first coming on in the plan of God. When nations come to worship in Jerusalem in the future as believers, it will be as comembers and coparticipants in the blessings of Christ. The gospel soteriologically is ultimately about the reconciliation God brings to all the world through the seed of Abraham, Jesus Christ (Rom. 4; Gal. 3). It is helpful to think about the relationship between Israel and Gentiles as one moves through Scripture. This discussion and the interplay between these two groups starts with the Abrahamic promise, continues in Romans 9–11, and runs through the Bible to the end of the story. It is always an important part of the discussion of promise in Scripture. I have benefited from discussions with Takashi Manabe, president of the Evangelical Biblical Seminary in Japan, on this point. On the other hand, the distinctions that exist in the dispensations are distinctions of structure, not distinctions of class of blessing. The church, with Jesus absent from earth and made up of people scattered throughout the world, is a distinct structure from the Millennium, in which Jesus shall rule over Israel and Gentile alike from Jerusalem while present on the earth. It is at this important structural level that the distinction between Israel and the church makes biblical sense.

22. I have elaborated how progressive dispensationalism is not covenant premillennialism or Laddian in approach in detail elsewhere. See "Why I am a dispensationalist with a Small 'd,'" *JETS* 41, no. 3 (September 1998): 383–96.

23. Ryrie, *Dispensationalism,* 178, cites the covenant theologian Vern Poythress as making this evaluation in his *Understanding Dispensationalists* (Phillipsburg, N.J.: Presbyterian & Reformed,

1994), 137. Ryrie uses the citation to make his point that progressives will eventually become Laddian in a "this is what they will become" argument.

24. The case of Abraham is one example of where looking to scriptural typological pattern and being canonically sensitive can surface the semantic complexity of a biblical concept. Here is a typology all traditions must reflect upon. Abraham is a type of faith for every era and race, even though he is at the same time the father of Israel. Abraham's seed also possesses an intriguing ambiguity. The seed is only found in one, Jesus Christ, according to Galatians 3:16; yet it is multiple when read as part of the story of Genesis or considering the history of Israel (Rom. 9:6–7). And yet even in Genesis it is specific at key points, for it is Isaac, not Ishmael, and it is Jacob, not Esau. By the end of the book, it has become like the sands of the sea and the stars of the sky, describing the nation of Israel (Gen. 48:16; Exod. 1:7). Yet that semantic ambiguity also appears in Galatians 3, for although the seed is only one, Jesus Christ, in Galatians 3:16, it is multiple, encompassing Jew and Gentile, in Galatians 3:28–29! The concept of Abraham's seed shows how inadequate it can be to have a one-size-fits-all prescriptive definition for some biblical terms, no matter which tradition does it. Each case must be worked out biblically, one set of terms and concepts at a time.

25. It is here that the relevance of progressive dispensationalism impacts the practical theology of the church in mission and evangelism, something Blaising initially addressed in *Progressive Dispensationalism*, 284–301, and that I discussed in "Current Messianic Activity and Old Testament Davidic Promise," 85–87, and in "The Son of David and the Saints' Task," 456–57. It is in this area that much promise for the development of dispensational theology exists.

26. See note 11 above and the discussion surrounding it.

27. The arrival of the new covenant is the only thing that can explain why the law no longer applies. It is because Christ has brought its fulfillment and end (Rom. 9:30–10:13, esp. v. 4; Heb. 8–10; 2 Cor. 3–4; 6:14–7:1). Israel should still be under law if the new covenant has not come in Christ, at least with respect to the presence of the forgiveness of sins and the initial promise of the arrival of the Spirit of God. It should also be clear by the celebration of the Lord's Table that part of what is celebrated is the work of the

messianic suffering servant to provide forgiveness of sins ("the new covenant in my blood"—looking back to Luke 22:20, ". . . the new covenant in my blood, which is *poured out for you*. . . ."), another manifestation of salvific blessing that is evidence of the activity of his messianic rule (1 Cor. 11:25). This rite is discussed in a predominantly Gentile church to cover an aspect of worship that is in place only until Jesus returns.

28. The discussion of mystery in this Romans 16 passage is important. Thomas criticized me as not being thorough in presenting options when I did not present the option of "prophetic writings" in Romans 16 as meaning "the utterances and writings of the NT prophets." See his "The Hermeneutics of Progressive Dispensationalism," 94, and my "The Son of David and the Saints' Task," 456, n. 26, where I briefly note Romans 16. Note also my "Current Messianic Activity and OT Davidic Promise," 80–85, in which I carefully define the OT and Jewish understanding of the term *mystery*. He is right to note that I should have raised this alternative sense as an option that has been discussed for the passage. However, it is not at all the most probable meaning. Not only does the phrase "prophetic scriptures" preclude a reference to utterances, but in the context of Romans as a book, the constant recourse throughout has not been to *any* New Testament prophetic texts, but to constantly cite the Scripture of the Old Testament! A normal, contextual, and historical reading of this phrase shows, then, that the most natural reading of this benediction is to see a reference to the prophetic Hebrew Scriptures here, especially in light of Paul's consistent practice throughout the book, not to mention his introduction to the book in 1:1–7. If this is so, then mystery, at least in this Romans context *must refer not to totally new truth, but to truth that was already somewhat revealed in those Scriptures.* This idea is not new with us as dispensationalists. The dispensationalist Sauer, in *From Eternity to Eternity*, 171–78, discussed this issue in careful detail. Every dispensationalist should read and reflect on these pages.

29. I have tried to make this point before; see my review of *Issues in Dispensationalism* in *BSac* 152 (1995): 101 (The parenthetical statement in the following citation reflects the real progressive view). There I said, "Much of what is heard in some quarters about progressive dispensationalism simply is not true. Some writers in

Issues in Dispensationalism suggest that progressive dispensationalists resignify the text (p. 197—but this is not so), that progressive dispensationalists believe the present church age is indistinct from the kingdom (p. 21—this is a false accusation because the kingdom is a theme broader than the church), that typology is a denial of prophetic fulfillment (but see p. 175), and that progressives, by appealing to pattern, deny a "literal" approach to the text (they instead argue that they are handling the text in its normal grammatical-historical way)." The point about the kingdom needs elaboration. We are arguing that the kingdom comes in two phases: "already-not yet." The already phase is the period of the church, whereas the not-yet phase involves the millennial hope and its move into the eternal state. Thus, the claim that for progressives *kingdom* = *church* is wrong. A better discussion will be possible when the positions are correctly described.

30. R. Lightner, *The Last Days Handbook*, 211.
31. Names we used for views we did not hold, such as "classical" or "revised," were not prescriptive, but descriptive. We named the earliest expression of the tradition ("classical") and then named the next stage "revised" because that view was distinct enough temporally and historically that a revised version of a study Bible was released as a result of the differences.
32. See, for example, Ryrie, *Dispensationalism*, 209–13. I would guess that he regrets the situation that some classically oriented dispensationalists who are around today call his expression of dispensationalism a historic departure (and thus hardly normative or historic at all). Again, who should decide such questions?

PART TWO

ABRAHAMIC, DAVIDIC, AND NEW COVENANTS

CHAPTER FOUR

Covenants in Traditional Dispensationalism

Elliott E. Johnson
with response by Darrell L. Bock

Traditional dispensationalism has been unified in its interpretation of the promissory covenants in broad principle, if not in every detail. These broad principles may be captured in two basic criteria: (1) the covenants, defined in the Old Testament, frame in stable terms the outworking of God's purposes with man on earth and in history, and (2) what was promised to Israel will be fulfilled with Israel.[1]

In the exposition that follows, we will adhere to these criteria in a fresh exposition based upon a consistent literal interpretation of the original framework of the covenants as instituted, and a consistent literal interpretation of the fulfillment of the terms of the covenant in the progress of revelation.

However, before we begin the exposition, it is important to have common ground in basic vocabulary:

1. *Promise* is a stated commitment to act in the future for the benefit of a specified recipient.[2]
2. *Covenant* is a formally stated agreement between specified partners to act in the future for the benefit of the other partner, confirming the agreement by an oath.[3]

a. The agreement may be *unilateral* when one partner alone assumes the responsibility to meet the provisions of the agreement toward the other partner.[4]

b. The agreement may be *bilateral* when both partners assume responsibility to meet the provisions of the agreement.[5]

c. A covenant is *instituted* when it is cut, concluded, or given so that provisions of the agreement may now be expected to be met.[6]

3. *Fulfillment* is either the keeping or the meeting (satisfying) of the commitments in the agreement with the specified recipient or partner.[7]

a. A covenant is *inaugurated* in fulfillment when all of the provisions agreed upon are kept but in a partial or limited scope.[8]

b. A covenant is *fulfilled* when all of the provisions are met in the complete, stated scope.

The Abrahamic, Davidic, and new covenants are promissory, unilateral covenants in which Yahweh assumes responsibility unconditionally to determine Israel's destiny and through Israel the destiny of all nations. Recent discussions between traditional dispensationalists and progressive dispensationalists have exposed disparity in the treatment of these fundamental agreements and their fulfillment that frame the progressive revelation of the Bible. Thus, the point of this chapter will be to examine the three covenants consistently with the criteria introduced and to highlight these disparities.

In broad terms, that disparity concerns the inaugural fulfillment of the promissory covenants. J. Dwight Pentecost in *Things to Come* related land, seed, and blessing to their fulfillment with Israel at the second advent of Christ. By distinction, Craig Blaising relates an inaugural or present fulfillment due to Christ's mediation of the covenants with the church after His first advent. Then, at Christ's second advent, a future fulfillment will feature Israel but include Gentiles in Christ. Israel will have a distinct role in that fulfillment but not a distinguishing relationship to the covenants as a covenant partner. The disparity concerns the determinacy and stability of the original statements of the covenants as they are fulfilled at later times in history and in the progress of revelation.

Similar disparity appears in various systems of interpretation because of different priority given to the reading of the New Testament theology and the view of the advents of Christ. Dispensationalists have traditionally assumed that the two testaments contribute in sequence to a view of progressive revelation rather than a priority be given to the New Testament such that the Old Testament is reread in some sense in light of conclusions reached about the New Testament.

Among evangelical interpreters, there are three disparate approaches that give the New Testament priority as a tool in exegesis:

1. Bruce Waltke[9] has carefully discussed an amillennial replacement theology based on a *resignification* of Old Testament passages.

2. George Ladd[10] supports a *reinterpretation* of Old Testament passages based upon proposed New Testament uses of Old Testament passages.

3. Darrell Bock[11] proposes an *expansion of the boundaries* of the message of Old Testament passages also based on a complementary reading in New Testament usage. This expanded meaning is conditioned on Christ's present work of grace but will be restored to an Old Testament reading in the future millennial kingdom.

Bruce Waltke, having abandoned a dispensational view of progressive revelation, has provided a reasoned case for his change. The value to be found in his extended discussion underlines the importance of adequate arguments in support of an epistemological priority given to the New Testament. In that sense of priority, his position represents all three approaches above. As such, that priority must be rejected for two reasons:

1. *Both testaments are verbal revelation.* To regard the revelation of the New Testament as capable of altering the original revelation of the Old Testament ignores the fact that the Old Testament is revelation. In spite of all that we do not know about the composition and collection of the old canon, what we do know sets our framework. The prophecies of Scripture came as holy men of God spoke as they were moved by the Holy Spirit (2 Peter 1:20–21). This leads

to the conclusion that Old Testament Scripture is true and stable in the expression of truth. This would be denied if that early revelation may be altered by later revelation, which would mean that the early revelation is either wrong or misleading and in need of correction.[12] If the early revelation were merely incomplete or temporary, the later revelation would simply add to what was said but not alter it.

Waltke's adoption of Martin Heidegger's argument that speakers and writers are at the disposal of language does provide a basis for arguing for cultural relativity and historical determination of what has been said. While there is clearly a cultural and historical influence to what has been said, influence does not equal relativity or determination. Rather, the Bible introduces language as God spoke creation into existence (Gen. 1) and as God communicated with the first couple (Gen. 2). Language remained as a basis for the functioning of God's relationship with human beings and their communication among themselves. So language came into existence from God and was shared with mankind, which portrays language as a tool and not as a controlling influence. Thus, interpretations of language may need to be altered, but statements in language find no grounds for being altered just because they are early.

2. *The New Testament progresses upon the Old.* The basis of a claim to see progress in revelation rests on both the determinate boundaries of each textual message and on the stability of what is meant by that message in history. Thus, the recognition of progress may take one of two forms: either the new enriches and deepens, as the implications fully unfold what we understand the old to mean (as in redemption); or the new adds meanings related to what had already been said (such as Israel as God's people and the church as God's people). If the old is subject to alteration, then the new is an altered revelation rather than a progressive revelation.

Thus, the Old Testament should be read as an introduction and a foundation, and the New Testament as the climax and conclusion. The climax and conclusion do not warrant rereading the Old Testament to alter it in some sense. Rather, there is a continuation that is in harmony with the climax and conclusion in the unity of the biblical canon.

The Structure of the Promissory Covenants

The Structure of the Abrahamic Covenant

The Abrahamic covenant is an unilateral, unconditional agreement given to Abraham (Gen. 15:18-19). This covenant is merely a formal expression of the relationship that already existed between Yahweh and Abram (Gen. 12:1-3). Yahweh appeared revealing His will to Abram (Gen. 12:1-3) and Abram responded as Yahweh had spoken (Gen. 12:4). The relationship thus introduced was unilateral since the terms of relationship were spoken by Yahweh alone. Within the terms were promises unconditionally stated even though they followed a "call" to leave his family and his homeland (Gen. 12:1 and Acts 7:2-3). That "call" was then followed by promises, the first of which was a promise of land, which Yahweh would show him.

Some would interpret the "call" as a condition based on which the promises were rewards. If Abram responded adequately, then he would be rewarded by what Yahweh promised. But as the narrative unfolds the response to the call, the response could not be identified as meeting a condition and thus as adequate. Abram arrived in the land God promised (Gen. 12:7) in spite of leaving with Terah (Gen. 11:31-32) and taking Lot, his nephew (Gen. 12:5). Further, Abram arrived in spite of the delay in Haran (Gen. 11:31-32 and 12:4) and maintained his relationship to promise in spite of departing from the land with disobedience (Gen. 12:10-13:1). So while obedience was associated with receiving what God had promised, it was neither a condition of that relationship with Yahweh nor a condition based on which he was rewarded by what was promised. Rather, the relationship was unilaterally originated and the promises unconditionally given. Obedience was associated with the occasion for Abram being blessed as necessary, but the promise was realized only because Yahweh was merciful.

The Promises Given to Abraham

The promises given to Abram were of three kinds: land, descendants, and blessings.

1. *Land.* God first promised to give land to Abram's seed (Gen. 12:7) and later promised land to Abram and his seed (Gen. 13:15). The land was promised to be owned forever.

2. *Descendants.* The descendants who were spoken *about* were going to be numerous (Gen. 13:6; 15:5), and those who were spoken *to* were going to be the recipients of what was promised (Gen. 12:7; 13:15). When descendants *(zera)* are referred to, an ambiguity exists because of the collective noun, "seed." It could refer to one descendant or many, and the context would provide the immediate clue to resolve the ambiguity.

3. *Blessings.* The blessings were not only personal (Gen. 12:2b, 2c) but also were to be mediated for others (Gen. 12:2c, 3). This role of mediation is what Caird called the job description. The job was greater than anything Abram could realize alone as well as anything Abraham's descendants ever did accomplish. Yet the promise provides the continuing basis for expecting that his descendants would be mediators of God's blessings to all nations.

The promise of land and the promise of posterity both seemed tenuous in Abraham's life. Almost ten years had passed without any land or even a descendant. Then, as Yahweh repeated His promise as an assurance that his reward would be great (Gen. 15:1), Abram burst into a question (Gen. 15:2). Abram's question concerning an heir was met with a clarification of the promise, promising a physical descendant (Gen. 15:3–4). That promise was amplified with the specification of many descendants (Gen. 15:5). Then Abram believed God and His word of promise (Gen. 15:6).

The Covenant Instituted with Abraham

God's promise, as Abram was in need of further assurance (Gen. 15:8), was confirmed by the institution of a covenant (Gen. 15:18–21). The covenant featured a land grant agreement given to Abram's seed. The extent of the territory was delineated in geographic and ethnographic terms. God contracted a solemn covenant with the patriarch, who became the passive beneficiary of His unilateral obligation, unconditionally assumed[13] as a legal document. That covenant provided Abraham with a title deed to the land, which was then passed on to Isaac (Gen. 26:3–4) and to Jacob (Gen. 28:13–15 and 35:9–13) because of the relationship each had with Abraham (Gen. 26:3, 5; 28:13). While the covenant was instituted with Abraham (Gen. 15:18–19), fulfillment was not inaugurated with either Abraham, Isaac, or Jacob, as none came into possession of any land by means of the promise.

The provision of the covenant focused on the land geographically and ethnically defined, but other provisions that had been promised were included in later summaries. The climactic and concluding provision had already been promised at the outset (Gen. 12:3) but was repeated for decisive emphasis; "in your seed, all nations of the earth shall be blessed" (Gen. 22:18; 26:4; 28:14). In addition, a further provision was repeated about the multiplication of his seed (Gen. 22:17; 26:4; 28:13; 35:11) to become a nation.

The Structure of the Davidic Covenant

The Davidic covenant is introduced in 2 Samuel 7:12–17 and 1 Chronicles 17:13–15. The covenant is then reflected upon by David in Psalm 2 and by other psalmists later in the history of the kingdom (Pss. 89 and 132). In addition, Yahweh revealed an oracle and an oath to David concerning His Anointed, who is also Lord (Ps. 110). The basic structure is revealed in these passages as a unilateral covenant with promises unconditionally assured in their outcome. While there is no record of its institution, the terms are referred to as a covenant (Ps. 89). Further, it is doubtful that the promise of David's house is a reward for David's desire to build God a house. Rather, God's promise is a stroke of unmerited favor, unilaterally given.

The Promise to Build the Davidic Kingdom

In distinction to the attention given by Blaising to the Davidic house,[14] equal attention ought to be given to the Davidic throne and kingdom (2 Sam. 7:16). Each one of these three components complement one another. A Davidic *house* refers to a dynastic succession of rulers in which a son was promised in each generation who would be qualified to reign. (Deuteronomy 17:15 announces God's plan for a monarchy while 2 Samuel 7:12, 16; 1 Chronicles 17:11; and Psalm 89:4 announce that the king will be a Davidic descendant.) A Davidic *kingdom* refers, in distinction, to the realm of reign which would include a chosen people as descendants of Abraham (2 Sam. 7:16; 1 Chron. 17:9; Ps. 89:15–17) and a chosen land (1 Chron. 17:9–10).

A Davidic *throne* refers to the "chair of state." Literally, it is a
seat, but in its use it is a symbol that refers to the power and authority of that reign, exercised while the king was ruling in that
kingdom. When Yahweh promises an "eternal" throne (2 Sam.
7:13, 16; 1 Chron. 17:12, 14; Ps. 89:4), Yahweh assures David that
at least his right to reign in Jerusalem would never be abandoned.
The power symbolized in David's throne was theocratic, political,
and righteous. However, the existence in Jerusalem of a continuing throne and kingdom was contingent upon the second feature
of the structure of the covenant related to the house.

The Promise of a Special Relationship with David's Son

In spite of the ancient Near Eastern setting, this language has
nothing to do with physical descent from God or with divine kingship. In the context of progressive revelation, this is the language
of adoption. Yahweh would adopt the king and share His life as a
father does with his son. It is the same language Yahweh used to
describe His adoption of the nation to be His son (Exod. 4:22–
23). In this history, the adoption of the king features him as *representative* "son" of the national "son." The relationship provided
two important privileges:

1. The son, if he were disobedient, would be disciplined like a
wayward child (2 Sam. 7:14–15). That discipline would not go
beyond parental correction. This pledge referred initially to
Solomon, as the rest of the sentence and the next verse make clear.
But it was coupled with the promise of an unending dynasty. "Verse
15 asserts that the grant of kingship will remain in effect regardless of the behavior of David's sons. . . . Such grants might be
patrimonial, in that they are sanctioned by adoption of the vassal
by the king, and—in special cases—inalienable, in that they were
not conditional upon the future behavior of the descendants of
the grantee."[15] Thus, discipline was promised in the context of
both assurance and hope of a father-son relationship that would
not end.

2. The son, adopted by the Father, was promised the privilege
of making request for an enlarged inheritance (Ps. 2:8). Although
Psalm 2 is not attributed to David in the Psalter, Acts 4:25 ascribes
the Psalm to David. Thus, the psalm envisions the context of
David's reign when such an astonishing and senseless rejection of

God's rule and ruler did occur. The language seems appropriate for David, who was repeatedly under attack (2 Sam. 8–10). In the context of such instances, God spoke by David to voice His response and to enlarge upon the pledge of adoption given to David's heir (2 Sam. 7:14). These words in Psalm 2:8 would have been originally spoken by David, a prophet, and then may have been read by the dynasty of kings in the coronation rite of each king. As the word *today* suggests, it marks the moment the new sovereign formerly took up the title combined with his inheritance and titles. Caird would call these words and the name "son," *mendicants*, meaning words thrown out at a not fully grasped object. The Old Testament is full of such words, and part of its inexhaustible usefulness to us lies in its "majestic mendicancy."[16] Kidner summarizes the same point: "Once again, in addressing the king as Son, the Old Testament has introduced a theme which, undeveloped, suits its immediate context but outgrows it utterly as its *implications* fully unfold."[17]

The Davidic covenant left a stamp of balanced expectation on each generation that followed. On the one hand, the Davidic covenant consisted of the inalienable rights for David's house, but on the other hand it consisted of the conditional warning of fatherly discipline open to any generation. While the warning threatened the survival of any individual king, it also assured the longevity of the dynasty because no wicked king could remove God's blessing nor would he remain unattended by God and, thus, risk gradual decay.

Different psalms reflected upon the expectations created by the covenant's terms and the king's responses to God. Psalm 132 celebrated the resolve of David in bringing the ark to Jerusalem to focus the attention of the nation on worshiping God. This resolve was matched only by Yahweh's promised resolve to stand by the Davidic dynasty. Kidner captures the heart of God drawing a response from the heart of David as "the warmth and wealth of these promises spring from love and require an answering love for their fulfillment."[18]

Similarly, Psalm 89 celebrates the promise of "forever" in the Davidic covenant (89:2, 4, 28, 36–37), which was based on the sure mercies of God (89:1–2, 14, 24, 28). This celebration issued into a prophetic addition in which "Yahweh's firstborn" would be elevated above *all* the Gentile's kings (89:26–27). The thrust of the psalm, however, concerned the time of judgment (89:38–39) when the promise of "forever" appeared to go into eclipse. Still, the "mercies of Yahweh" provided the confidence to pray to restore "the lovingkindnesses of David" (89:46–52) in Yahweh's truth. The hope of an eternal throne remained resting in the sure mercies of Yahweh in spite of judgment that came.

Thus, what did the Davidic covenant guarantee? Did it anticipate the discipline of foreign invasion to capture a disobedient king? The promises provided three assurances:

1. A descendant of David would be born in each generation who would meet the qualifications to be king. Although God could anoint the Davidic son to be king when the house was under discipline, He would not necessarily anoint him as king. Nevertheless, God's promise guaranteed an eternal house to David.
2. The descendants of Abraham would continue to exist, with the land promised subject to be occupied in the formation of the kingdom.
3. Yahweh continually possessed the right to delegate authority and power and promised readiness to enthrone the descendant of His choosing, on the occasion of the descendant's reception.

These promised assurances were all contingent upon God's discipline of any or all descendants. A captivity at the hand of Gentile nations could occur but not at the expense of invalidating any of the promises permanently.

One additional feature of the covenant was mentioned in 1 Chronicles 17:14: "I will establish him over My house . . . forever." Blaising uses this feature to relate the covenant to Psalm 110: "Since the Davidic king builds and maintains the house of God, it is not surprising that he is described in Scripture as a kind of priest."[19] But the proposal of this relationship between the Davidic covenant and Psalm 110 is unwarranted for two reasons:

1. The relationship between the Anointed One and the Aaronic priesthood had already been established when Eli and his sons had been judged (1 Sam. 2:30–35).

The Aaronic priesthood was to "walk before my anointed," which "means to function as a royal priest . . . to serve the king (as priest)."[20] That judgment on the priesthood anticipated this promise (1 Chron. 17:14) in the Davidic covenant.

2. Psalm 110 introduced Messiah into a new ministry, unrelated to any provision of the Davidic covenant.

Psalm 110 contains a new oracle (Ps. 110:1) and a fresh decree (Ps. 110:4). Unlike the decree in Psalm 2—which explored the "father-son relationship" more fully—and the revelation of Psalm 89—which seized on the clause "forever," which the turn of events seemed to flatly contradict—Psalm 110 introduces a new relationship and ministry.[21]

The new decree focused on a heavenly shared throne and the oracle on a Melchizedek priestly ministry from that throne rather than an earthly delegated throne in Jerusalem and an Aaronic priestly ministry. This distinction between a heavenly and an earthly throne had been recognized and maintained in both Psalm 2 and 89. In Psalm 2, "He who sits in the heaven" shall laugh at senseless rebellion on earth against Yahweh's anointed. Psalm 89 recognizes the Throne above the throne (Ps. 89:14). Thus, a strictly heavenly ministry is new and unexpressed in the Davidic covenant.

Finally, the heavenly ministry of Melchizedek is not based on descent from David as the king and is distinct from Abraham and his line of descendants. In fact, Melchizedek appeared in history without any relation to the descendants of promise (Gen. 5; 11:27–32) and is superior to the chosen Abraham in his relationship to God. Thus, Psalm 110 introduces a ministry to David concerning his descendant that is not based on the Davidic covenant promises. Rather, it anticipates a relationship and ministry of the One who is equal to God.

The Structure of the New Covenant

The name *a new covenant* first appears in Jeremiah, but the idea of a covenant subsequent to the Mosaic covenant is introduced by Isaiah. Most recent studies,[22] thus, begin with an exposition of Jeremiah 31:31–34, along with the broadly recognized parallel in Ezekiel 36:22–36, but in so doing overlook the essential perspective

Isaiah introduced. Thus, before examining Jeremiah, an examination of Isaiah and the servant-covenant is worthy of attention.

Isaiah and the Servant-Covenant

The book of Isaiah introduces the Mosaic covenant with a declaration that the nation is on trial based on the prophetic prosecutor's lawsuit presented in terms of violations of the covenant (Isa. 1:2ff.). The prosecutor pronounces that Israel is guilty of violation of the covenant with Yahweh (Isa. 24:5; 28:15, 18; 33:8). The nation, kings (Ahaz and Hezekiah), and people stand condemned and subject to impending judgment (Isa. 6–39).

Then the mood and tone of the prophecies dramatically change with the announcement of *deliverance*. The demands of such a deliverance are so great that only Yahweh can accomplish it (Isa. 40:3–10). In addition, the arm of Yahweh (i.e., the agent of Yahweh) was introduced, who would rule for Him (Isa. 40:10; 48:14). This prominent agent of Yahweh is introduced and briefly featured ("Behold, His reward is with Him and His work before Him") and then the prophet drops any further mention. The treatment raises questions in the reader's mind:

1. Who is Yahweh's arm?
2. What work shall He do?

The answer to these questions unexpectedly appears following the introduction of Israel as Yahweh's chosen servant taken from the ends of the earth (Isa. 41:8–10). Israel was assured of God's help. Then with similar abruptness, Yahweh's Servant is introduced, quiet and unobtrusive, who enjoys God's unqualified pleasure and accomplishes justice among the nations (Isa. 42:1–4). Isaiah speaks of His service for Yahweh. Thus, Isaiah introduces Yahweh's agent, the Servant, who is immediately identified with the nation but who is also the representative of the nation, who serves and accomplishes God's will for the nation. This representative Servant matches in prominence the arm of Yahweh in terms of realizing God's will without limit.

The work of this Servant is further developed as a new work of Yahweh (Isa. 42:6) is introduced. While the language is unusual, the basic thoughts can be unpackaged. The Servant is "given as a *covenant* of the people." Eichrodt interprets the statement to mean that "the Servant of God, (who) is defined as the mediator of the covenant to the nation."[23] Weinfeld speaks of covenant mediation as "the covenant is sponsored by a third party, i.e., through mediation. . . . Mediation of a covenant is especially characteristic of the covenant with God. . . ."[24] So the Servant of the Lord is the mediating party, serving Yahweh and representing the people. The people with whom Yahweh establishes a covenant are mentioned in distinction to the Gentiles (Isa. 42:6). Thus, Yahweh gives the Servant as a pledge, as the mediator of an agreement with Israel and based on His service, Yahweh assumes an obligation to the people. In other words, the Servant of Yahweh is given as the covenant basis of a fresh relationship with Israel. Prior to being given, Yahweh sustains the Servant as He serves ("I will take hold of your hand . . . keep you," Isa. 42:6; 49:8). That covenant with Israel also serves as a light to the Gentiles (Isa. 42:6; 49:6) who find their relationship with God brought to light through the Servant serving Israel. The Gentiles will see in Him justice (Isa. 42:4).

In the prophet's continued development, the servant-Israel is deaf, blind, and obstinate in disobedience (Isa. 42:18–25; 43:22–24), and yet Yahweh will redeem Israel (Isa. 43:1–21). In view of that, Yahweh "will not remember her sins" (Isa. 43:25–28) and "will pour My Spirit on your descendants" (Isa. 44:1–5). These themes, developed in the context of a "covenant" between Yahweh and His people, introduce themes that are developed by Jeremiah.

Jeremiah and the New Covenant

Jeremiah addressed "a new covenant established with the house of Israel and with the house of Judah" (Jer. 31:31–34). It is a covenant that is specifically distinct from the broken, Mosaic covenant (Jer. 31:32) and the one that will be established in the future (Jer. 31:33a). The text that follows spells out the terms of God's agreement and what He pledges (Jer. 31:33b–34). Ware[25] singles out four aspects of "newness" in the covenant agreement from which our summary is adapted:

1. *The new mode of implementation of relationship.* Yahweh's law will be internalized so that a response to the law will be

prompted from within rather than a response created by threat from without. The internalizing process will be done by Yahweh Himself as He "writes" His Torah upon their heart. Such a personal process correlates well with Ezekiel 36:27. No indication of a change in the content of the law is given in the language. The heart was always the focus of the law (Deut. 6:4; 8:2, 5, 14; 10:6), but now it becomes the focus of God's personal presence and work (Deut. 30:6). Wolff[26] features the "heart" as the focus of thinking, reasoning, reflecting, and considering—without a heart, one is without a clear sense of direction—and of the activity of the will where perception becomes choice, and hearing, obedience.

2. *The new scope of relationship.* All will know Yahweh, from the least to the greatest. "To know" often implies a personal relationship with Yahweh in Old Testament Scriptures (cf. Deut. 4:35, 39; Jer. 24:5–7; Ezek. 34:25–31).[27] As a result, the covenant community as a whole and individually will have a personal relationship with Yahweh. Thus, no longer will they exhort one another "to know Yahweh" as the Mosaic covenant demanded in the community. The decisive evidence of such a comprehensive scope is found in the next promise.

3. *The new basis of relationship.* Yahweh's forgiveness of sin is full and final. In such forgiveness, reconciliation with Yahweh is real.

4. *A new national relationship.* Yahweh first spoke of a national relationship at the Exodus (Exod. 6:7). The same promise is repeated here: "I will be your God and you will be My people." What is new are the mode, scope, and basis that now establish a national relationship, which also includes a personal relationship to every individual of the nation. What had been promised failed in the Mosaic agreements but now is again promised in the agreements based on the work of the Servant of Yahweh.

Fulfillment of the Promissory Covenants

There is an overwhelming influence among evangelical New Testament students as a result of the agreement of G. E. Ladd, F. F. Bruce, and I. Howard Marshall that fulfillment occurred in

Christ's first advent in an "already-not yet" pattern. Traditional dispensationalists do not agree that this is an adequate perception to sponsor nor is it a comprehensive exegesis of fulfillment.[28] Progressive dispensationalists have adopted this or a similar overview to explain New Testament fulfillment. Bruce Waltke, a former dispensationalist, assesses the state of study as "the overwhelmingly convincing evidence in the New Testament for the 'already' fulfillment of Israel's covenants and promises in Christ and his church. . . ."[29] Yet S. Lewis Johnson questions the consequences of such a theological conclusion because of the effect it has on subsequent interpretation of the Old Testament: "The problem of the authority of the New Testament apostle to 'reinterpret' the Old Testament needs careful consideration. I have strong misgivings about this, in spite of its sponsorship as a biblical truth."[30]

This active debate indicates the need to examine fulfillment carefully and will begin by considering definitions. On the one hand, the term "fulfill" has been defined in terms of quantity and space—full/empty. On the other hand, the term is used here to refer to statements. Thus, it is more appropriate to define "fulfill" in a linguistic context where it refers to "commissive statements" rather than to think metaphorically as space and quantity. A promise or a promissory covenant is a commissive statement in which the author commits himself to act in a specified way in the future. Fulfillment is then a satisfying of that commitment.

Commitments may be satisfied and thus fulfilled when one *keeps* what has been agreed upon to do. Some issues need further consideration to clarify what is involved in keeping a commitment. First, a commitment is fulfilled only when it is kept with the one addressed as recipient of the agreement. Second, commitments may take different forms of expression; in the Bible it is either a promise or a covenant. A promise involves a simple agreement or provision to act in the future. A covenant is a formal agreement, often involving a package of related provisions. Thus, a promise is fulfilled when the agreement is *kept*. A covenant is fulfilled only when *all* of the related provisions are *kept*.

An additional issue must consider the scope of the provisions. In the consideration of the historical progress of commitments, the question of the scope of those commitments is particularly relevant. The scope of a promise or a covenant may involve a series of actions, all of which are necessary to keep the commitment in an exhaustive sense. Then, the first action of the series would keep the commitment in an inaugural or initial sense.

These issues may be illustrated in the following manner. Suppose that I made a promise to a first-year student to pay for his college education. It all sounds simple enough. Would the first payment for the next semester's tuition keep the promise? Yes, in an inaugural sense but not in an exhaustive sense. In some future semester if I, for some reason, chose to make a similar payment for the student's wife, would I fulfill the commitment? It seems clear that the initial commitment was made to the student and *his* education, and thus must be *kept with him*. The fact that I paid for the student's wife is a blessing to her and unrelated to the promise I initially made to the student. Such an illustration is relevant when some claim that the covenant blessings given to the church constitute an inaugural or partial fulfillment of a covenant agreed upon with Israel. The confusion in the terms of agreement seems clear, and something else must be happening as the church is blessed.

The Fulfillment of the Abrahamic Covenant

The covenant was *instituted* with Abraham at a point of new revelation in his relationship with God (Gen. 15). The covenant, however, was never *inaugurated* in fulfillment either during his life or that of Isaac or Jacob. Yet it is important to recognize that individual promises that were provisions of the covenant were fulfilled, if only in an inaugural or partial fashion. A simple list of promises and the subsequent statements that represent some degree of fulfillment will demonstrate the point.

12:2b	blessed	13:2; 24:35
12:2c	make your name great	24:35
12:2d	you shall be a blessing	14:15–16; 18:22–33
12:3b	curse him who curses you	12:17; 20:3
13:16; 15:13	many descendants	21:1–7

These instances in Genesis illustrate that provisions of a covenant may be fulfilled in some sense after it has been instituted even though the covenant as a whole has not been inaugurated in fulfillment.

This same interpretive perspective is reflected in Exodus 6:3–5.

Cassuto captures that interpretation in the following restatement: "I revealed Myself (God declares) to Abraham, Isaac, and Jacob in My aspect that finds expression in the name Shaddai, and I made them fruitful and multiplied them and gave them children and children's children, but by the name YHWH, in My character as expressed by this designation, I was not known to them, that is, it was not given to them to recognize Me as One that fulfills His promises, because the assurance with regard to the possession of the Land, which I had given them, I had not yet fulfilled."[31] This perspective on fulfillment is then developed in the narrative of Moses and Joshua in their generation.

In particular, the narrative in Joshua introduces the inaugural or partial fulfillment of the covenant as given to Abraham. And in this narrative, what is meant by inaugural or partial fulfillment is clearly portrayed. At issue are summary statements which are both included in the text and which might appear to be mutually contradictory.

The first statement summarizes what happened to the promises or provisions of the covenant. *All* of these provisions were kept. Boling and Wright's translation captures this sense (Josh. 21:43–45):

> (43) Yahweh entrusted to Israel *all the land* which he had promised on oath to their ancestors to give. They took possession of it, and there they settled down. (44) Yahweh brought about a cessation of the hostilities toward them on every side, in strict conformity to the ancestral promise. And no one successfully withstood them—out of all their enemies! *All the enemies* Yahweh subjected to them. (45) Not a word of *all the Good Word* which Yahweh had spoken to the house of Israel proved untrue. *It all happened.*[32]

Inaugural fulfillment includes the keeping of all the provisions of the covenant; yet, it is inaugural or partial because of the limited scope. That limitation is indicated in a second summary statement (Josh. 13:1–7).

> When Joshua had reached a ripe old age, Yahweh said to Joshua: "Although you have reached a ripe old age, *much of the land remains to be taken. This is the land that remains. . . .*"

Thus, while all of the provisions had been *kept,* not all of the provisions had been *met* to the extent promised. Thus, the covenant
was partially fulfilled.

One final question remains: was the land given to Abraham's
descendants? At the outset the promised land was given, entrusted
to them, and there for the taking (Josh. 1:3, 6). For the transaction
of giving to be concluded, the gift must be received. Otherwise,
the gift is only offered or left out there on the table. To be given, it
had to be received. It is clear that Joshua's generation did not take
or receive all of the land. Boling and Wright thus translate the term
give (natan) used three times, nuanced in the context (Josh. 21:43–
45): *"entrusted . . . to give . . . subjected.* The verses display three uses
of the verb *ntn,* with three distinct nuances, thus underscoring the
free and gracious initiatives of Yahweh toward the house of Israel."[33]
Thus, all of the land had been *entrusted* to be taken but not all of it
was taken. What had been given to Abraham, he received (Gen.
22:13–14), and then "because Abraham obeyed . . ." (Gen. 22:16–
18), it was entrusted to Isaac (etc.) and to Joshua for occupation.
But no descendant or generation of descendants took all that had
been given to Abraham. Not even David took all in the sense of
occupying it all with Israelites in possession of the land. Thus, the
covenant remained unfulfilled, in a final and complete sense, while
Israel occupied only portions of the land. Their occupation of the
land continued until it was forfeited in God's judgment on their
evil (722 and 586 B.C.). The inaugurated covenant now went into
abeyance or into temporary inactivity[34] even though the provision
of numerous descendants of Abraham continued to be fulfilled in
spite of captivity. Thus, what had been given to Abraham had not
yet been given to his descendants.

In addition, God prophesied the length of the deportation to
be seventy years (Jer. 25:11). As a result, Daniel, near the end of
that prophesied time, prayed on the basis of it to the God "who
keeps His covenant and mercy with those who love Him and with
those who keep His commandments" (Dan. 9:2–19). Nehemiah
prayed similarly (Neh. 1:5–11). In these prayers, God is viewed as
open to keep and thus fulfill His covenant, but it is available only
to those who love Him and keep His commandments. These are
ones who, by their obedience, put themselves in a position to receive what God waited to give.

Israel's history unfolded to disclose in hindsight that there were none who fully loved nor any who completely kept His commandments until Jesus of Nazareth came to fulfill God's will (Luke 4:16–21). He came to be obedient to the will of the Father (Luke 22:41–42) and expressed that in the ultimate act of obedience in death on the cross (Luke 23:46). So it was that the Father raised Him from the dead (Acts 2:24) and having ascended to an exalted position, He received the Father's promise (Acts 2:33). Thus, Paul concludes: "Now to Abraham and his Seed were the promises made. He does not say 'And to seeds' as though there were many but as of one 'And to your Seed,' who is Christ" (Gal. 3:1 NKJV). This is the fulfillment of a provision of the seed to whom the blessing is given. Now the exhaustive fulfillment of the covenant awaits the Father's display of "mercy on all" (Rom. 11:32), the seed of Abraham, so that they would receive the Seed (Zech. 12:10), and what He would give.

The Fulfillment of the Davidic Covenant

The Davidic covenant was given unilaterally as Yahweh promised a Davidic house in response to David's offer to build Yahweh a house. The provisions of the covenant were unconditionally given even though one provision was a condition assuring God's discipline of each royal son who sinned. While a record of institution of the covenant does not appear in the text, later revelation recognized the *institution* (2 Sam. 23:5) and *inauguration* of the covenant (Ps. 89:3–4).

The *inaugural fulfillment* of the covenant rested upon revelation given in the Torah (Deut. 17:15–16). That revelation specified the two factors associated with the establishment of a monarchy. First, the people were given the freedom to choose a monarchy (Deut. 17:14). They then had the responsibility to establish a monarch by setting a king over them, but only a king of Yahweh's choosing (Deut. 17:15). Second, Yahweh would choose the one from among the Israelites who would be king (Deut. 17:15). In the history of the people in the land, God's choice was communicated by the prophet (1 Sam. 9:16–17; 10:20–24; 16:1–13; 1 Kings 1:10–49; 11:29–39; 2 Kings 9:1–13; contrast with Hos. 8:4). The prophet was thus the king-maker. Thus, the monarchy involved both Yahweh's choice of who would be king and the people's appointment or placing upon the throne of the anointed one. A brief history of the early monarchy will clarify how the choice and the appointment appear in the nation.

Saul was chosen by Yahweh through Samuel to be king (1 Sam. 9:15–16), after which the people hailed him as their king—"Long live the King" (1 Sam. 10:24). Since there were some who spurned him (1 Sam. 10:27), it was only after he was proven in defense of the men of Jabesh (1 Sam. 10:27b–11:12) that his kingship was renewed (1 Sam. 11:14) and all of the people "made" him king in Gilgal (1 Sam. 11:15).

In a similar fashion, David was chosen by Yahweh and anointed by Samuel to be king (1 Sam. 16:1–13). However, it wasn't until after Saul had died that "the men of Judah came and anointed David king over the house of Judah" (2 Sam. 2:4). From that time, David was king in Hebron (2 Sam. 2:11). Seven years and six months later, all the elders of Israel came to the king at Hebron. King David made a pact with them before Yahweh as he formally agreed to also represent Israel's interests, and they anointed David king over Israel. Thus, the people's appointment was an official, formal agreement sealed with an act of anointing by all the people.

The Davidic covenant was inaugurated when the first king was enthroned from the family of David. Although Absalom claimed the choice of the people (2 Sam. 15:10–12) and Adonijah claimed the choice of leadership (1 Kings 1:5–10), neither was chosen by Yahweh. Both lacked the support of a prophet of God. Yahweh's choice of Solomon (1 Kings 1:11–53) originated with Nathan the prophet (1 Kings 1:11). The people's appointment was originally stated by David to Bathsheba that her son would rule (1 Kings 1:28–30). Solomon was joined by leadership who represented the people—Zadok the priest, Nathan the prophet, and Benaiah the military commander. Based on the Davidic covenant, the people sought to make one of David's sons king (1 Kings 12:1). It wasn't until after the heavy hand of Rehoboam rebuffed the people that Israel abandoned the Davidic heir (1 Kings 12:16). This appointment of the people followed Yahweh's discipline of Solomon as the prophet Ahijah revealed Yahweh's choice to divide the kingdom and to choose Jeroboam (1 Kings 11:29–31). This discipline did not represent an abandonment of the Davidic covenant (1 Kings 11:32–36). So Rehoboam reigned over some of the children of Israel "who dwelt in the cities of Judah" (1 Kings 12:17).

As the Abrahamic covenant went into abeyance when the nation left the land and went into captivity, so also went the Davidic covenant. There was a lapse in the inaugurated Davidic covenant as the succession of enthroned kings in Jerusalem ceased. Yet, as in the Abrahamic covenant, provisions in the covenant continued to be kept. This continuance is reflected when Babylon releases Jehoichin from prison and acknowledges his right to royalty (2 Kings 25:27–30). So in each generation one would exist with the right to royalty even though Yahweh, in discipline, failed to support that right. God disregarded each heir's claim to the throne until the birth of Jesus. His rightful claim to the throne of His father David was carefully noted by Matthew (1:1–17), as the legal heirs are listed from captivity to Joseph. Further, all four Gospels record Yahweh's anointing of Jesus with the Holy Spirit and adoption of Him as Son (Matt. 3:13–17; Mark 1:9–11; Luke 3:21–22; John 1:32). Thus, the provision of an eternal house had been kept during the times of the Gentiles, but the provision of a throne and kingdom awaited the people's response to God's choice.

That response came to a focus at the triumphal entry and the resulting crucifixion. The multitudes who went along (Matt. 21:9–11), whom Luke specified as the multitude of disciples (Luke 19:37), pronounced praise to God for the coming of the Son of David. Yet before Pilate, the chief priests and the elders persuaded the multitudes to call for Him to be crucified (Matt. 27:20–23; Luke 23:13–24). From early in His ministry, many Pharisees had resisted His claim to be king (Luke 5:21ff.), and at His staged entry into Jerusalem even more resisted (Luke 19:36). The chief priests, the scribes, and the elders assembled as the Sanhedrin at Caiaphas's house and plotted to kill Jesus (Matt. 26:1–5). Caiaphas ironically reasoned that "it was expedient that one man should die for the people and not that the whole nation should perish" (John 11:49–50). Their decision to reject His claim to the Davidic throne (Zech. 9:9) was unanimous in the people's cry to crucify Him. The chief priests in particular rejected Him as King of the Jews (John 19:21), concluding that they would not have Him rule over them. This evidence of the people's decision is clear and established without any doubt.

A dispensational stress on the people's response has led some

to draw a faulty inference. That inference posits that dispensationalism held out the possibility in the people's choice (John 6:15)
that the political kingdom of Messiah might have been established
before the Cross. Thus, the dispensationalist's model misrepresents God's decreed will, which posited the Cross before the kingdom. This inference is faulty for two reasons.

First, even though the people must enthrone the king of God's
choice, yet during the "times of the Gentiles" Rome remained in
position to make the final decision. Thus, as Jesus approached
Jerusalem and wept (Matt. 23:37–37; Luke 13:34–35; 19:41–44), He
acknowledged this contingency from a human point of view. Had
Jerusalem recognized the time of her visitation and received God's
Messiah, Jesus would have protected Jerusalem as a mother hen
gathers and protects her chicks from the inevitable invasion by Rome
(Luke 19:43–44). As a mother hen, He would have died at the hand
of Rome for Jerusalem. The call for Israel's decision was real.

Second, even though Jesus' first advent involved a *real* presentation of the kingdom, yet it would not be a *realized* fulfillment
during the first advent (Acts 2:23–24; 3:13–15). The first advent
called for a *real* decision and provided the *real* Anointed One from
God. Had not the multitudes recognized this reality in the triumphal entry, the very stones as witnesses would have cried out about
the truth (Luke 19:39–40).

Yet at the same time, the ultimate determination of a generation's decision had been decreed and revealed by God (Isa.
52:13–53:12). That decision, according to the Mosaic covenant
responsibility, rested in the position of the nation and in the hands
of evil men in Rome. Thus, it would never have been a realized
Davidic kingdom, let alone an *already* or *inaugurated* fulfillment
of the Davidic covenant without the Cross first.

While the first advent of Jesus Christ does not represent a partial fulfillment of the Davidic covenant, it does represent a fulfillment "in part" concerning the provision of the Son of David. After
Jesus' death, God recognized His right to life (Acts 2:24) when
He raised Him from among the dead (Acts 2:31–32). Further, God
exalted Him in glory to His own right hand (Acts 2:33), where He
was seated in ascent to God's throne (Acts 2:34–35 quoting Ps.
110:1). There are at least three consequences of the fulfillment of
this provision of sonship that the New Testament examines.

A fulfillment of the promised relationship of the Son of David (Ps. 2:7)

The Davidic covenant had promised an adopted relationship between the Father and each Davidic son. Such an adopted relationship involved a share in God's life, initially in God's correcting presence in the reign of the son and that presence in mercy. Preeminently, adoption involved a share by anointing and enthroning to rule in God's stead. The language of Psalm 2 about God's anointed set on the throne in Jerusalem speaks of sonship that is pressed in the New Testament to speak of an unlimited share in life.

During Jesus' life, this share in God's life as a Son was proclaimed at His baptism. The unqualified pronouncement of the Father's pleasure indicated that Jesus had shared the Father's life without limit during His growing up years. All that remained was sharing it through all of life's experiences.

At His transfiguration, those experiences had been enlarged to include the temptations from Satan, the confrontations with the Jewish leaders resulting in their rejection, and even the slowness of the disciples to believe. In all this, God pronounced Him to be His Son whose words would represent Him in unqualified truth.

In resurrection, Jesus' share in life as a Son was completed (Acts 13:33). The ultimate surrender of human life came in death, when Jesus voluntarily gave His life to the Father (John 19:30). Now, only life from the Father could resurrect the life that was Jesus, and in resurrection He was thus designated to be the Son of God (Rom. 1:4). Now in resurrection it was evident for all to see that the life He had was life from God alone.

A fulfillment of the promised position of the Son of David (Ps. 89:26–27)

Psalm 89 explores the promise that the Davidic covenant would last "forever." Such longevity could survive only if the Davidic descendant shared the life and position of God. Israel had enjoyed an exalted position corporately, addressing God as *My Father* (Jer. 3:19), and they had been called His *firstborn* (Exod. 4:22) and *the highest* (Deut. 28:1). The psalmist borrowed these exalted terms to refer to the position of the Son of David as firstborn. Now in the resurrection and ascension of Christ, they aptly refer to His present position as firstborn over all creation (Col. 1:15). This position of preeminence is a fulfillment in part of the promise of Sonship forever and an anticipation of the promise of an eternal throne and kingdom.

An introduction based upon the prototype ministry of Melchizedek of a new ministry for the Son of David (Ps. 110:1)

The present ministry of Jesus as Lord is not the result of the Davidic order as reflected in Psalms 2 and 89. While Jesus had been chosen by Yahweh to be anointed, He had not been made king by Israel (Deut. 17:15–17). Rather, He had been made Lord by Yahweh Himself and Yahweh alone in His ascension and enthronement (Acts 2:34–36). And this is the position and authority of the order of Melchizedek (Ps. 110:1). The author of the book of Hebrews argues that the order of Melchizedek is based on criteria other than that which we have seen in the order of David.

- It is an order based on a superiority in position to Abraham rather than descent from Abraham (Heb. 7:4–5).
- It is an order based on an authoritative appearance in history rather than on a claim to authority based on descent from a line with promised blessings (Heb. 7:3, 6).
- It is an order based on righteousness and peace found in the realm over which his name pronounces his rule rather than on the discipline of sin in David's line (Heb. 7:2).
- It is an order based on unending life rather than a succession of lives in office (Heb. 7:3).

Thus, the rule and ministry of Jesus in the order of Melchizedek is accessed by believers in Him and His word. It is that rule which Jesus introduced in the parables of the mystery of the kingdom in which the word of the king produces life and fruitfulness in those who hear, believe, and obey.

Fulfillment of the New Covenant

To appropriately consider the new covenant, we must begin with the consideration of the Servant of the Lord as Isaiah did. The Gospels all tell the story of Jesus' anointing for the will and ministry of God the Father at His baptism (Matt. 3:13–17; Mark 1:9–11; Luke 3:21–22; John 1:32). It is clear that He arrived in Jerusalem as the Anointed Son of David (Matt. 21:1–11). The emphasis of the Gospel accounts, however, presents Him as the Servant anointed to serve the nation in its sinful condition (Luke 4:16–30). This narrative in Luke 4:16–30 "is at first sight remarkable for his first major example of Christ's public ministry . . . (yet it) makes a fitting introduction to Christ's public ministry. To identify himself and his mission Christ cited Isaiah 61:1–2a and 58:6, and it recalls the way Luke identified John and his mission at 3:4–6 by a similar quotation from Isaiah."[35] Matthew, also known for his focus on Jesus the King, presented Him in ministry as the suffering Servant (Matt. 8:17; Isa. 53:4) and as the Servant in spirit (Matt. 12:15–21; Isa. 42:1–2). Although Jesus was anointed to rule, He was "given" to the nation at His first advent as the Servant of the Lord, anointed to serve.

The popular expectation, however, was that He would be king. While this expectation was correct, the expectation obscured the order that suffering service must precede glory in rule. When the gathered crowd attempted by force to make Him king (John 6:15), He withdrew to be alone. When the crowds later found Him, He pressed them to receive the sacrifice that He would make of Himself (John 6:41–59). As a result, "many disciples went back and walked with Him no more" (John 6:66). When He challenged the Twelve (John 6:67), they responded that they had accepted His words as the source of eternal life (John 6:68–69). This does not suggest that they had put together their expectation with His teaching that He must suffer. It simply means that His words were more important than their present expectations. The Gospel narrative presents the One Anointed to serve whose words promise life.

While the remnant that received Him did not represent the nation so as to "make" Him king (Matt. 23:37–39), still that remnant did represent Israelites to whom the Servant had been given as a covenant (Isa. 42:6). And so, as He met to celebrate the Jewish Passover with His disciples (Matt. 26:17–25), He introduced a memorial meal. In particular, the cup introduced His blood to be what would institute the new covenant (Matt. 26:26–29 and Luke 22:19–20). Unlike the Abrahamic and Davidic covenants, the new covenant was not instituted in the Old Testament. In fact, Jesus was given as the covenant that was about to be instituted. The language of Isaiah 42:6 and 49:8 using *nathan* ("give as a covenant") means to institute or establish a covenant rather than to inaugurate fulfillment of a covenant.[36]

The distinction between institution and inauguration in fulfillment must be clarified further. To institute a promissory covenant is to introduce provisions of the agreement which are now available to be received. To inaugurate fulfillment is to keep all of the provisions of the agreement. The new covenant was instituted only after the death of Christ, the Mediator of the covenant, and then He and the provisions of the covenant were offered to the nation following His resurrection and ascension. Some of the provisions were then made available as given to the remnant gathered in Jerusalem for Pentecost. The new covenant will be inaugurated in fulfillment when Israel as a nation will accomplish her national destiny (Rom. 11:26–27).

In this way, some of the provisions (Acts 2:38) were offered as the promise of Christ is given "to you and to your children, and to all who are afar off" (Acts 2:39). These provisions—"the forgiveness of sins" and "the gift of the Holy Spirit"—are given to "as many as the Lord our God will call." This national offer was rejected by the national leaders (Acts 4:1–4, 13–22) and thus inauguration of fulfillment was postponed, but the same provisions were made available to the Gentiles as well (Acts 10:42–44).

Those provisions now became the basis for the ministry as described by Paul and the author of the book of Hebrews. For Paul, the ministry of the apostles (namely, setting the direction for the church) is the ministry/provision of the new covenant. In this context the ministry would entail the forgiveness of sins and the gift of the Holy Spirit (2 Cor. 3:4–4:18). Central to the church's worship is the Lord's Supper, where the cup is the occasion to remember the institution of the new covenant (1 Cor. 11:25). The perspective of Paul's gospel is to receive Christ in whom are offered these provisions of the new covenant. As we saw with the Abrahamic covenant, the provisions of the covenant were available to be received by faith by the patriarchs before the inauguration of fulfillment of all the covenant provisions that awaited the generation of Moses and Joshua. Provisions of these two covenants are combined by Paul as he develops the ministry to the Gentiles.

So in Galatians, the provision of the Holy Spirit was received by these Gentiles (Gal. 3:2–3) and that reception came in the provision promised to Abraham that "in you all nations shall be blessed" (Gal. 3:8 quoting Gen. 12:3; 18:18; 22:18; 26:4; 28:14).

The author of the book of Hebrews reasoned on the basis of Christ's resurrection and ascension (Heb. 8:1). Based on His position, He is the "Mediator of a better covenant, which was established on better promises" (Heb. 8:6). From His position, some of the provisions of the better covenant are now available (Heb. 8:1–10:25). Further from His position, all of the provisions are now ready to be inaugurated with the nation of Israel in the future.

This representation of some of the provisions of the Abrahamic and new covenants now available to Gentiles corresponds to the imagery of the natural olive tree (Rom. 11). As some of the natural branches are broken off, the original olive tree does not realize the outcome for which it was planted. As wild olive branches are grafted in (Rom. 11:17–25), they enjoy some of the provisions of being an olive tree without becoming natural olive branches or fulfilling the role of the tree. Rather, as Paul leaves the metaphor for a moment, he talks about a time when the fullness of Gentile opportunity will have come to an end (Rom. 11:19–25). After that the wild branches will be removed and natural branches again will be grafted in the tree, and then "all Israel will be saved" (Rom. 11:26–27). Then both the Abrahamic and new covenants will be inaugurated in their fulfillment and the natural olive tree (the nation of Israel) will realize its designed end. However, those who argue for an inaugural fulfillment of the new covenant at Jesus' first advent have challenged these above mentioned traditional conclusions and thereby need to be addressed.

1. *John the Baptist promised One mightier than he, who would baptize with the Holy Spirit and with fire (Luke 3:16–17).* Progressive dispensationalists argue that Jesus fulfilled John the Baptist's statement and inaugurated the fulfillment of the new covenant when the baptism of the Spirit occurred in Acts 2. In fact, Blaising[37] proposes that this is an aspect of Messiah's ministry in the history of redemption. As such, the ministry of Spirit baptism is no longer distinctive to the church age but is normative in the fulfillment of the ministry of the new covenant. Blaising's proposal will be

addressed by first advancing the claim for a distinctive ministry of Spirit baptism and then second by challenging the claim that the pouring out of the Spirit and the baptism of the Spirit are identical.[38]

The claim that baptism of the Holy Spirit is a distinctive term and ministry in the church rests first on its appearance in Acts. Spirit baptism in Acts is related to the birth and formation of the church. The ministry of the Spirit that was about to happen is defined by a promise from the Father but spoken by Christ (Acts 1:4–5). That promise was first spoken by John the Baptist (Luke 3:16–17). This distinguishing relationship will be considered. First, Jesus adds that this ministry of Spirit baptism was about to happen (Acts 1:5). As the church is born in Acts 2, neither Luke nor Peter described the work of the Spirit as baptism. Terms such as *filling, prophecy,* and *speaking in other languages* describe the ministry of the Spirit. Thus, the ministry of baptism is implied in context but it is not necessary to mention. The term *baptism,* however, does appear when the Spirit's ministry unexpectedly incorporates Cornelius into the body of believers (Acts 11:16), which was described as "the Holy Spirit fell upon all those who heard the word" (Acts 10:44). Thus, *baptism* is used to define what had happened in the formation of the church, but other terms are also used to describe aspects of the total experience of the Spirit.

Thus, when that defining term *baptism* appears in the writings of Paul and Peter, the traditional expectation is that the theological components of the Spirit's ministry would be developed. This is the second argument to advance the term as referring to a distinctive aspect of the Spirit's ministry. That ministry of the Spirit thus describes the formation of a body of believers with diverse members unified by the common Spirit (1 Cor. 12:12–13). In addition, it describes those members as identified in Christ's experience of death and resurrection, which introduces the potential of a believer's new life in Christ (Rom. 6:1–3; Col. 2:12; 2 Peter 3:21).

The third reason to interpret *baptism* as referring to a distinctive ministry of the Spirit is the field of terms used to describe the Spirit's ministries. This field of terms—"filled, indwelt, drink, seal, baptize, gift, guide, assure, and pray"[39]—does not appear in contexts presenting them as synonyms but rather appears as distinct in emphasis even though they are related works of the Spirit. Thus, based on New Testament usage, which is the *only* biblical usage, we have good reason to conclude that baptism is not a comprehensive term but rather descriptive of what God does in giving birth to and forming the church.

This claim for distinct usage must also refute the claim that Spirit baptism is synonymous with the Spirit's new covenant ministry. The first and strongest argument rests in John the Baptist's introduction to Israel of her Messiah as distinguished by the ministry of baptism with the Holy Spirit and fire. Blaising[40] challenges dispensationalists to define Spirit baptism in the context of Old Testament promises even as they are prone to define baptism with fire in the context of the Old Testament. He makes two points: the term *baptism* does not occur in the Old Testament for either fire or Spirit and yet the image of "fire" is used in the Old Testament (Isa. 61:2; Mal. 3:1–6; 4:1) to interpret John's words. Should that not also apply to the Spirit?

When the three Old Testament passages that promise the Spirit are examined (Isa. 44:3; Joel 2:28–32 [to be examined in detail later]; Ezek. 36:25–27) no basis is found to explain John the Baptist's image. The presence of two themes of water and spirit poured out by God suggest a link between the passages but certainly do not establish any connection. Ezekiel 36:25–27 speaks of the Spirit indwelling but with a different ministry than described in Spirit baptism. While Isaiah's promise of the pouring out of God's Spirit (Isa. 44:3) is related to the ministry of the Servant, it is insufficient by itself to be the basis of what John the Baptist announced.

Therefore, the substance of this ministry of Messiah has its origin in the wording of John the Baptist, who spoke in particular as a prophet. The problem that dispensationalists then face is that John was a prophet to Israel (Isa. 40:3–5), and the direct object of the reference "you" ("Messiah will baptize you," Luke 3:16) is clearly the Israelites. This raises a problem for those who distinguish between Israel and the church, since this promise of the Father addressed to Israel is fulfilled in the forming of the church (Acts). Does this not provide a basis for taking Israel's promises as fulfilled in the church? From the viewpoint of the historical participants, no awareness exists at this time of God's introduction of the church, yet from God's point of view the church did exist. This was a First Advent prophecy to Israel. While the Old Testament had clarified the distinction between Messiah's sufferings and Messiah's glories that would follow (1 Peter 1:11), it did not clarify how they were related. Peter, as a historical participant, came to understand that the First Advent had to be followed by Messiah's heavenly session (Acts 3:21). The length of the heavenly session remained unknown, but the fact of the session separated the suffering from the glory. As a First Advent promise, this promise to Israel is not a national promise but is historically related to Messiah's first advent and thus simply related to Messiah and His session in heaven, separated from believers on earth.

John the Baptist thus fashions his description of Messiah's ministry as similar to his own ministry, yet clearly John's ministry was inferior in element. What is the point in the similarity? Dockery[41] suggests that water baptism *identified* a repentant remnant with John and a shared consciousness of Messiah's coming. Thus, Spirit baptism would *identify* those responsive to Messiah in a spiritually effective fashion to Him and the benefits of His suffering. It would form His body on earth.

The final argument against the identification of Spirit baptism with Israel's new covenant is based upon a failure to appreciate a subtle distinction that the Lord makes in the beginning of Acts. After having introduced His baptism with the Holy Spirit, the disciples asked if this meant that the kingdom was being restored to Israel (Acts 1:5-6). While the disciples were not to know when the kingdom would be restored to Israel, they were to relate the coming of the Spirit with power given to them in their impending witness (Acts 1:7-8). Thus, a supposed connection between Spirit baptism and the new covenant ministry in a restored kingdom to Israel was not supported in these words of the Lord.

Although the arguments are strong supporting the thesis that Spirit baptism is distinctive to the formation of the church, they may not be conclusive. There are reasons that lend support to the idea that the effects of Spirit baptism are normative for any believer in Christ's finished work. Certain conclusions, however, need to be mentioned. First, Spirit baptism is not comprehensive of all the provisions of the new covenant. Rather, it is only a component of one provision of the covenant—"the pouring out of the Spirit." Second, the unity of diverse members in the group of the church is in need of an overarching Spirit of unification more than a nation which has both governmental and ethnic unity. Thus, one of the effects of Spirit baptism is uniquely necessary to the new entity, the church. Third, the Spirit's identification of the believer with the experiences of Christ on the cross and in resurrection is uniquely appropriate to a group known as the body of Christ. While it would be a helpful blessing to members of a nation, it is essential to members of His body (Acts 9:4).

2. *Peter's explanation of the phenomenon of Pentecost based on Joel 2:28–32.* Progressive dispensationalists argue that Joel 2:28–32 introduces the fulfillment of the new covenant. It is not without significance that Peter found a context to explain what had just happened at Pentecost in the promises to Israel found in Joel. While a reference to Jesus' words or John's words would have been true (this is what John spoke about), they would not have had the recognized authority nor the breadth of discussion found in Joel. Peter does not insist on a total discontinuity between the church and Old Testament saints. Rather, this promise of the Spirit not only explains the prophetic utterances being made, but it also anticipates what was impending in God's dealing with Israel in judgment.

The point of connection between the phenomena of Pentecost and the prophetic passage is found in Peter's phrase "this is that" (Acts 2:16). While this is not a direct announcement of fulfillment *(plāroō)*, it is a Qumran pesher mode of interpretation used to refer to contemporary fulfillment. The extent of that fulfillment depends upon the referent, "this," and the textual corresponding explanation, "that." Clearly, the antecedent of "this" is "we hear them speaking in our own tongues the wonderful works of God" (Acts 2:11). In the text, the "that" is the portion that corresponds to "I will pour out of My Spirit . . . shall prophesy . . ." (Acts 2:17). What corresponded was what they heard and what Joel announced that they would say. Joel's explanation traced this to the outpouring of the Holy Spirit "in the last days." As Zane Hodges concludes, "Peter meant to say that the outpouring of the Spirit fulfilled Joel's prophecy . . . (yet) it appears that Joel's prophecy about signs and wonders is not fulfilled here (or anywhere else in Acts either). For that matter, this prophecy has never yet been fulfilled."[42] So again we have a fulfillment of a provision of the covenant that does not represent an inaugural fulfillment of Israel's covenant. Rather, as Peter seems to say in Acts 3, national covenant blessing is contingent upon the repentance of the nation's leaders.[43] While the church was not self-consciously separate from Israel yet, added revelation would unfold the distinctive work of God in the church as Gentiles become equal partners of Christ in the body (Acts 10–11; Eph. 3:1–7).

Since this does not represent an inaugural fulfillment, it is erroneous to conclude, as Bock does, that "the allusion to Joel fulfills the new covenant."[44] The error of this conclusion is found in two reasons. First, the new covenant provisions, as found in Jeremiah 31:31–34 or Hebrews 8:7–12, do not even mention the Holy Spirit. Thus, taking the ministry of the Holy Spirit to define—or at least to represent—the covenant as a part used in place of the whole does not find support in this central passage, which often is used to spell out the covenant. Second, there is an error in logic. The logical fallacy that progressive dispensationalism makes is that *"linking* is not equivalent to *identification."*[45] The New Testament acknowledges that the Spirit is one provision of the new covenant that is being fulfilled, but one provision does equal all the provisions. Rather, "Joel's revelation . . . predicts a prophetic endowment brought to pass by the outpoured Spirit of God. According to Peter, this prophetic endowment was fulfilled at Pentecost."[46] The conclusion of covenant fulfillment that Bock reaches is not the result of textual reasoning but rather of theological reasoning. This line of reasoning must now be examined.

3. *The interpretation of an inaugural fulfillment of the covenant based on theological reasoning.* Ware, a progressive dispensationalist, states directly the problem that dispensationalists have been struggling with: "How can the church—a multiethnic and multinational spiritual organism, not given any such promise of national identity or land possession—participate in this same new covenant given to Israel?"[47] That is the question with which we struggle as we attempt to interpret Old Testament texts based on their own contexts (i.e., consistent literal interpretation). The answer that Ware proposed recognizes the influence that in fact governs some of the meanings interpreted. "The answer here requires an application of the other theological consideration mentioned above,

namely, the "already-not yet" eschatological framework."[48] In other words, the meaning of a text is *expanded* to include the church along with Israel based upon a theological framework. This leads to an alteration in the meaning of new covenant texts. The fulfillment of new covenant texts is described as *inaugural* fulfillment of the covenant. That leads, based on the theological framework, to select only "the spiritual aspects of new covenant promise" as fulfilled and this is "necessitated by the fact of ongoing sin and disobedience in the lives of new covenant participants."[49] This represents an altering of a text's meaning based on theological selections. Those selections force some to ask whether the agreements with the covenant do in fact represent fulfillment. Thus, the approach of progressive dispensationalism in regard to the new covenant must be rejected for textual and hermeneutical reasons.

Conclusion

Dispensationalism has been known for its emphasis on discontinuity, but as this examination of the promissory covenants has shown, this discontinuity is not absolute. Continuity exists in the fulfillment of some of the provisions of the covenants made with Israel. At the same time, it is important to recognize that this view of continuity is not that proposed in an inaugural or partial fulfillment of Israel's covenants. The fulfillment of individual provisions is based on a consistent literal treatment of the text rather than fulfillment of covenants, which is based on an "already-not yet" theology developed in the New Testament.

An examination of individual texts finds continuity in the unilateral and unconditional agreement that Yahweh assumed in each of the promissory covenants. When the agreement involves Yahweh's "I WILL . . . ," He assumes ultimate responsibility in word to accomplish what had been promised to Israel. Even in a unilateral and unconditional covenant, it still remains an agreement which shares responsibility to participate in fulfillment with Israel. This responsibility may be only to receive what was promised and to believe that God would keep the provisions that He promised. But when we propose unconditional promises and shared responsibility together, these seem to constitute a contradiction. This apparent contradiction finds resolution when the relationship between continuity and discontinuity is examined.

In the Abrahamic covenant, the final responsibility is stated *in word* in the promises of the provisions. The central provision of the covenant is that a land would be given to Abraham's descendant(s), which implies both the birth of descendants and one or a generation of descendants that would be willing to receive what was promised and would be able to mediate blessing which was promised for all nations. While God's promises assured without condition that there would be one or more such descendants, the question of how this would occur remained unspecified.

In the Davidic covenant, Yahweh once again assumes the final responsibility in a unilateral and unconditional agreement *in word*. The agreement again shared responsibility with such a son or line of sons who would be involved in fulfillment of God's reign over the kingdom of Israel and that forever. In other words, the provisions of the covenant implied that a son or a line of sons would appear who would be willing and able to reign in God's stead forever.

In the new covenant, Yahweh not only assumes final responsibility *in word* in specifying the promised provisions of the covenant with Israel, but He also assumes the responsibility that was shared with Israel as God's servant. Thus, the responsibility was assumed *in the Person* of the Servant. In the accomplishment of that Servant, an agreement would be instituted through which Israel-servant would accomplish its share of responsibility.

The Abrahamic, Davidic, and new covenants all converge in the implied promise of a descendant, in the promise of a son who would be begotten of God, in the promise of the Servant, Yahweh's arm, who would serve and in that service would become the basis of the agreement through which Israel would serve. This One, who would be willing to receive and able to fulfill all that God promised, is God Himself, who takes Israel's share as a descendant of Abraham. The agreement then, is the covenant that Israelites must be willing to receive and Gentiles are invited to see; by what they see, Gentiles are enlightened to see God for themselves (Isa. 42:6).

The discontinuity is disclosed in the individual texts describing the First Advent in which the covenant partner, Israel as a nation, rejected the Son of Abraham and the Son of David, who was the Servant. The covenants are unconditional because God would assume Israel's share, but God does not *replace* Israel in accomplishing her share when Israel rejects Him. That would be Waltke's position representing amillennialism. Nor does God *re-interpret* Israel's share when Israel rejects Him. That would be Ladd's position representing historic premillennialism. Nor does God *expand* those who share in fulfillment of Israel's role tempo-rarily when Israel rejects Him. That would be Blaising's and Bock's position representing progressive dispensationalism. Rather, God *sets aside* the nation temporarily and incorporates believing Gen-tiles along with a believing Jewish remnant to continue the minis-try of the Servant until He returns as the Son of David and the Son of Abraham for judgment and rule. That ministry is based on provisions of the new covenant received by faith in the provi-sion of Christ, the Son of David and the Son of Abraham. This setting aside of the nation-servant creates the discontinuity in the fulfillment of covenant agreements with Israel.

Therefore, all covenant agreements with Israel will be inaugu-rated in fulfillment when Israel receives the One whom they cru-cified—the Son of David, the Son of Abraham—when He returns (Zech. 12:10).

RESPONSE

Elements of Agreement

It is a pleasure to respond to Elliott Johnson's good and seri-ous effort to have a textual discussion about the differences be-tween progressive and traditional dispensationalists. The essay is a reasoned case that explains itself through clear definitions and engagement with the more difficult texts for a traditional view. The noting of the role of the Servant in the plan is a helpful dis-cussion that parallels points I make in my own presentation. Say-ing all of this does not mean that I find the presentation persuasive. Nonetheless, Johnson's presentation is a model of how to go about the discussion. The essay reflects why I enjoy interacting with my "traditional" colleague so much.

It might also be helpful to summarize where we have agreement. (1) We agree on the need to pursue textual stability in interpretation. (2) We both affirm a future for Israel in a land that is hers—a future existence of peace in the land that represents God's completion of fulfillment of His covenant promises for the nation of Israel. (3) We both affirm a national rejection of Jesus at His first coming that resulted in a setting aside of the nation's role in God's program for the present era, an era known as "the time of the Gentiles." (4) I also believe that we agree that current provisions from all three covenants have met with a form of realization now (namely, Abrahamic: Gentile blessing through Abraham's seed; Davidic: the provision of an everlasting ruler for David's house; New: forgiveness of sins and bestowal of the Spirit). Thus, in the midst of the disagreements about to be noted, it is important to affirm these points of extensive agreement.

Elements of Disagreement

Our disagreement about the text centers on a debate over what the biblical text does (especially in NT units that have roots in OT terminology) and how to correlate these data. There are two specific issues. (1) What is the nature of covenant fulfillment in the events tied to Jesus' first coming and the emergence of the church? Is it the recognition of the presence of individual covenant provisions today without covenant inauguration (Johnson)? Or is it that covenants are in a process of inauguration and realization, some "already," others "not yet" (Bock)? (2) A key question surrounding this discussion is hermeneutical and definitional. Does the signaling of fulfillment require the presence of all the provisions of a covenant (Johnson)? Or is the presence of and appeal to covenantal language about some of those provisions adequate to signal initial fulfillment (Bock)? To treat these issues, I will proceed in two steps. First, I will discuss definitions and hermeneutics, then I will consider textual issues, especially the nature of the each covenant's fulfillment. Obviously, I cannot respond in detail to all the textual points I might wish to treat. So I shall try to major on the majors.

1. Definitions and Hermeneutics. Johnson's opening definitional section is important to his task. It is important to appreciate that the definitions he gives as his principles have emerged

from his textual discussion that follows. He attempts to be textually inductive. If I were to accept the accuracy of these definitions as defining what Scripture does, then his conclusions might well follow. My fundamental contention, however, is that the technical distinctions he argues do not match what the text is doing nor do they fit the Bible's terminology about covenant realization. As Shakespeare once said on another topic, he "doth protest too much" to set up and maintain these distinctions.

The progressive argument is that the New Testament treats a wide scope of provisions as realized in the current era, while also noting the fundamental shifts in the administrative structure and operation of God's promise in this era. These provisions and shifts are proclaimed in terms that point to the realization and advance of the promises of God. They show that a covenantal stage has been reached as a result of Jesus' coming that is directly connected to the promises of old. In sum, some of what was promised in the covenants has come and has been instituted. The sheer scope of this covenantal language points to initial realization.

I also want to question how Johnson has characterized my hermeneutical approach as one that is like Waltke and Ladd in giving priority to the New Testament. This is not my understanding of what progressives are doing (and author's intent counts for a lot for both of us). Thus, I question the accuracy of his claim that lumps what progressives are doing with what Waltke and Ladd are doing. In my view, the New Testament does not have a priority. Rather, it has a place, a completing (complementary) one, in contributing evidence as a constituent piece of the canon that addresses God's covenant promise and advances our understanding of it as a result.

I also reject the way Johnson defined my view hermeneutically, when he says that I propose "an expansion of the boundaries of the message of Old Testament passages also based on a complementary reading in New Testament usage. This expanded meaning is conditioned on Christ's present work of grace but will be restored to an Old Testament reading in the future millennial kingdom." Rather, what I propose and what my essay tries to show is "an expansion *within* the boundaries of the *covenant backdrop and* message of Old Testament passages also based on a complementary reading in New Testament usage. This expanded meaning is conditioned on Christ's present work *but also affirms the* Old

Testament reading in the future millennial kingdom." These differences are significant because they show how stability of meaning and the right of the Old Testament to speak is maintained in the progressive approach (as the amount of time spent on the Old Testament in my covenants essay also shows). It also means that criticisms raised about the New Testament priority approach of Ladd and Waltke (and any implied postmodernism) at the beginning, middle (through the citation of comments by S. Lewis Johnson), and end of the essay do not apply to what we are doing hermeneutically. In our approach there is no "restoring" of Old Testament meaning, but there is the affirming of that meaning as applying ultimately to the later period of fulfillment, while affirming also what the New Testament says about the initial realization of such promises. This very difference is what makes the progressive proposal dispensational and thereby leaves the approach unaddressed by Johnson's hermeneutical critique on New Testament priority and postmodernism.

2. Textual Discussion on the Covenants and Their Initial Fulfillment.

a. The Abrahamic covenant. Here I wish to point out what Johnson did not dwell on in contrast to what our essay and earlier response to him treated. Texts such as Romans 4 (esp. vv. 10–11, 16–19) and Galatians 3:26–29 indicate specifically a realization involving the language of the Abrahamic covenant as the basis of Paul's ministry to the Gentiles (see also Eph. 2:11–3:13, especially the language "brought near to the promise of the covenants and co-partakers of the promise"; Rom. 1:1–4; and 16:25–27, where promise is invoked). When Johnson highlights the land as key to the Abrahamic promise, he decidedly underplays how the seed is the mediator of blessing for the nations, the point Paul finds so central. Johnson's treatment is unbalanced. The major and climactic point of the covenant to Abraham is to answer the problem of sin and separation that humanity has as a result of events described in Genesis 1–11. Paul's point is that Abraham is the father of us all, both circumcised and uncircumcised. In addition, Christ's distribution of the Spirit *in realization of promise to Abraham* is what shows that the era of realization has come, breaking down barriers that previously existed through His work on the cross (Eph. 2–3).

b. The Davidic covenant. There is much to treat here, but I have to be selective. So I limit myself to Johnson's argument that a Melchizedekian heavenly king-priesthood is distinct from Davidic, messianic earthly hope. I treat other points of contention on Davidic hope in my discussion of the covenants, which sets forth a whole range of covenant-driven features that Johnson does not treat.

Johnson argues for a distinction between the order of Melchizedek and Davidic order by making four points: (1) it is superior to Abraham, not descended from him; (2) it appears as an authority in history rather than claiming authority based on descent from a line of promised blessings; (3) it is based on righteousness and peace found in the realm rather than on discipline of sin; (4) it is based on unending life rather than a succession of lives. Each one of these arguments, however, fails because the other activities of Psalm 110 involve the victory of a king who would have been seen as a Son of David. A second reason is that Psalm 110 is already connected to the Davidic hope in Hebrews 1. So, Psalm 110 does not discuss two separate figures, one Davidic and one Melchizedekian, but discusses one figure who is both Davidic and Melchizedekian.

In addition, it should be pointed out that whereas the Melchizedekian connection to Psalm 110 is found in one New Testament context, the Davidic-messianic connection to Psalm 110 is repeatedly present throughout that testament. In fact, the basic textual point to note is that the Melchizedkian royal priesthood is seen as a development and explanation of Davidic, regal hope. The use of Psalm 110:4 in Hebrews 5–7 follows the basic Davidic category of son in the introductory argument of Hebrews 1, which also appeals to Psalm 110:1. It is crucial to note that the point of contrast in Hebrews is not Melchizedekian king-priest versus Davidic messiah, as Johnson's argument implies, but Davidic-Melchizedekian king-priest versus Aaronic priesthood. (After all, it is Christ, the Son, who is Melchizedekian.) Do we want to argue that Psalm 110:4 is a different figure than Psalm 110:1, a figure Jesus identifies as messianic in his question to the Pharisees about the meaning of Psalm 110:1 (Luke 20:41–44 and parallels)? I think the distinction fails to be persuasive textually.

How do Johnson's four specific claims for a distinction fail? (1) The messianic argument about Psalm 110:1 shows that one can speak of a superiority of position for David's son *despite* his descent from David. So the contrast of point one falls short. (2) The appearance in history and his Davidic descent is what the New Testament stresses (Matt. 1–2; Luke 1:31–35; Rom. 1:1–4). It is his superiority as son in line with Davidic hope that the New Testament stresses and consistently affirms (Heb. 1). (3) The righteousness and peace found in his realm is precisely the language that is applied to some of Jesus' current work, as my covenant discussion showed (see pts. 6–10). The Spirit is a major means by which the initial manifestation of this righteousness comes. The realm, expressed currently, includes Gentiles among God's people, as the use of covenant terminology shows (Eph. 2–3; 2 Cor. 3, 6—all of Gentiles, Acts 15; in fact, 2 Cor. 6:18 uses covenant language given to David and applies it in a democratized fashion to the Gentiles in Corinth; see also Rom. 15:7–13 and the use of Isa. 55:3 in Acts 13:34, a text that includes God-fearers). (4) The unending life explains how David can have one to sit on his throne forever over his house in conjunction with promise. Thus, none of these points argue for the distinction.

So if Jesus exercises a Davidic-Melchizedekian royal priesthood today, then some of the Davidic hope is being currently realized as a part of His executive authority over His people. Such examples also indicate the inadequacy of the technical definition Johnson attempts to sustain. How can one institute a covenant and have some of its provisions operative and yet *not* speak of partial or initial fulfillment *unless* one creates a technical definition to guard against a connection (especially when the practices of God's people are radically altered [i.e., things such as circumcision, foods, the Sabbath, the way of Gentile inclusion, and the institution of the Lord's Table as commemorative of the establishment of the new covenant through Christ])?

c. The new covenant. Here the discussion of the Spirit, baptism, John the Baptist, and Acts 2 merge (making a point I made in my essay that the covenants are tightly linked). An initial difference surfaces immediately in Johnson's claim that the emphasis of the Gospel accounts is limited to presenting Jesus as the servant. Rather, the Gospels stress that Jesus is the Servant-Son. John's baptism appeals to Psalm 2 and Isaiah 42; one is a regal text, the other is a Servant text. Luke 4 looks back to this anointing in this combined role. Luke 1–2 and Matthew 1–2 both start their gospels with a highlight on Jesus as Davidic son. John the Baptist's point is that the way to know Messiah has come is that He baptizes with the Spirit (Luke 3:15–17). In sum, if Spirit baptism comes, then know that the Messiah has been here. This is John the Baptist's message about identifying Messiah, a point that matches Peter's in Acts 2:16–36.

Johnson works the hardest at attempting to argue for different kinds of baptisms (see his n. 31). He argues for a uniqueness on behalf of the body of Christ to baptism "by" the Spirit or "into" Christ. In fairness, even after working through the case in several pages, he notes that the argument may not be persuasive. *In fact, this distinction will not work. Thus, the distinctions failure means that the baptism announced by John (Luke 3:15–17) is linked and identified with the Spirit's activity that created the church (Acts 2:16–36). This promised baptism with the Spirit is the act that links the covenant program of God tightly together and connects it to this age.*

The link is further observed elsewhere in Acts. Not only does receiving the Spirit and being baptized in the name of Jesus appear side by side in Acts 10:47–48, but also, being baptized by/in (ἐν) the Spirit appears in Acts 11:16 to refer to the Acts 10 event (i.e., the Spirit baptism of Gentiles). The Acts 10 event, in turn, is being referred back and compared to what took place in Acts 2 (see 11:17). In addition, in John 1:33, John the Baptist's announcement concerns one to come who is "the One who baptizes with/ by (ἐν) the Holy Spirit." So the terminology of John's announcement overlaps with the language one sees of baptism to create the church. In other words, Johnson's claim that the New Testament evidence for baptism is that it is *not* a comprehensive term but refers only to a baptism that gives birth to and forms the church is not correct, if one looks at the connection of eras the reference of John the Baptist brings.

The overlap between John the Baptist and the New Testament baptismal language of Paul also shows that what the last of the Old Testament prophets talked about *is* what came through the Christ in fulfillment of long-awaited expectation (Col. 2:12; ἐν and εἰ" used interchangeably in Gal. 3:26–28 with the image of clothing; Luke 24:49). That is why John announced the approach of the kingdom of God. The coming of the Spirit through the Christ is how one could know that it had come. Again, this is the very point that Peter makes in Acts 2, showing that we are conceptually discussing new-covenant hope. *Israel* can know that Jesus is the Christ because the *promised* Spirit has been poured out, which is an initial fulfillment of the new covenant. From where else does that promise for Israel come but from new-covenant hope? John the Baptist does not speak unattached to Old Testament hope as he proclaims that which represents the founding element of what later became known as the church.

So the promised benefits and the kingdom have come in an initial form, even as Israel's national role is temporarily set aside, only to be reintroduced into that program in its final stages associated with Jesus' return (see also Acts 3:19–21; 8:12; similar is Paul's argument in Rom. 9–11). The distribution of the Spirit is both the arrival of the first advent promise and of the covenant promise. The "that" of Acts 2 is the beginning of that realization. A confirmation of this is Paul's use of new covenant language in association with the Spirit and Corinthian Gentiles in 2 Corinthians 3. Another confirmation is the Old Testament context of Luke, where reference is to the promise of the Father, power from on high, and being clothed with the Spirit (the language of baptism; see Gal. 3:26–29).

My fundamental textual and hermeneutical claim is that the alteration to meaning coming from the New Testament is an extension and development based on the boundaries coming from the Old Testament, namely, the sending of Abraham's seed (Christ) as the source of blessing for the nations. It is not alteration *ex nihilo* (i.e., read into the text from nothing) but alteration *ex Christi* (i.e., coming canonically through the details as Christ's own life and ministry are made evident). Such a reading is both stable and bounded, while also honoring the fact that all Scripture points to Him. The expansion takes place on the basis of incorporation in Christ (Davidic Messiah-Exalted Son) and His work involving the Spirit now. This incorporation includes both Jews and Gentiles, a realization of the promise made to Abraham about blessing through the seed to the nations (Gen. 12:3; Gal. 3). It is not an alteration of original promises, as nothing about the original promise to Israel is changed or lost for her. Rather, the alteration involves a complementary addition to promise. Hope is declared and promise opens up to involve Gentiles directly in ways that had not been anticipated by those who had only the broad outlines of the original promise. The specification contains things both old and new, as the kingdom parable of Jesus promised (Matt. 13:52). These are the textual reasons why I reject the distinction in Johnson's technical definition on initial fulfillment.

One final point needs to be made. When Johnson concludes by arguing that God does not expand fulfillment as progressives claim, but rather God sets aside the nation temporarily as traditional dispensationalists claim, I want to reply that this either/or is better seen as a both/and. God both expands the scope of blessing according to promises made to Abraham, even as he temporarily sets aside Israel in the bestowal of blessing. This is Paul's point in Romans 11. The olive tree, which pictures access to hope and promise, has lost natural branches for a time while unnatural branches are grafted in, *but the tree* where the branches experience the blessings *is the same*. One day those "set aside," natural branches will be grafted in, as the promise begun now in Him is completed in Him. The difference between Johnson and me is that the incorporation of blessed Gentiles and remnant Jews today, which Johnson acknowledges as the realization of covenant provision, is for me based on the initial realization of core covenant promises. By the covenants' very linked nature, these core promises, activated in part, involve the initial fulfillment of all of the covenants of promise.

Let me conclude by noting that Elliott Johnson's interest in this area of study and the interaction in which he and I have been engaged throughout the years at Dallas Theological Seminary have been among the greatest treasures of my professional career. He has been a model of what Christian mentorship, friendship, and dialogue should be. (As a student, I served as his grader for three years.) Even in the midst of our disagreements, we both affirm one thing—our oneness in Him.

Chapter Notes

1. These broad principles are simply another way of viewing consistent literal interpretation and the distinction between Israel and the church as proposed by Charles Ryrie.

2. J. L Austin, *How to Do Things with Words,* 2d ed. (Cambridge, Mass.: Harvard University Press, 1975). *TDOT,* 1978 ed., s.v. דָּבָר, esp. 84–124. Speech act theory has analyzed the commissive sense of promises.

3. *TDOT,* 1975 ed., s.v. בְּרִית, esp. 253–78. Covenant is a formal set of commitments to act in the future.

4. *TDOT,* 1975 ed., s.v. בְּרִית, esp. 270–72. Covenant royal grant is a promissory type of commitment.

5. *TDOT,* 1975 ed., s.v. בְּרִית, esp. 255–70. The Mosaic covenant is an obligatory type of commitment.

6. *TDOT,* 1975 ed., s.v. בְּרִית, esp. 262–65. Covenants are established with a ceremony that includes sacrifices.

7. *TDOT,* 1978 ed., s.v. דָּבָר, esp. 102, 107, 108. "God did what He said" to denote the fulfillment of what God said about the future.

8. The distinction between inaugural and exhaustive fulfillment must focus on what has been promised and not on provisions individually included within what had been promised.

9. Bruce K. Waltke, "A Response," *Dispensationalism, Israel, and the Church,* eds. Craig A. Blaising and Darrell L. Bock (Grand Rapids: Zondervan, 1992), 358.

10. George Ladd, "Historic Premillennialism," in *The Meaning of the Millennium: Four Views* (Downers Grove: InterVarsity, 1977), 20–21. His claim for "reinterpretation" of the Old Testament text by the New Testament author is summed up thus: "The fact is that the New Testament frequently interprets Old Testament prophecies in a way not suggested by the Old Testament context." On Matthew 2:15 and the use of Hosea 11:1 he says, "The Old Testament is reinterpreted in light of the Christ event." Clark Pinnock adopts a similar point of view: "Let us by all means begin with the original sense and meaning of the text," adding a new paragraph, "But when we do that, the first thing we discover is the dynamism of the text itself. Not only is its basic meaning forward looking, the text itself records a very dynamic process of revelation, in which the saving message once given gets continually and constantly updated, refocused, and occasionally revised. Just consider the progression between the Old and New Testament, how the coming of the Messiah introduced crucial reinterpretations into the earlier process." Cf. Clark Pinnock, "The Inspiration and Interpretation of the Bible," *TSF Bull* 4 (October 1980), 4–6.

11. Darrell L. Bock, "Interpreting the Bible—How We Read Texts," in *Progressive Dispensationalism,* coauthors Craig Blaising and Darrell L. Bock (Wheaton, Ill.: Bridgepoint Books, 1993), 57–105. Although progressive dispensationalism would resist descriptions such as "resignification" or "reinterpretation," the language Bock uses is similar to Pinnock's: "Since Scripture is about linked events and not just abstract ideas, meaning of events in texts has a dynamic, not a static, quality," p. 64. The dynamic quality is the result of a summary of the New Testament view of Old Testament fulfillment. In the earlier and more theoretical book *Dispensationalism, Israel, and the Church,* each chapter assumes a summary of fulfillment: "already/not yet" (chaps. 1, 2); "both/and" (chaps. 3, 6, 7, 8); "continuous/discontinuous" (chap. 4); "identity/distinction" (chap. 5); "progression/distinct" (chap. 9); "progressive fulfillment" (chap. 10). Each summary influences the dynamic meanings understood in an Old Testament text as the meaning expands or is altered due to the perspective introduced by the interpretation of events of the New Testament. *Dispensationalism, Israel, and the Church,* eds. Craig A Blaising and Darrell L. Bock (Grand Rapids: Zondervan, 1992).

12. S. Lewis Johnson, "Old Testament in New: Response," *Hermeneutics, Inerrancy, and the Bible,* eds. Radmacher and Preus (Grand Rapids: Zondervan, 1984), 799.

13. Nahum M. Sarna, *Genesis,* The JPS Torah Commentary (Philadelphia: The Jewish Publication Society, 1989), 114.

14. Craig Blaising, "The Structure of the Biblical Covenants: The Covenants Prior to Christ" in *Progressive Dispensationalism,* coauthors Craig Blaising and Darrell L. Bock (Wheaton: Bridgepoint Books, 1993), 159–60.

15. P. Kyle McCarter Jr., *II Samuel,* AB (Garden City, N.Y.: Doubleday, 1984), 208.

16. G. B. Caird, *The Language and Imagery of the Bible* (Philadelphia: Westminster, 1980), 58.

17. Derek Kidner, *Psalms 1–72* (Downers Grove, Ill: InterVarsity, 1973), 20 (emphasis mine).

18. Derek Kidner, *Psalm 73–150* (Downers Grove, Ill: InterVarsity, 1975), 451.

19. Blaising, "The Structure of the Biblical Covenants," 161.

20. P. Kyle McCarter Jr., *I Samuel,* in AB (Garden City, N.Y.: Doubleday, 1980), 90–91.

21. While Bateman argues that Psalm 110 is related to the Davidic covenant enthronement, I argue that it is a unique expression of only *one* heir and thus not incorporated in the covenant. Compare Herbert W. Bateman, "Psalm 110:1 and the New Testament," *BSac* 149 (October–December 1992): 438–53 with Elliott E. Johnson, "Hermeneutical Principles and the Interpretation of Psalm 110," *BSac* 149 (October–December 1992): 428–37.

22. Blaising, "The Structure of the Biblical Covenants," 151–59; Ralph H. Alexander, "A New Covenant—An Eternal People (Jeremiah 31)," in *Israel: the Land and the People,* ed. H. Wayne House (Grand Rapids: Kregel, 1998), 169–208; John R. Master, "The New Covenant," *Issues in Dispensationalism,* eds. Wesley R. Willis and John R. Master (Chicago: Moody, 1994), 93–112; Bruce A. Ware, "The New Covenant and the People(s) of God" in *Dispensationalism, Israel, and the Church,* eds. Craig A. Blaising and Darrell L. Bock (Grand Rapids: Zondervan, 1992), 68–97.

23. Walter Eichrodt, *Theology of the Old Testament,* vol. I (Philadelphia: Westminster, 1961), 61–62.

24. *TDOT,* 1975 ed. s.v. "בְּרִית‎," by M. Weinfeld, 264.

25. Ware, "The New Covenant and the People(s) of God," 75–84.

26. Hans Walter Wolff, *Anthropology of the Old Testament* (Philadelphia: Fortress, 1973), 45–58.

27. Alexander, "A New Covenant," 198.

28. Elliott E. Johnson, "Prophetic Fulfillment: The Already and Not Yet," *Issues in Dispensationalism,* eds. Wesley R. Willis and John R. Master (Chicago: Moody, 1994), 183–202.

29. Waltke, "Response," 355.

30. S. L. Johnson, "Old Testament in New: Response," 797.

31. V. Cassuto, *A Commentary on the Book of Exodus* (Jerusalem: Magnes, 1967), 79.

32. Robert G. Boling and G. Ernest Wright, *Joshua,* in AB (Garden City, N.Y.: Doubleday, 1988), 499 (emphasis mine).

33. Ibid., 498.

34. The appropriate term to describe what happened in Gentile occupation and political control is difficult. Eclipse means that the covenant continues to exist but that there is a lapse in occupation. Thus, the title deed to the land remains intact but it awaits a recipient to receive all that God promised.

35. David Gooding, *According to Luke* (Grand Rapids: Eerdmans, 1987), 81.

36. "The verbs *heqim*, "to erect," *nathan*, "to give," and *sim*, "to set," which are used with *berith*, imply the notion of "establish" or "institute"; cf. *heqim/nathan/sim* in connection with appointing a judge, a king, a prophet . . . whereas in the piel of *qum* the idea of fulfilling is prevalent, in *heqim* the idea of establishing is dominant." *TDOT*, 1975 ed., s.v. "בְּרִית" by M. Weinfeld.

37. Craig A. Blaising, "The Fulfillment of the Biblical Covenants Through Jesus Christ," in *Progressive Dispensationalism*, coauthors Craig Blaising and Darrell L. Bock (Wheaton: Bridgepoint Books, 1993), 199–210, and "The Baptism with the Holy Spirit in the History of Redemption," unpublished preliminary draft of a paper.

38. The ministry of Spirit baptism has been distinguished by some in its various New Testament uses based on the effects of that ministry: Matthew 3:11 and Acts 1:5, baptism *with* the Holy Spirit in the sense of pouring out of the Spirit; 1 Corinthians 12:13, baptism *by* the Spirit in the sense of uniting together with Christ the head; and Romans 6:3, baptism *into* Christ in the sense of relating to the life and death experience of Christ. While all of these are distinguishable by effects and distinguishable in the role the Spirit has, yet they are related in the use of the common image—baptism.

39. Charles Ryrie, *The Holy Spirit* (Chicago: Moody, 1965), 74–79.

40. Craig A. Blaising, "The Baptism with the Holy Spirit in the History of Redemption."

41. D. S. Dockery, "Baptism," *Dictionary of Jesus and the Gospels*, eds. Green, McKnight, and Marshall (Downers Grove, Ill.: InterVarsity, 1992), 57.

42. Zane C. Hodges, "A Dispensational Understanding of Acts 2," in *Issues in Dispensationalism*, eds. Wesley R. Willis and John R. Master (Chicago: Moody, 1994), 168–69.

43. Haenchen, speaking as a nonevangelical, seems to infer a similar conclusion: "If the Jews turn from their old ways, there will come 'seasons of refreshing from the presence of the Lord' (i.e., God) and God will send the Messiah Jesus forechosen for the Jews." Ernst Haenchen, *The Acts of the Apostles: A Commentary* (Philadelphia: Westminster, 1971), 208.

44. Darrell L. Bock, "The Reign of the Lord Christ," *Dispensationalism, Israel, and the Church*, eds. Craig A. Blaising and Darrell L. Bock (Grand Rapids: Zondervan, 1992), 49.

45. Hodges, "A Dispensational Understanding of Acts 2," 176.

46. Ibid., 178.
47. Ware, "The New Covenant and the People(s) of God," 94.
48. Ibid.
49. Ibid., 95.

CHAPTER FIVE

Covenants in Progressive Dispensationalism

Darrell L. Bock
with response by Elliot E. Johnson

Although the complex topic of biblical covenants lies outside
our immediate purview, we must note at least the general recognition that the so-called Mosaic covenant differs both formally
and functionally from other biblical covenants. It is also conceded that there are important connections and correspon-
dences between the Abrahamic and Davidic covenants. This is
most apparent in Ruth itself. The narrator is writing, among
other reasons, to clarify that the Davidic dynasty did not spring
out of the conditional Mosaic covenant, but rather finds its historical and theological roots in the promises to the patriarchs.
Israel as the servant people of Yahweh might rise and fall, be
blessed or cursed, but the Davidic dynasty would remain intact
forever because God had pledged to produce through Abraham
a line of kings that would find its historical locus in Israel, but
would have ramifications extending far beyond Israel. (Eugene
Merrill, *Kingdom of Priests*, p. 185)

This quotation by my Old Testament colleague nicely sets up our
topic. It is not my goal to overview the entire covenant program
of the Old Testament. Rather, my aim is more modest. Two

questions dominate this study: (1) What is the relationship between the covenants of promise as laid out in the Old Testament? (2) How does the New Testament portray the realization of these promises? With these modest goals in place, it will not be possible to develop in detail how what I call the covenants of promise (Abrahamic, Davidic, and New) connect to other potential covenants, such as the covenant made with all mankind in Noah or the Mosaic covenant. One need only note that it is not debated that the program begun with Abraham gives Israel a central role in God's plan and represents part of God's activity to restore a relationship lost with man at the fall. It is also generally held, as the above quotation already suggests, that the structure and nature of the Mosaic covenant differ from that of the covenant to Abraham and to David, marking a distinction between them. Formally, this means that whereas the covenants with Abraham and David are unilateral covenants of grant that God made with each partner, the Mosaic covenant is a suzerain-vassal treaty, which is a bilateral covenant of relationship and obligation for both partners.[1] This difference alone, about which dispensationalists agree, justifies a discussion of covenants of promise that does not include the Mosaic covenant in that category.

Another focus of our study will be to point out where a progressive dispensational reading of the covenants differs from more traditional expressions of dispensationalism. The points argued for in this essay and the differences between progressive and more traditional expressions of dispensationalism can be summarized briefly. This contrastive discussion is often done in the endnotes alone.

I shall argue that (1) the covenants of promise are linked together, each containing many elements. To appreciate how fulfillment works, it is important to see the parts of the promise and recognize that the realization of one part is portrayed in Scripture as a realization of an aspect of fulfillment. One does not need every element of the promise to be fulfilled to have the beginning of fulfillment.[2] In contrast to more traditional approaches, fulfillment is not an "all elements present" or "no fulfillment present" affair. One can quickly see the point of this argument, for if fulfillment were an all-or-nothing affair, then one could not speak of fulfillment in the first coming of Jesus for many texts.

There are still elements of fulfillment that many of these promises will experience in His second coming. Just as our salvation is a process of realization in stages (and everyone accepts this), so is the eschatology of which it is a part. Thus, to argue that fulfillment is missing because one element of realization is absent is a biblical *non sequitur.*

(2) The initial fulfillment of one covenant necessarily involves the realization of aspects of another covenant *because of the way they are linked.* This linkage is set up in the Old Testament and is elaborated in the New Testament. As was argued in the hermeneutical essay, to see how promise is realized in Scripture requires that one read the entirety of the canon, noting the associations each text in context makes. The result of this reading is another difference between progressives and more traditional dispensationalists in how they correlate the various texts of Scripture.

(3) All of the covenants of promise are initially realized in the church. This has never been disputed for the Abrahamic covenant in dispensationalism. It has been a subject of discussion for the new covenant and, more recently, for the Davidic covenant. A major burden of this study is to defend this claim. To say that such realization occurs in the church is not to deny that these covenants were originally or ultimately for national, ethnic Israel. It is rather to note that because of the work of Christ, who is the key to fulfillment, initial fulfillment becomes possible in the context of the church (see point 5 below).

(4) There awaits, in the age to come, an even more complete fulfillment of these promises in a period when Christ returns to reign on the earth from Israel. This fulfillment will give the nation peace in her land and give the nations peace on earth, as the promise to Abraham suggests in the promise of a seed through whom the world is blessed. This continued expectation of a central role for Israel in the future means that progressive dispensationalism does not hold to "replacement" theology as some of her critics have erroneously contended. In fact, this approach remains dispensational by maintaining a distinction at the structures level between Israel and the church in the plan of God.[3] On this point the various expressions of dispensationalism are in basic agreement.

(5) Ultimately, the key to fulfillment of the covenant promise resides in its Christological-messianic core as realized in the person and work of Christ. This work benefits both Israel and the world, allowing both to be heirs according to promise. This shared heirship reflects Paul's proclamation of the gospel to the Jew first and then to the Greek, a proclamation that is according to Scripture and its promise (see also Luke 24:43–49; Acts 26:15–23). This Christological center is what requires the recognition of the connection of the covenants, a connection that the New Testament repeatedly makes. Progressive dispensationalism's emphasis of this point of continuity in Christ represents one of its more prominent features that makes it different from previous expressions of dispensationalism.

The Covenants of Promise in the Old Testament

The Abrahamic Covenant

It is crucial to note that this covenant is doing two things at one time. First, it marks out the unique role that Abraham's seed will have in the plan of God. This seed, as the story of Genesis and Exodus makes clear, is both particular and plural at the same time. It is seen as plural in the emergence of the nation of Israel with descendants as numerous as "the dust of the earth" (Gen. 13:16). The seed is particular in that it is through Isaac, not Eliezer or Ishmael. It is through Jacob, not Esau. Through Jacob, it becomes the twelve tribes and then an entire nation that multiplies and fills the earth (Gen. 12:2; 28:3; 35:11; 46:3; 47:27; 48:4; Exod. 1:7).[4] Eventually it emerges in a promised king, the Christ, not through anyone else (Gal. 3:16). Yet even that particular seed, in turn, yields a plurality that includes Jew and Gentile (Gal. 3:28–29). In other words, this promise contains all of the elements necessary for God to redeem mankind and to do His special work through the nation of Israel.

The second feature of the covenant is the uniquely prominent role it gives to the ethnic nation of Israel in the plan. Here is where all dispensationalists differ from other interpretive systems. This covenant is the basis for the irrevocable role the nation has in God's plan. Some of what God does serves as an illustration of His grace. His actions on behalf of Israel are the model, the pattern (typology) of what gracious redemption looks like. The importance of this point is that even though God does have a plan for the world, as revealed in the promise to Abraham, and will work out that plan through His promise, some of what He is doing is mirrored in and through Israel. What He does specifically for Israel as a people models what He is doing and will do for mankind as a whole.

The issue of God's faithfulness to His promise and His gracious, persistent extending of redemption to this nation, despite their history of disobedience, shows just how much the character of God and His unfailing love are manifested in His entire plan. To argue that the promises to Israel have been exclusively transferred elsewhere in such a way that the original recipients are largely excluded from its benefits, a move nondispensational approaches to the plan of God make, is to destroy the model of God's faithfulness and enduring mercy that the story of God's relationship to Israel is designed to portray. Such a transfer undercuts the very pattern of deliverance that Israel represents as a microcosm of the larger work of God's salvation. This point, which emerges from the Abrahamic promise, is the reason progressive dispensationalism is a dispensational approach. It argues for a future for national, ethnic Israel, even as it emphasizes continuities in the plan of God that bring the church and nations into the fulfillment of God's plan. Scriptural promise can be Christological, dispensational, and covenantal in a way that respects how God is dealing with His promises to humanity and to ethnic Israel. The Abrahamic covenant with its two sets of concerns is the basis for all of this hope and realization. The unity of God's plan has its origins ultimately in the unity of the promise made to Abraham. This also explains why God's kingdom program for the world both involves Israel and extends beyond her.

It is important to note that this covenant is presented in four places in the Genesis narrative involving Abraham. The basic covenant appears in 12:1–3. It is restated and formally ratified in a unique ritual God performs for Abram in 15:1–21. It is here that the promises are called a covenant for the first time. It is also here that God unilaterally offers a sacrifice that shows that the promises made are His alone. His commitment to these promises is something that is entirely in His sovereign hands. The covenant is restated in 17:4–21, where the rite of circumcision is added. (As

Paul notes in Romans 4, this is after the covenant was established and ratified in Genesis 15.) Here also a promise is extended to Sarai (who becomes Sarah) as she is promised that she shall be a mother of *nations* and that kings of peoples shall come from her (17:16). It is also here that God makes clear that the promise runs through Isaac, not Ishmael (17:18–21). The promise is repeated throughout Genesis, first to Abraham (22:15–18), then to Isaac (26:3–5, 24), and finally to Jacob (28:13–15; 35:9–12; 46:1–4). Here is why God is the God of the patriarchs, the God of Abraham, Isaac, and Jacob (2 Kings 13:23).[5]

So what are the provisions of this unilateral promise by God, this grant covenant? In 12:1–3, the promise is set up by the call to Abram to leave his country, relatives, and father's house. In an ever-narrowing circle, God calls Abram to a new start in a new setting to make a new people. Away from all past biological ties, Abram will have a unique relationship to the only true God. Five promises are a part of the basic text in 12:1–3. In addition, three more promises surface in the reaffirmation of this covenant.

The first covenantal promise in 12:2 is that Abram will become a great nation. That this nation is ethnic Israel is clear from both the story of Genesis and Exodus. This is also evident in the remarks made in the covenant's reaffirmation in 15:12–21, where not only are the descendants ("the seed") discussed, but the dimensions of the land are detailed.

The second and third promises involve a commitment to bless Abram and make his name great. Tracing specifically what these promises include is a little more difficult, but it appears that the point is elaborated and summarized in Genesis 22:17–18, after the famous incident of Abraham's faithfulness to God in bringing Isaac for sacrifice. Here the promise of blessing is associated with the multiplication of seed—the promise of taking possession of the land *and* the promise that through this seed all nations on earth will be blessed. Here the relationship of the promise is related to Abraham's obedience. Obedience allows the promise to move forward. Three elements of blessing are named here: promise of offspring, victory-security for Abraham's posterity, and the seed as a mediator of universal blessing.[6] Note how elements of this blessing are both material and spiritual. Note also how the promise has two tracks: one involving the nation of Israel and another involving humanity. Note also *how both tracks are linked together* in the work of the seed. The promise of the great name indicates the renowned reputation Abram would possess because of the unique role he has in the plan. In fact, Abram's reputation and name will be so great that he is called to be a blessing. The Hebrew verb here is imperative, unlike the imperfect, which surrounds the line. In a sense, Abram not only is receiving a promise, he also is receiving a call. Here is a commission of the Old Testament like the Great Commission we often note in the New Testament (Matt. 28:18–20; Luke 24:43–49; Acts 1:8). His call, and that of his seed connected to him, is to be a blessing to the humanity he is being called to serve. The unilateral act of God's grace is a call to serve and be faithful.

The fourth promise is that blessing would come to those who favor Abram and cursing would come to those who do not. Again, it is important to note that though the promise goes to Abram, the seed that he contains are also beneficiaries of this promise. Here is another promise whose outworking is difficult to trace. Yet it appears that the argument of Isaiah 41:5–16 is rooted in the promise made here (esp. v. 11).

The final line of the promise in 12:1–3 is crucial for our concerns. In Hebrew, the structure of this line differs from the other promises. Here we have a perfect tense, a shift that points to a result clause.[7] There is also debate over the kind of force the reflexive/passive has in the reference to nations blessing themselves or being blessed. This latter problem is particularly complex as the restatements of this promise alternate between using the hithpael (reflexive, two times, Gen. 22:18; 26:4) and the niphal (passive, two times, Gen. 18:18; 28:14). A credible solution is to see ambiguity in the phrase and render it "acquire blessing (for) themselves."[8] Regardless of exactly how one renders the difficult syntax, the point is that these many promises have a singular result. It is that by/through Abram all the families of the earth shall gain for themselves blessing. Here God joins the program for Israel and the program of the world in such a way that the channel of blessing to the world comes through what God does through the seed of Abram. In other words, the two tracks of the promise connect here and *are linked* as God works to redeem humanity through what He does through Abram and his seed. As we shall see later, this is the point at which Paul makes his case for Gentiles against the Judaizers appealing to the promise of the Old Testament as his basis for preaching the gospel and conducting his *current* ministry as he does (Gal. 3; Rom. 4).

An important principle of God's promise giving is that He often states a promise in general terms and then elaborates on its specifics later, filling in details. The giving of the promise to Abram follows this pattern. Shortly after the initial promise in Genesis 12:1–3 there follows the passage where Abram has actually traveled to the land. In this new and separate context, God elaborates on the promise of a nation and its land with some detail. A key methodological point surfaces here. To understand the covenants one has to check all of the contexts where the promises appear or are developed. If we limit our definition of God's promise to Abram to the first offer of that covenant, the land promise would be absent. (The other covenants need to be treated similarly.) In two new contexts, God specifically says that to Abram God will give *this land*. It is for his seed. Thus, the nation will have a home. That promise receives more elaboration in 13:14–18 and again in 15:12–21, including its dimensions. Thus, *one part of one track of the promise to Abraham* is the track that deals with the nation. It is the promise of land for her in which she will live in peace.[9]

Two more promises can be briefly stated. First, Genesis 17:7–8 notes that God will be the God of His people. Here is the commitment of an intimate relationship to God, in which Abraham's seed are also God's children. This image becomes important when we get to the promise of a line of kings.

Another promise of a line of kings surfaces in Genesis 17:7–8. This detail is important because it suggests that there is a regal element to how the blessing is mediated from God to His children. There is next to no detail here, but as is common with promise, as revelation proceeds God fills out how the promise works out. This promise also helps to explain why the next great covenant of promise is the one made to David.

How do we summarize such a comprehensive and significant covenant? The words of H. J. Kraus do so nicely:

> In this word of God to Abraham is to be found a master clue to the understanding of the whole of Old Testament history. The

starting point of the history of man's salvation is God's call to man and nothing else. . . . This call, with its trenchant demand for separation, is at the same time promise. Out of Abraham a great people will grow, and this people will be the bearer of blessing to all peoples. *By way of Abraham and Israel God enters into the world of the nations.* The Old Testament message is based on the first call and the first promise of which Abraham was the recipient.[10]

In sum, God has unilaterally committed Himself to Abraham. We have noted eight promises above: (1) seed for Abram, (2) blessing for Abram, (3) a great name for Abram, (4) blessing or cursing for those who bless or curse Abram, (5) blessing for the families of the earth through Abram, (6) land for the seed of Abram, (7) that God would be God to this seed, and (8) that kings would be descended from Abram. This commitment involved three key elements: (a) the establishment of seed that would grow into a distinct nation, (b) the promise of the formation of that nation in a land where they would dwell in peace, and (c) the provision of a mediatorial role through that seed that would become the basis of blessing for all families of the earth.[11] In fact, the result of the formation of the nation would be that she would become the means by which humanity is blessed. What is important to see is how *linked* the promise of the nation and the working out of blessing for humanity are. Though the promise contains two tracks of concern (one involving ethnic Israel and another involving all of the families of the earth), they are ultimately linked together to form one fundamental promise as God moves to redeem a fallen humanity. God always promised that the seed of Abram had a call to be a blessing to the world.

The Davidic Covenant

The promise to David of an eternal line of kings comes in a context where God and the nation have been debating the wisdom of the nation possessing a king, a process that began in earnest with Saul.[12] When David brought the ark to Jerusalem in 2 Samuel 6, it was clear that Yahweh had directed events in such a way that Jerusalem would be Israel's capital and set location for the representation of His presence. In this context, David asked

for permission in 2 Samuel 7 to build an appropriate house for
God, one not made of tent material (v. 2). The reply that comes
through Nathan begins with God noting that He never asked for
anything more (vv. 5–6). The remarks that follow make up the
base declaration of the Davidic covenant (vv. 7–16). Even though
the term *covenant* does not actually appear in this text, later references to it describe it that way, so there is no doubt that we have
a unilateral, grant promise of God present (2 Sam. 23:5; Ps. 89:3,
28; 1 Kings 8:23; 2 Chron. 13:5; 21:7).[13]

David is told initially that God took the initiative with him, calling him out of the role of a shepherd to be a ruler over Israel.
The image of a shepherd as ruler is common. The connection at
the start of the covenant is no accident. David's history in one
role pictures his ultimate function before the people. A shepherd
leads and guides the people as well as protects them. The image
defines the function and activities of a ruler. This introduction is
often skipped over in discussing the covenant, but the image sets
a background for the remarks to come. This image is raised in
Psalm 78:71 to describe the role of David on behalf of the people.
In this text, the shepherd functions with integrity of heart and
guides the people with skillful hands. The text summarizes the
kingship of David himself. The same image appears in 1 Chronicles
11:2, when David is told that he will be a shepherd to Israel. The
remark stands in parallelism with the observation that he will be
a prince over God's people, Israel. In Ezekiel, when the nation is
overrun, the people are described as those without a shepherd
(34:5). One shepherd, that is, one king, is promised to the nation
in the future, David. He will guide the people to walk in God's
ordinances, having made Israel one nation again, living on the
land. The shepherd gives them a covenant of peace, a place to
dwell and worship God forever as God shows that Israel is related
to God (37:21–28; see also Mic. 5:4). Thus, the image of shepherd
is fundamental to the promise to David, identifying his regal, guiding, and protective role on behalf of the nation. The use of the
image in the rest of the Old Testament shows that this is more
than a historical reminiscence. Rather, it is a fundamental description of the king's function.

The survey of shepherd makes a methodological point that is
important to understand about how the promise to David is pre-

sented in the Old Testament. It is a point we also saw in the Abrahamic covenant. This imagery, introduced initially in very basic categories, is filled out as revelation proceeds. As that imagery reemerges and is filled out, more detail about the promise surfaces. This is why discussing the Davidic covenant cannot be limited to 2 Samuel 7 or to its parallel in 1 Chronicles 17.

Nonetheless, it is important to look carefully at the promises God makes in 2 Samuel 7. Once again there are several elements, all of them relating to His role as king over Israel. God begins the promise by reviewing how He has given David victory over all of the king's enemies. So just as God had promised Abram (Gen. 12:2), so God now promises David a great name (2 Sam. 7:9). This points to the significant rule and line that will develop from David as the rest of the promise shall make clear. Here is God's first promise to David.

Second, David will establish a place of rest for the nation (2 Sam. 7:10–11). This language also looks back to the Abrahamic promise of security in its own land (Gen. 12:7). The point highlights the important theme of a land for the nation, which is so prominent in the Old Testament. Rest means that neither enemies nor the wicked will afflict the people. It is the role of David's rule and that of the line coming from him to provide this for God's people. Thus, the promise assumes that the people desire to live righteously before God. They are free to honor Him.

Third, there will be seed from David to rule after him when he is dead and gone (2 Sam. 7:11b–13; note how this promise also parallels that to Abram, Gen. 12:2). This descendant will establish a kingdom. He will also build the house for the Lord that David requested to build. More than that, however, God will build a house (a dynasty) for God's name, and will give him a throne on which his kingdom will reside forever. The reference here is to Solomon, who begins a line of kingship that will never end. We know Solomon is meant because it is he who builds the temple as God promised. Thus, God promises an everlasting rule on behalf of His people, the nation of Israel. It is the role of this kingship to provide a rule that is on behalf of God's name. With this rule comes the image of establishing a throne that will never end. The point in this remark is not to discuss a chair or its location, but its function. The king of the Davidic line is charged with shepherding the nation of Israel and of guiding God's people into a life of rest, free from the wicked and from God's enemies. The remark about a line of kings connects back to the promise to Abram that kings would descend from him (Gen. 17:6, 16).

Fourth, God's relationship to the king in this dynasty is special (2 Sam. 7:14–15). It will be a father-son relationship. Like a father, God will correct and discipline the king when he sins. It is this remark that lets us know that the text is not about a sinless king, but about the line of kings as a whole. This familial relationship has one abiding benefit. God will never remove the kingship from this family as He did from Saul. Lovingkindness (covenant faithfulness) will always belong to the family of David. It is this remark that allows the Davidic king to be thought of as the Son of God. The title points to a regal function and the special relationship the appointed one has with God.

Fifth and finally, there is the reassurance that this line and its throne will endure forever (2 Sam. 7:16). Again, the point about the throne is not a particular chair but is about a rule and its unending character. This promise is expressed as something God will yet do, given that it looks to Solomon's arrival. Solomon establishes the line of kings and sets the dynasty in motion.

David's response is one of amazement and praise (2 Sam. 7:18–29). A phrase in verse 19 is much disputed. It is David's declaration that what God has said is the "custom of man" (NASB) or the "usual way of dealing with man" (NIV) or, more literally rendered, "the law of humanity."[14] David is making one of two points, depending on how the phrase is rendered. Either he is simply saying that God has dealt marvelously and unusually with him in a manner out of custom with His normal dealings with humanity, or he is noting that what God has said has universal significance for the affairs of mankind. The phrase refers back to the establishment of this dynasty (v. 19a) and the relationship of that dynasty to the nation of Israel and the victory that will come with this kingship. So it is more likely that the remark points to the universal significance of the promise ("a law for humanity"). McComiskey summarizes the point well:

> Taken in its simplest and most literal sense, the phrase may denote that the promise that David's house would continue is the

established body of teaching for mankind. There is only one body of teaching that relates the concept of the offspring to the destiny of mankind, and that is the promise given to Abraham. This understanding of 2 Samuel 7:19 emphasizes the continuity between the offspring of the Abrahamic promise and the offspring of David. Both are viewed as mediating the divine blessing to all mankind (cf. Gen. 22:18).[15]

McComiskey makes two points here. First, David realizes that the promise has implications for those outside of the nation as well as for those inside. Second, the Davidic covenant is *linked* to the Abrahamic covenant in goal and purpose, as both this verse shows along with the numerous parallels to the Abrahamic promise discussed above.[16]

Nevertheless, David's remarks of praise leave no doubt as to the national focus of the promise. Second Samuel 7:23–24 speaks of God's action for one nation during the Exodus. God saved the nation to make for Himself a people, to make a name for Himself, and to do awesome things in giving them land and rescuing them from idolatry. It is Israel that is established as God's people forever through the promise He has made in this kingship, this everlasting house.

Here is the core Davidic promise. It has one image and five elements. David and his line are called to shepherd Israel as their rulers. (1) David will have a great name. (2) Rest for the nation will come from this promise. (3) David will have a line of descendants that will become a dynasty, even as one of those descendants builds a house for God. (4) This line will have a special father-son relationship with God. Discipline by God will also be a part of this relationship, a point which shows that the kings will not always be perfect rulers. (5) This dynastic house will last forever.

This covenant expectation exercised much influence on the nation's thinking and hope. So it is a mistake simply to read this covenant promise as it is introduced here. Davidic covenant hope involves more than this one text says. As we saw in the repetition of the Abrahamic covenant, sometimes elaboration and further detail and expansion come into the promise in further revelation. Thus, a treatment of Davidic promise in the Old Testament must consider other texts where the promise is raised. I shall proceed by discussing Davidic promise in the Psalter and then in the Prophets.

Psalm 72 is a good place to begin as it is a psalm ascribed to Solomon, one of the main beneficiaries of the promise to David. This text lays out his expectation of Davidic dynastic kingship. The king asks to receive judgment and righteousness. This includes the ability to judge on behalf of the poor and to bring peace to the people. He also will deliver the children of the needy and break in pieces the oppressors (vv. 1–4). In his presence the righteous shall flourish (vv. 5–7). His dominion shall extend "from the river to the ends of the earth" (v. 8). Here the note in the *Thomas Nelson Study Bible* (NKJV) is significant, "The promises of God to Abraham included a promise that his descendants would have dominion over the land of Canaan (Gen. 15:18–21). The verses here expand the geographical dimensions to include the entire earth (p. 951)." Once again a connection between promises to Abraham and the activity of Davidic kingship are made. The Septuagint's version of Psalm 72:17 makes this connection explicitly through this language. So the connection was recognized early on in Judaism. There is a recognition that enemies will bow before him (vv. 9–11). Deliverance of the poor and needy will be his calling (vv. 12–14). He will receive tribute from abroad as prayer and praise are offered for him (v. 15). Blessing will abound because of him (v. 16). His name shall endure (v. 17a). Men shall be blessed in him, a phrase recalling Genesis 12:3 (v. 17b). Nations will call him blessed (v. 17c). God is then praised for designing this to take place (vv. 18–19). It is easy to see how the regal mandate is understood by Solomon as he paints the portrait of the call of the king. This kingship does impact the world as the authority of the sovereign is manifest and recognized, even among the nations. In particular, the language of verses 8 and 17 is important to show that the Davidic mandate was seen as impacting the nations of the world.

Similar in thrust is Psalm 89. Here is a psalm written in the face of the failure and unfaithfulness of kingship. As God's mercy is extolled, the promise to David is explicitly recalled (vv. 1–4). Praise of God's creative power and sovereignty follows (vv. 5–18). The key verses for us appear in 19–29. It also begins with the recollection of the promise to David (vv. 19–20). This one has the support of the Lord's arm (i.e., His strength, v. 21). He will defeat

David's enemies and strike those who hate him, a phrase whose language is like Genesis 12:3 (vv. 22–23). God's faithfulness will be with him. In God's name the horn (i.e., the strength) of this one will be exalted. Here is an explanation of how the name of this regal figure is made great. The authority of this ruler will extend over seas and rivers (v. 25). The king will call God his Father, His God, while God will make him his "first-born," the highest of the kings of the earth (vv. 26–27). God's lovingkindness will be with him forever, and His covenant will be confirmed to him (v. 28). So his seed will be established forever, and his throne like the days of heaven (i.e., endless). The language here clearly alludes back to 2 Samuel 7, with its promise of an eternal line and a throne established without end.

But all is not good. Even despite their sin, the reign will not end, but discipline shall be given (vv. 30–37). In fact, currently the king rules in shame and defeat because of sin (vv. 38–45). The psalm ends with a request that God remember the reproach (vv. 46–52). The hope is that restoration will come to the line that has shamed its God.

The psalm is important because verses 19–28 describe the role of the king according to Davidic promise and hope. Here is the greatest of kings, the one with authority over the rivers and seas, the one who will defeat the enemies of His people, and the one who belongs to a line that will never run out.

Psalm 132 is written in a similar context of despair. Here the cry is also for the Lord to remember the affliction of David, who agonized to give God an appropriate place of worship (vv. 1–5). As the nation is called to worship, the promise to David is explicitly recalled (vv. 6–12). From the fruit of David's body, God will set one upon David's throne (v. 11). This is a truth from which God will not turn. In addition, if the sons keep God's covenant, their sons will sit upon David's throne forever (v. 12). Once again the promise to David is invoked. The reason it can be invoked is that God has chosen Zion for His habitation and His resting place forever. Here He will dwell. Here God will bless, satisfy the needy with bread, clothe the priests with salvation, and godly ones will sing (vv. 13–16). Here the horn of David will spring forth as God prepares a lamp for His anointed (v. 17). The king's enemies will be shamed, but the crown of the king will shine (v. 18). Once again the image is of a victorious king on behalf of God's people bringing victory. The key image at the end of the passage is the king's association with the presence of light as God's people, the godly, are at rest to worship the presence of God.

Psalm 2 acknowledges that many stand opposed to the king and fight against the Lord and His anointed (vv. 1–3). Yet the Lord laughs at the opposition given to the King established in Zion (vv. 4–6). Here is the Lord's Son proclaimed by decree (v. 7). The reference to decree refers to an article of covenant (2 Sam. 7:14; Ps. 89:20–28). This king will receive the nations as an inheritance and the ends of the earth for a possession (Ps. 72:8). He will break them in victory (Ps. 2:9). So the kings of the earth are warned to worship the Lord and "kiss" (i.e., do homage) to the Son. Those who take refuge in the king will be blessed. Once again the sovereignty the king enjoys because of his covenant-sonship relationship to God is affirmed. What is said of this king is said of kings of the Davidic line, as the parallels to what is affirmed here note.

Psalm 45 is the wedding psalm of Solomon. Kingship involves truth, meekness, and righteousness (vv. 3–5). The throne on which he sits is forever (v. 6; 2 Sam. 7:12–16). The king loves righteousness and hates wickedness (v. 7). After addressing the bride (vv. 10–15), the psalm goes on to note that it is the greatness of this king that causes his name to be remembered in all generations. Peoples will give thanks forever (v. 17).

Psalm 110 is another song that praises the authority of the king, who serves according to the order of Melchizedek. He is a king-priest, serving much as David and Solomon did as they oversaw the bringing of the ark and the building of the temple.[17] Here is one who bears the title of David's Lord and who sits at God's right hand until God is finished with the job of bringing all of the king's enemies into submission (v. 1). A day comes when this king will rule from Zion in the midst of all of his enemies (vv. 2–3). The Lord will fight with him as he defeats the enemies that lie before him (vv. 4–6). At the end, the king will drink from the brook at rest and peace (v. 7). Once again the psalm is full of imagery that has its roots in Davidic hope of victory and giving rest to the nation.

We have quickly overviewed these psalms without any elaborate comment to let their cumulative force have an impact. The themes of (1) the international scope of the victory of the king

(Pss. 2:8–12; 72:8–12; 89:25, 27; 110:2–6; 132:18), (2) the extent of his sovereignty (Pss. 2:8; 89:25–27), and (3) the righteousness and justice of his rule on behalf of the people who serve him (Pss. 45:3–5; 72:2–4, 12–16) are major ideas running through these psalms. The theme of (4) the everlasting character of this rule is also reaffirmed (Pss. 89:4, 28, 36–38; Ps. 110:4). Each of these themes has its roots in the promise to David. In theme (5) God will set up a lamp for the king, a light that continually shines for him (Ps. 132:16–17; note also 2 Chron. 21:7). In theme (6) the role of the king for Israel is also prominently displayed in virtually all of these psalms (esp. Pss. 2; 72; 89; 132). Here is how the Davidic covenant is seen in its development through the Psalter.

What do the prophets add to the picture? This survey can provide only a summary of the six elements the prophets raise. It is important to see both how parallel the portrait is to what has been said and to show what this material adds. The prophets do not discuss the term *Messiah*. Rather, they raise the issue by discussing the rule of a Davidic heir who meets all of the national ideals of the promised kingship on behalf of the nation.

1. This king will *come from the line of David and introduce a lasting rule of righteousness and peace*. Several texts simply name him as "David" (Isa. 9:6–7, 16:5, 28:16; Jer. 23:5). These passages all stress the righteous character of this rule, a point to which we shall return. Perhaps the most interesting text, Isaiah 28, is the one that does not mention David directly. Nonetheless, the laying of a precious stone in Zion, a stumbling stone, is designed to counter Israel's covenant with the death that her disobedience brings. The righteous and just character of the stone laid will bring a rule that cancels out this covenant of death. The imagery here involves the activity of the promised king in reversing a tide of unfaithfulness in the nation. The parallelism is also seen when Isaiah 9 and 16, and Jeremiah 23 are considered. This king is "the Branch" (Jer. 23), who rules with good counsel and wisdom. He can be considered a "Prince of Peace" (Isa. 9) as he is established in the tent of David (Isa. 16). These descriptions of the king's role show that although the name David does not appear in Isaiah 28, it is this promise that is being invoked. The Isaiah 28 text notes the importance of believing in this stone.

2. The kingship to come *rebuilds something that was broken down*

in the house of David. Here stand three texts, Amos 9:11–15, Isaiah 11:1, and Ezekiel 17:22–23. Whether speaking of the rebuilding of the fallen tent of David (Amos 9), the shoot that springs forth from the stem of Jesse and becomes a branch (Isa. 11:1, 10), or the spring that comes from the cedar that will be planted on a lofty mountain (Ezek. 17), the point is the reemergence of a king of the Davidic line. His coming means that hope for Israel and victory are on its way. When this king comes, a tree begins to grow in Israel that will be a shaded place of peace for the birds and a locale of great fruit and strength. This nation will take possession of places such as Edom, long a Gentile enemy of the people.

3. The third note is *about national security for the nation.* Here is the rest that the covenant promised, described in texts such as Amos 9. Others include Isaiah 11:12–16, where the division in Israel is removed and victory over the nations follows. Among the defeated are Edom, Moab, the Sea of Egypt, those of "the River," and Assyria. The allusion to the "river" recalls Psalm 72:8. In this context, those who have been dispersed are regathered. The rule of the Branch in Jeremiah 23:5–6 leads to the secure dwelling of people in Judah. The ruler is known as "the Lord our righteousness," a point repeated in Jeremiah 33:15. Jeremiah 33:17–21 makes the point that there shall be no lack of kings or priests for Israel if the nation is obedient. Disobedience will mean a temporary end to the line of kings and priests, a point that was being applied in the very time in which Jeremiah wrote. Micah 5:2–5 promises one from Bethlehem, who will shepherd the people in strength. He brings stability "because at that time he will be great to the ends of the earth. This one will be peace." Note again the language connection with Psalm 72:8 and Isaiah 9–11. Ezekiel 37:16–28 takes place in a similar context, where the nation is restored securely in its land as is pictured in the image of the dry bones brought to life.[18] The nation will have one shepherd, David, to be king over them. The result is a people who live righteously and experience a covenant of peace, an everlasting covenant, that God will make with them. In the midst of this security, all nations will know that God is the God of Israel, the One who sanctifies them.

4. The impact of this king on the nations has already been noted in some of the texts in the other categories. *His rule involves the nations, both in victory and in peace.* Amos 9 and Micah 5 fit here.

Isaiah 11 should be noted as well. The victory leads eventually to a great peace (Isa. 11:6–9). Isaiah 11:10 says, "Then it will come about in that day that the nations will resort to the root of Jesse, who will stand as a signal for the peoples; and his resting place will be glorious." The work of this king extends to the nations, both in judgment-conquest and in peace.

5. Most of the texts already noted also *highlight the character of this king's rule and the character of the people as a result.* Terms such as *righteousness, wisdom, justice, counsel, lovingkindness,* and *walking in the ordinances* are present. Whether one looks at Isaiah 9, 11, 16; Jeremiah 23; Ezekiel 37; or Micah 5, the unsurpassed character of this king is a major feature prominent in the character of his rule. The influence of his presence is transferred to the people, who also live in peace and walk in righteousness.

6. One text yields the final category. It is *the democratization of the regal promise,* so that the beneficiaries of the Davidic promise are the people. By democratization, we mean that the promise originally given to the Davidic line has its beneficiaries explicitly extended to the people. Democratization is not, as some Old Testament critics argue, at the expense of the Davidic line, but rather shows how the subjects of this ideal rule will benefit from this promise. The text is Isaiah 55:1–5. Here there is a call to people who thirst to come and experience the everlasting covenant. This is probably an allusion to the promised covenant of peace that all of these regal passages highlight. But in verse 3 this covenant is "with you" (plural). The promise is extended to all of the people. Its identity is also noted, "the sure mercies of David." This line is in appositional parallelism to the invocation of everlasting covenant hope. Here is a leader and commander who will lead to great blessing for those who thirst—"for the peoples." But note that this thirst is widespread. Isaiah 55:5 reads, "Behold, you will call nations you do not know, and nations who do not know you shall run to you, because of the Lord your God and the Holy One of Israel; for he has glorified you." The presentation of this universal scope of promise becomes a major emphasis in Isaiah 60. This text comes just after the announcement of the Redeemer coming to Zion and the Spirit coming upon the people (Isa. 59:20–21). The hope extends to the description of final glory in Isaiah 65–66.

Here is a hint of where the promise is headed. The Septuagint shows that Jews understood the text this way, as Isaiah 44:3 in this version explicitly connects the theme of water with the Spirit placed on the nation's seed and the giving of blessing upon her children. In fact, the Septuagint and the Masoretic text agree here. Though the nation is in view in Isaiah 44, by the time we get to Isaiah 55, the potential for the promise's extension to others is affirmed through the use of the same water image. A careful consideration of Isaiah 55's context shows that the blessing that comes with the Spirit is not a military victory but the bestowal of righteousness, an act of salvation that is a part of the eschaton. If the Spirit has come, the Messiah has been present as he brings the righteousness to the people. If the Spirit has come, the eschaton is also present. All of this teaching sets up the development of this theme in the New Testament, which also must be allowed to speak on its own terms to develop and complete what God is doing through this image.

God has selected a nation and a seed through whom the family of nations is blessed. Isaiah's statements echo that which was promised to Abraham. God has also selected a king of Davidic descent who is to be the incarnation of the presence of God's rule in justice, righteousness, and peace. He will redeem Israel but also will bless the world with peace. Thus, Isaiah also echoes that which was promised to David about his dynasty. That blessing extends to those who thirst and looks to a day when Israel and the nations are gathered before this king. This also is promised in the Davidic hope. Those people also will be characterized by a righteous response to God and will be called to believe in the stone that was rejected, a precious cornerstone.[19] How will they be able to be so responsive? That leads us to the next element of the promise, the New Covenant.

However, before we consider the last element of the covenants of promise, one outstanding point requires attention. It is the very interlocking nature of these promises. They are tightly knit together. A nation leads to a king for both the nation and the earth. That king's rule has contained within it, both because of his character and his gifts, the enablement to render his people vindicated, secure, and righteous. In other words, the covenants of promise contain *many linked elements,* but those elements ultimately tell *one fundamental story* about the redemption of all humanity. It is this promised king who stands at the center of realization in all of its stages as he engages in all of the elements of his executive, regal activity and rule. That movement of rule toward redemption and the establishment of peace for the nation and humanity is the most fundamental element of the promise made to David, which itself is designed to lead to the fulfillment of the promise made to Abraham.[20] How will the people share in this great blessing and transformation? That is where the new covenant enters into the portrait.

The New Covenant

Only one passage in the Old Testament actually has this phrase, though numerous texts mention the themes raised in this promise. Jeremiah 31:31–34 gives the provisions of the covenant, while texts in Jeremiah 32:40 and 50:5 and in Ezekiel 16:60–63, 34:25–31, and 37:26–28 speak either of "my covenant" or a "covenant of peace." An "everlasting covenant" is discussed in Isaiah 55:3 and 61:8. The servant appears with reference to a covenant where peace and deliverance come in Isaiah 42:6 and 49:8. Isaiah 59:21 also discusses "my covenant."[21] The association of the Spirit with the acts of deliverance are also noted in several texts where the concept of covenant is not explicitly named (Isa. 42:1; 44:3; 59:21; Ezek. 36:27; 39:29; Joel 2:28). Of these texts, the only one we have considered up to this point is Isaiah 55. But the concept of the everlasting covenant appears with the activity of promise tied to the blessings of David. The links show that the eschatological activity associated with the presence of the Davidic heir and the events tied to the new covenant are united in Old Testament eschatological expectation. The *linking* indicates that the new covenant itself is an extension of the realization of promises made to Abram and David. In fact, it has been rightly claimed that the eschatological teaching of both Ezekiel and Isaiah 40–66 can be characterized as new covenant oriented.[22] As can be seen with the Davidic promise, the nation of Israel ultimately has a key role in the realization of these promises, though it is also clear that the key figure in its realization is the presence of the activity of the promised "David."

Three features are prominent in the presentation of the new covenant in Jeremiah.

1. It is *a covenant made with Israel and Judah,* representing the reuniting of a divided nation (v. 31). The promise comes in a context in which God is declaring the future redemption of the nation and its full restoration according to the promise of God. In this goal, all of the covenants of promise are united. Progressives do not debate this point. In fact, on this they are agreed with other dispensationalists.

However, none of this nullifies the significant question of what Scripture does with this promise and hope from this point on in Scripture. It is here that our conceptual and hermeneutical discussion with more traditional forms of dispensationalism begins. Progressives contend that the covenants are tightly linked. In fact, the New Testament is forthright in declaring the initial realization of the covenant promise in association with Jesus' first coming and His resurrection-ascension. To deny the initial stages of this fulfillment is to understate what the New Testament affirms, even as more traditional dispensational approaches are right to highlight how Israel is always prominently in view in the foundational Old Testament texts.[23] In other words, this observation about Israel's participation and central role in the covenantal promise does not close the question of whether God can extend the promises made here to include others.[24] *To treat these Old Testament passages on the covenants as if they end the question is to close the question before all of the Scripture has been brought to bear on a theme that Scripture has been constantly developing.*

2. It is a covenant *unlike* the covenant made with the nation during the Exodus, an allusion to the Mosaic covenant (v. 31). It is this distinction that leads to marking off the Mosaic covenant as of a different class than the new covenant. The remarks also suggest that although the new covenant provides for an obedience that has in mind what the law sought to accomplish, some fresh divine initiative was required for God to get His people to respond to Him. This distinction is part of what caused the early church to de-emphasize specific Mosaic covenant stipulations or rites that come after the giving of the promise of Abraham (Gal. 3).

3. It is fundamentally *a covenant of restored and transformed relationship,* which seeks to restore a husband-wife relationship that the nation had violated (vv. 32–34).[25] *Here are the central elements of*

the restoration and redemption of God's people. This idea establishes the basis for the bridge that the New Testament development of this hope will bring. It will allow Gentiles to share in its scope.

What are the stipulations of this covenant? Four elements are central.[26]

1. *God will change from within the nature of those included in the covenant,* so that they are able to know Him. Jeremiah speaks of the law on the mind and the law written on their hearts (v. 33). This probably alludes back to the call for a circumcised heart that was a part of the Mosaic obligation (Deut. 6:6; 30:6). Jeremiah 32:39 speaks of God giving "a singleness of heart and action" that leads to the fear of God.

2. A *special relationship* is the result of this transformation, as "I will be their God, and they will be My people" (v. 33). This imagery has been fundamental to that seen in the Abrahamic covenant and in the father-son relationship of the Davidic promises (Gen. 26:3, 24; 28:15; 2 Sam. 7:14, 24).

3. The result is *a new, more direct, more intimate, more faithful relationship with God as those transformed will know God.* All of his children will know Him. The point here is not that instruction is abolished; rather, it is the loss of a need for any other mediator in conducting the relationship with God. All "from the least to the greatest" will have direct access to knowledge of Him (v. 34). This promise is probably what underlies the earlier eschatological revelation that a day was coming in the midst of the restoration when all of the people of God would experience the outpouring of God's Spirit (Joel 2:28–29). This is also what underwrites Ezekiel's remark about the promise of a new heart and Spirit within them (Ezek. 36:26–27).[27]

4. Finally, there is a promise of *the forgiveness of sins.* It is the dealing with sin that allows the changed relationship to exist. Thus, though this element comes last in order, in a real sense it is the provision that clears the way for everything else that was mentioned.

The promises are sealed with a statement of surety that these things will come to pass (vv. 35–37). The promise is sealed by the sovereign Creator. These promises can fail only if the creation can be measured and searched out. In other words, they cannot fail.

Before looking to see how the other prophetic texts take up

this theme, it is important here to make one point about the New Testament use of the image of this passage. When Jesus speaks of the blood of the new covenant in the Last Supper (Luke 22:20; 1 Cor. 11:25), a meal that the church also commemorates in the Lord's Table, He is explaining how the new covenant is being established and thus initiated with His death. Thus, the provision of forgiveness of sins is made possible in Jesus' death. This shows that at least this element of covenant realization is tied to His first coming, as it is *that* forgiveness applied on the basis of that act that established the transformed relationship that emerged from Acts 2 on.[28]

What do the prophets add to our new covenant portrait? Really, much of what is presented has already been said in what was promised to Abram and David.

Isaiah 61:8–9 promises that the nation's offspring will be known among the nations, and their descendants will be known in the midst of peoples. They will be recognized as offspring whom God has blessed (Gen. 12:2–3; 2 Sam. 7:24). The people will be clothed in salvation and righteousness, like a bride adorned with jewels. The context is one of national restoration as Israel is restored before the nations (61:10–11). This "everlasting covenant" has two key qualities: its focus on Israel and its salvation resulting in praise to God.

Ezekiel goes in a similar direction. Ezekiel 16:63 grounds the establishment of "my covenant" in the forgiveness of sins (v. 60 speaks of the "everlasting" covenant). The result is that the nation will know the Lord. In Ezekiel 34:25–31, David is the one shepherd of the people. Thus, this period involves the rule and activity of one promised to come from David. Here the "covenant of peace" discusses a secure life in a fruitful land. Again, the imagery recalls the promises to Abram and David (Gen. 13:14–18; 2 Sam. 7:10).

Ezekiel 36:22–32 maintains this perspective about a covenant of peace. It raises the issue of forgiveness and a transformed relationship through a washing that allows for a new heart and spirit to be placed within the people. "His Spirit" will be placed in them. The parallels to Jeremiah are evident. Here is the source of the New Testament imagery on rebirth. All of this is being done to keep God's name honored among the nations, vindicating the holiness of His name before them.

Ezekiel 37:15–28 follows the vision of the resurrection of the nation. Here God makes his people into one nation again. David again is king. The people walk in God's ways. They live in the land. It is a "covenant of peace," an "everlasting covenant." God's sanctuary is in their midst and His dwelling place is with them. The result will be that "I will be their God, and they will be my people. And the nations will know that I am the God who sanctifies Israel, when my sanctuary is in their midst forever."

What these promises indicate is that the new covenant hope involves the nation and her promised king in a major spiritual transformation of God's people. That transformation is equated *to a resurrection* in Ezekiel 37:14, where God promises to put His "Spirit within you and you will come to life, and I will place you in your own land." When this takes place, the nation will *know* God has spoken.

At the center of the transformation stands the promised mediatorial ruler. Isaiah explains this role in the figure of the servant, one who embodies the nation. Yet distinct from her, he redeems her. The servant does what the nation was called to do. Two texts associate him with covenant. The *link* is important for it shows that with the new covenant comes "My covenant" or "the everlasting covenant" or "the covenant of peace." In other words, the covenants of promise are ultimately one covenant commitment of God *for Israel and for the nations,* since Abram's promise is ultimately a blessing for the world (Gen. 12:3). In addition, the accomplishment of that covenant promise resides itself in the activity of one promised to shepherd and enlighten the nation and the world out of darkness. Thus, the servant is a "covenant to the people, as a light to the nations, to open blind eyes, to bring out prisoners from the dungeon, and those who dwell in darkness from the prison" (Isa. 42:6–7). Thus, the Lord declares "new things" (v. 9). The events will lead into the praise of God to the end of the earth (v. 10).

Also in Isaiah 49:6, the servant is raised up to gather Israel. Yet, here also, he is a "light unto the nations," so that God's "salvation may reach to the end of the earth." Kings and princes shall rise up and bow down as a result. Isaiah 49:8–13 specifies the point. The servant himself is given as "a covenant for the people, to restore the land, to make them inherit desolate heritages." They, that is, Israel, will be regathered to a land of plenty. People, that is, from other nations, will come from everywhere. Then the Lord will comfort the people through His servant.

The promise of the servant certainly looks to the restoration of the nation, but this point should not cause us to miss one other central point. At the center of the covenants that are linked together stands one figure, the servant-Davidite. It is his work, *all of it,* that makes the complete realization of promise possible.[29] The blessing he brings is for Israel, but it also is light for the world. That is the lesson of the Old Testament covenants of promise. They all come together in this one figure.

What does the New Testament do with this hope, especially those elements tied to the promise made to David? What does the coming of the Messiah and the arrival of the Spirit in the same period tell us about the plan of God?

The Covenants of Promise and the New Testament

Most of this essay concentrates on the Old Testament, for it is there that the groundwork for covenant promise is laid. Space prevents us from as detailed a look at the New Testament, but our basic premise is simple. The covenants look to Israel and eventually to the world (Abrahamic covenant). The promises contain many parts but come together in one figure (Davidic covenant and the servant of the end). That figure brings forgiveness, peace, light, the Spirit, and rest in the land to his people (new covenant). Though salvation is to the Jew first and then to the Greek (Rom. 1:16), it is not for Israel alone, as God in the New Testament expands the beneficiaries to include the nations, something He evidences explicitly when He gives to Gentiles the sign of the new era, the Spirit of God along with the forgiveness that this indwelling presupposes (Rom. 15:7–13). As shocking and surprising as this was, when the apostles and the early church recognized this, they also understood the equality of blessing into which the nations had come (Acts 11; Rom. 4; Eph. 2:11–22; Col. 1:24–29), while also continuing to maintain a hope for Israel. The expectation was that Jesus' return and the Gentiles' inclusion would one day bring Israel's response to the gospel (Acts 3; Rom. 9–11). It was also for this reason that the Mosaic covenant came to be replaced in the church's thinking by the presence of the new covenant (2 Cor. 3–4; Heb. 8–10). In the New Testament era, God was still revealing and developing His salvation plan in covenant promise for Israel and the world. At the center of it all stands Jesus Christ.

Dispensationalists have never debated the presence of some realization of the Abrahamic covenant in the current era. I have highlighted the connections of realization of the new covenant as we discussed that covenant. Though a point still contended—and while some expressions engage in some subtle semantics in discussing this promise—many, if not most, dispensationalists recognize the church's participation and see elements of fulfillment of the new covenant today. In the remaining space I will once again concentrate on the Davidic covenant and hope because it remains a point of contention between progressive dispensationalism and more traditional views. Which themes tied to this promise and current activity appear in the New Testament? I concentrate only on texts related to the present era because that is where the discussion lies. As one can see, there is far more involved here than just an appeal to Acts 2. *What we are discussing is Davidic-messianic activity of the current era, undertaken as an expression of his rule and authority in light of Old Testament descriptions of the activity of the promised ideal king. These realized promises are part of the reason why we confess Jesus as the Christ, not merely as a Messiah-designate.*

1. *Shepherd.* At the head of the announcement to David comes the picture of the Shepherd. It is an image Jesus used quite explicitly. Whether it was when He discussed looking on the people and having compassion for them because they were like sheep without a shepherd (Matt 9:36; Mark 6:34) or when He described Himself as the Good Shepherd (John 10), Jesus was invoking the imagery that the promised Davidite had come. In fact, Jesus explicitly makes the point in John 10 that He has sheep who are not of this fold (10:16). Here is the surfacing of the inclusion of more than Israelites in the plan of God. The image of sheep in peaceful pastures also invokes the imagery of Davidic rest. Here is a declaration that the salvation Jesus brings, the ability to know how one can have life, shares in promises made to David (also Heb. 13:20; 1 Peter 2:25).[30]

2. *Regeneration.* Once again it is John's gospel that makes the connection. Here the imagery is found in John 3. For John, entry into the kingdom is a function of being born from above, born of

the Spirit. Those who study John note how "realized" the eschatology of John is.[31] John 14–16 show how it is Jesus as the raised Christ who provides this Spirit. This theme is also connected to the idea of eternal life in John, which is defined as "knowing God" (John 17:3). Knowing God is a major goal of the covenant promise. For John as well, regeneration and possession of the Spirit mean that the Lord teaches the believer directly about the truth of the gospel (1 John 2:27).

3. *Thirst.* The invitation to come and drink appeared in a text that democratized the Davidic hope (Isa. 55:1–5). In John 4, Jesus offers the woman at the well water that will never leave one thirsty. He then goes on to discuss true worship later in the chapter as the woman raises the issue of Messiah and where one should worship. To be sure, Revelation 22:1–2 also uses this imagery of the future. John's usage reflects the presence of an "already-not yet" theme.

4. *Father (to His Children).* Perhaps nothing is so dramatic in terms of picturing the democratization of Davidic hope as what Paul does in 2 Corinthians 6:18. Here he takes the "I will be a Father" language from 2 Samuel 7:14, as well as language from Isaiah 43:6, and fuses it to include the idea of sons and daughters. The passage combination supports a claim that God has made the Corinthians a part of God's people, a fundamental theme of the Abrahamic and new covenants (see Ezek. 37:27; Jer. 31:1; 2 Cor. 6:16). Paul is able to do this because of the benefits Christ gives as the promised Son of David (v. 15 mentions the Christ). These are promises that the Corinthians possess (2 Cor. 7:1). Thus, Paul feels perfectly comfortable using the language of Davidic and new covenant hope, bringing them together and applying them to the church and to Gentiles. The move is not surprising since the goal of the new covenant is to bring the transformed people into a special relationship to God.

5. *Light.* This image appears in several locales. John 1:9 contrasts Jesus as the true light to John, an image developed in John 8:12; 9:5; and 12:46. This image is also present in Matthew 4:14–17. It reappears in association with the kingdom and the image of rescue in Colossians 1:14. Here, it is the kingdom Jesus brings that is characterized as light (Ps. 132:18; Isa. 11:10). But this image recalls the description of the character of the rule of the promised king from the Davidic and new covenant hope of the Old

Testament and the promised one as light. He is also light for the Gentiles in Luke 2:32, citing Isaiah 42:6 (see also 49:6). Here Jesus' work for Gentiles, the topic of the book of Acts, is explicitly present. This shows the unity of Jesus' work and activity as His work for Israel is also noted here.

More traditional dispensational interpreters will argue that these images from the Gospels do not count as they relate to the period when Jesus was offering the promised kingdom to Israel, an offer that was made again in Acts but was postponed when the nation rejected the offer. Here is another difference between progressives and more traditional dispensationalists. The continuity of this covenant imagery extending from the Gospels through the Epistles, the teaching of texts such as Isaiah 52:13–53:12, the presence of texts citing the presence of the kingdom now—including in parables where rejection is a given—all argue against a parenthesis of the kingdom idea. For example, when the invitation to come to the banquet is rejected in the parable of the great banquet (Matt. 22:1–10; Luke 14:16–24), the banquet goes on with others present, including outsiders who picture Gentiles. The banquet is not postponed; who attends is altered! The invitation to come to the banquet pictures the message of Jesus. What others are offered is what Israel is offered. What emerges is *the appearance of a parenthesis* or a break in how the program relates to Israel as an entire nation, but the kingdom program itself *continues and continues to be linked and described using the language of Old Testament promise and realization.*[32]

6–10. *Morning Star-Light, Horn of David, Peace, Defeat of Enemies.* This image of light, viewed as a morning star, is also present in the hymn of Luke 1:78–79, where Jesus is compared to the morning light who shines on the people and leads them in the way of peace. The theme of peace is a Davidic theme. The hymn raises it by speaking of the visitation of God through the horn of the Son of David (Luke 1:68–70). This Davidite will defeat the enemies so that the people of God may worship God without distraction (Luke 1:71–74). All of this is done according to covenant promise. Zechariah is combining the covenants here and showing how they can be brought together. In Luke's narrative, these enemies are developed to include Satan, demons, and the foes of darkness, which is why the light needs to appear.[33]

11–13. *Authority over Sea and Rivers, Blind See, Messiah Anointed by the Spirit.* Another aspect of Davidic authority shows itself in the calming of the waters of the sea by Jesus (Luke 8:22–25). The act represents an allusion to Psalm 89:25, "I will set his hand on the sea, and his right hand on the rivers." This kind of miraculous activity is like the reply Jesus gave to John the Baptist about whether Jesus was "the one to come" (Luke 7:20–22). Jesus' reply centered around the activity of His ministry, drawing on a collection of texts that all refer to the events of the eschatological end (Isa. 29:18; 35:5–6; 42:18, 26:19, 61:1: "the blind see, the lame walk, lepers are cleansed, the dead are raised up, the poor have the good news preached to them").

Also in this category are the servant texts about giving sight to the blind. Here Jesus' declaration from Isaiah 61:1 in Luke 4:18–21 is relevant. Verse 21 explicitly says, "Today this Scripture has been fulfilled in your hearing." A corollary to this theme is also present. The declaration in the use of Isaiah 61:1 that the Spirit has anointed him is a declaration of God's marking out Jesus at the baptism as the Christ-Servant in language that alludes back to Psalm 2:7 and Isaiah 42:1. The invocation of Psalm 2 is the invocation of Davidic hope as Hebrews 1:5 shows, citing both Psalm 2:7 and 2 Samuel 7:14 side by side as texts already realized in the naming of Jesus as Son.

Also relevant is the healing of the blind man in Jericho (Luke 18:35–43; Matt. 20:17–19; Mark 10:46–52). Here the blind man knows to ask the Son of David for this healing. He understands, as the request is made, that eschatological power resides with the Promised One.

All of this relates to the realization of Old Testament hope and promise as Jesus gives thanks to the Father for the activity associated with this ministry. Jesus tells His disciples that they are blessed because "Blessed are the eyes which see what you see! For I tell you that many prophets and kings desired to see what you see, and did not see it, and to hear what you hear, and did not hear it." That what Jesus is doing is related to Old Testament hope could not be stated any more directly (see also 1 Peter 1:10–12, which shows the same point being made in the era of the church).

14. *The First Born, the King of Kings.* This title from Psalm 89:27 is reflected in both Colossians 1:15 and Revelation 1:5. Jesus' cur-

rent authority is named and associated with the presence of a kingdom in Revelation. The kingdom exists for those to whom John writes in the churches.[34] One day that authority will be totally manifest, but that represents the completion of something Jesus has already started.

15. *Revealed Sitting at God's Right Hand, Already Exercising Messianic Authority in King-Priestly Ministry, Forgiveness for Israel, Cleansing, the Offer of Repentance, Authority over Cosmic Forces, and the Giving of the Spirit.* This category deals with those activities associated with the Davidic-messianic activity linked to Psalm 110:1. Acts 2 is actually one of several New Testament texts that appeal to the language of Psalm 110:1. The roots for Acts 2 go back to Jesus raising this text as a crucial text about Davidic promise in Matthew 22:44; Mark 12:36; and Luke 20:42. The fulfillment is seen as beginning from the moment of Jesus' death-resurrection-ascension. As He tells His Jewish interrogators in Luke 22:69, "From now on you will see the Son of Man seated at the right hand of God." So we see Jesus standing to receive Stephen at the right hand of heaven in Acts 7:56. Other texts highlight the fact that at the right hand the Christ is already given authority over a host of cosmic forces and is ministering on behalf of the people in what the book of Hebrews calls the true sanctuary (Rom. 8:34; Eph. 1:15–23; Heb. 1:3–4, 13; 8:1; 10:12). Hebrews 10:13 notes that the final defeat of the enemies in terms of Psalm 110:1 is yet to come, but this point does not annul the fact that the initial steps of realizing this victory have begun with His ascent to God's right hand, as the epistle also declares. Another clear text is 1 Peter 3:21, where the subjection of cosmic forces and the idea of cleansing are related through the use of an aorist (past tense) verb to the effects of Christ's resurrection. The Ephesians text is also significant because it occurs in a context where Paul highlights Jesus' headship (authority) relationship for the church and the benefits that stem from His exaltation. Finally, Acts 5:31 makes the point that from the right hand Jesus can offer repentance to Israel and forgiveness of sins, so that once again His position opens up His authority and power to give benefits in this era.

This brings us to the Acts 2 text, which explicitly notes the promise of throne seating from Psalm 132:11, which itself alludes to the throne language of 2 Samuel 7. Many of the exegetical points were made in the hermeneutical essay as they related to the claim of the association of an initial fulfillment because of current activity. What the above survey of "right hand" passages shows is that in the New Testament, though Jesus awaits the completion of the defeat of enemies, He is neither inactive nor passive at the right hand. No comparison can be made to the Old Testament example of David's being anointed and reigning later—because Jesus is active at the right hand of God. He is performing messianic activities. In Acts 5 it is in the offer of repentance to Israel and the availability of forgiveness. In Acts 2 it is distributing the promised Spirit of God, the ultimate sign of the arrival of the period of fulfillment in conjunction with new covenant hope.

16. *Democratization of the Promise and Justification.* Acts 13 cites Isaiah 55:3 specifically alongside Psalm 2:7 and Psalm 16. Paul is preaching here to an audience of God-fearers (i.e., Gentiles) and Jews in the synagogue. He makes the point that "to you" are given the "faithful and holy things of David." Included in the benefits are forgiveness and justification from sins (Acts 13:37–39). This kind of linkage is possible because Paul is combining the Davidic hope with the New Covenant hope. Everything Paul preaches about here is on current offer.

17. *Forgiveness of Sins Offered Once and for All.* The relationship of Jesus' activity to forgiveness in Acts 5 and 13 has already been discussed as it related to Psalm 110:1 and Davidic-messianic activity. Here we treat forgiveness as offered for all time. Added to those earlier forgiveness texts is the exposition of Hebrews 8–10, which discusses new covenant hope in relation to the sacrifice Jesus offered once for all. The roots of this teaching must be Jesus' own teaching about the suffering of the Servant and His explicit reference to the new covenant at the Last Supper. Once again, hope involving the ideal king and the eschatological age are united in a New Testament text.

18. *Spirit as Proof that the Promised Messiah Has Come.* Perhaps the most complex set of texts presenting the promise comes in the Luke-Acts theme concerning the Messiah as the bringer of the Spirit. The key corollary point is that the distribution of the Spirit proves that the Messiah is present.[35] This hope starts with John the Baptist in Luke 3:15–17, where he makes clear that the way to know that Messiah is present is when He baptizes with the

Spirit. The idea continues in Jesus' reference to the Father's promise of the coming of power from on high in Luke 24:49. This idea, in turn, is picked up in the reference to the promise of the Father in Acts 1:4–5 with allusion back to John the Baptist. The cycle is completed in Acts 10–11, when the coming of the Spirit is marked in 10:45 as coming amazingly on Gentiles and then is commented on by Peter in 11:15–17. Peter's remarks are worth citing: "As I began to speak, the Holy Spirit fell on them just as on us at the beginning (i.e., at Pentecost in Acts 2). And I remembered the word of the Lord, how he said, 'John baptized with water, but you shall be baptized with the Holy Spirit' (see Luke 3:15–17; Acts 1:4). If then God gave the same gift to them as He gave to us when we believed in the Lord Jesus Christ, who was I that I could withstand God?" The conclusion comes in verse 18: "Then to the Gentiles God has granted repentance unto life." In other words, through the Lord Jesus Christ the same offer made to Israel (Acts 5:31) has come to Gentiles. There is no analogical or metaphorical reference in this citation. A real epoch-changing event has taken place. In Jesus, eschatological, regal, messianic promised activity has come to realization in the giving of the Spirit and the granting of a transformed relationship to Gentiles.

19. *Salvation to the End of the Earth.* This image rooted in Abrahamic hope, declared from Psalm 72:8 and reaffirmed in the work of the Servant as covenant, is also in the process of being realized. Here is an aspect of the mission and commission of the church as Acts 1:8 asks for the gospel to be taken to "the end of the earth." The apostle Paul, in another bold application of Scripture, cites Isaiah 49:6 and describes his commission and that of Barnabas with this phrase. He applies the servant imagery of light and proclamation of salvation to the Gentiles to their message. This fits with Paul's view of his ministry as the extension of the work and mission of Jesus. In fact, to call the church Christ's body is to make a similar point about her call. The church today represents Christ's presence on earth.

20. *Spirit from the Christ as Proof that Gentiles Are in the Promise.* This final text puts the entire package of this essay together. The result of Christ's redemptive work is Paul's topic in Galatians 3:13. The goal of that work is stated in verse 14. It reads, "that in Christ Jesus the blessing of Abraham might come upon the Gentiles, that

we might receive the promise of the Spirit through faith." The "we" is specified in verses 26–29, where the key statement is in verses 27–28, "for as many of you as were baptized into Christ have put on Christ. There is neither Jew nor Greek, neither is there slave nor free, there is neither male nor female; for you are all one in Christ Jesus. And if you are Christ's, then you are Abraham's seed, heirs according to promise."

Conclusion

Our study has come full circle. The Abrahamic promise leads to the great king of blessing according to Davidic hope, the Christ. He will sit on David's throne forever and exercise the prerogatives of regal rule. He, in turn, gives out the Spirit, the promise of transformed relationship marked out in the new covenant as the sign of the arrival of the new era. In Galatians 3:13–14, all three covenants converge to explain how the seed of Abraham is both Gentile and Jew thanks to the gift of the Spirit which comes through Christ in the current age. There is a beautiful unity to the linkage of these promises. The Abrahamic covenant shows what God commits to do as Father. The Davidic covenant shows how the Son fits into the plan. The new covenant details the role of the Spirit. The one plan is rooted in the activity of the triune God.

I have noted twenty themes in the New Testament that touch on current elements of the Davidic covenant promise. Much more could be said. I have purposefully avoided bringing in the full range of servant motifs that one could connect to this hope. In other words, this list could be longer. I hope that I have shown why progressives discuss the element of fulfillment that has already taken place in conjunction with God's covenant program. It explains why the New Testament teaches that all Scripture teaches fulfillment about Jesus as the Christ. This teaching is not a declaration that one day fulfillment will come or that what has taken place today is like what will be fulfilled tomorrow, but rather that much has been fulfilled already. We already share *directly* in much promised blessing.

As a result, our preaching should be filled with praise for what God has already done for all of us according to a plan He devised and revealed long ago. The reign and rule of our great Messiah, the promised Son of David, has begun, highlighted by the executive and mediatorial outpouring of many divine blessings of His grace. Much of what the Christ will do has not yet come, including much involving national Israel.[36] When those days appear, all will see Israel's special place in the plan, especially as it is focused in the work of her great king. Both Jews and Gentiles will rejoice in the share they have in that salvation. One thing is clear, however; the three covenants of promise meet with their initial fulfillment in Christ's first coming, the activity of the church, and especially in the blessings that provide the church with a transformed relationship to God. These three covenants of promise culminate in Jesus Christ to provide forgiveness, salvation, peace, and the Spirit to the seed of Abraham, both Jew and Gentile alike (Eph. 2:11–22). These things have been written from long ago in the Law, the Psalms, and the Prophets. They are affirmed as already present in the New Testament.

RESPONSE

The appearance of progressive dispensationalism has occasioned a challenge for dispensationalists "to examine the Scripture to see if these things are so." Rather than simply revisiting an older answer, which some found unconvincing, the challenge invites a fresh consideration of the texts in view of the traditional *sine qua non.* Well-educated and primarily younger scholars, representing a wide range of schools with a dispensationalist heritage, advanced arguments from texts to adopt some new conclusions. Viewing progressive dispensationalism from a distance, there are a number of attractive elements: a posture that emphasizes continuity between the Old Testament and the New Testament that moves closer to a view shared by other evangelicals; an exegetical and scholarly rigor in dealing with biblical texts; and a presentation of the position as a natural development of changes already having appeared in the heritage.

Darrell Bock presents a wide ranging study of the promissory covenants in the Old Testament and argues that each, with an emphasis on the Davidic, reaches an "already" or "inaugural" fulfillment in the church. The presentation provides a simple mode and a neat package of parallel treatment of the covenants in an "already-not yet" view of fulfillment. Yet when examined in Scripture, a number of issues must be questioned:

- Are the Old Testament records of the covenants to be read from the perspective of New Testament issues?
- Does the universal influence of the Davidic reign over Gentile nations expand the scope of the Davidic covenant?
- Are not Gentiles reached as proselytes in the Old Testament so that the salvation of Gentiles is not unique to the New Testament?
- What are the foundation blocks of progressive revelation and complementary fulfillment?

While all of the questions raised have consequences, the answers to the last question must be considered in this brief response.

Bock is quite right in highlighting the difference between the two points of view (pp. 168–70), but the differences are more basic than mere differences in emphasis, vocabulary, or strategy of explanation. It is a difference in conception of progressive revelation that is based on disparity in interpretation. As dispensationalism is both a theology and a hermeneutic, so the disparity concerns interpretation of texts and some doctrines as well as introducing a disparity in the interpretation of other texts and in the *sine qua non*. The foundational doctrines that form the building blocks are two: the inaugural fulfillment of the promissory covenant occurs at the first advent of Christ; and thus, the church is a covenant people of God. This conception of what Christ realized at the First Advent and of the nature of the church must be rejected for the following reasons.

The Relationship Between the Two Stages of Fulfillment

Although both constructs of dispensationalism agree that there is some fulfillment concerning the Promised One at the First Advent and that the remainder awaits the Second Advent, the disparity concerns the relationship between the two stages of fulfillment. Bock addresses that relationship: "Just as our salvation is a process of realization in stages (and everyone accepts this), so is the eschatology of which it is a part" (p. 169). This argument by analogy from salvation to eschatology does not follow because the plan of salvation involves man as both the *object* of salvation and the *agent* of salvation. This distinction is first implied in the protoevangelium (Gen. 3:15), where the seed of the woman, man, is promised to be the *agent* of deliverance from the serpent and the curse against the serpent implies that man is the *object* of God's deliverance. The fallacy in the analogy is that it reasons from the provision of salvation in Christ (an "already" stage and a "not yet" stage) where man is the *object* of salvation to interpret the promissory covenants where man is the *agent* of salvation. In other words, *what* God provides *for man* in Christ does not parallel *how* God provides *through* Israel, which is the issue common to each of the covenants.

What, then, is the relationship between what is fulfilled at the First Advent and at the Second Advent? It seems clear that the Lord and His apostles interpreted the Old Testament to refer to suffering at the First Advent (Luke 24:26, 46; Acts 17:2-3; Heb. 2:9-10; 1 Peter 1:11). Such suffering by itself would not fulfill the covenants. However, the argument is that certain provisions of the covenant were fulfilled in an inaugural fashion in the death, resurrection, and *ascension of the Lord into glory.* For instance, Scripture says that "all nations of the earth would be blessed through Abraham and his seed (Gen. 12:3; 22:18) and the Son of David is declared to be "the begotten" Son in the resurrection (Ps. 2:7) as He received "the sure mercies of David" (Isa. 55:3) in His resurrection (Ps. 16:10). The question is this: Does the fulfillment of these provisions mean that the covenants are fulfilled?

Bock's answer is that "fulfillment is not an 'all elements present' or 'no fulfillment present' affair" (p. 160). In other words, inaugural fulfillment is a partial fulfillment of some provisions. He adds two arguments to support this position: (1) unless one held Bock's position, "one could not speak of fulfillment in the first coming of Jesus for many texts"; and (2) "the proposition that "fulfillment is missing because one element of realization is absent is a biblical *non sequitur.*" This position and the arguments are by no means conceded as true.

Bock's position does not harmonize with the definition of a covenant: "formal stated agreement (involving interrelated provisions) between specified partners." This position is subject to challenge on two grounds: (1) the provisions of the agreement were not satisfied in the fulfillment of some (one or two of the provisions); and (2) the agreement involved Israel, who rejected her Messiah and thus refused any national participation (Luke 19:28–21:4; Acts 4:1–22).

An everyday example demonstrates that an agreement involves provisions (terms) that must be kept. If I agreed to pay a student's tuition to complete his degree, then I would be expected to pay the tuition each semester as tuition came due until the degree is earned. If for some reason I decided one semester to pay the student's wife's tuition, but not the student's, would that payment fulfill my agreement? It is clear that it would not. The student neither received what was promised nor could fulfill his role in completing his degree.

Based on such a definition, traditional dispensationalism does not view any promissory covenant fulfilled at the First Advent. Rather, the Abrahamic and Davidic covenants were inaugurated in the Old Testament and then went into eclipse during the times of the Gentiles. After the First Advent, neither the land nor the Davidic kingdom were restored to Israel as promised. The new covenant, which had been promised in the Old Testament (Jer. 31 and Ezek. 36, etc.), was instituted at the death of Christ (Luke 22:20). But such an institution ought not be regarded as fulfillment with Israel who rejected Him (Acts 4:8–20) nor even with the church. The church is merely the beneficiary of some of the provisions of the new covenant (2 Cor. 3:4–6) without becoming a covenant partner. In this way, numerous promises and provisions are fulfilled at the First Advent without a covenant having been fulfilled (Gen. 3:15; 22:18; 17:19; 49:10; Num. 24:17; Isa. 9:7; 7:14; 53:9; Pss. 16:10; 22:6–8, 18 [two references]; 34:30; 68:10; 69:21; 109:4; Jer. 31:15; Dan. 9:25; Mic. 5:2; Zech. 12:10).

The biblical *non sequitur* refers to many of these passages in which direct references to fulfillment are found in the New Testament. While this is true, none of these direct statements refers to fulfillment of a promissory covenant. Therefore, a strategy based on allusion must be advanced to argue for fulfillment of the covenants. Bock argues here that the twenty references to realized promises "means that Jesus is the Christ, not merely messianic-designate." It is inferred that since Jesus is the Christ, His ministry (represented by the twenty themes) means that His Davidic reign has begun. That inference must be challenged for several reasons.

First, in Nazareth (Luke 4:16–21) Jesus drew a similar but different conclusion. Since He has been anointed with the Spirit, the anointed ministry meant that He was Messiah in fact (Isa. 61:1, 2a). Jesus did not claim that His ministry meant that His reign had begun.

Second, the pattern of themes, as imposing as it is (although a commentary on a number of the themes needs to be questioned) lacks at least three themes to identify the Davidic reign on earth. The themes of the nation of Israel (even though the kingdom was supposedly democratized), the city of Jerusalem, and the conquest of Rome—which ruled on earth during the times of the Gentiles— are all absent. The pattern argument rests on recognizing sufficient defining themes to make the identification. Otherwise, the pattern represents a general association which demonstrates commonality but not identity. The themes recognized by Bock demonstrate reigning but *not Davidic* reigning.

Third, following His resurrection He was identified as the Christ (Acts 2:31), and following His ascension into heaven He was identified as Lord (Acts 2:34). His ministry from heaven (the twenty themes) is an expression of the kingdom of God but in a form announced in the parables of the kingdom (Matt. 13) rather than in the form of the kingdom promised to David.

The first foundation block concerns the concept of progress in revelation, which is the heart of dispensational theology. The issue is how what Christ fulfilled at His first advent represents progress in the promissory covenants. Progressive dispensationalism argues that continuity exists between an inaugural fulfillment of the covenants and Christ's first advent. Traditional dispensationalism contends that the continuity exists in the fulfillment of the covenants and Christ's second advent. The First Advent includes the fulfillment of some provisions of the covenants concerning Jesus, who is the Christ, and the inauguration of the new covenant in the death of Christ. There is real disparity between the conception of the covenants and the interpretation of passages.

The importance of this discussion relates to the *sine qua non*. In interpretation, a literal, contextual reading of Old Testament covenants is challenged by the complementary context of the New Testament. In doctrine, issues in eschatology and ecclesiology are affected. Progressives claim that no Old Testament meanings will be lost, yet fail to clarify how additions to the meaning of these texts at the First Advent do not distort the expectation that no meaning will be lost. In ecclesiology, does the limited presence of fulfillment of Israel's covenants in the church not affect the nature of the church? It is to answers of this question that we now turn.

The People of the Church as a Covenant People

Although both agree that the church believers are recipients of blessings promised in the Old Testament, the disparity appears in the conception of the people of the church as a covenant partner or a covenant people. This conception is based upon the covenants finding some fulfillment in the church. Bock states it this way: "Though a point still contended and while some expressions (of dispensationalism) engage in some subtle semantics in discussing this promise, many, if not most, dispensationalists recognize the church's participation and see elements of *fulfillment* of the new covenant today" (p. 193). The semantic distinction we proposed is not subtle at all but is the distinction between "institution" and "initial" or "inaugural fulfillment." The distinction is between "the formal commitment to the terms of the covenant" (institution) and "the actual keeping of the terms of the covenant with the specified recipient" (fulfillment). This distinction is well established in both the Abrahamic and Davidic covenants in the Old Testament. In the period of time between the institution and the inaugural fulfillment, some terms of the covenant were fulfilled (such as the birth of Isaac or Solomon) without the covenant being inaugurated.

At issue then is the *institution* of the new covenant. To appreciate that institution of the new covenant, it ought to be compared to the previous covenants. The Abrahamic and Davidic covenants were unilateral covenants as Yahweh assumed unconditionally to bless the descendants of Abraham and David. From the perspective of the history of these descendants, it soon became evident that this was a commitment to sinful and repeatedly sinning descendants. How does God guarantee blessing upon Israel in her sins?

Alongside the Abrahamic covenant, Yahweh formulated a bilateral, vassal covenant with Israel as the covenant-partner. The partnership was not formulated with Israel because of her ability to obey but rather on her acceptance of Yahweh's proposal (Exod. 19:8; 24:3). The role that Israel would have was as a "special treasure," "a kingdom of priests," and "a holy nation," but the role was contingent upon her obedience. In her covenant partnership, Israel repeatedly displayed sinfulness and disobedience. This finally brought judgment upon the nation in captivity.

When Jesus was born, He was born of a woman, under the law (Gal. 4:4). He assumed a responsibility under law (Matt. 5:1) and to represent the nation in her covenant partnership (Matt. 3:15). When Jesus died, He bore the nation's guilt and sin as representative partner, so as "to give repentance to Israel and forgiveness of sins" (Acts 5:31). In addition, in His death, God the Father instituted a new covenant *for* Israel (Luke 22:20) through the mediation of God the Son. Thus, a covenant was instituted between God the Father and God the Son whereby a righteous basis was provided in His blood for God to unilaterally and unconditionally bless sinful man.

In the same vein, Jesus revealed His role as the True Vine (John 15:1–8). "There are numerous Old Testament passages which refer to Israel as a vine (Ps. 80:8–16; Isa. 5:1–7; Jer. 2:21; Ezek. 15:1–8; 17:5–10; 10:10–14; Hos. 10:1). The vine became symbolic of Israel and even appeared on some coins issued by the Maccabees. The Old Testament passages which use this symbol appear to regard Israel as faithless to Yahweh and/or the object of severe punishment" (*Net Bible,* 316). Israel was Yahweh's vine in the role of covenant partner. Christ as Israel's representative assumed the role in Israel's place and claimed to be the True Vine. Now disciples united to the life of the Vine are nourished and in that nourishment are fruitful in the Vine. In time, the church would not be a covenant people nor a covenant partner but an extension of Christ's presence on earth.

But in view of these dramatic events, how would the covenant be fulfilled? It is important to note that Jesus claimed to be the

True Vine as the representative of Israel, not as the replacement for Israel. As representative, Christ will enable Israel to fulfill her role as covenant partner (Exod. 19:4–6). But this will be fulfilled in the new covenant relationship instituted in Christ ("I will be their God and they will be My people" [Jer. 31:33], as compared to "I will take you as My people, and I will be your God" [Exod. 6:7]). Then these descendants of Abraham will realize the role determined at their election: "Through you all nations shall be blessed" (Gen. 12:3). Paul portrays this future reality in the image of the olive tree into which the natural branches will be engrafted again to be fruitful (Rom. 11:11–32).

Not only is the church not a covenant partner, it is not comprised of a covenant people because their relationship is circumscribed by God's *grace* rather than the terms of a covenant. To mention such an emphasis on grace often brings confusion, but it does not deny that every believer in every age has a relationship grounded in grace. Grace is always the basis of election as it was for Abraham or for David (Rom. 4:1–25). Likewise, grace is always an aspect of the forgiveness God provides for His own.

However, grace for the church is distinct because of the availability now made known through the finished work of Christ. It is grace revealed in Christ—in person (John 1:14) and in work (Rom. 4:5). Not only is it the ground of a believer's election but equal access is now open to all people. Gentiles without a national claim have the same access (Acts 10–11) as Jews whose national claim is in eclipse due to spiritual blindness (2 Cor. 3:14–16; 4:3–6).

Grace is not spelled out in terms of a covenant but in facets of a personal relationship with a gracious God. Prayer promises do not guarantee the answer to prayer but do invite believers to wait upon the graciousness of His answer. It is a relationship that is less like a contract and more like a handshake resting in personal trust.

As a result, the relationship between Israel and the church is more sharply distinguished. It is not that the church replaces Israel as the spiritual people of God, as in amillennial theology. Nor is it that the church is integrated with Israel as a covenant people, as in historic premillennial theology. Nor is it even that the church is added to Israel as God's covenant people in succession, as in progressive dispensationalism. Rather, the church appears as an unannounced mystery, based upon God's gracious desire to see all people come to be saved (1 Tim. 2:3). This is the position of traditional dispensationalism. The church emerges unexpectedly in history yet is blessed in Jesus, the Messiah promised to and for Israel.

Conclusion

Each generation and every tradition that sees the Bible as the basis of its confession can expect to face challenges to formerly accepted interpretations. That is, unless the tradition dies. Thus, a contention for what is true can be a mark of health. But Paul warns believers to pursue that contention in humility (2 Tim. 2:25–26). Such humility exhibits itself in a willingness to listen and to learn from other believers, while at the same time vigorously contending for what one believes to be the truth. In our contention, I want to express my appreciation for Darrell Bock's use of humor so that we do not take ourselves too seriously, yet at the same time we can forcefully advance what we believe to be true.

Chapter Notes

1. For a detailed discussion of the form of ancient covenants, see Moshe Weinfeld, *The Promise of the Land: The Inheritance of the Land of Canaan by the Israelites* (Berkeley: University of California Press, 1993), 222–64. He distinguishes between what he calls obligatory covenants (treaties) and promissory covenants (grants), comparing the forms of the agreements to other treaty types in the ancient Near East. The Abrahamic and Davidic covenants are "grant" type agreements, while the Mosaic covenant is a suzerain-vassal treaty. One other point should be made here. We do not discuss the so-called Palestinian covenant, because (1) there is no text that names such a covenant, and (2) the promise of land for Israel is part of the promise made to Abraham so that this so-called covenant does not promise anything new to make it a distinct promise. This point responds to an observation made in Charles C. Ryrie, *Dispensationalism* (Chicago: Moody, 1995), 163. The textual point annuls the important rhetorical question he raises about initial fulfillment of the Palestinian covenant. One final point needs attention. The Mosaic covenant's different form and role as an administrative covenant of obligation justifies its not being discussed as a covenant of promise. The actual relationship of the

Mosaic Law to the New Testament is quite complicated and beyond the scope of this essay. However, in relationship to promise, Paul makes the point that it is brought in alongside the promise with a temporary function and subsidiary role (Gal. 3:19).

2. It is important to note that the issues of covenant and kingdom are very interrelated. Ultimately, the promise to Abraham is a promise of God to reestablish His rule on the earth, a blessing that comes to the world through Israel and her king (i.e., Messiah). This means that the discussion of promise and messianic rule is inevitably a discussion about God's kingdom program. Now that rule has various phases and structural expressions (Israel, the church, millennial phases). Our point will be that the covenant scheme, linked together as it is to messianic presence and executive, ruling activity, indicates a fundamental unity in that kingdom program as it is realized in the two comings of the King *and his activity in the interim between them.* In other words, Israel and the church are distinct structures in God's program and should not be confused, but this does not mean that they work with entirely distinct promises and programs. (Texts such as Acts 2:14–39; 13:16–41; Rom. 1:1–7; 4; 16:25–27; Eph. 2:11–22; Heb. 1; 8–10; and 1 Peter 2 suggest otherwise with regard to *current* activity in the church by this promised messianic figure.) Seeing this unity is not to engage in "the fallacy" of "merging spheres of rule" since it is the biblical texts that associate Old Testament promises with the *current* activity of the Messiah Jesus. I respond here to the thoughtful critique of John F. Walvoord in *Issues in Dispensationalism,* eds. Wesley R. Willis and John R. Master (Chicago: Moody, 1994), 88–91. The question needs to be answered by more traditional dispensationalists: Why cite these Old Testament promise texts in association with these actions unless there was a connection? The traditional dispensational appeal to analogy understates what these texts are affirming in terms of the connection of promise and realization. An attempt to affirm that different spheres of rule exist is the imposition of a distinction where the text lacks one, suggesting that a defining principle has controlled how the New Testament text is read, as I noted in the essay on hermeneutics. For my response to Walvoord's request that I define kingdom more precisely, see "Why I am a dispensationalist with a Small 'd,'" in *JETS* 41, no. 3 (September 1998): 383–96.

3. This point is explicitly noted by a more traditional dispensationalist, John Witmer, *Immanuel: Experiencing Jesus as Man and God* (Nashville: Word, 1998), 120. His response to progressive dispensationalism is a good example of someone engaging our view textually and representing us fairly. Our objection to his critique resides in our fundamental point that the activity of the Davidic king according to promise and the details of new covenant fulfillment are inextricably linked in Scripture, even in the way they are tied together in the Old Testament. The most obvious example of their linkage comes in the remarks of John the Baptist in Luke 3:15–17, where he states that the way to know Messiah has come, is that He will baptize "with Spirit and fire." John, speaking like an Old Testament prophet, links messianic activity and the new covenant promise of the Spirit so tightly that to have one come means that the other is present as well. This linkage is treated as a united promise marking the arrival of the new era in the New Testament as Luke 24:43–49; Acts 1:3–8; 2:14–41; 10:44–45; 11:15–18 show. I would also challenge his attempt to argue that Melchizedekian priesthood is not a part of Davidic promise. When Jesus invokes Psalm 110:1 as a messianic text, He is invoking the whole psalm as Davidic, something Hebrews 1 also does. Just reading Hebrews in sequence shows that what is said in Hebrews 5 is built upon what has been said about his fulfilling kingship in Hebrews 1. As we hope to show, despite Witmer's claims otherwise, the text does not sustain the attempt to separate the activity of Jesus in distributing the Spirit from the *promised activity of the great Son of David, the Christ* (Gal. 3:14). *Even if it is the New Testament alone that makes this point explicitly, that still constitutes a biblical substantiation for the activity as promised, messianic, and Davidic.* Attempts to argue that a future realization in traditional dispensational terms involving national Israel form insuperable objections to this claim are no objection at all, because Scripture deals with the entirety of Christ's activity, both current and future, as a process of fulfillment. This process is evidenced by the fact that current activity is seen as part of what Scripture calls the "last days" or "the end of the ages," which are currently present (Heb. 1:1–2; Rom. 1:1–4; 1 Cor. 10:11; Acts 2:17), not to mention the many Christological fulfillment texts that argue that the Scripture addresses the whole of His career and the message of the church following it (Luke 24:43–49 and

Acts 26:15–23 are but two texts that discuss fulfillment surrounding Christ's current activity *and the church's message that came from it*). Even the concept of mystery is *not always* new revelation, but represents more detail about elements already revealed, as its use in Romans 16 shows, a point we covered in the essay on hermeneutics. The details on these points of New Testament correlation are found in two essays of mine, "The Son of David and the Saints' Task: The Hermeneutics of Initial Fulfillment," *BSac* 150 (1993): 458–78, and "Current Messianic Activity and Old Testament Davidic Promise: Dispensationalism, Hermeneutics, and New Testament Fulfillment," *TrinJ* 15ns (1994): 55–87. These essays fill out important, additional methodological and textual ground not covered in my initial treatment of fulfillment in *Dispensationalism, Israel, and the Church: A Search for Definition,* eds. Craig Blaising and Darrell Bock (Grand Rapids: Zondervan, 1992), 37–67. See nn. 20 and 34 below.

4. Note how the language of these texts echoes the command to all of mankind to be fruitful and multiply, showing how Israel is a microcosm of the command to all humanity in Genesis 1. This does indicate a connection between what God is doing with Israel and what He is doing with humanity as a whole. What He is doing for them, He will also do eventually for all.

5. Robert L. Saucy, *The Case for Progressive Dispensationalism: The Interface Between Dispensational and Non-Dispensational Theology* (Grand Rapids: Zondervan, 1993), 41.

6. Thomas McComiskey, *The Covenants of Promise: A Theology of the Old Testament Covenants* (Grand Rapids: Baker, 1985), 38–40.

7. William J. Dumbrell, *Covenant and Creation: A Theology of Old Testament Covenants* (Nashville: Nelson, 1984), 64–65.

8. H. W. Wolff, "The Kerygma of the Yahwist," *Int* 20 (1966): 137 n. 31; Dumbrell, *Covenant and Creation,* 71; and McComiskey, *The Covenants of Promise,* 57.

9. I do not have time to develop in detail the tracing of the land promise in the Old Testament. This is nicely done in McComiskey, *The Covenants of Promise,* 42–55. The concept of "rest" in the land, of Israel living in peace in the territory God gave her, is an important one in this testament. It is rooted in this promise of God to Abram on behalf of the nation. In this section, McComiskey also develops how the land promise is handled in the New Testament, how it retains

and expands its force as a territorial reference, an expansion that has parallel as well in Jewish tradition itself as Ecclesiasticus 44:20–21, Jubilees 32:19, and a later midrashic text in *Mekilta* (Lauterbach, 1:253) show. The Jubilees text reads, "I will give your seed the whole earth which is under heaven . . . and they shall then inherit the whole earth and possess it forever." The parallel to Matthew 5:5 is interesting to consider. The point is that when redemption comes on the earth for Israel and for all those properly related to God, then the restoration of their relationship and possession of the entire earth will be theirs to enjoy. Here is another case where the plan for Israel and the plan for humanity come together as the covenant serves both simultaneously. See also the remarks of Saucy in *The Case for Progressive Dispensationalism*, 50–57, which are parallel to McComiskey. Both McComiskey and Saucy note that the expansion of the scope of the promise in the New Testament does not annul the initial commitment God made to the nation. Here is a fundamental interpretive premise we argue for in a canonical reading. God can extend his promise, but He does not do so in such a way that what is originally promised is lost.

10. H. J. Kraus, *The People of God in the Old Testament* (New York: Association Press, 1958), 26–27.

11. Outside of Genesis, Israel's connection to Abraham is noted or alluded to a few times in the Old Testament (Ps. 49:7; Isa. 29:22; 41:8; 51:2; 63:16; Jer. 33:26; Mic. 7:20). Most of these references simply allude to the Abrahamic roots of the nation.

12. The details of this setting are noted by Dumbrell, *Covenant and Creation*, 127–41.

13. The parallel from 2 Chronicles 21:7 is particularly significant because the image of light ("a lamp to him and his sons forever") is present. The image of the "lamp . . . forever" highlights the presence of God's blessing and light (2 Sam. 21:17; 1 Kings 11:36; 15:4; 2 Kings 8:19; Prov. 13:9). The "grant" covenant is seen in language that says what the Lord promised to David (2 Sam. 7:28; 1 Kings 2:4, 24; 5:12; 8:20, 24–25, 56; 9:5; 2 Kings 8:19; 1 Chron. 17:26; 2 Chron. 1:9; 6:10, 15–16; 21:7). The conditional nature of the covenant relates to the blessing that comes on any individual Davidic king on the basis of his obedience or to the right to have a king on the throne at any particular time (1 Kings 6:12; 8:25; 2 Chron. 6:16; 1 Kings 9:4–9; 2 Chron. 7:17–22).

14. On this phrase, see McComiskey, *The Covenants of Promise,* 21–24.

15. McComiskey, *The Covenants of Promise,* p. 23. The note in the NKJV (p. 519) seems to go a similar direction, stating that "God has now extended the promise concerning David's dynasty far into the future. All of human history leads inevitably to the rule of Christ on earth. This is its destiny, its prophetic fulfillment, the final meaning of all history." See also Saucy, *The Case for Progressive Dispensationalism,* 64–65.

16. *TDOT,* 1974 ed., s.v. "אֲבְדְּהֲמ," by Ronald E. Clements, 56.

17. Some wish to contend whether Davidic kings ever served as priests of a non-Aaronic order and thus whether Psalm 110 is about Davidic kings or the Messiah alone. This is a difficult question to resolve. Nonetheless, there is significant evidence of a non-Aaronic, priestly role for David and Solomon and other Davidic kings related not to the daily operation of the cult but to the oversight of it in accordance with instructions David gave. (See 1 Chron. 16:4–6; 37–39; 1 Kings 8:22–66; 2 Chron. 23:18; 29:25–30; 35:2–6; Ezra 3:10; Neh. 12:24; and Eugene Merrill, *Kingdom of Priests: A History of Old Testament Israel* [Grand Rapids: Baker, 1987], 265–67, 274–76, 295–96.) Merrill explicitly connects Psalms 2 and 110 with Davidic promise and hope. In one sense, determining whether the psalm is about a son of David or the ultimate Son of David is irrelevant, because either way it expresses the hope of what Davidic kingship one day will involve. For another defense of the Davidic background of Psalm 110, see Herbert W. Bateman, "Psalm 110:1 and the New Testament," *BSac* 149 (1992): 438–53 and his *Early Jewish Hermeneutics and Hebrews 1:5–13: The Impact of Early Jewish Exegesis on the Interpretation of a Significant New Testament Passage* (New York, Peter Lang, 1997), 175–76. The invocation of an oath, like the decree of Psalm 2:7, is the language of covenant invocation; see Craig Blaising and Darrell Bock, *Progressive Dispensationalism,* 162. To present this king as seated on a throne and discuss current activity in association with it is to discuss aspects of this king's authority and rule. See note 34 below.

18. It is texts like this one emerging out of the disaster of the Exile that suggest that the covenant theologians who deny a future for ethnic, national Israel are wrong. The very way in which this text sets up the redemption of *this particular people and nation* as a model for God's name, faithfulness, and relationship to His people means

that this specific entity also has a guaranteed future in the way described here. Thus, whatever partial fulfillment of covenant promise exists in Israel's history (as it relates to national security, peace, and the land) does not nullify this hope. There are such significant points of partial fulfillment in Israel's history, but they do not remove the promise made here (after all those points of fulfillment). This means that Israel will again come to life and have the totality of redemption always expected for her. This point is most emphatically and eloquently made by Alva J. McClain, *The Greatness of the Kingdom: An Inductive Study of the Kingdom of God* (Winona Lake: BMH Books, 1974), 149–50 (emphasis ours). He says, "Attempts have been made, however, to deny the historical continuity of the Israel of the future kingdom with Israel of Old Testament history. Two hermeneutical schemes have been devised to implement this denial: first, certain of the Old Testament promises to Israel are treated as having been fulfilled in the historic return of the exiles from the Babylonian captivity; and second, those prophetic promises which cannot be thus handled are stripped down to a tenuous "spiritual" content and transferred to another "Israel" *having no genuine nexus with the historical nation.* Such attempts to eviscerate the promises of God to the Israel of history cannot be sustained in the face of biblical history." He then goes on to defend his point with seven reasons (pp. 150–52).

19. I have not developed, as I could have, the entire servant portrait as a part of Davidic promise. This would bring in a whole series of texts from Isaiah 40; 42; 49; 52:13–53:12; and possibly 61:1–4. They would add a dimension of suffering to the expectation. I have not included these texts because although they look eventually to one regal figure who is the embodiment of the nation, her need, rule, and hope, no servant text makes an explicit connection to Davidic themes and covenant concepts. The argument from these texts for its connection to Davidic, messianic hope is strictly conceptual and ultimately canonical, as it is Jesus' and the New Testament's invocation of these themes that makes them canonically relevant. Our story is proceeding in canonical order and *is designed to illustrate how the story and promises are deepened and connected as revelation proceeds.* Thus, the exclusion of the servant theme from a Davidic or ideal king heading at this point in the sequence is strictly historically and methodologically driven. Interestingly,

no dispensationalist debates the relevance of these servant of the Lord themes for messianism or for the hope of Israel as well, nor does anyone doubt that there are elements fulfilled in the first coming of Jesus, *even though there are elements of the glorification of the servant related to the return of Christ and the completion of His program for Israel.* Thus, the question could be posed, why include some elements of the servant themes as already realized, when elements related to the nation are still not yet fully realized? Or to flip the question around, why is it all right to read the servant texts in this "already-not yet" way but not other categories of promise such as those made in the Davidic covenant? Progressives argue that this hermeneutical inconsistency is a major problem for more traditional approaches and shows that their way of correlating these promise texts needed revision. That revision is what resulted in the emphases that progressive dispensationalism possessed, including the affirmation of aspects of realization of Davidic hope in this current, church era. For a consideration of these texts, see McComiskey, *The Covenants of Promise,* 31–35. See also n. 20 below.

20. It is in this fundamental dimension of the promise that we see the definition of the rule of God and of this promised king, as well as the ultimately unified nature of kingdom hope. It is here as well that our definition of rule and reigning will differ from that of my fellow progressive dispensationalist, Robert Saucy. His definition of rule includes the idea of the demonstration of coercive authority, something Jesus will not exercise until His return. Thus, he argues that Jesus has fulfilled elements of the Davidic promise but not those that involve His reigning *(The Case for Progressive Dispensationalism* [pp. 67–80]). I would simply contend that his definition is too narrow (as he would argue that mine is too broad). I will contend in the New Testament section that Jesus being seated at the right hand of God and distributing the promised Spirit, giving forgiveness or providing justification are acts of executive rule in providing the means of righteousness for God's people that is part of the exercise of Davidic messianic blessing and hope (Acts 2:14–39; 13:16–41; 15:12–21; 26:12–23; Gal. 3 [esp. vv. 13–14]; Heb. 1; Rev. 1:1–7). As such, they represent aspects of realization of Davidic *regal* hope and rule. See also n. 34 below and n. 3 above.

21. I have chosen to discuss the servant passages here because although the connection of the servant to the promise of David is not explicit and the movement between a reference to the nation and an individual in the songs is complicated, the eschatological connection of these texts with the nation's hope is the context of the original elements of this promise. It is not debated among dispensationalists that the servant is ultimately a messianic image. Nor is it contested that the texts originally appear in contexts that focus on the nation. Thus, it is appropriate to mention these texts within a discussion of the new covenant hope of peace and relationship with God that the new covenant represents.

22. Dumbrell, *Covenant and Creation*, 185–99.

23. In this section I will note in subsequent endnotes how new covenant themes are invoked in the New Testament because we have now surveyed all of the covenant texts. I do this mainly out of consideration of space, which will prevent me from noting in any detail all of the New Testament allusions to this category of texts. The final New Testament section of this essay can then concentrate on the more debated aspect of Davidic hope, though, as we shall see, what often happens in the New Testament is that references to the various covenants cluster together in one context.

24. As Saucy correctly states, "The fact that the prophetic statements are addressed only to Israel cannot logically be understood to *exclude* others from participating even though they are not a part of Israel" (emphasis his) (*A Case for Progressive Dispensationalism*, 114).

25. The image of a husband-wife relationship is fundamental for understanding God's relationship to His people. It is at the core of God's remarks in Hosea and His imagery of His relationship to Israel in Ezekiel 16. The repetition of the imagery in Ephesians 5:22–33 shows a fundamental unity in God's relationship to His people that encompasses both Israel and the church. How this move can be made is a burden of the New Testament section of this essay.

26. Our summary largely follows McComiskey, *The Covenants of Promise*, 83–89.

27. Here is a passage to which Jesus certainly alluded in John 3 in His discussion with Nicodemus in mentioning being born from above. It is the fundamental gospel imagery of regeneration that the New Testament presents from this hope.

28. Note the sequence in Ephesians 1:7–14, where redemption through

the forgiveness of sins is an ongoing state that emerges as those who believe (including Gentiles) receive the promised Spirit as a down payment/guarantee on their inheritance (in other words, the transaction has begun to be realized and awaits the remaining elements of its consummation). This is also why Paul calls himself the minister of a new covenant of the Spirit in contrast to the written code of Moses recorded on stone as he addresses the mostly Gentile Corinthians (2 Cor. 3). This new covenant cannot be "a" new covenant separate from Jeremiah, as has been argued as recently as this decade by some dispensationalists (see Ryrie, *Dispensationalism,* 172; and John Master, in *Issues in Dispensationalism,* 100–2). Ryrie's attempted distinction between payment, which is made, and fulfillment, which apparently is yet to come, ignores the fact that forgiveness *is an attained benefit now* as a result of this act of Jesus The imagery in 2 Corinthians is parallel to Jeremiah in its contrast with the Mosaic, as well as in its language of the Spirit on the heart, fusing Ezekiel 36 with Jeremiah 31 (2 Cor. 3:3, 6–7). In addition, Paul's description of the resulting period as a "ministry of righteousness" fuses images seen in the transforming character of the covenant with the ethical character of what the promised king's presence would bring, showing the connection of Davidic hope and new covenant hope. This is why Paul can say that in his ministry is revealed "the light of the *knowledge* of the glory of God in the face of Christ." This is yet another fusion of Davidic and new covenant imagery (Isa. 9–11). One final text is the well-known Hebrews 8–10, where the very cancellation of the need for sacrifice is made from the fact that the new covenant has come (note the perfect tense in Heb. 10:14). The very reason the author of Hebrews argues for a nonreturn to sacrifices of the Mosaic order for sin is because the sacrifices of the Mosaic covenant are no longer valid now that Christ has made his once-for-all sacrifice in fulfillment of new covenant promise (actually cited in 10:14–18). Hebrews closes with the comment after citing the provision for forgiveness of sins in Jeremiah that "where there *is* forgiveness of these (i.e., sins), there *is* no longer any offering for sin." The verbs to be supplied in the understood construction of v. 18 are clearly present tense in light of what the author is contending as the current application. More accurate is the remark by Ralph Alexander in *Israel, the Land and the People,* ed. H. Wayne House (Grand Rapids: Kregel, 1998), 197. He says, "When 2 Corinthians 3, Acts 2, and Hebrews 7:22; 8:6–13; 9:15; 12:24 are compared with the prophecies of Joel 2:28–29; Jeremiah 31:31–34; and Ezekiel 36:26–27, it becomes evident that the new covenant was instituted with the death of Christ on the cross and the outpouring of the Spirit in Acts 2. The full appropriation of this new covenant by the nation of Israel is still future, as argued by Jeremiah 31. But for both Israelite and Gentile believers since the time of Christ's sacrifice for sin, the new covenant has become the covenant under which they live in covenant relationship with God." (See also his remarks on Rom. 11:27 and Eph. 2:11–13 on p. 198.) Here is initial and ultimate fulfillment as we would argue for it. For a good critic of the "multiple covenants" view of Masters and his claim that the new covenant is "a new covenant" see Paul R. Thorsell, "The Spirit in the Present Age: Preliminary Fulfillment of the Predictive New Covenant According to Paul," *JETS* 41 (1998): 397–413. For the issue of an anarthrous reference to eschatological covenant as common in the LXX see his page 406 n. 31. Jeremiah 38:31 LXX (= Jer. 31:31 Eng.) is an anarthrous reference to "the new covenant."

29. The issue of the suffering of the servant is not explicitly tied to this covenant language, yet it is an example of how a concept tied to an ultimate realization is tied to the package of divine activity. It is also a part of the activity of realization. No one debates that behind the work of glory yet to come stands the work of suffering already undertaken. That "already-not yet" is one that applies to Israel and to the nations. The question still begs to be answered, if other fundamental concepts of the plan of salvation are "already-not yet," then why not those involving the structures of covenant and salvation? One other point needs treatment. Numerous texts refer to "David" coming in the future. Ezekiel 37:24 is a good example and refers to the *one shepherd* who will rule. This focus on oneness means that the point is not about the original David, but a second David of the fulfillment of promise, whom the New Testament reveals to be Jesus Christ.

30. Some more traditional dispensationalists give John a special place among the Gospels, as this gospel is seen as not being as influenced by the perspective of the law as the synoptics are. Thus, it is particularly significant that this image appears in this gospel.

31. For a consideration of these issues, see W. Hall Harris, "A Theology of John's Writings," in *A Biblical Theology of the New Testament* (Chicago: Moody, 1994), 196–201, 230–33, 235–37.

32. The idea of a parenthesis is legitimate only to the extent that it refers to the progress of the program as it relates to the positive involvement of the majority of the nation. It is here that Daniel's seventy weeks belongs, a text, in light of the New Testament, that pictures a break. Progressives read this text as more traditional dispensationalists read it.

33. The hermeneutics of this important passage is the burden of my essay "The Son of David and the Saints' Task: The Hermeneutics of Initial Fulfillment," *BSac* 150 (1993): 458–78.

34. A discussion among progressive dispensationalists is whether all of this activity and display of titles represents evidence of Jesus' current reign. Though I regard this as a minor point, because all progressives agree about some fulfillment of Davidic promise today, it is worth clarifying my argument for a current reign in light of the critique by Mark Saucy, *The Kingdom of God in the Teaching of Jesus* (Dallas: Word, 1997), 343–47. Saucy has erred with regard to the lexical biblical data when he claims in n. 104 that *basileia* language is not applied to the present function of Christ. Revelation 1:5 uses *ho archōn*, a synonym for "king." The verse describes Jesus' current status as He addresses the churches as the one who has and is exercising this authority in writing the church. The reference is to Psalm 89 and His status as the "ruler of the kings." This term is in the semantic range, Saucy claimed; he provides no examples. In addition, he begs the question more than once. (1) He treats 1 Corinthians 15:24–25 as an exception (even though it uses the verb form of *basileuō*). (2) He falls into a major semantic error in claiming that terms for ruling in the semantic field are not used when he ignores the presence of the term *Christ*, which is another way (a Jewish way, not Greek) to say *king* (i.e., the anointed Messiah). (3) He also begs the question again when he argues that the nouns *shepherd, Lord,* and the *exalted Christ's* current leadership as head over the church (and the creation, including evil cosmic forces, Eph. 1:22–23) do not count as evidence for reigning, though it does count for evidence of messianic activity. This means that Saucy's argument can work only if it excludes or explains away significant pieces of evidence. Saucy is right to note that this current reign is not where

emphasis is placed in the biblical use of the concept of Christ's rule and that a key element of this rule eventually is the Lord's corule with the saints. Ultimately, the hope is of a totally exercised authority, including the submission of all enemies. Nonetheless, the biblical terminology and conceptual field (even the name Christ) show that the authority of Jesus is received now (Matt. 28:18–20, contra his explanation of the parable in Luke 19) and involves the exercise of that authority at certain key soteriological points. Jesus' executive authority in a variety of areas as shown in this listing indicates that His activity is messianic and thus regal, not merely high priestly, as Saucy claims. If it is messianic and Davidic, then it is regal and indicates initial manifestations of Jesus' rule. In fact, even in Hebrews, the high priestly ministry is part of a rule as king-son, as the introductory Hebrews 1 shows, citing a series of regal Davidic promise texts. This messianic sonship the author develops to connect to the priesthood later in the book. The discussion of texts below from Psalm 110:1 under theme 15 shows that more than priestly intercession is in view for Christ's executive authority (contra Saucy, p. 345). This activity includes forgiveness and the giving of the Spirit as a messianic act, a major eschatological act of the new era of fulfillment. To say that intercession is the essence of current ministry, as Saucy does, is not to say that it is the only dimension of current ministry. Note that Saucy's study is a fine one, except for this detail. See also nn. 3, 17, and 20 above.

35. An earlier addition of this argument treating these linkages appears in my "Current Messianic Activity and Old Testament Davidic Promise," 55–87.

36. For a discussion of the debate about millennial eschatology, including discussions of premillennialism, amillennialism, and postmillennialism, see Darrell L. Bock, ed., *Three Views of the Millennium and Beyond* (Grand Rapids: Zondervan, 1999). The presentation of premillennialism in this volume is by Craig Blaising, who is a well-known progressive dispensationalist. His essay highlights what remains to be fulfilled, including much for national Israel.

PART THREE

ISRAEL AND
THE CHURCH

CHAPTER SIX

Israel and the Church of a Traditional Dispensationalist

Stanley D. Toussaint
with response by J. Lanier Burns

Importance of the Subject

In his classic work *Dispensationalism Today,* Ryrie sets forth a threefold *sine qua non* of dispensationalism—a distinction between Israel and the church, a literal hermeneutic, and the glory of God as His purpose on earth.[1] Of these three, undoubtedly the most important is the distinction between Israel and the church. Ryrie calls this "the most basic theological test of whether or not a man is a dispensationalist."[2] He calls it the "essence of dispensationalism."[3] He goes so far as to say, "The nature of the church is a crucial point of difference between dispensationalism and other doctrinal viewpoints. Indeed, ecclesiology, or the doctrine of the church, is the touchstone of dispensationalism."[4] All dispensationalists would agree that these statements are true. However, the degree of the difference has been and still is a matter of debate. If the church and Israel become so blurred in dispensationalism that there is no separation between them, dispensationalism will become as extinct as the pitied dodo bird.

Changes in Viewpoint

In the original form of Darby's dispensationalism, the line drawn between Israel and the church was heavy, dark, and broad. According to Darby, the promises to the church are spiritual and heavenly whereas those to Israel and the nations are earthly. The Tribulation and the Millennium do not concern the church for those prophecies are earthly. This distinction in Darby's theology has been summarized succinctly and accurately by Blaising.[5] In brief, in classical dispensationalism the Jews are God's earthly people and the church is God's heavenly people. This dualism was maintained by dispensationalists for more than a hundred years by men such as Gaebelein, Larkin, Scofield, and Chafer.

Gaebelein, whose commentary on Matthew was published in 1910, wrote that the promises to Israel are "all earthly" and then asserted, "The church, however, is something entirely different. The hope of the church, the place of the church, the calling of the church, the destiny of the church, the reigning and the ruling of the church is not earthly, but it is heavenly."[6] In 1920 Larkin wrote, "Again the 'wife' (Israel) is to reside in the earthly Jerusalem during the Millennium, while the 'Bride' (the Church) will reside in the New Jerusalem."[7]

C. I. Scofield, whose annotated Bible first published in 1909 influenced so many both pro and con regarding dispensationalism, made a distinction between God's purposes for Israel and the church. In the train of his predecessors, he believed that God's goal was earthly for Israel and spiritual for the church.[8] *The New Scofield Reference Bible* is not as clear in its statements although it implies an earthly destiny for Israel.[9]

Lewis Sperry Chafer, a founding father and the first president of Dallas Theological Seminary, was very influential in making a division between God's earthly purpose for Israel and His heavenly purpose for the church. Concerning Israel he wrote, "The particular point in view here is the fact that all her blessings, her riches both temporal and spiritual, become her portion when she enters the land. This is the heart of Old Testament prediction. Israel can never be blessed apart from her land."[10] He draws a sharp line between God's purposes for Israel and those for the church: "Every covenant, promise, and provision for Israel is earthly, and they continue as a nation with the earth when it is created new. Every covenant or promise for the church is for a heavenly reality, and she continues in heavenly citizenship when the heavens are recreated."[11] Such statements can be found throughout Chafer's *Systematic Theology.*

With Ryrie's *Dispensationalism Today,* published in 1965, a definite shift is seen, a revisionism that had been in process for some ten or fifteen years. Blaising notes, "It is amazing that in the writings of Walvoord, Pentecost, Ryrie, and McClain published in the 1950s and 1960s, the heavenly/earthly dualistic language is gone. A distinction between Israel and the church is vigorously asserted and all the theological structures of distinction are present except that the eternal destinies of the two peoples share the same sphere. Consequently the heavenly/earthly descriptions are dropped. Thus is begun a slow movement away from the scholastic, classic, absolute distinction found from Darby to Chafer. . . ."[12]

Walvoord, Pentecost, Ryrie, and McClain take various positions as to the destinies of Israel and the church. Pentecost believes that during the Millennium saved Jews and Gentiles who survive the Tribulation will inherit Christ's kingdom on earth. The Jews will have prominence in the kingdom as they enter into their blessings promised in the Old Testament. The resurrected saints of both Testaments will inhabit the heavenly Jerusalem from which the Lord and the saints will rule during the Millennium. This heavenly Jerusalem will be in the air over the earth. During eternity, the New Jerusalem will be on earth to be inhabited by God's saints while Israel, all of whom will have glorified bodies, reside on the purged earth.[13]

Sauer believes that all saved—resurrected and nonresurrected—will be on earth during the Millennium and then in eternity will be inhabitants of the New Jerusalem on a renovated earth.[14] Interestingly, Ice and Demy state, "Scripture is not clear as to whether Israel, the church, and other believer groups will maintain their distinctions throughout eternity."[15]

Fruchtenbaum sees the church ruling with Christ over Gentiles during the Millennium with Israel as the leading nation, but then projects that the New Jerusalem on a new earth will be the eternal abode of all the redeemed.[16] McClain believes that the resurrected saints will rule with Christ during the Millennium but in the eternal, refurbished earth the church will have a special place in the

New Jerusalem. He wrote, "The members of the Church will be its honored citizens (Phil. 3:20 asv). But the saved of all ages will have free access to its glories and benefits (Rev. 21:24–26)."[17]

Progressive dispensationalism[18] has taken a new tack. It still makes something of a difference between Israel and the church,[19] but that distinction is not nearly as sharp. Those who hold to this position believe that the promised kingdom has already begun; progressive dispensationalists assert that the Old Testament covenants and promises have had a beginning, a partial fulfillment in the church, but will have their ultimate fulfillment in the Millennium and eternity.[20] Their view of the kingdom is similar to Ladd's; that is, progressive dispensationalists believe that the kingdom was present when Christ ministered on earth[21] but His reign was not initiated until His ascension. At that time He took His seat on the throne of David.[22] Thus, the kingdom has been inaugurated but will come in its fullness only in the millennium and eternity.[23] The terms "already-not yet" punctuate their discussion. Undoubtedly this does represent a shift from classical and revised dispensationalism. For progressive dispensationalists, the primary distinction between Israel and the church is found in the Old Testament covenants, promises, and prophecies. These were made with and spoken to Israel. Even though the Davidic kingdom has already been inaugurated, according to this view, the church has been brought into Jewish blessings today. It is alleged that although the church may be called "the new Israel,"[24] national ethnic Israel will yet see the fulfillment of its promised blessings in God's future program. In this they see a distinction between the church and Israel because the covenants— Abrahamic, Davidic, and new—were given to Israel.

The Kingdom: A Crucial Issue

Of great importance in this whole discussion of progressive dispensationalism is the concept of an inaugurated kingdom. Without the doctrine of an inaugurated kingdom, the cohesion of that entire system is basically destroyed. In addition, the concept of an inaugurated kingdom tends to lend itself to replacement theology, as is seen in the church being called "the new Israel," as noted above.

All dispensationalists agree that the prophesied kingdom of the Old Testament is a major theme of the Scriptures. Kenneth Barker says that this is the major motif of the Bible.[25] In fact, this is such a dominant idea in progressive dispensationalism that Ryrie suggests that it more aptly may be called "revised," "reconstructed," "new," or "kingdom" dispensationalism.[26] According to progressive dispensationalists, because the promised kingdom has been inaugurated, the church is the first stage of the millennial kingdom. Is this the New Testament sense of the kingdom covenanted and prophesied in the Old Testament? Has that kingdom been inaugurated? To these questions progressive dispensationalists would answer, "Yes."

The viewpoint presented in this chapter is neither new nor novel; however, it is not held by the majority of dispensationalists in either the classical or revised camps. It certainly is not a tenet of progressive dispensationalism for it is totally contradictory to that system. The doctrine propounded here holds to a consistent meaning of *kingdom* in the New Testament. This means that the term *kingdom* always refers to the promised yet future fulfillment of Israel's Old Testament covenants, promises, and prophecies. The kingdom was not present when Christ Jesus was here and it is not here even in "mystery form" in this church age. It is totally future, awaiting fulfillment in the Millennium and eternity. Although this is not the normative view of dispensationalism, it does bear up under careful exegetical scrutiny.

The Kingdom in the Early Chapters of the Gospels

In dealing with this subject, Blaising very ably defends the idea that the gospel narratives from the preconception of Christ, to His birth, to His worship by the magi, to His baptism by John the Baptist, to John's warning of coming judgment are related to the kingdom envisioned in the Old Testament. Interestingly, Blaising says only that at this point the kingdom was near.[27] It is not without significance that Blaising acknowledges John's emphasis on judgment *preceding* the coming of the kingdom. He states, "The kingdom itself is understood in the terms of Old Testament prophecy. Its coming would be marked by judgment, a Day of the Lord."[28] This, of course, causes one to ask, "If the kingdom began in the ministry of Christ, where is the prophesied judgment in the Gospels? Were the Old Testament prophets and John incorrect in their message?" Concerning John the Baptist, Blaising states, "Like the earlier prophets, he expected the kingdom to come in a revelation of judgment and wrath."[29] This is exactly what dispensationalists of every kind have taught about the Millennium; it is preceded by judgment! After the prophesied judgment, the kingdom will come.

The Proclamation of John the Baptist and Jesus Christ

Both John the Baptist and Christ Jesus pronounced the kingdom as being at hand (cf. Matt. 3:2, 4:17; Mark 1:15). This same message was proclaimed by the Twelve (Matt. 10:7) and the seventy (Luke 10:9, 11). In every announcement, the verb ἤγγικεν is used. Blaising consistently translates it as "near" or "at hand." However, he also states that the kingdom was present in the person of Jesus when He was ministering on earth.[30] To buttress his viewpoint he uses Matthew 11:12; 12:28 (Luke 11:20) and Luke 17.21.[31] These verses will be discussed later. Bock, however, argues that the clause "The kingdom has drawn near," means "here" in the sense of "arrival."[32] However, none of the illustrations used by Bock support the meaning of arrival. In discussing the meaning of the verb ἤγγικεν, Lane concludes, "The linguistic objections to the proposed rendering 'has come' are weighty, and it is better to translate 'has come near.'"[33] Note that the Old Testament uses קָרוֹב, an adjective meaning "near," sometimes not in the sense of proximity but with the idea of imminence, of something impending. This is especially true of passages pronouncing the nearness of the Day of the Lord (Isa. 13:6; Ezek. 30:3; Joel 1:15; 2:1; 3:14; Obad. 15; Zeph. 1:7, 14). It is best to conclude that the kingdom was not proclaimed as being present by John the Baptist, the Lord, the Twelve, or the seventy, but only as being in a condition of nearness.

The Lord and the Message of the Kingdom

It is often alleged that the Lord in several passages said that the kingdom had arrived. One such interpretation is made by Blaising concerning Matthew 11:12.[34] He argues that the kingdom was present because it suffered violence from the days of John the Baptist until that very moment. He contends that the kingdom had to be present for it to be treated so harshly. However, this is not necessarily true. The preceding verse says, "Truly I say to you, among those born of women there has not arisen anyone greater than John the Baptist; yet he who is least in the kingdom of heaven is greater than he" (Matt. 11:11 NASB). The same term *kingdom of heaven* occurs in both verses 11 and 12, a fact that Blaising recognizes. He also acknowledges the obvious, that in verse 11 "the kingdom of heaven is a future reality."[35] But then he argues the same expression, "the kingdom of heaven," in verse 12 refers to some form of the kingdom then present. It would be far better to seek for a more consistent meaning of the phrase. If it is future in verse 11, its meaning most probably is future in verse 12.

The question then may be asked, "How can the future kingdom 'suffer violence' if it was not present during the Lord's ministry on earth?" The explanation is found in a parallel passage, Luke 16:16 (NASB), "The Law and the Prophets were proclaimed until John; since then the kingdom is preached, and everyone is forcing his way into it." The translation and meaning of the last clause of Luke 16:16 is debated, but whatever interpretation is given to it, the idea of a violent response to the message is clear. The proclamation of the future kingdom of heaven in Matthew 11:12 was suffering violence at the hands of evil men in that the message of the kingdom was being so violently rejected. Luke's gospel emphasizes the preaching of the message, and Matthew's the response to it. The message was being violently rejected. That this is the correct meaning is seen in the following clause, an admittedly difficult saying, "Violent men take it by force." Concerning Matthew 11:12, Nigel Turner writes, "The words of Jesus are still puzzling but we need have no doubt that St. Matthew understood him to mean that the kingdom was now facing opposition."[36] This is true; the kingdom was facing opposition because the message was being rejected.[37] This interpretation is confirmed by the Lord's own explanation in Matthew 11:16–19, where He compares that generation of Jews to children in the marketplace who could not be pleased by either the asceticism of John or the ministry methods of the Lord Jesus. Matthew 11:12 can hardly be used to say that the kingdom was present during the Lord's earthly ministry.

Another passage used by Blaising to show the presence of the kingdom during the Lord's earthly ministry is Matthew 12:28: "But if I cast out demons by the Spirit of God, then the kingdom of God has come upon you." In commenting on this verse he writes,

"The kingdom of God is present (it *has* come) by virtue of the fact that He is exorcising demons by the power of the Holy Spirit. . . . The fact that the King Himself is there, acting in the power of the Spirit, forms a basis for speaking of the presence of the eschatological kingdom."[38] The question revolves around the meaning of the verb *has come* (ἔφθασεν). The same verb with the identical following prepositional construction occurs in Luke 11:20: "But if I cast out demons by the finger of God, then the kingdom of God has come upon you." After a lengthy discussion of the verb φθάνω, A. J. Mattill Jr. summarizes his findings by noting that there are three basic meanings of φθάνω.

1. *Phthano* = precede, come before, come first, reach before, come sooner, go ahead of. . . .
2. *Phthano* = reach, arrive at, attain, just arrive, come up to, overtake, come into contact. . . .
3. *Phthano* = come near, come close, draw near, approach, advance toward, be about to. . . . But neither of the translations sanctioned by 2) bare contact, or by 3) imminent contact, gives support to the thesis of realized eschatology that for Luke the kingdom is a present process at work in this age on this earth.[39]

Mattill goes on to say that even if his research on the meaning of φθάνω is faulty, the aorist could be taken as a prophetic past tense.[40] The idea then would be the future coming of the kingdom is viewed as being so certain that the kingdom is looked upon as having already arrived. In other words, the normal translation of the verb still does not vindicate inaugurated eschatology. That the kingdom had not yet arrived is implied in Matthew 12:29, the verse that follows the Lord's statement regarding the approach of the kingdom seen in His exorcism. "Or how can anyone enter the strong man's house and carry off his property, unless he first binds the strong man? And then he will plunder his house" (Matt. 12:29). Satan is not yet bound and Christ has not yet taken possession of the "strong man's house."

Perhaps the passage most often used to support the idea that Christ said the kingdom was present during His earthly ministry is Luke 17:20–21 (NASB): "Now having been questioned by the Pharisees as to when the kingdom of God was coming, He answered them and said, 'The kingdom of God is not coming with signs to be observed; nor will they say, "Look, here it is! Or, "There it is!" For behold, the kingdom of God is in your midst.'" Concerning this passage Blaising writes, "He is in their midst, the very King of the kingdom. There is no greater sign of the kingdom than Himself, for in fact all other signs point to Him. . . . But for our purposes, we note that His presence at that very time was the occasion for speaking of the kingdom being *present*."[41]

The Authorized Version, better known as the King James Version, gave impetus to the idea of a spiritual kingdom in the hearts of individuals by translating ἐντὸς ὑμῶν as "within you," "the kingdom of God is within you." Many scholars have abandoned this idea because the Lord was speaking to Pharisees. Certainly the kingdom was not in the hearts of these people who so bitterly opposed Him. Furthermore, the Lord Jesus never spoke of the kingdom entering people; He only said that people will enter the kingdom. The phrase ἐντὸς ὑμῶν is more commonly taken to mean "among you" or "in your midst." The present tense of the verb is used to say that the kingdom was then in the midst of the people in the person of the King, the Lord Jesus. If this position is taken, it becomes a potent argument for saying that the kingdom was indeed present in Christ's presence during the Lord's earthly ministry. However, there is another interpretation that fits the context far more suitably.

The best way to take the words of the Lord Jesus in Luke 17:21 is to say that His return with His kingdom would not be gradual so that it can be observed in a slow metamorphosis, but it will be so sudden that it will be said of the kingdom, "Lo, it is in your midst." This interpretation is vindicated by a number of factors.

The Pharisees had inquired about when the promised eschatological kingdom was going to come (v. 20). To this question the Lord answered, "The kingdom of God is not coming with signs to be observed." The clause "signs to be observed" translates one noun, παρατήρησις, which occurs only here in the New Testament and basically means "observation." The translation "with signs to be observed" is a bit of a paraphrase or interpretation. The verbal form of the noun is found in Mark 3:2; Luke 6:7, 14:1, 20:20; Acts 9:24; and Galatians 4:10. This verb basically means to observe or watch carefully, closely. What, then, does the noun παρατηρήσις mean? Bock summarizes four views.[42]

First, it means "legal observation" in the sense that if one observes or maintains a certain level of righteousness, the kingdom will come. Christ Jesus would be denying this. Second, it means visibly. Christ then would be denying a visible manifestation of the kingdom. Third, it describes Israel's keeping or observing of the Passover. If this is the meaning, the Lord Jesus would be saying that the kingdom will not come by observing the Passover. Fourth, it refers to signs of the coming of the kingdom. Bock takes this view, "Most likely παρατηρήσις alludes to general apocalyptic signs, so prevalent in early Jewish eschatological speculation, including the desire to calculate the kingdom's arrival by what is seen. . . ."[43] Bock then would agree with the translation of the New American Standard Version.

However, there is a fifth view as to the significance of παρατηρήσις. This noun, which does not occur in the LXX, was used in the Greek world of observations made by scientists and physicians.[44] It looked at "empirical 'observation' as distinct from logical deductions."[45] The Lord is saying that the kingdom will appear so rapidly that its coming will not be able to be observed. It will be no gradual development as can be seen by scientific observation; it will be cataclysmic and sudden. This is supported by verse 21, "Nor will they say, 'Look, here it is!' or 'There it is!' For behold, the kingdom of God is in your midst." Verse 24 fits this interpretation as well. "For just as the lightning, when it flashes out of one part of the sky, shines to the other part of the sky, so will the Son of Man be in His day."

The present tense of *is* in the clause "the kingdom of God is in your midst," in verse 21 is no problem; it is futuristic in its significance, a common enough phenomenon.[46] That it should be taken as a futuristic present meaning "will be" is supported by the future tense of "nor will they say" in the same verse. Furthermore, the two occurrences of ἔρχεται ("comes") in the present tense in verse 20 look ahead to that future apocalypse. In addition, the immediately following verses describe the return of the Son of Man.

That verse 21 should be taken in a future sense is further seen in its parallel with verse 23. Verse 23 is describing the words of false teachers who will say that the Messiah can be seen "there" or "here." Those teachers will be erroneous because when the Son of Man comes the next time, He will arrive with His kingdom as suddenly and visibly as a huge bolt of lightning that flashes from horizon to horizon. Then "the kingdom of God will be in the midst" of humanity. It will be as cataclysmic as the flood in Noah's day and the fire and brimstone on Sodom in Lot's time (vv. 26–30).

The demonstrative particle ἰδού ("lo, behold") is used like the Hebrew הִנֵּה to enliven a narrative and often to point to something new. At the same time it may emphasize the importance of a statement.[47] So it is used here. The Lord Jesus, then, is not saying that the kingdom was present when He ministered on earth. Rather, He said that the kingdom does not come gradually so that its coming can be observed as in a scientific experiment so one can say that it is here or there, but "Behold, the kingdom of God will be in your midst '*suddenly.*'" In reality, Luke 17:21 becomes a potent apologetic for the future coming of the kingdom.

The Kingdom in the Parables of the Lord

It is often alleged that the Lord predicted a form of the kingdom for the church age in His parables, particularly those in Matthew 13. For many years dispensationalists have referred to these parables as teaching a mystery form or a new form of the kingdom. Blaising uses the same term.[48] However, nowhere in Matthew 13 or anywhere else does the Lord Jesus use the term *mystery form.* Rather, He refers to the "mysteries of the kingdom of heaven" (v. 11); that is, the Lord in these parables is giving to His disciples new truths about the kingdom that were hitherto unknown.

It is strange that so many dispensationalists claim that a new form of the kingdom is introduced in Matthew 13. Dispensationalists argue strenuously for a literal, earthly kingdom that is the fulfillment of the Old Testament when John, Jesus, and His disciples announce its nearness. Then suddenly these dispensationalists change the meaning in Matthew 13. How much better to say that the same kingdom is being discussed but now the Lord Jesus is providing further revelation about that kingdom.[49]

Note that when the Lord says, "The kingdom of heaven is like" or "may be compared to," He does not mean that the kingdom is like a man, or a woman, or a seed, or leaven, etc. He means that there is a truth in the parable that is related to the kingdom. A good illustration is the parable of the unforgiving slave in Matthew 18:23–34. The kingdom itself is not like any specific thing in the parable. The truth taught in the parable is obvious: heirs of the kingdom should be forgiving because they have been forgiven an impossible debt. So then, the clause "the kingdom of heaven (or God) is like" means that some truth tangential to the kingdom is found in the parable. In Matthew 13, the truths are ones that had not been revealed before.

Matthew 13 has eight parables, with the first and the last serving as introductory and concluding parables.[50] Because they function in this way, they do not give any new truths about the kingdom. Interestingly, in neither of these does the Lord use a form of the formula, "The kingdom of heaven is like." It is in the interior six parables that Christ presents new truths.

In the first of these, the parable of the wheat and tares, the new truth is clear: there is going to be a previously unforeseen age preceding the kingdom in which good and evil coexist. The kingdom had been proclaimed as being near at hand; it was so near that the ax was already at the base of the tree (Matt. 3:10). Now that imminent judgment is being postponed and a new age has intervened. This is a new and unexpected revelation.

Blaising, however, contends that this parable teaches that the kingdom is present in this age. It must be noted first that the term *sons of the kingdom* in verse 38 does not imply that the kingdom is present in this age; it simply describes those who are or should be heirs of the future kingdom (cf. Matt. 8:12). The clause Blaising uses to defend his position is, "they will gather out of His kingdom all stumbling blocks, and those who commit lawlessness." He argues:

> This would appear to identify a situation *before* the coming of the Son of Man as *His kingdom*. Both those who belong to Him and those who will be condemned are present in that form of the kingdom. After His coming, only the saved will be present in the kingdom. Both conditions, before and after His coming, are called "kingdom."[51]

Blaising seems to be drawing his line at the wrong place. Precisely when does the kingdom begin? The Lord will return *with* His angels, according to Matthew 16:27 and 25:31. In Matthew 24:30–31, the Lord Jesus appears and then sends forth His angels. It would seem that His earthly kingdom begins with His appearance and return. The judgment is the introduction to His kingdom; judgment marks the beginning of His reign. This being so, it would be natural to say that angels will gather sinners out of His kingdom. Matthew 13:41 does not prove there is a present form of the kingdom.

The parable of the mustard seed (13:31–32) does not argue for a present form of the kingdom either. On the contrary, a new truth is revealed about a new age preceding the kingdom. In this age, the number of the sons of the kingdom (that is, the heirs) will grow in this present age from an insignificant number to a very large group. The analogy of a tree large enough to house birds looks back to the Old Testament, which uses this to picture something as being large and prosperous (Ezek. 17:23, 31:3–9; Dan. 4:12, 21). The disciples were expecting judgment and the coming of the kingdom. Instead of a cataclysmic soon-coming of the kingdom, there will be an interadvent age for gathering heirs of that kingdom.[52] This was a whole new truth.

The parable of leaven in Matthew 13:33 is something of an enigma. Many take the leaven to portray good so that this parable parallels the preceding parable. It illustrates the growth in the number of the heirs of the kingdom. This is a very possible interpretation. However, it has a couple of difficulties. First, what does the Lord mean by "until it was all leavened?" If the leaven represents good, this appears to teach a form of postmillennialism. Furthermore, why does Christ Jesus say the woman "hid" (ἐγκρύπτω, a verb used only here in the New Testament) the leaven? It appears that she is doing something sinister. But the main objection is found in the New Testament usage of leaven. Although it must be conceded that leaven in the Old Testament does not consistently typify evil, leaven when used figuratively in the New Testament *always* portrays evil (Matt. 16:6, 11–12; Mark 8:15; Luke 12:1; 1 Cor. 5:6–8; Gal. 5:9; the only other occurrence of "leaven" [ζύμη] in the New Testament is Luke 13:21, where it is used in a parallel passage in the same parable).

It may be better to take the leaven as picturing the growth of evil in this age. This parable, then, would be in contrast to the preceding. In spite of the growth in the number of the heirs of the kingdom, there will be the increase of apostasy until the man of sin will be ruling the world when Christ returns. In either interpretation there is a new revelation concerning the new age between the Lord's two comings.

The two parables of the hidden treasure and the precious pearl (Matt. 13:44–46) likewise have differing interpretations. One commonly taken view asserts that the purchaser is a person who gives up everything to purchase the field and the pearl. Again, this is a possible explanation. However, it founders on one major problem: No human can buy his ticket into the kingdom. The reception of the gospel may prove costly to some, but no one can pay something in order to receive it.

It would seem that the purchaser is the Lord Jesus. If this is correct, the hidden treasure that is unearthed represents the kingdom. For centuries it has been buried, but when the Lord announced its nearness, it was unburied. With His rejection it was hidden and then purchased by His death. When He returns, it will be unearthed. At any rate, neither interpretation says that the kingdom is present in this age.

The parable of the costly pearl may have the same two different interpretations as the parable of the hidden treasure. On the one hand, it may portray a lost person giving up everything for the sake of the kingdom. But, again, no one can purchase the privilege of entering that future kingdom. More probably it describes the Lord's redemption to ransom the body of the redeemed. Neither explanation of the parable proves the present existence of the kingdom.

The final "kingdom parable" is the parable of the dragnet (Matt. 13:47–50). It simply describes the postponement of judgment that had formerly been proclaimed as near. In this sense it parallels the parable of the tares and wheat.

The concluding parable, like the introductory parable, gives no new revelation regarding God's kingdom program; therefore, it is not introduced with the formula "the kingdom of heaven is like" or some such similar clause. Rather, this parable places the responsibility for teaching the truths of the kingdom on the disciples. They now have things that are old, that is the Old Testament revelation regarding the kingdom, and things that are new, the "mysteries" taught by the Lord Jesus in the kingdom parables.

In Matthew 13 there is no new form of the kingdom that is being revealed. McClain pointed this out a generation ago when he wrote:

> The fiction of a present "kingdom of heaven" established on earth in the Church, has been lent some support by an incautious terminology sometimes used in defining the "mysteries of the kingdom of heaven" (Matt. 13:11). The parables of this chapter, it is said carelessly by some, describe the kingdom of heaven as now existing in "mystery form" during the Church age. Now it is true that these parables present certain *conditions* related to the Kingdom which are contemporaneous with the present age. But nowhere in Matthew 13 is the establishment of the Kingdom placed within this age. On the contrary, in two of these parables the setting up of the Kingdom is definitely placed at the end of the "age" (vss. 39 and 49 ASV, with 41–43). And it is to be noted that in each of these references, our Lord is speaking as the infallible interpreter of His own parable.
>
> What is certain in the teaching of these difficult parables is that the present age, viewed from the standpoint of the Kingdom, is a time of *preparation*. During this period the Son of man is sowing seed (vs. 37), generating and developing a spiritual nucleus for the future Kingdom, a group called "sons of the kingdom" (vs. 38, ASV). At the same time He is permitting a parallel development of evil in the world under the leadership of Satan (vss. 38–39). It is the purpose of God to bring both to a "harvest," when the good and bad will be separated, and then to establish the Kingdom in power and righteousness (vss. 41–43, 49).[53]

The Kingdom in Acts

Clearly the apostles were anticipating the coming of the kingdom in Acts 1. Significantly, the Lord invested His forty-day postresurrection ministry to these apostles in instructing them about the kingdom of God (Acts 1:3). After this teaching they were still expecting a future kingdom. Blaising cogently notes, "This passage in Acts, standing as it does at the close of Jesus' preascension ministry, is a most significant testimony to the continuity of Jesus' teaching with that of the Old Testament prophets. The notion of a political, earthly kingdom has not dropped out or been resignified."[54] As part of His concluding message, the Lord Jesus told the disciples to wait in Jerusalem for the promised Holy Spirit (1:4–5). After this command from Christ, the apostles asked, "Lord, is it at this time you are restoring the kingdom to Israel?" This was a completely logical inference because in the Old Testament the future manifestation of the Holy Spirit was associated with the coming of the Holy Spirit (Isa. 32:15; 44:3; Ezek. 36:27–28; 39:28–29; Joel 2:28–3:1; Zech. 12:8–10).

Very significantly, the Lord did not answer yes to their question. His answer was much more ambiguous. "It is not for you to know times or epochs which the Father has fixed by His own authority" (1:7 NASB). By this response Christ did not say that they had an incorrect view of the future kingdom; it was not for them to know the time of its coming. As Bock states, "Jesus simply notes that the time is not theirs to know, not that the question is improper."[55] What the Lord does is to separate the time of the coming of the kingdom from the time of the coming of the promised Holy Spirit. The coming of the Holy Spirit did not automatically mean the coming of the kingdom. After all, the presence of the kingdom was contingent upon Israel's response (cf. Acts 3:19–21).[56]

Acts chapters 2 and 3 are crucial to the question of whether the kingdom is present in this age. Chapter 2 describes the fulfillment of the promised baptism by the Holy Spirit. Progressive dispensationalists also claim that the Lord Jesus took the Davidic throne in heaven at this time and inaugurated the promised kingdom. But was the kingdom inaugurated here? Several factors say that it was not. First, the word *kingdom* does not occur in Acts 2, a fact that Bock concedes.[57] However, he claims, "the imagery of rule and the features of God's covenant are present."[58] It is difficult to explain why Luke suddenly does not use the term if the kingdom is being inaugurated. He employs it forty-five times in his gospel and uses it two more times in Acts 1. Of course, one can discuss kingdom concepts without using the term *kingdom,* but one would expect Luke to use the word if such a startling thing as the inauguration of the kingdom had taken place. The fact that Luke uses *kingdom* only eight times in Acts after such heavy usage in his gospel implies that the kingdom had not begun but was, in fact, postponed.

Progressive dispensationalists assert that the Lord Jesus, by being seated at the right hand of the Father, is now seated on the throne of David. But such an outstanding theological statement is never made anywhere in the New Testament, even though the name David occurs fifty-five times. Nevertheless, Bock, by using terms such as *link, allusion,* or *association,* contends that Christ is now on the Davidic throne. He states emphatically, *"Being seated on David's throne is linked to being seated at God's right hand"* (emphasis his). It seems, however, that Bock is missing the point of Peter's argument in his Pentecostal sermon.

First, in Acts 2:22–32 Peter is arguing for the resurrection of Christ by using Psalm 16:8–11. That the resurrection of Jesus is the theme is seen in the repetition of "God raised again" in verses 24 and 32, which bracket the paragraph; the Greek text uses the same vocabulary, θεὸς ἀνέστησεν. Peter does this by making it clear that Psalm 16:8–11 is predictive of the Lord Jesus. Paul uses the same argument in Acts 13:34–37. The reference to Psalm 132:11 in Acts 2:30 is not included to say that Christ is now on the throne of David but that He is the One who will sit on that throne. Because that future great king was to be incorruptible, but also human, it was necessary for Him to be resurrected. That is the logic of the passage. The ascension of Christ is not in this paragraph (2:24–32); the point is the resurrection of Christ.

The ascension of the Lord comes to the fore in Acts 2:33–36. It was the ascended and exalted Jesus Christ who poured forth the promised Holy Spirit. This was in accordance with the words of the Lord Jesus in John 14:16, 15:26, 16:7 (cf. John 7:39). Peter than quoted Psalm 110:1 to defend the doctrine of the Lord's ascension, which in turn proves who He is: Lord and Messiah. It says nothing of being seated on David's throne. The emphasis in verses 33–36 is on Christ's ascension and His present session, not on the throne of David. In brief, Acts 2:24–36 strongly sets forth two crucial doctrines—the Lord's resurrection and His ascension.

Evidently Peter believed that the kingdom would come in the near future. This is seen in the warning of Acts 2:40, "Be saved from this perverse generation." Peter knew that judgment preceded the coming of the kingdom, and he evidently is warning his hearers about this assize. It also may be implied in the quotation of Joel 2:28–32 in Acts 2:17–21, especially verse 21.

The kingdom is certainly future in Acts 3:19–21: "Repent therefore and return that your sins may be wiped away, in order that times of refreshing may come from the presence of the Lord; and that He may send Jesus the Christ appointed for you, whom heaven must receive until the period of restoration of all things about which God spoke by the mouth of His holy prophets from ancient time." Concerning this passage, Bock writes, "After calling the people to repentance (v. 19), Peter outlines Jesus' remaining career in three parts: the coming of periods of refreshing, the sending of the appointed Jesus, and the necessity of heaven receiving Jesus until the promised times of restitution come (vv. 19–21)."[59] The problem with Bock's interpretation is found in his explanation of "seasons of refreshing." He takes it to refer to the present time.[60] This simply does not suit the Greek text. Two purpose clauses separate two time periods. The first is the present time and deals with forgiveness of sins. The second looks ahead to the future return of Christ when there will be seasons of refreshing, the return of Christ, and the restoration of all things. This, of course, anticipates the kingdom yet to come.[61]

Still another passage in Acts used to support the idea that Christ is now reigning on the throne of David is Acts 13:32–35.[62] "And we preach to you the good news of the promise made to the fathers, that God has fulfilled this promise to our children in that He raised up Jesus, as it is also written in Psalm 2, 'THOU ART MY SON; TODAY I HAVE BEGOTTEN THEE.' And as for the fact that He raised Him up from the dead, no more to return to decay, He has spoken in this way: 'I WILL GIVE YOU THE HOLY AND SURE BLESSINGS OF DAVID.' Therefore He also says in another psalm, 'THOU WILT NOT ALLOW THY HOLY ONE TO UNDERGO DECAY.'"

Verse 34 refers to the "sure blessings of David," an obvious quotation of Isaiah 55:3: "Incline your ear and come to Me. Listen, that you may live; And I will make an everlasting covenant with you, According to the faithful mercies shown to David." The everlasting covenant with David clearly looks ahead to the reign of His greater Son in the coming kingdom. In Isaiah 55:3, the faithful hearer is promised life in that future kingdom. For the covenant to be everlasting, the Son of David must be incorruptible. This is why it was necessary for the Messiah to be resurrected from the dead. That is the logic of Acts 13:34: "And as for the fact that He raised Him up from the dead, no more to return to decay, He has spoken in this way: "I WILL GIVE YOU THE HOLY AND SURE BLESSINGS OF DAVID.'" This also explains why the following verse is introduced with "therefore" (διότι) or "because" and goes on to discuss the Lord's resurrection. Acts 13:34 does not indicate the kingdom is present.

It is clear from Acts 14:22 that the kingdom is future: ". . . strengthening the souls of the disciples, encouraging them to continue in the faith, and saying, 'Through many tribulations we must enter the kingdom of God.'" The kingdom here is eschatological.

Some may argue that because the kingdom is proclaimed by Stephen and Paul in the book of Acts (8:12; 19:8; 20:25; 28:23, 31), it must have a present form. But this is not necessarily so. After all, the Lord Jesus went about proclaiming the gospel of the kingdom when it was not present (Matt. 4:23; Mark 1:14; Luke 4:43; 8:1). In Luke 9:2, the Twelve announced the kingdom (cf. 9:60); this evidently means that they proclaimed the message of how people may enter the future kingdom. Concerning Acts 28:23, Harrison wrote, "He talked about 'the kingdom of God.' Here, as elsewhere in Acts, this is a comprehensive term for the Gospel."[63] Haenchen is more direct in commenting on the same passage, "If, on the other hand, as here and in 8:12 and 28:31, it is mentioned along with the events of Jesus, then it has the 'futuristic' meaning of which 14:22 speaks. At the Parousia the future kingdom will come with the returning Jesus: Lk. 21:31."[64] This means that in 28:23 Paul related the Old Testament to Christ's ministry and the future kingdom. This same message was extended to Jews and Gentiles in Acts 28:31.

As in the Gospels so also in Acts, the kingdom is seen as being future and eschatological.

The Kingdom in the Pauline Epistles

Several passages are used from Paul's epistles to argue for a present form of the kingdom. Romans 14:17 is one such passage: ". . . for the kingdom of God is not eating and drinking, but righteousness and peace and joy in the Holy Spirit." Ladd states, "The Word of God *does* say that the kingdom of God is a present spiritual reality," and then he quotes Romans 14:17 to prove his point.[65] He goes on to say, "Righteousness and peace and joy are fruits of the Spirit which God bestows now upon those who yield their lives to the rule of the Spirit."[66] This interpretation is fortified by the present tense *is* (ἐστίν).

But does this passage say that the kingdom is here now? One must be careful about arguing from the present tense because Paul normally looks at the kingdom as being future (1 Cor. 6:9, 10; 15:24, 50; Gal. 5:21; Eph. 5:5; Col. 4:11; 1 Thess. 2:12; 2 Thess. 1:5; 2 Tim. 4:1, 18). If this is his usual view of the kingdom, then it is probable that he is looking at the future in Romans 14:17 also.[67] Wallace, who makes a careful distinction between "aspect" (points of view) and *Aktionsarten* (kinds of action), says the futuristic use of the present tense is relatively common. He goes on to say that only the context makes clear whether the emphasis is on immediacy or certainty.[68] Here it is on certainty.

Note that the statement "the kingdom of God is not eating and drinking" by no means denies the material aspects of the future kingdom. It was common for the Jews to say "not . . . but" and simply mean that the emphasis is not this but that (cf. Matt. 6:19–20, 1 Cor. 4:20, 1 Peter 3:3–4). In that coming kingdom the emphasis will not be on food but on spiritual realities. If that will be true in the future, the Christian's present conduct should reflect it. The future does influence the present (cf. 2 Peter 3:11).

What was said of Romans 14:17 may also be stated about 1 Corinthians 4:20, "For the kingdom of God does not consist in words, but in power." There is no verb in the Greek text, so it must be supplied. That Paul is anticipating the future is seen in verses five and eight of the same chapter. When the kingdom comes in the future, it will arrive with power and not mere propaganda. Paul's ministry could demonstrate the authority of that future kingdom. In discussing the kingdom of God in this passage, Barrett states, "It is always an eschatological concept. . . ."[69]

A third Pauline passage is used to defend the idea of a present form of the kingdom, Colossians 1:13: "For He delivered us from the domain of darkness, and transferred us to the kingdom of His beloved Son."[70] Again, one must note that in eleven other references to God's kingdom in Pauline literature it is looked at as being future. One should, therefore, be biased toward a future interpretation here. It is true that both verbs are past tense (aorist indicative) and refer to past action. But these are also both positional in their theology. Just as Ephesians says that believers are blessed with every spiritual blessing in the heavenlies, so positionally Colossians 1:13 sees Christians as no longer being under the authority of Satan but now heirs of the coming kingdom. McClain writes, "The context here suggests that the action must be regarded as *de jure* rather than *de facto*."[71] He goes on to assert:

> Although we are not yet *de facto* seated in the heavenlies, the thing is so certain that God can speak of it as already done. In the same sense, we have been (aorist tense) transferred *judicially* into the Kingdom of our Lord even before its establishment. Being what He is, God "calleth the things that are not, as though they were" (Rom. 4:17, ASV). Such at times is the language of divine inspiration.[72]

It must be concluded, then, that in Paul's epistles the kingdom is seen as a future glorious kingdom.

The Kingdom in Hebrews

Two passages in Hebrews may be used to attempt a proof of a present form of the messianic kingdom. The writer of Hebrews exalts the Lord Jesus in Hebrews 1:8 (NASB), "But of the Son He says, 'THY THRONE, O GOD, IS FOREVER AND EVER, AND THE RIGHTEOUS SCEPTER IS THE SCEPTER OF HIS KINGDOM.'" Because this is a quotation from Psalm 45, this anticipates Christ's future rule. Hodges notes, "The quotation found in verses 8–9 is derived from Psalm 45:6–7 which describes the final triumph of God's messianic King."[73]

A second passage in Hebrews that may be used to show a present form of the kingdom is Hebrews 12:28: "Therefore, since we receive a kingdom which cannot be shaken, let us show gratitude, by which we may offer to God an acceptable service with reverence and awe." The participle translated "we receive" is present tense, but because it is a participle it is inherently timeless. The previous verses clearly look ahead to the shaking of the world in judgment. That future kingdom will not and cannot be shaken. Bruce notes, "The present participle παραλαμβάνοντες suggests that the people of Christ have not finally entered into their royal heritage with him, although it is already theirs by promise."[74] That kingdom is future.

The Kingdom in the General Epistles

The only times the term *kingdom* occurs in the General Epistles are in James 2:5 and 2 Peter 1:11. In both cases the kingdom is clearly eschatological.

The Kingdom in the Apocalypse

Several passages are taken from the book of Revelation to substantiate the idea of a present kingdom. One of these is Revelation 1:6 (NASB): "And He has made us to be a kingdom, priests to His God and Father; to Him be the glory and the dominion forever and ever. Amen."

The explanation of this verse is found in 5:10 (NASB), which anticipates the future reign of believers with Christ: "And Thou hast made them to be a kingdom and priests to our God; and they will reign upon the earth." Clearly, the kingdom in 1:6 is eschatological.

The same may be said of Revelation 1:9 (NASB): "I, John, your brother and fellow partaker in the tribulation and kingdom and perseverance which are in Jesus, was on the island called Patmos, because of the word of God and the testimony of Jesus." Thomas notes, "Little difference of opinion exists over the meaning of *basileia* in 1:9. It is the millennial kingdom described more fully in Revelation 20. . . ."[75]

Bock places stress on Revelation 5:5 (NASB): "And one of the elders said to me, 'Stop weeping; behold, the Lion that is from the tribe of Judah, the Root of David, has overcome so as to open the book and its seven seals.'" The verb "has overcome" is aorist. Concerning this Bock writes, "The victory, or at least the decisive act, has already occurred. He is qualified to open the scrolls and the seals because of what he has already done as a Davidite."[76] He goes on to say, "The timing of Revelation 5:5 is crucial, since it precedes the seal judgments and the second coming, so the text shows Jesus has his regal victorious status before he returns in Revelation 19."[77] But this does not prove a present form of the kingdom. Christ's death and resurrection have defeated Satan but the kingdom is clearly future; this is especially seen in the Apocalypse. As McClain notes, "That the second advent and the Kingdom are brought together as the main subjects of the last book of Scripture, will occasion no surprise to those acquainted with divine revelation. For these two great eschatological events are inseparable as the goal of history, as we have already noted especially in the teaching of Christ Himself. The personal and glorious coming of Messiah will bring in the Kingdom, and without such a coming there can be no Messianic Kingdom."[78]

It must be concluded that the kingdom in Revelation anticipates the millennial reign of Christ, which in turn merges and extends into the eternal kingdom (1 Cor. 15:24).

Conclusion

This long discussion concerning the futurity of the kingdom has many implications. Two are pertinent to the present discussion. First, if the Lord's messianic kingdom is totally future, then the "already-not yet" view set forth by progressive dispensationalists crumbles. There is no "already" kingdom of Christ. He is still waiting to rule, as the Scriptures so plainly state (Ps. 110:1; Heb. 10:12–13).

A second important implication relates to the distinction between Israel and the church. If there is no present form of the messianic kingdom, then the present age is something of a parenthesis. From Genesis 12 through the Gospels and deep into Acts, God's primary purpose dealt with Israel. In the Gospels and Acts, the Lord Jesus is offered to Israel as Messiah. The coming of the kingdom was contingent upon their response.[79] Because of Israel's negative response, God is now working with the church, distinct from Israel (Rom. 9–11; Eph. 2:11–22, 3:1–12). The church, therefore, is a mystery, never prophesied in the Old Testament (Eph. 3:4–6). It is neither a "new Israel" nor a new form of the kingdom.

The term *Israel* occurs sixty-six times in the New Testament. It is never used of the Church. Galatians 6:16 is often used to show that the church is the new Israel; however, Johnson has shown decisively that such an equation cannot be drawn.[80] It must be conceded that the promises to Israel (Acts 3:25, Rom. 9:4–5, Eph. 2:12) are not being fulfilled in the church as a form of the messianic kingdom. The fulfillment of those kingdom prophecies and promises awaits the future (cf. Rom. 11:15, 25–27).

The Church and the Promises to Israel

If the kingdom is not now in existence and the Church is living in a sort of parenthesis in God's program, the question must be asked, "What is the relationship of the church to Israel's promises?" At the beginning of this discussion, various answers were introduced, most of which seemed to be unsatisfactory in some way.

It is my position that the New Testament church enters into Israel's millennial promises. Several factors support this conclusion. The first is Matthew 19:28 (NASB): "And Jesus said to them, 'Truly I say to you, that you who have followed me, in the regeneration when the Son of Man will sit on His glorious throne, you also shall sit upon twelve thrones, judging the twelve tribes of Israel.'" Much the same is stated in Luke 22:28–30. When one recognizes that these same twelve apostles (except Judas Iscariot) are the foundation stones of the church in Ephesians 2:20, the conclusion becomes inescapable. The apostles, who are part and parcel of the church, are going to reign over Israel in the land during the Millennium.

The figure of the olive tree in Romans 11 confirms the same truth. The root of the tree (11:16) may refer to the patriarchs or to the early church, which was Jewish. In either case, the hopes of each anticipated the millennial kingdom (cf. Acts 3:20; Rom. 9:4–5, 11:26–27). If the wild olive branches are grafted into the olive tree, then it must indicate that the believing Gentiles participate along with believing Jews in earthly blessings.

It would seem that 1 Corinthians 6:2 looks at the church as ruling with Christ in the future kingdom age, "Or do you not know that the saints will judge the world? And if the world is judged by you, are you not competent to constitute the smallest law courts?"

The same idea is found in Galatians 3:29: "And if you belong to Christ, then you are Abraham's offspring, heirs according to promise." The same chapter of Galatians refers to the promises spoken to Abraham and to his seed (v. 16). The phrase "and to your seed" includes the land promises in Genesis (Gen. 13:15, 17:7–8; cf. 15:18; 24:7; 26:3; 28:4, 13; 48:4). The church, then, must somehow be related to the land promises.

Ephesians 2:19 says that the church comprises those who "are no longer strangers and aliens [to the covenants of promise, v. 12], but you are fellow citizens with the saints." It is interesting to notice the duplication of "strangers" in verses 12 and 19. Both are looking at the covenants of promise given to Israel. One must assume that the church becomes a participant in the Jewish hope and covenants.

Hebrews 11:39–40 (NASB) clearly associates the church with the heirs of Old Testament promises. "And all these, having gained approval through their faith, did not receive what was promised, because God had provided something better for us, so that apart from us they should not be made perfect." The pronouns *us* and *they* look at the church and Old Testament believers as being joined somehow in participation in future blessings.

The famous parable of Luke 19:11–27 looks at the Lord returning to reign. His faithful servants are given responsibilities to rule over cities in His kingdom, depending on their faithfulness in this age.

How this will be accomplished is difficult to describe. Dillow believes that the co-reigning with the Lord Jesus involves the universe.[81] Walvoord sees the raptured and resurrected church as inhabiting the New Jerusalem, which may be in orbit about the earth. He writes:

> Though the Bible does not comment on this, it is possible that the New Jerusalem will be a satellite city in relation to the millennial earth and that those with resurrected bodies, as well as the holy angels, will occupy the New Jerusalem during the thousand-year reign. They will be able to commute to the earth, much as people go from the country to their city offices and participate in earthly functions without necessarily living in the city. In the descriptions of the millennial kingdom, the saints are described as those who are still in their physical bodies, building houses and planting crops (Isa. 65:21–23), but no picture is ever drawn of the resurrected saints as living beside them. Accordingly, while this provides a possible solution, it should be borne in mind that there is very little direct Scripture to back this up, and it therefore cannot be a dogmatically held doctrine.[82]

The reigning of the church with Christ on earth does not blur the distinctions between Israel and the church. They are distinct in this age and they will be in the future millennium. That such a distinction exists is seen in the difference Paul makes between the natural branches and the wild branches (Rom. 11:17–18). This separation is carried into the Millennium, as Romans 11:24 indicates. Furthermore, the promises were made to Israel, not the church. The church only enters into the promises because of their association with and being joined to the promised Messiah (Gal. 3:29). If the New Jerusalem has twelve gates named after the twelve tribes of Israel and twelve foundation stones identified with the twelve apostles of Christ, it should not be thought strange to have one body of the redeemed with two peoples in it.

In summary, it may be stated that progressive dispensationalism errs in making the church a present form or "sneak preview" of the promised kingdom. There is no promised kingdom on earth in this age; the church is a unique mystery. However, it will enter into the Millennium and its promised blessings because of her association with the promised Messiah.

RESPONSE

I regard the present discussion with Stan Toussaint about this crucial subject as a privilege. Stan, his wife, and generational peers have taught us what it means to "live a lifetime worthy of the Lord" (Col. 1:10). Nothing could be more important for this fellow student of the Scriptures.

Toussaint's position is stated on pages 229 and 247. His primary presupposition is that the term *kingdom* is synonymous with the Millennium, "the promised, yet future fulfillment of Israel's Old Testament covenants, promises and prophecies." A corollary of the assumption is that eschatology is practically reduced to Millennium, the subject being narrowed to the study of millennial topics and issues. A less explicit assumption is that Israel and the church are antithetically distinct to the extent that the Davidic kingdom "was not present when Christ Jesus was here and it is not here even in 'mystery form' in this church age. It is totally future awaiting fulfillment in the Millennium and eternity" (p. 229). "There is no promised kingdom on earth in this age; the church is a unique mystery" (p. 257). His method is a brief survey of dispensational options followed by an *a priori* concordance study of the term *kingdom* in successive blocks of New Testament writings. His conclusion is that the present age of the church "is something of [or 'sort of' below] a parenthesis" in God's program (p. 247). The reluctant language seems to be a hesitancy between "parenthetical" or "intercalatory," as in his "Contingency of the Coming of the Kingdom" article. His fear is that "Israel and church become so blurred" that "there is no separation between them, [so that] dispensationalism will become as extinct as the pitied dodo bird" (p. 225). "Intercalation," with Toussaint's assumptions, would be a clearer designation of his position.

As a prelude to criticisms, we must state our agreements with Toussaint's chapter. Israel's Messiah will return, inaugurating the millennial kingdom that will ultimately fulfill God's unconditional promises to Israel. The Millennium is not present in any other age of the earth's history. The church is not Israel, even though it is the people of faith in the present age. Finally, "the church only enters the promises because of their association with and being joined to the promised Messiah (Gal. 3:29)" (p. 250).

We need to comment, however, on Toussaint's method, his exegetical conclusions, and the theological implications of his position. Methodologically, I differ with the reduction of Israel/church distinctions to the "kingdom." This is undoubtedly a crucial issue, but it reduces a comprehensive, biblical subject to the Davidic covenant, leaving a mere two and a half pages (pp. 247–50) for a summary of critical passages that directly bear on the peoples of God.

Toussaint cites sources such as Barrett about Paul's eschatology, but in fairness he should note that his and Barrett's conclusions differ. Barrett emphasizes resurrection and *parousia* (pp. 18–19), rather than the millennial kingdom, which he considers "possible" but "unthinkable." Toussaint should have cited as well Barrett's context for his quote:

> It is always an eschatological concept (though sometimes brought forward into the present), and the power with which it works is the power of the Holy Spirit (cf. Rom. xiv.17 [we add, a present New Covenantal blessing as in Acts 3:19–21]), by which God's purpose is put into effect and the future anticipated in the present.[83]

Barrett clearly does not support Toussaint's thesis.

We note, as well, that Toussaint is incorrect to imply that progressive dispensationalists believe that the Millennium has already begun. I do not know of anyone in that position who would say that we are in the Millennium. This criticism is appropriate only with his assumption that the kingdom is only future. A fairer assessment would be that replacement theology and ultradispensationalism are equally undesirable alternatives for a biblically balanced position.

Two vital topics are not discussed: the concepts of kingship and kingdom in the Bible, and its backgrounds and the use of the Old Testament in the New Testament. Ancient kingship was a multifaceted, absolute office that is obviously far removed from our assumptions about democratic rights and a republic's "checked-and-balanced" powers. Royal prerogatives mandated an ideal of total commitment (e.g., Luke 9:23) rather than a minimalist acceptance of "heavenly insurance" with materialist realities. Assuming a strictly political office and realm seems to regress to the postresurrection view of "the Christ" that Jesus corrected twice with His comprehensive exposition of the Old Testament (Luke 24:13-49; cf., John 18:28-40). In other words, the despairing disciples lost hope because they had anticipated a millennial-type kingdom without the necessary suffering kingship and exemplary, prophetic, Spirit-enabled kingdom. Their exhilaration ("burning hearts") came when Jesus' exposition demonstrated that the kingdom program of God had not been terminated by the cross. Instead, it was validated by His glorification (cf. Luke 24:26). His kingship is now evident in His commission of the Spirit (Acts 2) as He promised (John 14-16). At least three functions of messianic kingship are discernible in the New Testament: prophetic, priestly, and imperial.

The use of the Old Testament in the New Testament takes us "back to the exegetical basics." All dispensationalists agree that the unconditional Davidic covenant ("I will . . . forever"), with conditional generational blessings ("when he does wrong") was inaugurated in 2 Samuel 7:14-17. The office was patterned on an anointed, father-son relationship (2 Sam. 7:14; Ps. 89). The Davidic promises are repeatedly developed and reaffirmed in messianic texts such as Psalms 2 and 110, texts that with other covenantal promises frame the advents of the Son in the New Testament. An illustration of the point is Psalm 2:6–7, the coronation formula of the Davidic king that is cited at crucial transitions in Jesus' kingship.

First, the formula is quoted at the Transfiguration, a preview of the Lord's millennial glory (Matt. 17:1–8), the words recalling the divine affirmation at John's baptism. There is little debate among dispensationalists about the regal splendor of Messiah's millennial, imperial reign; the application of this event to pastoral settings; and the encouragement that it has brought throughout the age in the context of the Cross.

Second, as a precedent to the Transfiguration, the Davidic formula was quoted by the Father with the anointing of the Spirit at Jesus' baptism by the eschatological prophet John (Matt. 3:17 with parallels, 11:1–5, 17:11–13, and Rev. 11:1–10 in the context of the Second Advent). Jesus healed as the victorious son of David, even as He prepared to enter Jerusalem (Matt. 20:29–33 with parallels). He explained the significance of His authenticating miracles as an evidence of the kingdom's victorious power over sin's effect (Matt. 12:25–29, Luke 11:17–23). The text includes a parable that Toussaint ignores, teaching Jesus' power over Satan as a contextual issue. The "more powerful" one had come. The connection of kingship and John's baptism was supported by the Lord in Matthew 21:23–27. He responded to His critics with a question about His authority in the prophetic, servant role of Davidic kingship (cf. 13:53–58) that has been inaugurated by baptism. The realm of the Davidic servant was distinguished in values that reflected humble faith more than "sphere" (chaps. 20–22), a realm that pointed in its completeness to an imperial return in glory (chaps. 24–25) and that was crowned with glorious victory over sin at the Cross (Matt. 26–28, Col. 2:13–15). Does not the heavenly chorus resound with "Worthy is the Lamb that was slain . . . [in coequal, coeternal trinitarian terms] to Him who sits on the throne, and to the Lamb, be blessing and honor and glory and dominion forever and ever" (Rev. 5: 12–13)? The "fulfillment of righteousness" (3:15) was related to "the way of righteousness" (21:32, cf. John 14:6); it was Messiah's identification with the humble crowd that had believed John's cry in the wilderness. These believers entered "the kingdom of God" rather than unbelieving Jewish leadership that could not truthfully respond to the Davidic implications of Psalm 110:1 because of their political priorities (22:41–46 with parallels). The judgment for this phase of kingship was pronounced by Messiah in Matthew 23, a unique passage that gains added significance when its kingdom implications are considered. In short, Toussaint's title for his Matthean commentary, *Behold the King*, is apt for the "King of the Jews" (27:37 with parallels), whose servantly realm was vindicated at the Cross (Acts 4:23–30, John 1:29–42). The notion of a "condition of nearness" is too abstract and anemic for the advent of the King and the details of the texts noted above. An aspect of Davidic kingship had arrived in fulfillment of prophecy, so, according to a "plain and normal" hermeneutical emphasis, messianic fulfillments at the First Advent assure believers that the unfulfilled aspects of kingship would be completely fulfilled in the present and especially in future ages. The repeated appeals to futuristic present tenses and the fluidity of participial forms, in Toussaint's discussion, take the place of the "plain, normal" meaning of the Scriptures.

Third, the formula is quoted in Acts 13:32–33. Toussaint correctly connects the Resurrection with the soteriological implications of Isaiah 55:3 and Psalm 16:10. But why does he ignore the eschatological implications of Psalm 2:7 in verse 33? We must surmise that the inauguration of Messiah's priestly kingship as validated in Romans 1:3–4 and Hebrews 5:1–10 does not accord with his assumption about the millennial futureness of Davidic kingship in its entirety, so it must be dismissed. The question is serious, because it has implications for the correctness of the biblical text and the hermeneutical precision of the apostles' use of the Old Testament. Toussaint's treatment of Hebrews ignores the textual connection between the glorification of Messiah (1:3–4) and the citations of Psalm 2:7 and 2 Samuel 7:14 as the basis for worship of the reigning messianic Son alone. He ignores the Davidic connection (chap. 1) with the priest-king Melchizedek through Psalm 110. He also ignores the comparatively full statement of the new covenantal blessings (chaps. 8–10) that the church enjoys, selectively but not completely in the present age. If the participial form is "timeless," which we would question from the context, then why does 12:28 read with the NASB as more apropos for the preacher's appeal, "Therefore, since we receive a kingdom that cannot be shaken [cf. Rom. 11:29], let us show gratitude, by which we may offer to God an acceptable service with reverence and awe . . ."? In verses 22–24, the preacher had affirmed that his readers "have come" (perfect tense) to "Mount Zion," the "heavenly Jerusalem," to "Jesus the mediator of the New Covenant." Such an appeal would truly be "timeless" rather than merely future.

A couple of theological reservations must be addressed as well. First, his view of the "contingency" of the kingdom is not convincing, though it is necessary for his position. There is a significant biblical difference between the condition of faith for God's blessing and the "contingency" of God's unconditional kingdom. "Contingency" undermines the divine certainty that undergirds Romans 9–11 and raises substantial questions. As a premise, no one would agree that "all Israel" means every Israelite in a comprehensive sense, for that would mean a "second-chance" salvation for the unbelieving majorities at their future resurrection. It would not seem to mean every Israelite in the tribulational generation, for a number of those people will die in the persecutions. Therefore, a large remnant will accept Messiah before His return, sufficiently representative to be "all Israel." If the Millennium would have come with Israel's positive response, then how do we account for the significant number of Israelites who believed at His first coming and, in Pentecost's context (even leaders, John 12:42), the messianic Christians who formed the distinctive core of the infant church in Acts? If the Millennium is contingent, then is Christ's return contingent on a similar remnant, however large, of Israelite believers in the Tribulation? Is the contingency of saving faith consistent with the biblical doctrine of election (Rom. 8, 1 Peter 1–2)? If there is a contingency in God's sovereignty in this matter, which I doubt, it would appear to be in the "subjection of enemies" (Ps. 110, 1 Cor. 15) rather than the salvation of an end-time remnant which, we all agree, is a noncontingent promise. In other words, God knows when His tribulational wrath, Second Coming, and Millennium will come, and they assuredly will be in His time.

An additional reservation is that Toussaint's chapter is given to overstatement that will keep his readers off balance. More than twenty times he explicitly uses language of certainty such as "clear(ly)" or "prove(s)," yet he affirms a view "not held by the majority of dispensationalists" (p. 229). A view so clearly proven would seem to lead to a consensus. Arguably, of course, his view is now "novel." We should note that almost all New Testament scholars hold to a present form of the kingdom, including many traditional dispensationalists. Toward progressive dispensationalists, he is catastrophic. Without "an inaugurated kingdom the cohesion of the entire system is basically destroyed" (p. 228). Some of us would say that he has not even identified the basic issue of how the apostolic generation used the Old Testament, the issue of the intrabiblical, Christocentric hermeneutic. He emphasizes that his view is "totally contradictory to that system [that is, progressive dispensationalism]" (p. 229). With such language, Toussaint will polarize his fellow pretribulational, premillennial dispensationalists and undermine the significant agreements that all dispensational theologians share. Are we comfortable with this kind of language about our long-time coworkers in the ministry of the Word? We need a friendlier tone for our biblical interactions, recognizing with Ryrie that "we must be constantly reminded that the test of doctrine is whether or not it is Scriptural." (*Dispensationalism Today* [Chicago: Moody, 1965]: 132).

Chapter Notes

1. Charles Caldwell Ryrie, *Dispensationalism Today* (Chicago, Moody, 1965), 43–57.
2. Ibid., 45.
3. Ibid., 47.
4. Ibid., 132.
5. Craig A. Blaising, "Development of Dispensationalism by Contemporary Dispensationalists," *BSac* 145 (July 1988): 273–74.
6. A. C. Gaebelein, *The Gospel of Matthew,* vol. 1 (Wheaton: Van Kampen Press, n.d.), 11.
7. Clarence Larkin, *Dispensational Truth or God's Plan and Purpose in the Ages* (Philadelphia: Clarence Larkin Est., 1920).
8. *The Holy Bible,* ed. C. I. Scofield (New York: Oxford University Press, 1945). Cf. notes on Isaiah 11:10; Romans 11:1, 26; Revelation 19:7.
9. *The New Scofield Reference Bible* (New York: Oxford University Press, 1967). Cf., notes on Isaiah 10:12; Romans 11:1, 26.
10. Lewis Sperry Chafer, *Systematic Theology,* 8 vols. (Dallas: Dallas Seminary Press, 1948), 4:323.
11. Ibid., 4:47.

12. Blaising, "Development of Dispensationalism by Contemporary Dispensationalists," 276.

13. J. Dwight Pentecost, *Things to Come* (Findlay, Ohio: Dunham Publishing, 1958), 532–80.

14. Erich Sauer, *From Eternity to Eternity* (Grand Rapids: Eerdmans, 1954), 19, 30–31, 38–39, 41–42, 54–55, 93, 193.

15. Thomas Ice and Timothy Demy, *Fast Facts on Bible Prophecy* (Eugene, Oregon: Harvest House, 1997), 45.

16. Arnold G. Fruchtenbaum, *The Footsteps of the Messiah* (Tustin, Calif.: Ariel Press, 1982), 275, 280–82, 367.

17. Alva J. McClain, *The Greatness of the Kingdom* (Grand Rapids: Zondervan, 1959), 511; cf. 210–11.

18. This movement is the result of the Dispensationalism Study Group, which met preceding the meetings of the Evangelical Theological Society. The first of these meetings was in the fall of 1986. The title, "Progressive Dispensationalists," introduced in the 1991 meeting, is not meant to be pejorative of other dispensational viewpoints but to indicate the progressive nature of God's work. However, to an uninitiated student it does give the impression that all other dispensationalists are not up to date. Cf. Charles C. Ryrie, "Update on Dispensationalism," in *Issues in Dispensationalism*, eds. Wesley R. Willis and John R. Master (Chicago: Moody, 1994), 20.

19. Craig A. Blaising and Darrell L. Bock, *Progressive Dispensationalism* (Wheaton: Bridgepoint Books, 1993), 267.

20. Ibid., 53.

21. Ibid., 248–50, 279; Darrell L. Bock, "The Reign of the Lord Christ," *Dispensationalism, Israel, and the Church*, eds. Craig A. Blaising and Darrell L. Bock (Grand Rapids: Zondervan, 1992), 38–45.

22. Blaising and Bock, *Progressive Dispensationalism*, 175–90, 257; and Bock, "The Reign of the Lord Christ," 47–55, 65.

23. Blaising and Bock, *Progressive Dispensationalism*, 251–83; and Bock, "The Reign of the Lord Christ," 55–64, 66.

24. Turner refers to the church as the "New Israel," cf. David L. Turner, "The New Jerusalem in Revelation 21:1–22:5: Consummation of a Biblical Continuum" in *Dispensationalism, Israel, and the Church*, eds. Craig A. Blaising and Darrell L. Bock (Grand Rapids: Zondervan, 1992), 288. This is precariously close to replacement theology.

25. Kenneth L. Barker, "The Scope and Center of Old and New

Testament Theology and Hope," *Dispensationalism, Israel, and the Church,* eds. Craig A. Blaising and Darrell L. Bock (Grand Rapids: Zondervan, 1992), 306-18.

26. Ryrie, "Update on Dispensationalism," *Issues in Dispensationalism,* 20.

27. Blaising, "The Kingdom in the New Testament," 232-34.

28. Ibid., 234.

29. Ibid.

30. Ibid., 248.

31. Ibid., 248-51.

32. Bock, "Reign of the Lord Christ," 40-41.

33. William L. Lane, *The Gospel According to Mark,* NICNT (Grand Rapids: Eerdmans, 1974), 65, n. 93. Cf. Stanley D. Toussaint, "The Contingency of the Coming of the Kingdom," in *Integrity of Heart, Skillfulness of Hands,* eds. Charles H. Dyer and Roy B. Zuck (Grand Rapids: Baker, 1994), 231-32. For a more thorough defense of the meaning "near," see A. J. Mattill Jr., *Luke and the Last Things* (Dillsboro, N.C.: Western North Carolina Press, 1979), 70-77.

34. Blaising, "The Kingdom in the New Testament," 248.

35. Ibid.

36. Nigel Turner, *Grammatical Insights into the New Testament* (Edinburgh: T & T Clark, 1965), 60.

37. The normally deponent verb βιάζομαι is here used in a passive sense. Cf. James Hope Moulton, *A Grammar of New Testament Greek,* vol. 3, *Syntax* (Edinburgh: T & T Clark, 1963), 58; and Turner, *Grammatical Insights into the New Testament,* 60.

38. Blaising, "The Kingdom in the New Testament," 249.

39. A. J. Mattill Jr., *Luke and the Last Things* (Dillsboro, N.C.: Western North Carolina Press, 1979), 175-76.

40. Ibid.

41. Blaising, "The Kingdom in the New Testament," 249.

42. Darrell L. Bock, *Luke 9:51-24:53* (Grand Rapids: Baker, 1996), 1412-14.

43. Darrell L. Bock, *Luke 1:1-9:53* (Grand Rapids: Baker, 1994), 1413-14.

44. *TDNT,* 1972 ed., s.v. "τηρέω," by Harald Riesenfeld, 148.

45. Ibid., 8:149.

46. F. Blass and A. Debrunner, *A Greek Grammar of the New Testament and Other Early Christian Literature.* Trans. by Robert W. Funk

(Chicago: The University of Chicago Press, 1961), 168; Ernest DeWill Burton, *Syntax of the Moods and Tenses in New Testament Greek* (Edinburgh: T & T Clark, 1955), 9; C. F. D. Moule, *An Idiom-Book of New Testament Greek* (Cambridge: At the University Press, 1960), 7; Turner, *Grammar,* 63.

47. BAGD, s.v. ἰδού, 371.

48. Blaising, "The Kingdom in the New Testament," 253.

49. Cf. Stanley D. Toussaint, *Behold the King* (Portland: Multnomah, 1980), 172–76.

50. Cf. Stanley D. Toussaint, "The Introductory and Concluding Parables of Matthew Thirteen," *BSac* 121 (October 1964): 351–55.

51. Blaising, "The Kingdom in the New Testament," 252.

52. The present tense of ἐστίν in verse 31 does not prove that the kingdom is present; it means only that the Lord is presently making a comparison.

53. Alva J. McClain, *The Greatness of the Kingdom* (Grand Rapids: Zondervan, 1959), 440–41.

54. Blaising and Bock, *Progressive Dispensationalism,* 237.

55. Bock, "The Reign of the Lord Christ," 45.

56. Cf. Toussaint, "The Contingency of the Coming of the Kingdom," 232.

57. Bock, "The Reign of the Lord Christ," 47.

58. Ibid.

59. Ibid., 55–56.

60. Ibid., 56–57.

61. For a more complete discussion of this passage, see Toussaint, "The Contingency of the Coming of the Kingdom," 229–30.

62. Bock, "The Reign of the Lord Christ," 51–52.

63. Everett F. Harrison, *Acts: The Expanding Church* (Chicago: Moody, 1975), 403.

64. Ernst Haenchen, *The Acts of the Apostles* (Oxford: Basil Blackwell, 1971), 723. Cf. Kirsopp Lake and Henry J. Cadbury, *The Beginnings of Christianity, The Acts of the Apostles,* eds. F. J. Foakes Jackson and Kirsopp Lake (Grand Rapids: Baker, 1965), 4:4; and Homer A. Kent Jr., *Jerusalem to Rome* (Grand Rapids: Baker, 1972), 195.

65. George Eldon Ladd, *The Gospel of the Kingdom* (Grand Rapids: Eerdmans, 1959), 16.

66. Ibid., 16–17.

67. This is the only occurrence of βασιλεία in Romans.

68. Daniel B. Wallace, *Greek Grammar Beyond the Basics* (Grand Rapids: Zondervan, 1996), 535–37. Cf. Turner, *Syntax,* 3:59–60.

69. C. K. Barrett, *Commentary on the First Epistle to the Corinthians* (New York: Harper & Row, 1968), 118.

70. Blaising and Bock, *Progressive Dispensationalism,* 126, 178, 257, 266.

71. McClain, *Greatness of the Kingdom,* 435.

72. Ibid., 435–36.

73. Zane C. Hodges, "Hebrews," in *BKC,* 2 vols., eds. John F. Walvoord and Roy B. Zuck (Wheaton: Victor Books, 1983), 2:782.

74. F. F. Bruce, *The Epistle to the Hebrews* (Grand Rapids: Eerdmans, 1990), 364.

75. Robert L. Thomas, *Revelation 1–7, An Exegetical Commentary* (Chicago: Moody, 1992), 87.

76. Bock, "The Reign of the Lord Christ," 64.

77. Ibid.

78. McClain, *Greatness of the Kingdom,* 443.

79. Toussaint, "The Contingency of the Coming of the Kingdom," 222–37.

80. S. Lewis Johnson Jr., "Paul and the 'Israel of God': An Exegetical and Eschatological Case-Study," *Essays in Honor of J. Dwight Pentecost,* eds. Stanley D. Toussaint and Charles H. Dyer (Chicago: Moody, 1986), 181–96.

81. Joseph C. Dillow, *The Reign of the Servant Kings* (Miami Springs: Schoettle Publishing, 1992), 561–63.

82. John F. Walvoord, *Major Bible Prophecies* (Grand Rapids: Zondervan, 1991), 414–15.

83. Barrett, *Commentary on the First Epistle to the Corinthians* (New York: Harper and Row, 1968).

CHAPTER SEVEN

Israel and the Church of a Progressive Dispensationalist

J. Lanier Burns
with response by Stanley D. Toussaint

The Importance of the Subject

Discussions of the relationship between Israel and the church gravitate to Romans 9–11. These chapters can be called Paul's theodicy, his vindication of God's justice in light of "the divine purpose in history."[1] They are sufficiently comprehensive to serve as a unifying focus for texts and themes that concern the relationship of Israel and the church and will be so used in this chapter.

Paul's three contextual emphases have a significant bearing on Israel's distinctive past, "provocative" present, and promised future. The themes are the distinctiveness of the nation Israel as evidenced by her divinely bestowed privileges and promises, the justice of God as proven by the righteousness of faith in Christ, and the distinctiveness of the church as indicated by Gentiles' equal, ecclesial standing before God based on the Christ's atonement. Paul transitioned the themes with rhetorical questions in his unfolding argument in behalf of God's future for Israel. These themes will structure two arguments in this chapter: that the Jewish-Christian remnant in the church is God's assurance of the future fulfillment of His promises to Israel, and that the present age of the church is vitally connected to God's past promises and His future fulfillments. Hopefully, the chapter will enrich discussion between dispensationalists on the vitally important biblical relationship between the church and Israel. The latter statement, with its focus on the Scriptures, acknowledges that a significant tradition of hostility exists between Christians and Jews that is beyond the scope of the chapter.

No one has done more to highlight the importance of this subject than Charles Ryrie, who made it the first of three distinctives of dispensational theology in his *Dispensationalism Today:*

> A dispensationalist keeps Israel and the Church distinct. This is stated in different ways by both friends and foes of dispensationalism. [Quotes follow by Daniel Fuller, Arno Gaebelein, and Lewis Sperry Chafer.] . . . This is probably the most basic test of whether or not a man is a dispensationalist, and it is undoubtedly the most practical and conclusive. . . . The essence of dispensationalism, then, is the distinction between Israel and the Church. . . . Indeed, ecclesiology, or the doctrine of the Church, is the touchstone of dispensationalsim.[2]

Ryrie's point is validated by the connection of the Israel/church distinction with issues regarding the fulfillment of biblical covenants, the existence of an intermediate kingdom, and overarching questions about proper hermeneutical approaches to a variety of texts in different contexts and genres. Darrell Bock reflects more recent discussions, when he reduces the distinctive to its millennial expression: "So progressives speak openly, as other dispensationalists do, of a future for national Israel among the nations in the Millennium. It is this detail that makes a premillennial view dispensational."[3] Thus, the relation of Israel and the church has been an abidingly determinative issue for evangelical theologians.

Limiting such a broad subject will be difficult, but the purpose of this chapter is to deal with the topic per se as it concerns dispensationalists. It easily blends with both kingdom and covenants, but those are comprehensive topics in their own right and can be mentioned only in passing here.

Crucial questions surface in the more restricted topic and

purpose. How was Israel distinctive as a people of God among the nations? Why has Israel rejected the incarnation of Torah while Gentiles have found favor with Yahweh seemingly apart from the Torah? Has the church "replaced" Israel as a "reconstituted" people of God? Is Israel distinct from the church as people of faith in God? To what extent or degree are the two biblical entities distinct? Does the olive tree metaphor describe a simultaneous or a successive salvation of Gentiles and Jews in the present age? Why does the New Testament discuss the relationship of "Jews" and "Gentiles" more explicitly than implied "Israel" and "church" contrasts? Is there a key text, or a limited number of crucial passages, for debating the differences between divergent theological approaches to the subject? Can "integrative questions," involving a number of texts and issues, result in a clarification, or even resolution, of polarizing differences between evangelicals about Israel and the church? What is the future of theological discussion, when many scholars in different traditions agree about most eschatological issues except for the Millennium? Answers to these and related questions must begin with the distinctiveness of Israel as evidenced in its divinely bestowed privileges and prerogatives.

The Distinctiveness of Israel

Paul's sentiment about "his people Israel" in the present age is rooted in her unique calling as recorded in the Old Testament. He emphatically expressed his lament for the nation's unbelief and a passion for her salvation "my brothers, my kinsmen according to the flesh": "I could wish that I myself were cursed and cut off from Christ for the sake of my brothers . . . my heart's desire and prayer to God for the Israelites is that they may be saved" (9:1–3; 10:1). In 1:16 he had underlined his enthusiasm for the gospel, "the power of God for the salvation of everyone who believes: first for the Jew, then for the Gentile," a priority and order that resonates throughout the letter. The Jews, however, had largely rejected their privileged opportunities and, in Paul's context, regarded him as a traitor to his formerly zealous persecution of the church. In spite of the breach, Griffith Thomas notes, "His heart was rent in twain by the trouble of his nation's rejection of his Savior. . . . It is noteworthy that each chapter commences with a warm personal testimony to his pity for Israel (ch. ix.1; x.1; xi.1)."[4]

He describes Israel's distinctiveness (9:1–5) in terms of its unique call to be Yahweh's people. Seven distinctives are enumerated, perhaps in climactic order, in terms of a divinely bestowed ancestry, worship, and revelation. The nation was "adopted as sons"; chosen, that is, for a unique relationship with the only living God (cf. Exod. 4:22; Hos. 11:1), ultimately an inheritance of the earth under the Davidic son. It was chosen as the "dwelling" of the glorious, divine presence (cf. Exod. 33:14). It received patriarchal "covenants of promise" that would bless the earth through their mediation. Israelites had received the revelation of the Law to make them wise about righteousness (cf. Rom. 2:17–28).[5] The divinely prescribed temple worship was the awe-inspiring center of national life. Within the adoption, law, and covenants were messianic promises for a lineage that led to Christ. The Jewish Messiah is the hope and doxological focus of the world, "God over all, forever praised!" This crescendo of unique blessings begs for faith to break through the persistent hardness of "the apple of God's eye."

Paul's pathos stems from these distinctive blessings and privileges. Israel's collective memory, however, had been marred by a majority's persistent unbelief, a wilderness pilgrimage of unlearned lessons, a seemingly endless rupture of the national fabric, and harsh disciplines from Yahweh at the hand of pagan empires. Habakkuk asked the larger questions about divine "silence," as believing remnants had wondered about the pervasive prosperity and injustices of wicked enemies: "Why are you silent, while the wicked swallow up those more righteous than themselves?" (1:13b). If the law was privilege, as tradition had taught, then zeal for laws must be virtuous, but this approach to divine favor had led to an endemic legalism that obscured the righteousness of faith (2:4). Wasserberg's observations are perceptive:

> The key issue for Paul, as I see it, is not whether or how the Gentiles have access to God's promises but, rather, why Israel has by and large thus far rejected Jesus as its Messiah. Why is [sic] that the Gentile world has accepted what is first offered to Israel (Rom. 1:16)? That the Gentiles now have access to God's promises through Christ is not a problem for Paul. What is a problem is the way in which they have gained this access, for it

challenges the core of Jewish identity: the validity of Torah. To claim that Gentiles without the law are now part of the people of God is not acceptable for observant Jews.[6]

Besides Torah, "circumcision of the heart" lacked the exclusive punch of the distinctive national sign. Even messianic promises were elusive, since Jesus of Nazareth experienced a criminal's death instead of a heroic initiative against Rome. In Calvin's words, "Either . . . there is no truth to the divine promise, or . . . Jesus, whom Paul preached, is not the Lord's Christ, who had been peculiarly promised to the Jews."[7] Jesus' work, though legally impeccable and irrefutable, prioritized mercy over sacrifice, exposing the majority's spiritual lesions. As Saul, Paul had breathed murderous threats against the Christ's people for blasphemy against Moses and God. But God's grace blessed "the Way" of the Son of David. "The Way" was largely Hebrew Christian, a core of messianic believers who divided the nation with the line of faith. Paul, one of these newly elected kinsmen, was graciously and miraculously called to bring Habakkuk's justice of faith to the Jew first as well as to the Gentiles. In the eyes of Moses' elite, he could only be a traitor and an apostate. The Judaizers' hostility predictably polarized them from the apostle's fervor for grace. Even more disturbing than Paul's conversion was the lingering conviction that God had reneged on His promises and, consequently, compromised His Word.

Israel's unbelief surfaced questions about the trustworthiness of the Scriptures, since Yahweh had unconditionally promised a blessed future for Israel. Had God's Word failed (9:6)? Paul's answer is that not all of Abraham's natural descendants are God's "children of the promise": "not all of Israel's descendants are Israel . . . it is not the natural children who are God's children" (vv. 7–8). The reason is that the covenantal recipients are an elect seed as exemplified in God's particular selection of Isaac and Jacob (vv. 9–13). Confusion of the chosen part for the national whole has sometimes obscured Paul's emphasis on Jewish remnants, a point that ultimately is used as evidence for continuity between the ages. Thus, Morris's caveat is correct: "It was an error to assume (as many Jews of his day did) that descent from Abraham gave them total security and a favored position before God. . . . The significance of what God had done should be pondered by those who put such an emphasis on God's choice of Israel."[8] If this emphasis is not acknowledged, then God's Word would have justifiably appeared untrustworthy to Abraham's physical descendants. On the other hand, the chosen remnant that received the promises were Jews, so that a denial or de-emphasis of Abraham's physical offspring is inappropriate as well.

The truth of sovereign election raised a further question about the justice of God (v. 14): Was God unfair to promise blessing for some but not all of Abraham's offspring, and by extension, some but not all of humanity? Paul responds with an emphatic μὴ γένοιτο and reminds his readers, in the remainder of chapter 9 and in chapter 10, that God's mercy and standard of righteousness by faith alone are equitable. Far from being an aside or digression in Paul's argument, we may infer that God's sovereign plan is the answer to the historical relationships of Jews and Gentiles in every age, an answer that had been neglected in the presumptuous self-interests of various interpreters from Paul's day to the present. Instead, the key to Israel's past and future is the character of God as specifically expressed in the covenantal integrity of His relationships and promises. The emphases on total depravity and divine mercy that keynote the midsection of Paul's argument are further highlighted in his doxological conclusion in 11:30–36.

Paul's argument is two fold. First, God's justice is grounded in His sovereign mercy (9:15–29). His emphasis was not on a vindictive judgment of hardened reprobates but rather on divine patience in exercising wrath on a people who had become ripe for discipline. Paul used Exodus 33:19 to demonstrate that God's mercy created the nation at the Exodus, rather than Israel's zeal for personal attainments (cf. 10:2). The same creative prerogatives were evidenced in His calling of faithful remnants, both Jewish and Gentile (9:24). Citations from Hosea and Isaiah validate his point.[9]

Second, God's justice is proven by the principle of righteousness by faith alone (9:30–10:21). By faith, Gentiles obtained righteousness while unbelieving Jews did not. Paul had discussed this point of justification at length in chapter 4. In that context, he had argued against "boasting rights" for salvation. At the same time he affirmed salvation as a divine gift, a credit for righteousness predicated on "Abraham-like faith." Romans 4:9–17 overlaps chapter 9 to the point that Paul assumed a knowledge of his use of Genesis 15 in the latter passage, demonstrating that Abraham

> received the sign of circumcision, a seal of the righteousness that he had by faith while he was still uncircumcised. So then, he is the father of all who believe but have not been circumcised, in order that righteousness might be credited to them. And he is also father of the circumcised who not only are circumcised but who also walk in the footsteps of the faith that our father Abraham had before he was circumcised.

He proceeded to affirm that the inheritance of the world "was not through Law" but rather through "the righteousness that comes by faith." Therefore, he concluded:

> The promise comes by faith, so that it may be by grace and may be guaranteed to all Abraham's offspring—not only to those who are of the Law but also to those who are of the faith of Abraham. He is the father of us all. As it is written: 'I have made you a father of many nations' [citing Gen. 17:5]. He is our father in the sight of God, in whom he believed. . . .

This passage, in a word, forbids any discussion of a people of God apart from the principle of righteousness by faith alone. Israelites that will receive divine promises are necessarily believing Jews. The point has sometimes been obscured by well-meaning people who overgeneralized Israel/church distinctions; the focus is to be on the physical seed of faith rather than mere descent from Abraham.

Justification by faith alone in the finished work of Christ alone emerges in 9:30 with messianic proof texts (Isa. 8:14; 28:16): "Christ is the end of the Law so that there may be righteousness for everyone who believes" (10:4).[10] Israel's zeal for God was based on self-attainment rather than God's provision, or personal righteousness rather than submission to the perfect standard (vv. 2–5). The problem was misdirected zeal. The Jews were sprinting on the wrong path. Paul used Leviticus 18:5 to point to the perfection of the Law's righteousness which Christ alone fulfilled, so that He could provide salvation by faith (cf. Matt. 5:17; Heb. 5:9).

Previous allusions to Christ as the culmination of the messianic line (9:5), Zion's "stumbling stone" (v. 33), and "the end of the Law" (10:4) are developed to the conclusion of the just "word of faith"; namely, that "there is no difference between Jew and Gentile. For the same Lord is Lord of all and richly blesses all who call on Him" (10:8–9, 12). The bracketing truth from Isaiah 28:16 is that "anyone who trusts in Him will never be put to shame" (9:33, 10:11), for "everyone who calls on the name of the Lord will be saved" (Joel 2:32).[11] Obviously, there had been mutual shame between Jews and Gentiles apart from faith. However, Paul's point is that salvation has always been by faith alone, a truth that had been accomplished by Christ. Chapter 10 closes with Old Testament citations that demonstrate that Israel had the messianic word of righteousness but had maintained an obstinate rejection of God's provisions (Isa. 65.2).

Accordingly, the Lord had decreed through Moses that He "would make Israel envious by those who are not a nation . . . and make you angry by a nation that has no understanding" (10:19; quoting Deut. 32:21). The importance of this *testimonia* from the song of Moses (cf. 1 Cor. 10:20–22; Phil. 2:15; Heb. 1:6) centers on his use of παραζηλόω ("to make envious") and παροργίζω ("to make angry").[12] The verbs introduce God's "strategy of provocation," which Paul will develop in 11:11–29 and by which God will bless Gentiles to their "fullness" as a means of fulfilling His promises through Israel's full salvation. The emphatic placement of "Israel" and the first person pronoun in 10:19 brings the question of Israel's unbelief to the fore. Had Israel, with its many privileges, acted in ignorance or in rebellion? Both the Law and the Prophets testify that obstinate disobedience was an abiding problem that had not frustrated God's revealed plan. Thus, Paul appealed to Scripture rather than to the success of his ministry among Gentiles. Bruce accurately summarizes the divine provocation of Israel:

> "Because they had provoked God to jealousy by their worship of a 'no-god' (Heb. *lo'-'el*), he would provoke them to jealousy by means of a 'no-people' (Heb. *lo'-'am*). That is to say, in the course of history He used as the instruments of His judgment on Israel this or that Gentile nation—those whom they regarded

as being a 'no-people' in the sense that they did not enter into
God's electing purpose as a people in the way that Israel did."[13]

The next stage of Paul's argument concerning "strategic envy"
is the merciful interchange of wild and natural branches on the
basis of irrevocable, patriarchal roots.

He briefly introduces prophetic testimony from Isaiah 65:1–2
to bring Israel's guilt to a climax. His singular use of ἀποτολμᾷ
highlights Isaiah's astonishing contrast of Gentile faith and Israelite unbelief: "If the Gentile perceived, it is the Jews' own fault
that he did not."[14] However, consistent with his following arguments about the "non-rejection of God's people" and the "irrevocability of patriarchal roots," the "people" in Isaiah maintain their
chosen status in spite of their unbelief.

The Distinctiveness of the Church

Romans 11 describes the eschatological relationship of Jews and
Gentiles from the vantage of the present age. Paul uses his prior
arguments for Israel's distinctive calling and God's just righteousness by faith as preludes to his exposition of how the church relates to Israel's future. In fact, it is the one chapter in which Paul
"thematically discusses the future of Israel,"[15] and is, therefore, a
proper place to delineate various views of Israel vis-à-vis the church.

From among a plethora of nuanced options, two basic positions
emerge. First, covenant theologians have identified or equated
Israel and the church as a single people of God, the latter having
replaced Israel as the people of faith. Perhaps a more contemporary way of expressing the position is to say that Israel has been
"incorporated" or "reconstituted" into the church as the "new
Israel," having superseded Israel's special covenantal relationships
and promises. Accordingly, the present age for most non-
premillenarians is a kingdom age of unspecified length before the
return of the Lord.[16] Since the issue of corporate identity in this
position is the faith of the elect, some theologians like Louis
Berkhof link the church only with the Israelite remnant of believers.[17] The emphasis, however, may be latent in the continuity, indeed identity, between the testaments and the people of God.
Although covenant theologians have sometimes disagreed on
whether Old Testament promises are now fulfilled in heaven or

on earth, a point of agreement is that issues of fulfillment are centered in Christ as "the true Israel":

> Since Christ is the true Israel, the true seed of Abraham, we who are in Christ by faith and the working of his Spirit are the true Israel, the Israel of faith, not of mere natural descent. . . . We Christians are the Israel of God, Abraham's seed, and heirs of the promises, only because by faith we are united to him who alone is true Israel.[18]

If Christ is the true Israel, and surely His comprehensive fulfillment of biblical predictions and righteousness suggests that He exemplifies such a premise (cf. Luke 24:13–45; Rev. 19:10), then covenant theologians go on to infer that Israel's rejection of the Messiah forfeited its distinctive privileges and promises and transferred them to the church, the people of faith in Christ. Thus, in Romans 11 the "engrafting" of Gentiles and "regrafting" of Jews are simultaneous processes until the return of the Lord.

Covenant and dispensational theologians have long debated this issue and corollary themes like hermeneutics and kingdom. However, the chapter is focused specifically on intradispensational disagreements, so the covenantal Israel-Christ-church identity must be reduced to its tangential significance for insights about degrees of Israel/church discontinuities. These insights are important, however, because their questions about the text expose preunderstandings of dispensationalists that might otherwise be glossed.

Second, dispensational premillennialists have distinguished between Israel and the church in various ways. An older approach treated Old Testament covenantal texts as exclusively Israelite in reference and, accordingly, deflected their fulfillment to the Millennium. The underlying premise was that national Israel, as the physical seed of Abraham, was to be eternally bifurcated from the church, a heavenly mystery that could not have been known in a dispensation of earthly issues. Lewis Sperry Chafer's statement is representative:

> In fact, the new, hitherto unrevealed purpose of God in the outcalling of a heavenly people from Jews and Gentiles is so

divergent with respect to the divine purpose toward Israel, which purpose preceded it and will yet follow it, that the term parenthetical, commonly employed to describe the new age-purpose, is inaccurate. A parenthetical portion sustains some direct or indirect relation to that which goes before or that which follows; but the present age-purpose is not thus related and therefore is more properly termed an intercalation. The appropriateness of this word will be seen in the fact that, as an interpolation is formed by inserting a word or phrase into a context, so an intercalation is formed by introducing a day or a period of time into the calendar. The present age of the Church is an intercalation into the revealed calendar or program of God as that program was foreseen by the prophets of old. Such, indeed, is the precise character of the present age. . . . [Then Chafer concludes a chapter on 24 contrasts between Israel and the church with . . .] Each [Israel and the church], in turn, has its peculiar relation to God, to righteousness, to sin, to redemption, to salvation, to human responsibility, and to destiny."[19]

The New Scofield Reference Bible, Ryrie's *Dispensationalism Today,* and other dispensationalists in the mid-twentieth century modified the heavenly/earthly dualistic language, diminished future distinctions between the peoples of God, and debated about how the new covenant should be applied in the present age.[20]

A more moderate dispensational position has arisen in recent years. On the basis of the New Testament's use of crucial Old Testament texts, progressive dispensationalists acknowledge degrees of Old Testament content in the church, though complete fulfillment of Israel's promises awaits the Millennium as an intermediate kingdom that exists with Israel's Messiah ruling in the midst of the nations.[21] The progressives insist on distinguishing Israel and the church, but they see both continuity and discontinuity in Israel/church and Old/New testamental relationships. Thus, the fulfillments of messianic promises relate to both present and future ages and both advents of Messiah, an "already-not yet" mediating position. Accordingly, this position would see both continuity and discontinuity between Israel and the church.

As an initial question, do elements of discontinuity in Romans 11 support the view that the church has superseded Israel's distinctive calling and promises? The chapter is keynoted by two rhetorical questions about Israel's unbelief and the possibility of God's rejection of "His people." Paul asks: "Did God reject His people?" (11:1), and again he asks, "Did they stumble so as to fall beyond recovery?" (11:11). Twice Paul answered with his emphatic denial (μὴ γένοιτο). In answer to the first question (vv. 1–10), an issue of divine rejection, he included himself as part of a remnant that proved that God had not rejected His "foreknown people" (v. 2). The connection of the remnant to the "people" bridged the "lonely" minority to a larger ethnic "fullness" in verse 26. Stated obversely, had God rejected Israel, then Paul would not have been chosen for salvation and, by implication in view of his theology, for apostleship to the Gentiles (v. 13).[22] He introduced the precedent of Elijah (v. 26) to illustrate God's faithfulness at a time when national unbelief had seemed to short-circuit His program for Israel, a situation that he paralleled with his own (οὕτως οὖν).[23] Elijah had turned away from the majority of his country-men in despair, discounting the grace of God that had preserved a sizable remnant. The parallel with Israel's misdirected, hardened zeal in rejection of Messiah in 10:1–4 is unmistakable. As God's faithfulness had graciously carried His people forward in former times, so now the believing remnant could see itself as an earnest of God's commitment to the fulfillment of His covenants. By combining Deuteronomy 29:4 and Isaiah 29:10, Paul established a continuum for the remnant-majority theme as a basis for Israel's mysterious future fullness as Isaiah had predicted as well (11:26). He then introduced Psalm 69:22–23 as an ironically merciful imprecation that the burden of rejecting Messiah (cf. 9:33) would be lifted, so that he could provoke some of his kinsmen to faith.[24]

The preceding discussion has underscored a crucial point for the question of divine rejection; namely, has the church not superseded Israel's distinctive calling and promises? Paul's remnant was a part of the church, but ecclesial coequality between Jews and Gentiles had not obscured their distinctive ethnic identities. Instead, the second question (11:11), one that focused on the possibility of human disqualification, introduced the constructive tension between Jews and Gentiles as the divine strategy of provocation (cf. 10:19). The church had not taken Israel's place in God's program. Instead, it validated God's faithfulness to His people through its Jewish remnant of faith, and it has served as the provocative means of Israel's future fullness that will bountifully enrich the world (11:12). There is a present continuum between past promise and future fulfillments, and there is ethnic identity in the coequality of the church. This point makes language like "replacement" and "supercession" inappropriate.[25]

The remnant theme is insightful for Galatians 6:16 as well. This problematic verse has been used to defend the equation of Israel and the church.[26] The context is clear; Paul argues against the boasting of legalistic Judaizers in behalf of God's gracious "rule," walking in the Spirit based on Christ's cross. The blessing of believers, as Burton renders the verse, is "as many as shall walk by his rule, peace be upon them, and mercy upon the Israel of God."[27]

S. Lewis Johnson has summarized the various textual problems succinctly: exegetical, contextual, and theological.[28] Specifically, these problems concern the apostle's use of καί, the relation of Israel and the church in the history of Christian doctrine, and the apostle's arguments about the status of Israel in his generation. Theologically, debate centers on the phrase "Israel of God." How does the New Testament use the designation "Israel"? In more than sixty-five uses, fifteen in Paul's epistles, it refers to ethnic Israel: "There is no instance in biblical literature of the term *Israel* being used in the sense of the church, or the people of God as composed of both believing ethnic Jews or Gentiles."[29] The case for Israel as an ethnic nation in Paul's theology is conclusive to the point that Cranfield disclaimed his own "replacement" language:

> It is only where the Church persists in refusing to learn this message, where it secretly—perhaps quite unconsciously!—believes that its own existence is based on human achievement, and so fails to understand God's mercy to itself, that it is unable to believe in God's mercy for still unbelieving Israel, and so entertains the ugly and unscriptural notion that God has cast off His people Israel and simply replaced it by the Christian Church. These three chapters emphatically forbid us to speak of the Church as having once and for all taken the place of the Jewish people. . . . And I confess with shame to having also myself used in print on more than one occasion this language of the replacement of Israel by the Church.[30]

Additionally, the prepositional phrase "of God" marks the "Israel" in question as Hebrew believers, either as the present remnant in the church (Rom. 11:1–10)[31] or as a future, converted mass at Messiah's return (11:26).[32] Without denying the psychological appropriateness of Israel's hope for a future conversion in Paul's theology, the most exegetically apt interpretation for Galatians would be the apostolic confirmation of faithful Jewish believers in the Galatian churches. With this conclusion, Galatians 6:16 serves as a theological validation of Paul's remnant theme in Romans 11:1–15, a validation as well of abiding ethnic as well as gender and social distinctions (cf. Gal. 3:28) in spite of the coequality of all believers in the church.

Contextually, "what more fitting thing could Paul write, it is said, in a work so strongly attacking Jewish professing believers, the Judaizers, than to make it most plain that he was not attacking the true believing Jews?"[33] This conclusion is reinforced by the well-known fact that Justin Martyr's *Dialogue with Trypho* is the first writing to identify Israel with the church.[34]

Grammatically, the debate has keyed on Paul's use of καί. Is the nuance in 6:16 appositional as amillenarians contend, equating "the Israel of God" with "those who walk by the Spirit (= the church)? Or is the conjunctive particle continuative in nuance, encouraging Jewish believers who faced Judaizing hostility? The problem is the rarity of the appositional use: "An extremely rare usage has been made to replace the common usage, even in spite of the fact that the common and frequent usage makes perfectly good sense in Galatians 6:16."[35] The debate is important, because Galatians apparently advanced a Pauline perspective that does not accord with the supercessionist position.

In the remainder of the Romans 11, the firstfruit and olive tree metaphors encapsulate the tensions that characterize the Israel/church debate. Consonant with the remnant theme, the part of the firstfruit cake (cf. Num. 15:17–21) and the root of the tree consecrated the full harvest and the branches, respectively. As the Numbers passage addressed mutually edifying worship by Jews and Gentiles in the land, so Paul apparently was calling for a similar reciprocation among the Romans. The part-for-whole parallel (11:16) in both cases prepares his readers for a future "fullness" of "all Israel," a process that he hoped to employ in the salvation of a kinsman-remnant in his own ministry (v. 14).

The olive tree figure combines the themes of divine sovereignty, faith, and provocation in an extended description of how Gentiles and Jews are engrafted, pruned, and regrafted until God's covenantal promises reach their fulfillment. The tree and its root are single. Thus, the passage clearly supports a measure of continuity in God's soteriological and eschatological plan.

The root is given greater space, indicating that ecclesial privileges are "nourished" by irrevocable, patriarchal promises (vv. 17, 32). Beneath the present expressions of divine mercy ("now," v. 31), we can discern a "sustaining" root (v. 18), even as divine election proceeds to its perfect conclusions in spite of pervasive human presumptions throughout history. Verses 17–21, in the context of the chosen remnant, emphasize that the root cannot mean human claims on God's gracious blessings, patriarchal or otherwise: "do not boast . . . do not be arrogant, but be afraid . . ." (cf. v. 25). On the other hand, Cranfield notes: "There is a very widespread agreement that it *[riza]* must refer to the patriarchs and that Paul's meaning is that the unbelieving majority of Jews are followed by their relation to the patriarchs."[36] However, if the patriarchs are the living root ("the nourishing sap"), then their physical lineage would seem to be efficacious and the removal of unbelieving Jews as "natural branches" as well as the "engrafting" of believing Gentiles would be extraneous. Furthermore, such a view without qualification would undercut Paul's "not all of Israel is Israel principle." Perhaps the best way to reconcile patriarchal promises and the irrevocability of divine "gifts and calling" (vv. 28–29) would be to identify the root as God's loyal love to His covenantal stipulations (notably faith, v. 20) and promises.

The tree, accordingly, would refer to a saving program that would be theocratically based on Israel's covenants. In Romans 11 the new covenant is more relevant because it incorporated Gentiles under Messiah's forgiveness, and its misapplications led to ethnic tensions in the Roman church.[37] The point is the preservation of Paul's divine center rather than notions of ethnic privilege or supremacy that were problematic in the background. At stake are Paul's appeals for unity in the body of Christ, the Roman church in particular.

From the "engrafting" of Gentiles by faith with an emphatic caveat about pride, Paul transitions to the "regrafting" of believing Jews as "natural branches" into their own tree (vv. 22–24). The single tree remains as a point of continuity between past and present ages. The need for humble faith in the former verses shifts to an apostolic appeal "to consider the kindness and sternness of God" (v. 22) as it applied to the grafting process.

Two related questions come to the fore with the regrafting of believing Jews. First, if root and tree affirm intertestamental continuity, then Paul's consistent distinction between wild and natural branches undermines continuum in a "replacement" sense, for the text is forward looking to divine vindications that only "regrafting" can accomplish. This part of the chapter, far from being incidental, is a crucial point in Paul's argument that God has not rejected Israel. The remnant of Hebrew Christians, in turn, becomes an earnest of a future fullness of Israel in fulfillment of God's covenantal promises. What is the point of the grafting process and divinely sanctioned provocation, an interpreter should ask, if Israel has merely become "church"?[38] When combined with the coequality of believers in Ephesians and Galatians, then the interpreter must add discontinuity between the testaments to the provocation of abiding ethnic identities. In other words, the tree remains "natural," awaiting the faith of its own branches as faithful "wild branches" thrive on its "nourishing sap." Even in its discontinuity of branches, there is continuity in the tree but not to the extent of "replacement" or "supercession," as traditionally held by covenant theologians.[39] Thus, the kindness and sternness of God achieve the fullness of His elect people without compromising His character and Word.

Second, an interpreter must ask whether the steps of the grafting process occur simultaneously or successively. These are the amillennial and dispensational, premillennial options, respectively.[40] A superficial inclination would be to dismiss the "simultaneous" view as irrelevant in dispensational discussion. Such a dismissal is unwise because the grafting process affects the precision of one's interpretation of textual details as well as his interpretation of how Israel's past distinctives and present coequality in the church relate to its future.

The "simultaneous" view of Israel's pruning and regrafting has been argued at some length by William Hendriksen and Anthony Hoekema.[41] Hoekema, for example, accepts an "eschatological" fullness of Israel's salvation ("more Israelites than could be described as only a small remnant") but not a national salvation as distinct from Gentiles:

> There is no need, however, to restrict this acceptance to a period of history at the end-time. . . . Every thought of a separate future, a separate kind of salvation, or a separate spiritual organism for saved Jews is here excluded. Their salvation is here pictured in terms of becoming one with the saved totality of God's people, not in terms of a separate program for Jews! It should also be noted that Paul does not say that the ingrafting of Jewish branches must necessarily follow the ingrafting of Gentile branches; there is no reason for excluding the possibility that Gentile branches can be grafted into the olive tree simultaneously. . . . The salvation of all Israel, therefore, does not take place exclusively at the end-time, but takes place throughout the era between Christ's first and second coming—in fact, from the time of the call of Abraham. All Israel, therefore, differs from the elect remnant spoken of in 11:5, but only as the sum total of all the remnants throughout history.[42]

Therefore, "fullness," for Hoekema, means the sum of the remnants. He supports the simultaneous salvation of Jews and Gentiles to their fullness with rather predictable emphases: the single olive tree, the elect remnant motif, an equation of Gentile and Jewish fullnesses, and "fullness" as understood by contemporary successes in Jewish evangelism.[43] These emphases are interpreted with the amillennial assumptions that textual issues like the unconditional, covenantal promises to Israel are fulfilled in Christ's first advent and the consequent formation of a "new Israel" in Christ.

A response to Hoekema will help to determine the boundaries of dispensational discussion. Paul's emphasis on the continuity of grafting will not allow an imbalanced discontinuity between Israel and the church. In other words, we must not lose the connection of the "now" (vv. 30–31) to the future fullness.[44] However, the details of Romans 11 do not support his denial of "a large-scale conversion of the nation of Israel either just before or at the time of Christ's return, after the ingathering of the fullness of the Gentiles."[45] Consequently, and admittedly without decisive textual evidence, the grafting process seems to support a successiveness that points to a future fullness of "national" Israel, a "bulk" or "mass" of the "people" as distinct from the present remnant of Jewish believers in the church. Paul may not be predicting specific future events, but he certainly indicates the general goal of God's strategic provocation. The future, for him, is a reversal for the collective nation/people (vv. 12, 15), apparently not to be equated with the present remnant of saved Jews, since "their" refers to the unbelieving majority that will be grafted in again. The issue is not as uncomplicated as Strimple would wish.[46] Are we to believe that elect Jewish remnants were "broken off" (11:19), that a continuum of remnants with their lingering questions of theodicy will somehow result in an extraordinary "riches of fullness," or that the rather obvious cumulative salvation of elect remnants would be "mysterious"? If Jewish and Gentile grafting are equivalent, then why does Paul say that "natural branches" will be "more readily grafted into their own tree" (v. 24)? If οὗτος has its normal demonstrative nuance of manner, then its nearest antecedence is with the preceding Jewish hardening and Gentile salvation rather than the "fullnesses" to follow.[47] In other words, a dispensational premillennialist may have desired a more sequential or temporal particle, but the effect of οὗτος is to recycle the above questions as a prelude to decisions about the "salvation of all Israel" and the composite Old Testament quotation that follows.

The meaning of "all Israel" and the Old Testament citation in 11:26–27 remain as related textual issues had lead to larger "integrative questions" about Israel's future:

> One's general approach to how the Old Testament works when cited in the New Testament determines how the details of New Testament fulfillment, or even of Old Testament promise, are read. All sides are making a textual appeal here. The question is which synthesis is the more persuasive and comprehensive in treating the material.[48]

The integrative questions should begin with Isaiah and Jeremiah, as quoted in Romans 11. However, they will extend to

Daniel, Ezekiel, the Olivet discourse, Revelation, and a host of other passages. The composite quotation underlies a proper understanding of "the salvation of all Israel." Paul combined the LXX form of Isaiah 59:20–21, 27:9 and Jeremiah 31:33–34 to remind his readers about the goal of God's covenantal promises to Israel, a goal that encompasses a number of events that are associated with the second coming of Christ. Isaiah 59 places Israel's salvation at the Parousia of Messiah, "a strictly eschatological event."[49] The focus is on the unconditionally promised Davidic deliverer. Perhaps with influence from Psalms 14:7 and 53:6, Paul substitutes ἐκ for ἕνεκεν of the LXX. Can this be explained as a part of a received *testimonia*?[50] Was it another reminder that Israel's deliverer would be one of its own?[51] Was it a reminder as well that the Davidic deliverer was also Israel's Savior from sin, a connection that seemed to escape Israel's contemporary expectations (cf. Luke 24)? To be sure, however one answers the above questions by integrating other texts, this is an affirmation that the process of the olive tree is not the final answer for Israel's unbelief. Instead, the grafting process is the present phase that leads to Messiah's personal deliverance of His people. Paul also substitutes a clause from Isaiah 27:9 (LXX), emphasizing the connection between Messiah's Parousia and the nation's salvation. Finally, Jeremiah 31:33–34 is integrated to identify the forgiveness of Israel's sins with God's unconditional new covenant (cf. Micah 7:18–20).

The new covenant's distinctive emphasis on forgiveness self-consciously addressed "all Israel" with language that would have answered the anxieties and questions of first-century Judaism. It was made with "the houses of Israel and Judah" (Jer. 31:31). It would solidify the "God and people" relationship from "the least of them to the greatest" (31:33b–34). So, does the salvation of "all Israel" mean every individual member of the nation? The prior emphasis on faith and remnant would indicate otherwise. An absurdly extreme conclusion of the concept would be a "second chance" for the unbelieving Israelite majorities after a future resurrection. Even as every Jew has not rejected messianic promises or Messiah himself at His first advent, so every member of the nation need not be saved for a representative, national mass of believers at the Parousia. A remnant, yes; but a representatively national number will be converted through the oppressions of "Jacob's trouble."[52]

Having arrived at a general conclusion about "the salvation of all Israel" in Christ that is predicated on covenantal fulfillments, we need not pursue eschatological details that have only indirect bearing on the identity of the peoples of faith. Even though the present remnant has been interpreted as a proof of God's continuing acceptance of Israel and as an earnest of His future fulfillments, the present experience of the remnant has not been equated with the future experience of the nation.[53] Waltke has faulted dispensationalists for reading land promises into the text, where it would have been "rightly expected."[54] He is correct about geographical silence in Romans 11. However, he is incorrect in his removal of eschatology from Israel's salvation.[55] Admittedly, these conclusions arise from *a priori* premises. He is also incorrect to assume that the epistles necessarily had to address issues of the land or that "the symbolic imagery of the Apocalypse" is necessarily less clear than the epistolary genre.[56] Did not Peter sometimes find Paul "hard to understand"(2 Peter 3:16)? Finally, his appeal to existential hermeneutics and the sociology of knowledge is too generic to be meaningful. Even if we can all agree about culturally conditioned knowledge, interpretation, and communication, then are we to read abiding ethnic distinctions in Romans 9–11 as "'weak and beggarly' shadows of the Old Testament"?[57] We think not, and we would conclude that Romans 11 does not support the view that the church has replaced Israel's distinctive calling and promises.

A final question about the peoples of God in Romans 9–11, other Pauline epistles, and the New Testament in general concerns evidences of continuity that would invalidate a complete discontinuity of Israel and the church, and perhaps a dichotomous relationship between the biblical testaments. This question, of course, is asked with the assumption that Israel is not to be equated with the church. Three topics are germane for the Israel/church relationship: Paul's use of the Old Testament, his focus on Jew/Gentile relationships rather than on Israel/church contrasts, and the centrality of Christ in the crucial passages.

Paul's arguments are grounded in the Old Testament. The crucial questions are, how did he use Old Testament precedents and why did he and his fellow apostles use Israelite materials as extensively as they did, if Israel and the church are unconnected or antithetical? Is the Old Testament cited to separate the ages of Israel and the church? If affirmative, he reasonably would have de-emphasized Jewish precedents in favor of new revelation about the church that would undercut ethnic identities in behalf of the coequality of believers in the church. He is not doing this in Romans 9–11. In behalf of God's promises to Israel, he alludes to God's choice of particular children of Abraham. In behalf of God's justice, he quotes and alludes to numerous passages to defend sovereign mercy, a pattern of the remnant to preserve His love toward disobedient Israel, and the principle of salvation by faith in Messiah. He promises messianic salvation for Israel and praises God for His glorious ways with a catena of precedents.[58] By precedent, we mean that Paul is defending New Testament principles and practices by appealing to Old Testament revelation, thus demonstrating that God had not contradicted Himself or capriciously voided the hopes that had guided faithful believers. Beyond question, these are arguments by precedent to prove God's unconditional promises to His children and to defend his emphatic denial of the threatening implications of the rhetorical questions. The arguments bridge the testaments, and they place the present dispensation in vital connection with Israel's past and future. If the purpose of the divine plan is doxological (11:33–36), then why must the mutually edifying relationships of Jews and Gentiles (11:30–32) be distinguished in purpose to the point that the single tree is diminished? Distinguishable parts should not obscure the singleness of the divine plan in Romans 11 that demonstrates the unique, uncompromising majesty and wisdom of the only living God. In sum, we should advance a proper moderation and avoid "false dichotomies," as Kenneth Barker has argued.[59]

On the other hand, is the Old Testament being used to equate Israel and the church as a single, continuous people of faith? In this case, as mentioned before, the rhetorical questions, the remnant, the distinct branches, and the irrevocability of divine gifts become relatively meaningless details in a "single-branched tree." The details of the text better fit "a present remnant chosen by grace" as a guarantee of the complete fulfillment of God's "irrevocable" promises to His Israelite children according to the "word of faith."

Second, we must observe that the apostles characteristically focused on "Jew/Gentile" relationships rather than sustained contrasts between Israel and the church. The matter is important because coequality in faith is a present distinctive of a trans-dispensational principle of salvation with Old Testament precedent (Rom. 9:24; 10:18–21). A primary distinctive of the church is the equal acceptance and organic union of Jews and Gentiles in the body of Christ, truths that are expounded in Ephesians 2 and Galatians 3–4.

Ephesians 2:11–22 contrasts past ("formerly . . . at that time," v. 11) and present ("but now," v. 13) dispensations in terms of Gentile nonprivilege with Christological focus. Contrary to Israel's elected status in Romans 9:4, Gentiles were uncircumcised and "separate from Christ" by birth and identity, excluded from citizenship in Israel, "without hope and without God in the world." In light of Romans 9, this means that Gentiles were born outside of the chosen seed of the children of promise. Also implied in the above change of status is Romans 11:24, where Paul described "wild branches" as "cut out of a wild olive tree, and contrary to nature grafted into a cultivated tree." Because of the normative principle of salvation by faith, they could be saved by messianic faith through a proselytizing relationship with Israel (cf. Jonah).

"But now" in "Christ their peace," believing Gentiles have been "brought near." That is, they have been made "one body" with Jews, a "new man" and "holy temple" with equal access to the Father through the Spirit. This is an eschatological dimension of the Cross that has sometimes been neglected because of Christ's soteriological accomplishments that are a transparent priority for every person. He is "our peace, who has made the two one . . . who destroyed the barrier, the dividing wall of hostility, by abolishing in his flesh the law . . . to reconcile both of them to God through the cross . . . we are no longer foreigners and aliens, but fellow citizens with God's people and members of God's household." These accomplishments validate the distinction between the ages and the peoples of God that dispensational theologians have insistently defended. Specifically, the passage assumes the traditional dispensational emphases like the church's beginning at Pentecost as a distinctive stage in the outworking of God's purpose for the earth.[60] The passage continues by affirming that Christ

Jesus, the chief cornerstone (cf. Rom. 9:23) of the whole temple, purposed a fellow citizenship of all believers in His household. Hence, by atonement, He destroyed the dividing wall between Jews and Gentiles as well as the separation of the Law. Consequently, Gentiles are no longer aliens, but as believers are united with Jews in a "dwelling in which God lives by His Spirit." The church is a "mystery" in that "through the gospel the Gentiles are heirs with Israel, members of one body, and sharers in the promises of Jesus Christ" (3:6).

Consistent with passages such as Acts 10 and Romans 11, Paul appeals to his Jewishness as an apostolic bridge to God's new, coequal relationships in the church. Paul's argument, as elsewhere in his epistles, is that Hebrew Christians should fully accept Gentile believers in the church based on the precedent of faith and the accomplishments of Christ. In other words, the acceptance of Gentiles by faith is continuous with prior revelation and history, but their coequal, ecclesial union with Jews in Christ is discontinuous.

In Galatians 3–4, Paul established continuity between the testaments on the basis of Abraham's "messianic family of faith." The covenantal promises were given to Abraham and his seed, leading to justification by faith in the messianic "Seed." The Law emphatically did not void the promise, but rather tutored a hunger for righteousness that could only be fulfilled in Abraham's Messiah. This means, as Paul repeatedly emphasized, that the Law did not provide justifying righteousness. Thus, all believers are sons of God, Abraham's seed of faith, and heirs according to the promise (3:26–29). The chapter tacitly acknowledges an Abrahamic seed that received the Law and the promises, the fulfilling, messianic Seed, and a seed of faith in the coequality of the church. Its distinctions do not confuse the respective physical and spiritual seeds. In the church, therefore, there is "neither Jew nor Greek, slave nor free, male nor female" (3:28, 5:6), an equality in believers' position that would have been inappropriate in an Old Testament context. In the church age, there is an equality that also affirms identity. Christ came "in the fullness of time" to redeem all believers as heirs that are indwelt by the Spirit according to the promise of the new covenant. Again, Paul's emphasis is on the oneness of the family of God in Christ in the present age in contrast to the "unchosen slavery" of Gentiles in the former age (4:21–31). As in the Ephesians passage, the Old Testament is used to show the continuity of the faith principle and the new equality that Christ's redemption accomplished for all who believe. As in Romans 9, Galatians 4:21–31 comforted "children of promise" (4:28), relegating the Judaizing opponents to the legalizing bondage that had led to the persecution of believers. All are not Israel that call themselves Israel, he consistently affirmed to his kinsmen in faith.

A similar continuity that invalidates "false dichotomies" between distinguishable dispensations is found in Peter's use of the "people of God" with reference to Israel and the church. He encouraged his scattered "fellow-pilgrims" with the fact that they "are a chosen people, a royal priesthood, a holy nation, a people belonging to God" (1 Peter 2:9–12)[61] as God's "elect, called from darkness into His wonderful light." These crucial descriptives of Israel as God's elect people are transferred to his readers with concomitant assurance that they were now God's people and aliens in the world.[62] Reminiscent of Ephesians 2:11–13 and 19, their status had changed from "not a people" to "the people of God" (cf. Rom. 10:19), from a nonrecipient of mercy to a recipient of mercy. The point resurfaces similar dispensational distinctives as noted in Ephesians. Finally, the notion of "aliens and strangers" has been transferred from a position "outside of the holy nation" to a call to be holy in opposition to the cosmos system.

The terms for God's people must be understood in light of the preceding stone metaphor in 2:4–8. As Jewish unbelief had compared with Gentile faith in Romans 9:30–33 (Isa. 8:14 and 28:16), so acceptance of the stone formed a chosen people of God in 1 Peter 2. In Shrenk's words, "the λίθον ἐκλεκτόν creates and upholds the γένος ἐκλεκτόν. . . ."[63] The mutual chosenness of Christ and His believers is the thread that forms the cloth of this epistle.

Three overlapping terms describe the corporate bonds of believers with Israelite nuances: γένος, ἔθνος, and λαός.[64] The terms refer to groups of people that are formed by common bonds. They are taken from Exodus 19:5–6, the foundational passage, Isaiah 43:20–21; Deuteronomy; and Hosea 1–2. An interpreter can compare them concentrically. The broadest term, ἔθνος, is used in 2:9 as "a holy nation" (cf. Exod. 19:6). Lexicons suggest that it is a mass of people living under common conditions, whether Jew or

Gentile. Thus, it means "nation," "holiness" connoting Israel's being set apart under the Mosaic Law of God from all other nations on earth. Related to ἔθνος in Exodus 19 is "a royal priesthood" (βασίλειον ἱεράτευμα), blending as well with 2:5, where Peter describes the church as "a holy priesthood, offering spiritual sacrifices acceptable to God through Christ Jesus."[65] The combined idea of nation and priesthood is that believers are bonded by common service of their divine sovereign, Yahweh, who is now Christ.

A narrower, concentric term is γένος that is used in 2:9 as "a chosen race." It refers to a people that share familial (or ancestral) bonds (cf. Isa. 43:20–21 and the related term φυλή as used for Israelite tribes in the New Testament). Synonymous expressions would be a nation of the same stock, a common offspring, or kinspeople. Perhaps here Peter is referring to believers that are bonded in the family of faith (cf. 2:2, 5), akin to Paul's "children of the promise" in Romans 9:8.

A similar term for "people" translates λαός in 2:9–10 as "a people belonging to God . . . now you are the people of God."[66] The Bible uses this term for a people that are bonded by God's elective choice as indicated by their reception of His saving mercy (cf. Deut.; Hos.; and Rom. 9:25–26). Applied to Israel, we can understand a nation with Law and geographical boundaries, an ethnic people that were ancestrally bonded, and a chosen people of God. Peter parallels these allusions to the church. The elements of continuity are a distinguishable people that are bonded by their common election, faith in the family of God, and royal service in a hostile world. Glenny summarizes the comparison as follows:

> Just as the three quotations in verses 6–8 are united in their application to Christ by the common term *stone,* so the three allusions in verses 9–10 are united in their New Testament application by the term *people* found in each context. In each of these Old Testament contexts the word people is used to refer to Israel as the people of God. The phrase people of God was used in the Old Testament, esp. Deuteronomy, to designate Israel as God's elect people (Deut. 7:6; cf. 4:37; 10:15).[67]

He proceeds to argue for a future for ethnic Israel in the epistle and the apostle's sermons in Acts.[68]

Third, Paul argued for continuity on the basis of the centrality of Christ. The mere fact of Christ's fulfillments and accomplishments may mean that His first advent either delineated the past and present ages or that it related them as a dispensational "hinge." The answer, as usual, must be found in the contextual emphases. We have noted that Christ's ancestry was a Jewish blessing (Rom. 9:5) and that His atonement established the righteousness of faith (9:30–chap. 10). Furthermore, He is the "end of the Law," who delivers all believers from sin's bondage (9:33–10:12). Dovetailing with the above facts about the fulfilling Jewish Messiah, he is the "Cornerstone" of the church as the present "temple" of God, a chosen people, "priesthood," and "nation" (Eph. 2; 1 Peter 2). The "living Stone," He has made the sacrifices of His "living stones" acceptable to God. He is the "Head" of church as his "body." He is the "Seed" through whom all believers are sons and fellow heirs in the family of the church according to the new covenant promises (Gal. 4:1–7). He is the peace who made Jews and Gentiles "fellow citizens" of God's household (Eph. 2:19). In short, the church is described with Old Testament imagery to assure the people of faith, notably concerned Jewish believers, that God's Word had not been voided by change. He has and will fulfill the Old Testament as appropriate, while serving as the foundation of the "new man" in the eschaton. He is the unifying center of the passages that form the argument of this paper, passages that assume His inauguration of the church age after His ascension to the right hand of the Father through the divine gift of the Spirit (John 14; Acts 2). As in other arguments of the paper, Christ represents continuity, even though the peoples of God and dispensations are distinguished. Further study will only reaffirm the Christocentrism of Scripture (Luke 24; Rev. 19:10).

Therefore, Paul's use of the Old Testament, his focus on Jewish/ Gentile relationships in Christ by faith, and the centrality of Christ for all dispensations are continuities that keep us from distinguishing Israel and the church without, at the same time, recognizing the continuities of progressive revelation from Genesis to the Revelation. In the present, the Jewish-Christian remnant, Paul argues, is God's assurance that He has not compromised His Word nor rejected His people. The remnant with the olive tree metaphor, as God's "provocative" present, teach us that the present church age is vitally connected to God's past promises and the future fullness of His covenantal fulfillments.

Conclusion

The chapter began with the importance of the subject for dispensational theology and, specifically, with Romans 9–11 as perhaps the most crucial passage for our understanding of Israel's distinctive past, ecclesial present, and promised future. The distinctiveness of Israel was founded on God's sovereign call of a chosen seed of Abraham to be His kingdom of priests and holy nation with a unique revelation, worship, and messianic ancestry. This section of the chapter is a reaffirmation of the traditional, dispensational emphasis about Israel's destiny, the earthly rule of Messiah from Jerusalem in the Millennium.

Dispensationalists must remember, however, that "children of the promise" were always believing Jews who could be joined in faith by Gentiles. At times, there has been a misplaced emphasis on Israel as "physical seed" that has led to misunderstandings about salvation as well as eschatology. The unbelief of Israelite generations was endemic, as was the majority's legalistic rejection of salvation by grace through faith in Messiah. God's character and Word have been vindicated through a believing remnant that had pointed to an uncompromised future for God's people and covenants. Romans 9–11 underlines the truth that God's sovereign plan is the "mysterious" answer to historical relationships between Jews and Gentiles in every age. Too frequently, other themes and contrasts, disconnected from their divine source, have taken center stage in discussions about Israel and the church. From Paul's initial passion for his kinsmen through the olive tree to the doxology, the divine commitment is the covenantal bridge from past remnants to distinctive ecclesial identities to the future "fullnesses" and fulfillments.

The distinctiveness of the church involved a brief summary and comparison of covenantal and dispensational theologians on this subject. Covenant theologians have equated Israel and the church as a single people of God, Israel having been "reconstituted" into the church as the "new Israel." Dispensational theologians have not equated the peoples of God, thus believing that a future intermediate kingdom, the Millennium, is a necessary fulfillment of God's unconditional promises to Israel. The difference between traditional and progressive dispensationalists is the extent to which Old Testament covenants are realized (in other words, fulfilled) in the church age. Two questions were asked regarding this difference in the context of Romans 9–11.

First, do elements of discontinuity indicate that a replacement theology has gone too far by saying that Israel's distinctive calling and promises have been superseded in the church? The textual details of Romans 11 support the irrevocability of God's promises to Israel, notably the remnant theme as validated by Galatians 6:16 and the consistently distinguished branches of the olive tree in the regrafting process that proceed to the fullnesses of God's fulfillments. Romans 11 does not support a "simultaneous" fulfillment of God's elective promises in this age, but it does connect Hebrew Christians to God's abiding commitment to Abraham's seed that will be realized through the return of Messiah the seed. The chapter, accordingly, suggests that a successive grafting process best explains the salvation of all Israel.

Second, the paper inquired about whether elements of continuity invalidate a dichotomous (or antithetical) relationship between the testaments and peoples of God. Paul's use of the Old Testament, his focus on Jewish/Gentile relationships rather than Israel/church contrasts, and the centrality of Christ in the passages and a proper theology indicate that a balance of continuity and discontinuity is required as a guide for accurate interpretation of these topics. The chapter has led to a "middle ground" that does not equate Israel and the church, thus preserving a distinctive future kingdom in which Israel's Messiah will rule the nations from Jerusalem. The distinctiveness of the church, in Israelite terms, does not mean a new ancestry and revelation, for, by nature, it is by the coequal family of Abraham's faith. The coequality in Christ's body is new but not the faith. It means an equal access and standing of all believers, who in faith live on the basis of Old Testament precedents, predictions, and the accomplishments of Messiah. In short, the church should celebrate its blessings in this age on Old Testament grounds that assuredly lead to a shared future beyond our present comprehension.

A number of issues and subjects with less direct bearing on the identities of Israel and the church have not been discussed in the chapter—notably kingdom, covenants, and future relationships of Israel and the church. These subjects require detailed analysis of other passages. Concerning the Davidic kingdom, fulfillment texts, such as those found in Acts and Hebrews 1, and crucial predictions, such as the ones recorded in Psalms 2 and 110, lead to a similar connection of the church with Israel's past and future in Messiah. Regarding the covenants, fulfillment texts of the new covenant, such as 2 Corinthians 3, Hebrews 8, and eucharistic passages, conclude in a degree of fulfillment in this age with complete fulfillment awaiting the world to come. Other covenants involve the same temporal conditions. Passages such as Revelation 21:9–14 indicate that eternity will be shared by all believers without loss of their identities; Israel and the church are distinguished by "gates" and "foundations" in the Holy City.

The aforementioned topics bring us back to Romans 11, which distinctively identified ethnic Jewish believers and encouraged them with a promised future that had not been voided. The greatest tragedy in discussions such as these is not only that differences arise from a failure to engage God's Word at a mature level, but also that we tend to lose the passion of the apostle: "Brothers, my heart's desire and prayer to God for the Israelites is that they may be saved."

RESPONSE

With consummate skill, Lanier Burns has written on Israel and the church in Romans 9–11. Very frankly, dispensationalists of a more traditional stripe will agree with the majority of what Burns says. He argues for discontinuity between Old Testament redeemed Israel and the New Testament church as two peoples in the body of the redeemed. Like all dispensationalists, he argues that Israel means "Israel" in the New Testament, including Galatians 6:16. He masterfully contends against replacement theology, which evacuates a future for Israel in the coming kingdom. He also shows how the figure of an olive tree is to be taken as a metaphor of the successive salvation of Jews, Gentiles, and Jews rather than as a picture of the simultaneous salvation of Jews and Gentiles in this dispensation. He defends the idea that saved Jews and Gentiles are coequal in the church that began at Pentecost. For instance, he states ". . . the acceptance of Gentiles by faith is continuous with prior revelation and history, but their coequal, ecclesiastical union with Jews is discontinuous." In other words, when Burns contends for discontinuity, traditional dispensationalists will "amen" his statements.

It is in the realm of continuity that disagreements arise. Burns argues for continuity between Israel and the church. He uses three evidences—"Paul's use of the Old Testament, his focus on 'Jew/Gentile' relationships rather than Israel/church contrasts, and the centrality of Christ in the crucial passages." All dispensationalists see some continuity between the Old and New Testaments. The question is: how much?

In connection with Paul's use of the Old Testament, Burns asks, "Is the Old Testament cited to separate the ages of Israel and the church? If affirmative, he most reasonably would have de-emphasized Jewish precedents in favor of new revelation about the church that would undercut ethnic identities in behalf of the coequality of believers in the church. He is not doing this in Romans 9–11." In response to the question of whether Paul uses the Old Testament to separate Israel and the church, it must be said that the church is a New Testament mystery. It would be difficult, if not impossible, to find the church in the Old Testament. How, then, could Paul cite the Old Testament to distinguish Israel from the church? Yet, Paul clearly distinguishes the ages of law and the church (cf. Gal. 3:23–28; Eph. 2:11–22; 3:4–6). The figure of the olive tree makes the distinction clear. Burns uses the Hosea 2:23 and 1:10 quotations in Romans 9:25–26 to show that the Old Testament is applied to the church. It is possible, as Burns concedes, that Paul is using Hosea analogically, that is, as an illustration of a principle. It is also very possible to say that Paul quotes from Hosea to apply it directly to Israel as Hosea did. He also uses 1 Peter 2:9–12 as an illustration of the Old Testament Jewish terminology being applied to the church. However, he never mentions the fact that the readers for the most part may be Jewish. Peter refers to them as being of the *diasporas* (1:1), a term used elsewhere only of Jews in the New Testament. It is true that they are in the church, but this gives a different slant to the emphasis. Once again, the Old Testament passages may be used analogically by Peter. These discussions indicate that each passage must be examined carefully before undue continuity may be claimed.

The major question of continuity comes in the matter of the fulfillment of the three major Jewish covenants in the church—the Abrahamic, the Davidic and the New. Sadly, Burns did not discuss these because he limited himself largely to Romans 9–11. He did use the expression "already-not yet" to describe some fulfillment of the Old Testament promises today. Would it not be better to employ New Testament terminology such as "pledge" or "down payment"? The expression "already" implies that the Old Testament promises are being fulfilled now. It also leaves the impression that the kingdom has already begun. The term *arrabon* is far more accurate in that it lays a proper emphasis on the future.

The second evidence Burns uses to show continuity is Paul's emphasis on Jew/Gentile relationships rather than Israel/church contrasts. But does not Paul make a strong contrast between Israel and the church in Romans 11:28–31? Certainly the entire section of Romans 9–11 looks back on Israel as a group distinct from the church. In fact, this is one of the undergirding theses of the book of Acts. But let Burns's assumed point stand. Does this show continuity? Justification by faith is transdispensational; there is continuity in this. No one disputes this. It is interesting, however, to note that Gentiles had to become Jews in the Old Testament to worship with them. The opposite is true in the New Testament; Jews needed to become Gentiles to be saved (Acts 15:11; Gal. 2:17; 4:12). In other words, Jews had to abandon any confidence in the law system for justification and sanctification. At any rate, there is continuity in justification by faith, even if Burns's point seems overstated.

The third argument for continuity is the centrality of Christ. On this point there can be no debate.

A few minor disagreements may be pointed out, such as the distinction Burns makes between the middle wall of partition and the Law. It seems the Law of Moses was the barrier between Jew and Gentile that Christ tore down. Such differences are small.

In conclusion, it is necessary to interact more on relevant issues such as the contingency of the coming of the kingdom, the debate over a present form of a kingdom, and the present reign of Christ. All in all, traditional dispensationalists will find much common ground in Burns's chapter on Romans 9–11.

Chapter Notes

1. C. H. Dodd, *The Epistle of Paul to the Romans* (London: Hodder and Stoughton, 1932), 161. Daniel Harrington, *God's People in Christ: New Testament Perspectives on the Church and Judaism, Overtures to Biblical Theology* (Philadelphia: Fortress, 1980), 66: "Romans 9–11 . . . remain the most serious effort to grapple with these problems in the entire New Testament."

2. Charles Ryrie, *Dispensationalism Today* (Chicago: Moody, 1965), 44–47, 132.

3. Darrell Bock, "Summary Essay," in *Three Views on the Millennium and Beyond,* ed. Bock (Grand Rapids: Zondervan, 1999), 292.

4. W. H. Griffith Thomas, *St. Paul's Epistle to the Romans: A Devotional Commentary* (Grand Rapids: Eerdmans, 1946), 244, 271. Cf. F. L. Godet, *Commentary on Romans,* reprint ed. (Grand Rapids: Kregel, 1977), 338–39. Also, C. K. Barrett, *The Epistle to the Romans,* Harper's Commentaries (New York: Harper and Row, 1957), 176: "So far from being an unfeeling apostate, Paul is racked with pain at the thought of Israel's unbelief. Further, like the best of all Jews, Moses (Exod. xxxii. 31 f.), he is willing to sacrifice himself for his people's good."

5. The Law, temple worship, and deeds of lovingkindness were viewed as preeminent privileges by the Mishnah, Aboth 1.2. A helpful summary of key components of Israel's identity can be found in N. T. Wright, *The New Testament and the People of God* (Minneapolis: Fortress, 1992), 215–33. Wright discusses temple, land, Torah, and ethnic ancestry as the primary symbols of the Israelite story.

6. Guenter Wasserberg, "Romans 9–11 and Jewish-Christian Dialogue: Prospects and Provisos," in *Society of Biblical Literature 1998 Seminar Papers* (Atlanta: Scholars Press, 1998), 7. An excellent summary of first-century polemics between Christians and Jews can be found in Craig Evans, "Introduction. Faith and Polemic: The New Testament and First-century Judaism," in *Anti-Semitism and Early Christianity: Issues of Faith and Polemic,* eds. Evans and Donald Hagner (Minneapolis: Fortress, 1993), 1–17. In Jewish perspective, see Claudia Setzer, *Jewish Responses to Early Christians: History and Polemics, 30–150 C.E.* (Minneapolis: Fortress, 1994).

7. John Calvin, *The Epistles of Paul the Apostle to the Romans and to the Thessalonians,* trans. Ross MacKenzie (Grand Rapids: Eerdmans, 1960), 190.

8. Leon Morris, *The Epistle to the Romans* (Grand Rapids: Eerdmans, 1988), 352.

9. Paul uses Hosea 2:23 to validate a principle of God's loving call of Jews and Gentiles to faith (9:24). Edward Glenny explains the Hosean citation as a pattern of God's restorative relationship with Israel, a principle of envy (10:19) that will be enlarged in Romans 11. Glenny, "The Israelite Imagery of 1 Peter 2," in *Dispensationalism, Israel, and the Church: The Search for Definition,* eds. Craig Blaising and Darrell Bock (Grand Rapids: Zondervan, 1992), 177–78. This view accords with the argument of this paper about God's use of provocation to fulfill Israel's future, adding the insight that it is characteristic divine behavior that is not restricted to the present age. S. Lewis Johnson, after a survey of the options, preferred an analogical interpretation based on elective grace, a focus on soteriological rather than national or ethnic meaning, "Evidence from Romans 9–11," in *A Case for Premillennialism: A New Consensus,* eds. Donald Campbell and Jeffrey Townsend (Chicago: Moody, 1992), 209–10.

10. The reader should note David Lowery, "Christ, the End of the Law in Romans 10:4," in *Dispensationalism, Israel, and the Church,* 230–47; Kenneth Barker, ibid., 295–302; and Willem VanGemeren, ibid., 341–43. A meaning that honors the believer's position in Christ as in Romans 3:31 seems closest to Paul's balance of freedom and love as expounded in 1 Corinthians 9:19–23.

11. Rudolf Bultmann notes that Old Testament "shame" words are sometimes linked with judgment, which may be the case here, *TDNT,* 1965, s.v. "αἰσχύνω," 190. Paul's tone is one of assurance; faith in Christ would deliver the majority of Jews from the current dilemmas of unbelief in which they found themselves. This amounts to Bruce's view of the divine vindication of faith for fearful Jews. F. F. Bruce, *The Epistle of Paul to the Romans: An Introduction and Commentary* (Grand Rapids: Eerdmans, 1963), 200. Cf. John 9:22, 12:41.

12. The verbs are followed by ἐπί, a use which BAGD places with "verbs that denote aroused passions" (s.v., ἐπί, II 1 b γ).

13. Bruce, *Romans,* 210. The verse is quoted substantially from the

LXX, substituting *umas* for *autous* to personalize Israel's problem with a divine *lex talionis* response.

14. James Stifler, *The Epistle to the Romans: A Commentary Logical and Historical* (Chicago: Moody, 1960), 182. N.B., C. E. B. Cranfield, *A Critical and Exegetical Commentary on the Epistle to the Romans*, ICC (Edinburgh: T & T Clark, 1979), 2:540. Isaiah's text referred to apostate Israelites. Paul applied them to Gentiles within the broader divine strategy that he had begun to explain.

15. N. A. Dahl, *Studies in Paul: Theology for the Early Christian Mission* (Minneapolis: Augsburg, 1977), 137.

16. Albertus Pieters, *The Seed of Abraham* (Grand Rapids: Eerdmans, 1950), 66–67, 98; and Herman Hoeksema, *Reformed Dogmatics* (Grand Rapids: Reformed Free Association, 1966), 818. A leading exponent of contemporary amillennialism is Anthony Hoekema, who reflects the Dutch legacy in the position: "Is it not abundantly clear from the passages just dealt with that the New Testament church is now the true Israel, in whom and through whom the promises made to Old Testament Israel are being fulfilled?" *The Bible and the Future* (Grand Rapids: Eerdmans, 1979), 198. In the Dutch tradition, a notable example is G. C. Berkouwer, *The Return of Christ, Studies in Dogmatics* (Grand Rapids: Eerdmans, 1972), chap. 11. Berkouwer cites the need for an entire chapter on Israel and the church because of residual anti-Semitism and the formation of the state of Israel. A lengthier survey of the position can be found in J. Lanier Burns, "The Future of Ethnic Israel in Romans 11," 212–17.

17. Louis Berkhof, *Principles of Biblical Interpretation* (Grand Rapids: Baker, 1966), 135–36.

18. Robert Strimple, "Amillennialism," in *Three Views on the Millennium and Beyond*, ed. Darrell Bock (Grand Rapids: Zondervan, 1999), 88–89. A similar emphasis, though hedged and ambivalent, can be found in George Ladd, "Historic Premillennialism," in *The Meaning of the Millennium: Four Views*, ed. Robert Clouse (Downers Grove: InterVarsity, 1977), 22–23, 28–29: "In these references the servant is both Israel and the one who redeems Israel. . . . I do not see how it is possible to avoid the conclusion that the New Testament applies Old Testament prophecies to the New Testament church and in so doing identifies the church as spiritual Israel. . . . Israel remains the elect people of God, a 'holy' people

(Rom. 11:16). We cannot know how the Old Testament prophecies will be fulfilled, except to say that Israel remains the people of God and will yet experience a divine visitation which will result in her salvation."

19. L. S. Chafer, *Systematic Theology*, 8 vols. (Dallas: Dallas Seminary Press, 1948), 4.41, 53. Cf., C. I. Scofield, *Rightly Dividing the Word of Truth*, repr. ed. (Findlay, Ohio: Fundamental Truth, 1947), p. 6; idem, *Scofield Bible Correspondence Course*, 19th ed. (Chicago: Moody Bible Institute, n.d.), 23–25.

20. Erich Sauer, *From Eternity to Eternity* (Grand Rapids: Eerdmans, 1951), 82, 89, 93; Alva McClain, *The Greatness of the Kingdom* (Winona Lake, Ind.: BMH Books, 1959), 439–41; John Walvoord, *The Nations, Israel, and the Church in Prophecy* (Grand Rapids: Zondervan, 1988), 57–61; and idem, *The Millennial Kingdom* (Grand Rapids: Dunham, 1959), 166–73, 187–92, 213–15, 273–74. These men, as noted by Ryrie at the beginning of the chapter, maintained the Israel/church distinction as the most basic theological issue and used Romans 11 for that purpose. For lengthier surveys of the position, see Burns, "The Future of Ethnic Israel," in *Dispensationalism, Israel and the Church*, 218–21; and Craig Blaising, "Development of Dispensationalism by Contemporary Dispensationalists," *BSac* 145 (1988): 133–40, 254–80.

21. Craig Blaising and Darrell Bock, *Progressive Dispensationalism* (Wheaton: Victor, 1993); Robert Saucy, *The Case for Progressive Dispensationalism: The Interface between Dispensational and Non-Dispensational Theology* (Grand Rapids: Zondervan, 1993); and Darrell Bock, ed., *Three Views on the Millennium and Beyond* (Grand Rapids: Zondervan, 1998).

22. Karl Barth, *Church Dogmatics*, vol. II.2: The Doctrine of God, trans. G. W. Bromiley et al. (Edinburgh: T & T Clark, 1957), 268: "To admit that God has rejected His people would mean the annulment, not only of Paul himself, but above all (and this alone is absolutely 'impossible') of his office, his commission, and its whole content."

23. William Sanday and Arthur Headlam, *A Critical and Exegetical Commentary on the Epistle to the Romans*, ICC, 5th ed. (Edinburgh: T & T Clark, 1902), 317: "This doctrine of a remnant implied that it was the individual who was true to his God, and not the nation, that was the object of the Divine solitude; that it was in this small

body of individuals that the true life of the nation dwelt, and that from them would spring that internal reformation, which, coming as the result of the Divine chastisement, would produce a whole people, pure and undefiled, to be offered to God [Isa. lxv. 8,9]."

24. By "burden," we refer to the contextual emphasis that many in Israel had tried too hard in a self-defeating system of legal salvation to fail (Romans 9:31–33; 10:1–5, 14–21; 11:6–10).

25. One of the most influential books on the use of the Old Testament in the New Testament is Richard Hays's recent *Echoes of Scripture in the Letters of Paul* (New Haven, London: Yale Univ., 1989). Hebrews excepted (p. 98), Hays repeatedly argues that supersessionist language is inappropriate for Paul: "It is no accident that Paul never uses expressions such as 'new Israel' or 'spiritual Israel.' There always has been and always will be only one Israel. Into that one Israel Gentile Christians such as the Corinthians have been absorbed" (pp. 96–97; cf. p. 102).

26. Donald Guthrie, ed., *Galatians*, The Century Bible (London: Thomas Nelson, 1969), 161–62; William Hendriksen, *Exposition of Galatians*, New Testament Commentaries (Grand Rapids: Baker, 1968), 246–47; Hans LaRondelle, *The Israel of God in Prophecy: Principles of Prophetic Interpretation* (Berrien Springs, Mich.: Andrews Univ., 1983), 108–14; R. C. H. Lenski, *The Interpretation of Saint Paul's Epistle to the Galatians, to the Ephesians and to the Philippians* (Columbus: Wartburg, 1937), 320–21; John Stott, *Only One Way: The Message of Galatians* (London: InterVarsity, 1968), 180.

27. Ernest DeWitt Burton, *A Critical and Exegetical Commentary on the Epistle to the Galatians,* ICC (Edinburgh: T & T Clark, 1921), 357.

28. S. Lewis Johnson, "Paul and the Israel of God: An Exegetical and Eschatological Case Study," in *Essays in Honor of J. Dwight Pentecost*, eds. Stanley Toussaint and Charles Dyer (Chicago: Moody, 1986), 181–96.

29. Johnson, ibid., p. 189, with validation from Acts; cf. Johnson, "Evidence from Romans 9–11," in *A Case for Premillennialism*, 200–203, for the same meaning in that context; and Burton, *Galatians*, 358, notes: "These facts favour the interpretation of the expression as applying not to the Christian community, but to Jews; yet in view of τοῦ‟ θεοῦ‟ not to the whole Jewish nation, but to pious Israel, the remnant according to the election of grace [Rom. 11:5], including even those who had not seen the truth as Paul saw it, and

so could not be included in ὅσοι . . . στοιχ."; W. D. Davies, "Paul and the People of Israel," *NTS* 24 (1978), 4–39, who finds it difficult to see the church here contrary to Pauline usage elsewhere.

30. Cranfield, *Romans*, 2:448.

31. Hans Dieter Betz, *Galatians*, Hermeneia: A Critical and Historical Commentary on the Bible (Philadelphia: Fortress, 1979), 320–23; Charles Ellicott, *A Critical and Grammatical Commentary on St. Paul's Epistle to the Galatians with a Revised Translation* (Andover: Draper, 1880), 154; Gottlieb Schrenk, "Was bedeutet 'Israel Gottes'?" *Judaica* 5 [1949], 81–95. *TDNT*, 1965, s.v. "'Ιουδαῖος,'Ισραήλ,'Εβραῖος," by Walter Gutbrod, 3:387–88. With reference to Romans 11, Gutbrod notes that Paul would not "separate the term from those who belong to Israel by descent."

32. F. F. Bruce, *The Epistle to the Galatians: A Commentary on the Greek Text*, The New International Greek Commentary (Grand Rapids: Eerdmans, 1982), 275; Franz Mussner, *Der Galaterbrief* (Frieburg: Herders, 1977), 417; and Peter Richardson, *Israel in the Apostolic Church*, Society for New Testament Studies Monograph Series, vol. 10 (Cambridge: Cambridge Univ., 1969), 74–84.

33. Johnson, "Paul and the Israel of God," 185.

34. *Dialogue with Trypho* 11:1–5; also, *Commentary on the Epistle to the Galatians and Homilies on the Epistle to the Ephesians of St. John Chrysostom*, rev. ed. (London: Walter Smith, 1884), 98. Cf. Richardson, *Israel in the Apostolic Church*, chap. 2.

35. Johnson, "Paul and the Israel of God," 188.

36. Cranfield, *Romans*, 2:565.

37. Burns, "The Future of Ethnic Israel," 203.

38. The incompleteness of Hays's thesis is at this point. He argues in *Echoes* on page 86 that a former Christocentric hermeneutic needs to be revised to an ecclesiocentric focus (pp. 84, 100–101, 107, 111, 117, *passim*), a biblical hermeneutic that "is a prefiguration of the church as the people of God. (By church, I mean, of course, not the institutional hierarchy that took shape over time but the community of people who confess that Jesus Christ is Lord.)" On the other hand, "This brings us to the heart of the matter. Typology is before all else a trope, an act of imaginative correlation. If one pole of the typological correlation annihilates the other, the metaphorical tension disappears, and the trope collapses. The viability of the Israel/church typology depends,

for Paul's purposes, on maintaining the separate identity of both poles. The church discovers its true identity only in relation to the sacred story of Israel, and the sacred story of Israel discovers its full significance—so Paul passionately believed—only in relation to God's unfolding design for salvation of the Gentiles in the church" (pp. 100–101). The view introduces paradox into the New Testament (cf. his view of Hebrews), which Hays would accept, as well as his own position (cf. separation with absorption). Specifically, for present purposes, Hays's "absorption" does not allow for a "regrafting" of the natural branches because they are already "absorbed" in the church. Therefore, I would say that a Christocentric hermeneutic that honors both advents of Messiah remains as the best explanation of the details of the olive tree and related issues in the New Testament.

39. See Burns's critique of Sanday and Headlam in "The Future of Ethnic Israel," 203–206.

40. These terms should not be caricatured so that they lose their intended meaning. "Simultaneous" means that the engrafting and regrafting are a present provocation and that the future fullness is a sum of the salvation of elect remnants, although some amillennialists will admit that there can be a large future conversion without the national implications that are a prelude to the Millennium. "Successive" does not mean that present remnants necessarily connect to the future conversion of "all Israel." It means that present Hebrew Christian remnants are the assurance that God has not rejected "His people," and that the future conversion in the content of the Lord's return represents a significant fulfillment of God's unconditional promises to Israel.

41. William Hendriksen, *Israel in Prophecy* (Grand Rapids: Baker, 1974), chaps. 3–4; and Anthony Hoekema, *The Church and the Future* (Grand Rapids: Eerdmans, 1979), 145–46. Cf. Strimple, "Amillennialism," in *Three Views,* 116.

42. Hoekema, *The Bible and the Future,* 143, 145. Herman Ridderbos, *Paul,* trans. J. R. DeWitt (Grand Rapids: Eerdmans, 1975), 354–61, refers to the grafting process as "the wave motion," a metaphor that is adopted by Robert Strimple, "Amillennialism," in *Three Views,* 115–17. Strimple also rejects the present-and-future connection: "This summary statement makes it clear that the apostle's concern in chapter 11 is not to predict the future but to explain

the motive and purpose of his present ministry" (p. 116). The correct answer, I think, is "both-and."

43. Ibid., 146–47.

44. Hoekema, *The Bible and the Future*, 143; Waltke, "A Response," in *Dispensatonalism, Israel, and the Church*, 352; and Strimple, "Amillennialism," in *Three Views*, p. 116.

45. Ibid., 144.

46. Ibid. The issue is not as (un)complicated as Strimple would wish.

47. Johnson, "Evidence in Romans 9–11," 214–15; Sanday and Headlam, *Romans*, 335; Hoekema, *The Bible and the Future*, 144; Strimple, "Amillennialism," 116; and Waltke, "Response," in *Dispensationalism, Israel and the Church*, 352.

48. Bock, "Summary," in *Three Views*, 293.

49. Cranfield, *Romans*, 2:578.

50. One of the most detailed discussions of the citation that also defends its conflation in Jewish oral tradition is Christopher Stanley, "The Redeemer Will Come 'ἐκ Ζιον,'" in *Paul and the Scriptures of Israel*, eds. Craig Evans and James Sanders, *JSNT*, Supp. Ser. vol. 83; and *Studies in Scripture in Early Judaism and Christianity*, vol. 1 (Sheffield: Sheffield Academic Press, 1993), 118–42.

51. Burns, "The Future of Ethnic Israel," 210. David Aune, *Prophecy in Early Christianity and the Ancient Mediterranean World* (Grand Rapids: Eerdmans, 1983), 252–53, interprets the mystery as a prophetic oracle that relieves a potential contradiction with Romans 9:6ff. The oracle, in his view, has three lines, "culminating with the salvation of the entire nation," a notion that is not found elsewhere in the New Testament yet "in no way diminishes the prophetic nature of this Pauline oracle."

52. Erich Sauer, *From Eternity to Eternity: An Outline of the Divine Purposes* ([Grand Rapids: Eerdmans, 1954], 159), has aptly referred to the remnant as "the theocratic kernel of the nation" from which a "national" conversion and restoration will eventuate. Belief in a future, mass conversion of ethnic Israel is not distinctively dispensational. Among amillennialists, see Gerhardus Vos, *The Pauline Eschatology*, reprint ed. (Phillipsburg, N.J.: Presbyterian and Reformed, 1930, 1991), 87–88. More recently, Stanley Grenz, *The Millennial Maze: Sorting Out Evangelical Options* (Downers Grove: InterVarsity, 1992), 171. An excellent summary of Reformed precedents for a mass conversion is Willem VanGemeren's "Israel as

the Hermeneutical Crux in *The Interpretation of Prophecy* (II)," *WTJ* 46 (1984), 254–97.

53. Cf. VanGemeren, "Response," in *Dispensationalism, Israel, and the Church*, 341.

54. Cf. Waltke, "Response," in *Dispensationalism, Israel, and the Church*, 352.

55. Ibid.

56. Ibid., 358. Cf. Blaising and Bock, *Progressive Dispensationalism*, 390.

57. Ibid., 354, 358.

58. Perhaps we have even understated Paul's indebtedness. Hays, *Echoes*, 92, observes: "This observation [about indirect allusions] should remind us how inadequate it is to restrict consideration of Paul's use of Scripture to the passages that he quotes explicitly. Israel's story, as told in Scripture, so comprehensively constitutes the symbolic universe of Paul's discourse that he can recall the elements of that story for himself and his readers with the sorts of subtle gestures that pass between members of an interpretive family."

59. Kenneth Barker, "The Scope and Center of Old and New Testament Theology and Hope," in *Dispensationalism, Israel, and the Church*, 293–328.

60. For example, Ryrie, *Dispensationalism Today*, 133–44; and idem, *Basic Theology* (Wheaton, Ill.: Victor, 1986), 399–402.

61. The future tense with conditional stipulations in Exodus 19:6 is changed to the present tense to assure his suffering friends that their obedience in accepting Christ's atonement (1:2) had assured them "as living stones" with "a living hope." Christ's resurrection was the guarantee of an eternal inheritance "in these last times" (vv. 3–25). His assurance is grounded in the doctrine of election as well. Wayne Grudem argued that "the nation blessed by God is no longer the nation of Israel," *1 Peter, TDNT* (Grand Rapids: Eerdmans, 1988), 113. Glenny countered that Grudem had missed not only the point of Peter's argument concerning election but also the meaning of election and noted that God's election is "irrevocable" from Romans 11:25–29, "Israelite Imagery of 1 Peter 2," in *Dispensationalism, Israel, and the Church*, 185 n. 131.

62. Glenny, ibid., stated: "Applying the Old Testament to the recipients of 1 Peter is foundational for the entire epistle and is developed in 2:4–10. In this passage Peter takes the central concept of

Israel's self-understanding, their status as the elect people of God, and using Old Testament texts that originally spoke of Israel, he transfers this status to his recipients" (pp. 156–57). Does this, he asks, mean that the church has become the new or true Israel of God? Arguing from a "typological-prophetic" perspective, he concluded that 1 Peter "does not present the church as a new Israel replacing ethnic Israel in God's program. Instead, Old Testament Israel was a pattern of the church's relationship with God as His chosen people" (p. 186). Like Israel, the church has been called as an elect people to conduct worship and ministry in the world.

63. *TDNT*, 1967, s.v., "ἐκλεκτός," by G. Schrenk, 4.191. Cf. J. H. Elliott, *The Elect and the Holy* (Leiden: E. J. Brill, 1966, 1966), 141–45.

64. Cf. *TDNT*, 1964, s.v. "ἔθνος," by K. L. Schmidt, 2:369, uses "practically interchangeable" to relate the terms. I would prefer to nuance them differently.

65. The phrase "kingdom of priests" in the LXX may be translated as two substantives ("a royal dwelling" and "a priesthood") or as an adjective and a substantive as above. A majority of interpreters have preferred the dual substantive rendering; however, a meaning of "service under the divine Sovereign" is the same in either case.

66. The reader should consult Markus Barth, *The People of God*, Studies for the Study of the New Testament, Supplement Series, vol. 5 (Sheffield: Sheffield Academic Press, 1983), 11–14.

67. Glenny, "Israelite Imagery in 1 Peter 2," 170.

68. Ibid., 185.

CONCLUSION

CHAPTER EIGHT

Dispensationalism Tomorrow

Herbert W. Bateman IV

Three Central Issues in Contemporary Dispensationalism has served as a forum whereby traditional and progressive dispensationalists might present frank yet congenial perspectives on (1) hermeneutics; (2) the application of their hermeneutic to the Abrahamic, Davidic, and new covenants; and (3) Israel and the church. As I reflect on the discussions in this work, two questions come to my mind: What has been accomplished, and where do we go from here? Much of what has been discussed may be summarized by identifying the unifying issue of dispensationalism, putting to rest secondary issues that tend to distract us from textual discussions, and highlighting primary issues such as hermeneutics and its effect on dispensational theology.

Unifying Issue

Three Central Issues in Contemporary Dispensationalism has argued that throughout the twentieth century, longstanding and universally held dispensational positions have been challenged and, as a result, have been clarified and at times changed (chap. 1). In 1965 and again in 1995, Ryrie stated, "Like all doctrines dispensational teaching has undergone systematization and development in its lifetime, though the basic tenets have not changed."[1] Dispensationalism, however, is still under systematization and development, for it is a tradition driven by a desire to be scriptural and a recognition that infallibility is what the text—not its interpreters—possesses. But regardless of the theological tradition with which we affiliate ourselves, the thought of change—even if it comes as a result of wrestling with the text—is difficult.

After affirming his premillennial-dispensational roots by citing his long term affiliation and association with dispensationalists and by listing his contributions to dispensationalism, a longstanding dispensationalist makes the following statement.

> I have recited these associations so as to affirm my position with the premillennial, dispensational, pretribulational movement. Therefore, when in this chapter I express a viewpoint that runs counter to the almost universally held position of prophetic teachers, I want to make it clear that I am a member of the *loyal* opposition! I am not trying to undercut the basic unity of the position we all hold dear. Rather, I am offering an alternate solution to one of the areas in which I have felt our hermeneutics as a movement has been faulty.

If you keep up with current dispensational discussions you may think this quote is taken from Darrell Bock's article, "Why I am a dispensationalist with a Small 'd.'"[2] It's not! The statement was made in 1973 by Clarence E. Mason in his book *Prophetic Problems*.[3]

According to Mason, the problems with which he interacts are difficult to address for two reasons: (1) a longstanding and universally held theological position was about to be challenged and changed, and (2) it involved dispensationalists employing a hermeneutic that Mason considered "faulty." Mason makes it perfectly clear, however, that he is "not trying to undercut the basic unity of the position we all hold dear."[4] Nevertheless, his understanding of the text resulted in his arguing for a change in a previously held dispensational position.

Today's dispensationalists continue to address questions to the text that involve the use of hermeneutical approaches that affect our theological understanding of the text. They do so, however, without trying to undercut the basic unity of dispensationalism. What, then, unites one dispensationalist to another? Simply put, the basic unifying issue for all dispensationalists is that Israel is not the church. In fact, Ryrie maintains that such a distinction is "the most basic theological test of whether or not a person is a dispensationalist."[6] What is contended among dispensationalists, as we have seen in these essays, is how to define the nature of the Israel/church distinction. Dispensationalists have never universally agreed on a single, unifying theme of Scripture. So definitional and synthetic debates have precedents in dispensationalism. Thus, this tradition is not monolithic, as some have believed and as our first chapter has shown. Dispensationalists are, however, agreed and like-minded in their stress on the uniqueness of the church and their confidence that a future exists for national Israel.

Despite this unifying issue, perpetual interaction with the text has created diversity among dispensationalists, thereby generating various types of dispensationalism. Diversity created because of textual study, however, has spawned some secondary issues that tend to sidetrack discussions away from the text. This is particularly true concerning discussions evident among today's dispensationalists, especially between the traditional dispensationalist (some may prefer the description "revised dispensationalist") and the progressive dispensationalist.

Secondary Issues

Three Central Issues in Contemporary Dispensationalism has put to rest, I hope, at least two secondary issues that are not only disparaging but also tend to derail relevant textual discussions among today's dispensationalists.

To begin with, I hope we can put to rest the charge that progressive dispensationalists are not dispensationalists. When progressive dispensationalism first hit the press, it was associated with Ladd's historical premillennialism and amillennialism. Despite the differences,[7] the accusations pervaded dispensational circles. Such charges, however, are conspicuously absent in this work. Johnson clearly recognizes that Bock is neither Laddian nor amillennian. In fact, Johnson writes:

> Each generation and every tradition which sees the Bible as the basis of its confession can expect to face challenges to formerly accepted interpretations. That is, unless the tradition dies. Thus, a contention for what is true can be a mark of health. (p. 218)

Johnson *does not advance* the notion (nor does Toussaint) that progressive dispensational perspectives are something outside our dispensational tradition. This is a significant observation in light of the fact that both of these men teach at Dallas Theological Seminary. In fact, Johnson readily believes that the contentions that exist between them reflect the sign of a healthy tradition. That "tradition" is dispensational.

I also hope that we can put to rest the secondary issue concerning labels. While labels have been created to define positions, the designation "progressive dispensationalism" is frequently misunderstood. Johnson rightly notes, "By connotation one might conclude that all previous statements and, in fact, all other statements, are regressive or outdated" (p. 103). However, the original intention of the designation "progressive dispensationalism" did not seek to support such a connotation. Progressives simply were trying to describe the inherent structure of their approach. In fact, they have had great respect for those dispensationalists who went before them. Dispensationalism has never been a stagnant theological system. Throughout the twentieth century, dispensationalism evidenced continual evaluation, development, and systematization. In fact, Johnson himself has taken traditional perspectives and presented fresh textual evaluations of them in this very work (chap. 4). Thus, the idea that "all other statements are regressive or out dated" should be viewed as unwarranted and not the intention of the label.

Yet, in looking at the choice of the label from the outside, Johnson correctly noted that "the connotations felt painful for all of us who are 'non-progressive'" (p. 103). Although the initial introduction of the label "progressive dispensationalism" may have seemed disparaging for nonprogressives, Blaising and Bock made it clear in their very first work that

> The label *progressive dispensationalism* is being suggested because of the way in which this dispensationalism views the interrelationship of divine dispensations in history, their overall orientations to the eternal kingdom of God (which is the final, eternal dispensation embracing God and humanity), and the reflection of these historical and eschatological relations in the literary features of Scripture.[8]

In addition, Bock has gone to great pains in this work to state and restate *the motive* for choosing such a label. Thus, the label is intended *to describe* the inner nature of *a type* of dispensationalism. Hopefully we can better understand the authors' choice and intent, lay to rest this particular secondary issue, and focus our energies on hermeneutical issues that affect our theological applications of the text.

Primary Issues

Three Central Issues in Contemporary Dispensationalism has presented the employment of two dispensational hermeneutical approaches that are more focused on this question than were previous discussions among dispensationalists. As a result, Johnson's and Bock's hermeneutical conclusions greatly affect today's dispensational theology.

First, Johnson and Bock present a historical-grammatical interpretive approach (chaps. 2–3) that specifically addresses the issue of semantic expansions between the Old and New Testaments. On the one hand, Johnson advances a "stable meaning approach" that further develops Ryrie's consistent literal hermeneutic. At issue is this question: Can a passage in the Old Testament be taken to refer to Israel in the future while at the same time it is taken to refer to the church? Thus, it involves a tighter correspondence between human authors of the Old and New Testaments and thereby minimizes an expanded understanding in the New Testament era.

On the other hand, Bock argued for a "complementary approach" that allows for a variety of ways by which the New Testament author may present an expanded understanding of the Old Testament promises. These meanings are supported frequently by extrabiblical material of the first century, in the teachings of Jesus, and in the working of the Holy Spirit as He inspired the New Testament writings. This is not to say that Johnson ignores extrabiblical material, the teachings of Jesus, and the working of the Holy Spirit. It is to say, however, that whereas Bock maximizes these aspects of the first-century apostolic period, Johnson tends to utilize them less.

Questions about semantic expansions within the canon *should not* be confused with postmodernism. Johnson recognizes, correctly, that Bock "*limit(s)* the interpretive expansion to the apostle's interpretation of the Old Testament" and that Bock is not a postmodernist. Bock's canonical limitations distinguish him from postmodernists. In fact, as long as dispensationalists remain canonically bound, they avoid the risk of a postmodern free-for-all. Thus, tomorrow's dispensationalists will continue to ask, "Do semantic expansions, which are connected to a unified meaning of Scripture, happen within the canon? If so, how do they work? To what extent do statements made in the Old Testament change or expand due to the perspective of added revelation? What part does the historical and theological milieu of the apostolic period play in our methods of interpretation?" As we address these and other questions, our approach to a canonical reading of the text will continue to mature and thereby challenge and strengthen our dispensational positions concerning God's Old Testament promises to national Israel and their application to the church.

Second, while applying their respective hermeneutic to Old Testament texts about the covenants (chaps. 4–5), Johnson and Bock make fresh suggestions about the relationship between God's promised covenantal provisions and their realization during the early church. On the one hand, Johnson's "stable meaning approach" leads him to conclude that inauguration of fulfillment occurs only when *all of the provisions* of agreement are *kept* with the one to whom those promises were made (specifically national Israel). As a result, only one covenant is inaugurated in fulfillment today and that is the new covenant in Israel's representative: Christ. The Abrahamic covenant promises a descendant *through whom blessing will come*, and that descendant is Christ. The Davidic covenant promises a descendant *who will reign*, and that descendent is Christ. However, neither of these latter covenants is fulfilled today. Thus, there is but one covenantal partner/beneficiary—national Israel. It is not the church.

On the other hand, Bock's "complementary approach" leads him to conclude that initial fulfillment exists for the Abrahamic, Davidic, and new covenants because these multifaceted covenants are linked together in both the Old and the New Testaments. Whereas the Christological-messianic elements that specifically benefit both Israel and the world are initially realized today in the church, an even more complete fulfillment of these covenantal promises is yet to come when Christ Jesus returns to reign on earth from Jerusalem. Thus, the church (both Jew and Gentile) shares *directly* in many of the covenantal blessings, although other promised blessings to national Israel are yet to come.

Through the employment and results of Johnson's and Bock's hermeneutical approaches, they not only challenge some long-standing dispensational perspectives, they also offer some fresh perspectives about God's covenantal promises. Tomorrow's dispensationalists will be no different. Dispensationalists will continue to inquire whether covenantal blessings are limited to national Israel (Johnson) or whether they are in some sense extended to the Gentiles (Bock). At least two questions must be addressed as a result of the work presented in chapters four and five. (1) If the institution of the covenants is merely something about which Gentiles are to be informed, do any covenantal provisions exist for the Gentile or the church today? (2) If the promises and covenants extend to the Gentiles or the church, what aspects of the covenantal promises are fulfilled? Thus, tomorrow's dispensationalist should evaluate and interface with these more recent dispensational hermeneutical approaches to the text and consider how they make legitimate impacts on the dispensational tradition.

Finally, there is the linchpin that distinguishes dispensationalists from nondispensationalists—the teaching that stresses the uniqueness of the church and the future for national Israel. Although they agree concerning the distinction between Israel and the church, Toussaint and Burns still contend over the boundaries of that distinction (chaps. 6–7). Whereas the line between Israel and the church was at one time quite boldly drawn by previous generations of dispensationalists (i.e., Darby, Larkin, Scofield, and Chafer all held to a total distinction), today's dispensationalists differ concerning the extent of that distinction. On the one hand, Toussaint maintains a relatively broad line of distinction between Israel and the church. He argues that the Lord's messianic kingdom is something totally future and thereby rejects the existence of a current mystery form of the kingdom (or "spiritual kingdom" for today, unlike Ryrie, Walvoord, Pentecost, etc., and most pointedly an inaugurated form of the Davidic kingdom (unlike Bock and Blaising, pp. 226–47). In fact, Toussaint denies any Old Testament connection with the New Testament's concept of *mystery* (pp. 247–48).[9] The church age is a "parenthesis," although it shares in Israel's millennial promises (pp. 248–51). Thus, Toussaint preserves sharply the discontinuity between Israel and the church with a resonant emphasis on the *sudden* and future coming of the kingdom for national Israel.

On the other hand, Burns's distinction is less comprehensive. While supporting a dispensational Israel/church distinction, Burns presents a more moderate position that recognizes both discontinuity and continuity in Israel/church and Old/New Testament relationships (pp. 277–99). Like Toussaint, Burns does not believe that the church supersedes national Israel's distinctive call and promises and detects in Scripture a coequality that presently exists between Jew and Gentile whereby covenantal promises have been extended to the church. This coequality comes as a result of an "already-not yet" fulfillment of the promissory covenants to Israel. Thus, while arguing that Israel has a distinctive past, ecclesial present, and promised future, Burns recognizes the coequality in Christ's church whereby all of God's saints now participate in the covenantal promises of the Old Testament initially fulfilled in the predictions and accomplishments of the Messiah's first advent. These promises also serve as the basis for further fulfillment at the Messiah's second advent.

Despite the agreement between Toussaint and Burns concerning the distinction between Israel and the church, the relationship of the church with the Davidic kingdom and the present rule of Christ are issues that tomorrow's dispensationalists will continue to discuss. Although dispensationalists are confident in a future millennial period in human history when God will establish His kingdom with national Israel, does any form of that kingdom exist today? Or, do various forms of "the kingdom" exist? The question involves at least two issues: (1) the understanding of *mystery,* and (2) the relationship between Jew and Gentile in the kingdom.

First, how is *mystery* to be understood? Does the concept of *mystery* refer to the church, totally separated from the promised kingdom (Toussaint, McClain)? Does *mystery* refer to a "spiritual kingdom" for today that is distinct from the future earthly kingdom yet to come (as Johnson, Walvoord, Pentecost, and Ryrie nuance in a variety of ways)? Or does *mystery* speak of an initial form of the Davidic kingdom inaugurated during Christ's first advent (Bock, Burns, Blaising, and Saucy)? Do connections exist between the Old and New Testaments that help in our understanding of *mystery*? If not, how does one interpret Paul's linking of *mystery* with the "prophetic writing" in Romans 16:26? What are they, if not the Hebrew Scriptures? If connections do exist, does *mystery* speak of an initial form of the promised kingdom inaugurated during Christ's first advent with a future consummation of the kingdom yet to come when Christ returns to fulfill God's promises to national Israel? This brings us to the second issue.

Whatever the conclusions about *mystery*, tomorrow's dispensationalists will also need to ask what the relationship is between Jew and Gentile with respect to promise today. What will be the relationship between Jew and Gentile in the kingdom to come? What do Jews and Gentiles actually share in the church now and in the millennium? What exactly are the distinctions between the Jew and Gentile in the church and in the kingdom to come? Are there any distinctions? Ultimately, tomorrow's dispensationalists will need to discuss whether believers (Jews and Gentiles) share directly (Bock and Burns) or indirectly (Johnson and Toussaint) in the Old Testament promises of God. If Jews and Gentiles are equal in Christ as Ephesians 2:11–3:13 argues, then how does that impact the Jew and Gentile relationship now and in the millennium to come?

In all of this what is being discussed is how best to synthesize what the Old Testament affirms alongside what the New Testament declares. Ultimately, the debate is about the degree of continuity in the Bible placed next to an acknowledged distinction that all dispensationalists have between Israel and the church.

Conclusion

As we enter the twenty-first century, those who study Scripture will continue to reflect upon our dispensational tradition because the authority of what the text says supersedes our theological system. Paramount to our future textual studies is the need for open and frank communication. Openness uncovers the strengths and weaknesses of conclusions being drawn. Thus, frank but congenial discussions about such issues are paramount for all dispensationalists, both leaders and students, because such discussions reflect an ultimate respect for the text of Scripture.

All of the contributors in this work believe that our dispensational tradition—a tradition that stresses the uniqueness of the church and confidence that a future exists for national Israel—is derived from the Bible. We continue to study Scripture in the hope that our dialogue with one another about the Bible will help us all appreciate the message of the text with more clarity and sensitivity, especially as it relates to the depth of God's promises. As a result, this book is not the end but the beginning of future examinations and systematization of dispensational theology. Thus, I conclude this chapter with a bibliography.

Although not exhaustive, the following bibliography (page 319) is provided for those who wish to study further dispensational history, hermeneutics, the covenants, and Israel and the church. While the basis for the bibliography was Gerry Breshears's "Dispensational Bibliography: 1965–1991," other sources have been compiled from the various articles in this book, the American Theological Library Association (ATLA), and the Religious and Theological Abstracts (RATA). I trust that tomorrow's dispensationalists will (1) be as driven by and committed to interpreting the biblical text as dispensationalists have demonstrated throughout our history as they (2) recognize that infallibility is what the text—not its interpreters—possesses.

Chapter Notes

1. Charles C. Ryrie, *Dispensationalism Today* (Chicago: Moody, 1965), 11; and idem, *Dispensationalism* (Chicago: Moody, 1995), 11.
2. Darrell L. Bock, "Why I am a dispensationalist with a Small 'd,'" *JETS* 41, no. 3 (September 1998): 383–96.
3. Clarence E. Mason, *Prophetic Problem with Alternate Solutions* (Chicago: Moody, 1973), 177–78.
4. Ibid.
5. Whatever the differences that exist among today's dispensationalists, the one area of uniform agreement is the distinction between Israel and the church.
6. Charles Caldwell Ryrie, *Dispensationalism* (Chicago, Moody, 1995), 39; originally stated in *Dispensationalism Today* (Chicago, Moody, 1965), 45.

7. Bock refutes the charges about being Laddian and an amillennialist in chapter two. See also this chapter, note 2 above. In that *JETS* article Bock discusses the Laddian charge in detail.

8. Craig A. Blaising and Darrell L. Bock, "Dispensationalism, Israel, and the Church: Assessment and Dialogue," in *Progressive Dispensationalism,* eds. C. A. Blaising and D. L. Bock (Wheaton: Victor Books, 1993), 380. Reiterations of the definitions are also stated by Bock in "Charting Dispensationalism: A Group of Progressive Scholars Is Mapping Out a Dispensational Theology for a New Era," *ChrTo* 38 (12 September 1994): 26–29.

9. Toussaint's position concerning the church age as a "parenthesis" closely parallels Alva J. McClain's position.

Select Bibliography

Bailey, Mark L. "Dispensational Definitions of the Kingdom." In *Integrity of Heart, Skillfulness of Hands: Biblical Leadership Studies in Honor of Donald K. Campbell.* Ed. C. H. Dyer and R. B. Zuck, 201–21. Grand Rapids: Baker, 1994.

Blaising, C. A. "Changing Patterns in American Dispensational Theology." *Wesleyan Theological Journal* 29 (spring–fall 1994): 149–64.

——. "Contemporary Dispensationalism." *Southwestern Journal of Theology* 36 (spring 1994): 5–13.

——. "Developing Dispensationalism." *BSac* 145 (1988): 133–40, 254–80.

——. "Dispensationalism at the End of the Twentieth Century." U.p. ETS of AAR paper, 19 November 1990.

——. "Dispensationalism: The Search for Definition." In *Dispensationalism, Israel, and the Church.* Ed. C. A. Blaising and D. L. Bock, 13–34. Grand Rapids: Zondervan, 1992.

——. "The Extent and Varieties of Dispensationalism." In *Progressive Dispensationalism.* Ed. C. A. Blaising and D. L. Bock, 9–56. Wheaton, Ill.: Victor Books, 1993.

——. *Progressive Dispensationalism: An Up-to-Date Handbook of Contemporary Dispensational Thought.* Wheaton, Ill.: Bridgepoint Books, 1993.

Blaising, C. A. and D. L. Bock. "Dispensationalism, Israel and the Church: Assessment and Dialogue." In *Dispensationalism, Israel, and the Church.* Ed. C. A. Blaising and D. L. Bock, 377–94. Grand Rapids: Zondervan, 1992.

Bock, Darrell L. "Charting Dispensationalism: A Group of Progressive Scholars Is Mapping Out a Dispensational Theology for a New Era." *Christianity Today* 38 (12 September 1994): 26–29.

———. "Why I am a dispensatinalist with a Small 'd.'" *JETS* 41, no. 3 (September 1998): 383–96.

Bowers, R. H., Jr. "Dispensational Motifs in the Writings of Erich Sauer." *BSac* 148 (1991): 259–73.

Bowman, J. W. "Bible and Modern Religions, Pt. 2, Dispensationalism." *Interpretation* 10 (April 1956): 170–87.

Chafer, Lewis Sperry. "Dispensationalism," *BSac* 93 (October–December 1936): 390–449.

Couch, M., ed. *Dictionary of Premillennial Theology: A Practical Guide to the People, Viewpoints, and History of Prophetic Studies*. Grand Rapids: Kregel, 1996.

Crutchfield, L. V. "The Doctrine of Ages and Dispensations as Found in the Published Works of John Nelson Darby." Ph.D. dissertation, Drew University, 1985.

———. *The Origins of Dispensationalism: The Darby Factor*. New York: University Press of America, 1985.

———. "Rudiments of Dispensationalism in the Anti-Nicene Period." *BSac* 144 (1987): 254–76, 377–99.

Darby, J. N. "The Dispensation of the Kingdom of Heaven." In *The Collected Writings of J. N. Darby*. Ed. William Kelly, 34 vols. Reprint, Sunbury, Pa.: Believer's Bookshelf, 1972.

Dollar, G. W. "Early American Dispensationalist: The Rev. F. L. Chapell." *BSac* 120 (April–June 1963): 126–36.

———. *A History of Fundamentalism in America*. Greenville: Bob Jones University Press, 1973.

Ehlert, A. D. *A Bibliographic History of Dispensationalism*. Grand Rapids: Baker, 1965.

Hannah, John D. "The Early Years of Lewis Sperry Chafer." *BSac* 144 (January–March 1987): 3–23.

Houghton, G. G. "Lewis Sperry Chafer, 1871–1952." *BSac* 128 (October–December. 1971): 291–9.

Kaiser, W. C., Jr. "The Promised Land: A Biblical-Historical View." *BSac* 138 (1981): 302–16.

———. "The Promise to David in Psalm 16 and Its Application in Acts 2:25–33 and 13:32–27." *Journal of the Evangelical Theological Society* 22 (1980): 219–29.

Larkin, Clarence. *Dispensational Truth*. Philadelphia: Rev. Clarence Larkin Est., 1918.

MacLeod, D. J. "Walter Scott, a Link in Dispensationalism Between Darby and Scofield? [tables]" *BSac* 153 (April–June 1996): 155–78.

McCune, R. "An Investigation and Criticism of 'Historical' Premillennialism from the Viewpoint of Dispensationalism." Th.D. dissertation, Grace Theological Seminary, 1972 (TREN, #009–0169).

Miller, W. C. "The New Apocalypticism [History of Dispensationalist Thought.]" In *The Second Coming: A Wesleyan Approach to the Doctrine of Last Things*. Ed. H. Ray Dunning. Kansas City: Beacon Hill Press, 1995, 221–45.

Poythress, V. *Understanding Dispensationalists*. Grand Rapids: Zondervan, 1987.

Radmacher, E. D. *Understanding Contemporary Dispensationalism*. Portland: Western Conservative Baptist Seminary, 1972.

Rosscup, J. E. "Crucial Objections to Dispensationalism." Th.M. thesis, Dallas Theological Seminary, 1961.

Ryrie, C. C. *Dispensationalism Today*. Chicago: Moody, 1965.

———. *Dispensationalism*. Chicago: Moody, 1995.

———. "Update on Dispensationalism." In *Issues in Dispensationalism*. Ed. W. R. Willis and J. R. Master. Chicago: Moody, 1994, 15–28.

Saucy, R. L. *The Case for Progressive Dispensationalism*. Grand Rapids: Zondervan, 1993.

———. "Contemporary Dispensational Thought." *TSF Bulletin* (March–April 1984): 10–11.

———. "The Crucial Issue Between Dispensational and Nondispensational Systems." *Criswell Theological Review* 1 (fall 1986): 149–65.

———. "Response to *Understanding Dispensationalists*." *Grace Theological Journal* 10 (1989): 139–45. Vern Poythress, "Response," 157–9.

Spencer, S. R. "Reformed Theology, Covenant Theology, and Dispensationalism." In *Integrity of Heart, Skillfulness of Hands: Biblical Leadership Studies in Honor of Donald K. Campbell*. Ed. C. H. Dyer and R. B. Zuck. Grand Rapids: Baker, 1994, 238–54.

Stallard, M. "Emile Guers: An Early Darbyite Response to Irvingism and a Precursor to Charles Ryrie." *The Conservative Theological Journal* 1, no. 1 (April 1997): 31–46.

Hermeneutics

Barker, K. L. "The Scope and Center of Old and New Testament Theology and Hope." In *Dispensationalism, Israel, and the Church*. Ed. C. A. Blaising and D. L. Bock. Grand Rapids: Zondervan, 1984, 293–330.

Bateman, H. W. *Early Jewish Hermeneutics and Hebrews 1:5–13*. New York: Peter Lang Publishing, 1997.

———. "Psalm 45:6–7 and Hebrews 1:8–9." U.p. ETS plenary paper presented at the Meeting of the Midwest Regional Evangelical Theological Society, February 1999.

———. "Psalm 110:1 and the New Testament." *BSac* 149 (October–December 1992): 438–53.

———. "Jewish and Apostolic Hermeneutics: How the Old Testament Is Used in Hebrews 1:5–13." Ph.D. dissertation, Dallas Theological Seminary, 1993.

Battle, J. R., Jr. "Paul's Use of the Old Testament in Romans 9:25–26." *Grace Theological Journal* 2, no. 1 (1981): 115–29.

Bock, D. L. "Interpreting the Bible—How Texts Speak to Us." In *Progressive Dispensationalism*. Ed. C. A. Blaising and D. L. Bock, 76–105. Wheaton: Victor Books, 1993.

———. "The Son of David and the Saints' Task: The Hermeneutics of Initial Fulfillment." *BSac* 150 (1993): 458–78.

———. "Evangelicals and the Use of the Old Testament in the New: Parts 1 and 2," *BSac* 142 (1985): 219–20; 306–19.

Book, M. "James' Use of Amos 9:11–12 in Acts 15:13–18." Th.M. thesis, Grace Theological Seminary, 1981 (TREN, #009–0249).

Chafer, Rollin. "The Science of Biblical Hermeneutics." In *BSac*. Dallas: Dallas Theological Seminary, 1939.

———. "A Syllabus of Studies in Hermeneutics." *BSac* 91 (October–December 1934): 457–62.

———. "A Syllabus of Studies in Hermeneutics, Second Installment." *BSac* 93 (January–March, 1936): 110–18.

———. "A Syllabus of Studies in Hermeneutics, II. Historical Sketch, Continued." *BSac* 93 (April–June, 1936): 201–17.

———. "A Syllabus of Studies in Hermeneutics, III. Some Axioms of General Hermeneutics." *BSac* 93 (July–September, 1936): 331–35.

———. "A Syllabus of Studies in Hermeneutics, Fourth Installment." *BSac* 94 (January–March, 1937): 72–94.

———. "A Syllabus of Studies in Hermeneutics, Fourth Installment, Continued." *BSac* 94 (April–June, 1937): 207–17.

———. "A Syllabus of Studies in Hermeneutics, Fifth Installment." *BSac* 94 (October–December, 1937): 470–78.

———. "A Syllabus of Studies in Hermeneutics, Seventh and Concluding Installment." *BSac* 95 (January–March, 1938): 91–101.

Cropper, C. "The Use of Amos 9:11,12 in Acts 15:13–18." Th.M. thesis, Capital Seminary, 1985 (TREN, #014–0036).

———. "Evangelicals and the Use of the Old Testament in New." *BSac* 142 (1985): 209–21, 306–19.

———. "The Son of David and the Saints' Task: The Hermeneutics of Initial Fulfillment." *BSac* 150 (October–December, 1993): 440–57.

Dyer, C. H. "Biblical Meaning of 'Fulfillment.'" In *Issues in Dispensationalism*. Ed. W. R. Willis and J. R. Master. Chicago: Moody, 1994, 51–74.

Edgar, T. R. "An Exegesis of Rapture Passages." In *Issues in Dispensationalism*. Ed. W. R. Willis and J. R. Master. Chicago: Moody, 1994, 203–24.

Feinberg, P. D. "Dispensational Theology and the Rapture." In *Issues in Dispensationalism*. Ed. W. R. Willis and J. R. Master. Chicago: Moody, 1994, 225–47.

Fuller, D. P. "The Hermeneutics of Dispensationalism." Th.M. dissertation, Northern Baptist Theological Seminary, 1957.

Gerstner, J. H. *Wrongly Dividing the Word of Truth: A Critique of Dispensationalism*. Brentwood, Tenn.: Wolgemuth & Hyatt, 1991.

Glenny, W. E. "Dispensational Hermeneutics: A Proposal." U.p. ETS paper presented at the Dispensational Study Group, November 1998.

———. "Typology: A Summary of the Present Evangelical Discussion." *Journal of the Evangelical Theological Society* 40 (December 1997): 627–38.

Gosnell, P. "Typology Reappraised and Redefined." Th.M. thesis, Western Conservative Baptist Seminary, 1983 (TREN, #002–0257).

Hodges, Z. C. "A Dispensational Understanding of Acts 2." In *Issues in Dispensationalism*. Ed. W. R. Willis and J. R. Master, 167–82. Chicago: Moody, 1994.

Howard, T. "The Use of Hosea 11:1 in Matthew 2:15." Th.M. thesis, Dallas Theological Seminary, 1984 (TREN, #001–0241).

Ice, T. D. "Dispensational Hermeneutics." In *Issues in Dispensationalism*. Ed. W. R. Willis and J. R. Master. Chicago: Moody, 1994, 29–50.

Jeremiah, D. "The Principle of Double Fulfillment in Interpreting Prophecy." *Grace Theological Journal* 13:2 (1972): 13–29.

Johnson, E. E. "Author's Intention and Biblical Interpretation." In *Hermeneutics, Inerrancy, and the Bible: [papers from ICBI Summit II]*. Ed. E. D. Radmacher and R. D. Preus (Grand Rapids: Zondervan, 1984), 409–29.

———. "Dual Authorship and the Single Intended Meaning of Scripture." *BSac* 143 (1986): 218–27.

———. *Expository Hermeneutics: An Introduction*. Grand Rapids: Zondervan, 1990.

———. "Hermeneutics and Dispensationalism." In *Walvoord: A Tribute*. Ed. Donald K. Campbell. Chicago: Moody, 1982, 239–56.

———. "Hermeneutical Principles and the Interpretation of Psalm 110." *BSac* 149 (October–December 1992): 428–37.

———. "Prophetic Fulfillment: The Already and Not Yet." In *Issues in Dispensationalism*. Ed. W. R. Willis and J. R. Master. Chicago: Moody, 1994, 183–202.

———. "What I Mean by Historical-Grammatical Interpretation and How That Differs from Spiritual Interpretation." *Grace Theological Journal* (fall 1990): 157–69. Reply, T. Longman III: 153–5.

Kaiser, W., Jr. *The Uses of the Old Testament in the New*. Chicago: Moody, 1985.

Longman, T. "What I Mean by Historical-Grammatical Interpretation— Why I Am Not a Literalist." *Grace Theological Journal* 11 (fall 1990): 137–52.

Mattison, M. M. "A Revised Hermeneutic of Premillennialism." *Journal from the Radical Reformation* 1:2 (1992): 24–9.

Oss, D. "The Hermeneutics of Dispensationalism within the Pentecostal Tradition." U.p. ETS paper, 21 November 1991.

Sheppard, G. "Pentecostals and the Hermeneutics of Dispensationalism: The Anatomy of an Uneasy Relationship." *Pneuma* 6, no. 2 (1984): 5–33.

Smith, R. "The Kingdom of God in Luke with Special Reference to Luke 17:20,21." M.A. thesis, Trinity Evangelical Divinity School, 1983 (TREN, #006–0014).

Stallard, M. "Literal Interpretation, Theological Method, and the Essence of Dispensationalism." *The Journal of Ministry and Theology* 1, no. 1 (spring 1997): 5–36.

Tan, Paul Lee. *The Interpretation of Prophecy*. Winona Lake: BMH Books, 1974.

Taylor, H. "The Continuity of the People of God in Old and New Testaments." *Scottish Bulletin of Evangelical Theology* 3 (autumn 1985): 13–26.

Thomas, R. L. "A Critique of Dispensational Hermeneutics." In *Where the Trumpet Sounds,* Ed. Thomas Ice and Timothy Demy, 413–25. Eugene, Ore.: Harvest House, 1995.

———. "The Hermeneutics of Progressive Dispensationalism." *Master's Seminary Journal* 6 (spring 1995): 79–95.

Turner, D. "The Continuity of Scripture and Eschatology: Key Hermeneutical Issues." *Grace Theological Journal* 6 (1985): 275–87.

VanGemeren, W. A. "Israel as the Hermeneutical Crux in the Interpretation of Prophecy." *Westminster Journal of Theology* 45 (1983): 132–44, 146; (1984): 254–97.

Covenants

Blaising, C. A. "The Fulfillment of the Biblical Covenants Through Jesus Christ." In *Progressive Dispensationalism.* Ed. C. A. Blaising and D. L. Bock. Wheaton: Victor Books, 1993, 179–211.

———. "The Structure of the Biblical Covenants: The Covenants Prior to Christ." In *Progressive Dispensationalism.* Ed. C. A. Blaising and D. L. Bock. Wheaton, Ill.: Victor Books, 1993, 128–78.

Bock, D. L. "Current Messianic Activity and Old Testament Davidic Promise: Dispensationalism, Hermeneutics, and New Testament Fulfillment." *Trinity Journal* 15 (spring 1994): 55–87.

———. "The Reign of the Lord Christ." In *Dispensationalism, Israel, and the Church.* Ed. C. A. Blaising and D. L. Bock. Grand Rapids: Zondervan, 1984, 37–67.

Couch, Mal. "Progressive Dispensationalism: Is Christ Now on the Throne of David?, Part I." *The Conservative Theological Journal* 2 (1998): 32–46.

Decker, R. J. "The Church's Relationship to the New Covenant [tables: 2 pts.]" *BSac* 152 (July–September 1995): 290–305; and (October–December 1995): 431–56.

Dumbrell, William J. *Covenant and Creation: A Theology of Old Testament Covenants.* Nashville: Nelson, 1984 (Reformed).

House, H. Wayne, and Thomas Ice. *Dominion Theology: Blessing or Curse?* Portland: Multnomah, 1988.

Kaiser, W. C., Jr. "Davidic Promise and the Inclusion of the Gentiles (Amos 9:9–15 and Acts 15:13–18): A Test Passage for Theological Systems." *Journal of Evangelical Theological Society* 20 (1977): 91–111.

Master, J. R. "The New Covenant." In *Issues in Dispensationalism.* Ed. W. R. Willis and J. R. Master, 93–112. Chicago: Moody, 1994.

———. "Where Are We Now? The Kingdom, the New Covenant, and the Church." U.p. ETS paper, 19 November 1998.

McComiskey, Thomas. *The Covenants of Promise: A Theology of the Old Testament Covenants*. Grand Rapids: Baker, 1985.

McGahey, John F. "An Exposition of the New Covenant." Th.D. dissertation, Dallas Theological Seminary, 1957.

Nichols, S. J. "The Dispensational View of the Davidic Kingdom: A Response to Progressive Dispensationalism." *Master's Seminary Journal* 7 (fall 1996): 213–39.

Peer, P. "The Church and the New Covenant of Jeremiah 31:31–34." Th.M. thesis, Grace Theological Seminary, 1982 (TREN, #009–0273).

Pentecost, J. Dwight. "The Biblical Covenants and the Birth Narratives." In *Walvoord: A Tribute*. Ed. Donald K. Campbell. Chicago: Moody, 1982, 257–70.

Strauss, Mark. *The Davidic Messiah in Luke–Acts: The Promise and Its Fulfillment in Luke-Acts*. JSNTSup 110 (Sheffield: Sheffield Academic Press, 1995).

Thorsell, Paul R. "The Spirit in the Present Age: Preliminary Fulfillment of the Predicted New Covenant According to Paul." *JETS* 41 (1998): 397–413.

Townsend, Jeffery L. "Fulfillment of the Land Promise in the Old Testament." *BSac* 142 (1985): 320–37.

Walton, John H. *Covenant: God's Purpose, God's Plan*. Grand Rapids: Zondervan, 1994.

Walvoord, John F. "The New Covenant." In *Integrity of Heart, Skillfulness of Hands: Biblical and Leadership Studies in Honor of Donald K. Campbell*. Ed. C. H. Dyer and R. B. Zuck, 186–200. Grand Rapids: Baker, 1994.

——. "The New Covenant with Israel," *BSac* 110 (1953), 193–205.

——. Ware, B. A. "The New Covenant and the People(s) of God." In *Dispensationalism, Israel, and the Church*. Ed. C. A. Blaising and D. L. Bock, 68–97. Grand Rapids: Zondervan, 1984.

Israel and the Church

Bock, Darrell L. *Three Views of the End of History and Beyond*. Grand Rapids: Zondervan, 1999.

Brashear, R. "Cornerstone, Stumblingstone: Christian Problems in Viewing Israel." *Union Seminary Quarterly Review* 38, no. 2 (1983): 203–24.

Burns, J. L. "The Future of Ethnic Israel in Romans 11." In *Dispensationalism, Israel, and the Church*. Ed. C. A. Blaising and D. L. Bock, 188–229. Grand Rapids: Zondervan, 1984.

Campbell, Donald K. "The Church in God's Prophetic Program." In *Essays in Honor of J. Dwight Pentecost*. Ed. Stanley D. Toussaint and Charles H. Dyer, 149–61. Chicago: Moody, 1986.

Dean, R. L. "Is There a Special Future of Ethnic Israel?" *Biblical Perspectives* 1, no. 6 (November 1988): 1–6.

Dekar, P. "Does the State of Israel Have Theological Significance?" *Conrad Grebel Review* 2, no. 1 (1984): 31–46.

Fruchtenbaum, A. "Israel and the Church." In *Issues in Dispensationalism*. Ed. W. R. Willis and J. R. Master, 113–32. Chicago: Moody, 1994.

Gade, R. M. "Is God through with the Jews?" *Grace Journal* 11, no. 2 (1970): 21–33.

Glenny, W. E. "The Israelite Imagery of 1 Peter 2." In *Dispensationalism, Israel, and the Church*. Ed. C. A. Blaising and D. L. Bock, 156–87. Grand Rapids: Zondervan, 1984.

———. "The 'People of God' in Romans 9:25–26." *BSac* 152 (January–March 1995): 42–59.

Greenburg, G. "Fundamentalists, Israel, and Theological Openness." *Christian-Jew Relations* 19, no. 3 (1986): 27–33.

Hoch, C. B., Jr. "The New Man of Ephesians 2." In *Dispensationalism, Israel, and the Church*. Ed. C. A. Blaising and D. L. Bock, 98–126. Grand Rapids: Zondervan, 1984.

———. "The Significance of the Syn-Compounds for Jew-Gentile Relations in the Body of Christ." *Journal of Evangelical Theological Society* 25 (1982): 175–83.

Johnson, S. L. "Paul and 'The Israel of God': An Exegetical and Eschatological Case-Study." In *Essays in Honor of J. Dwight Pentecost*. Ed. Stanley D. Toussaint and Charles H. Dyer, 181–96. Chicago: Moody, 1986.

Johnston, R. "The Centrality of the Jewish Temple in the Affairs of God, Israel, and the Nations—Part I—Historical Temples." *The Conservative Theological Journal* 1, no. 1 (April 1997): 61–84.

———. "Does Scripture Teach Millennialism: An Exegetical-Expositional Study of the Passages of Scripture Which Are Used to Support the Millennial Doctrine." S.T.M. thesis, Wisconsin Lutheran Seminary, 1983 (TREN, #041–0002).

Penney, R. L. "Why the Church Is Not Referenced in the Olivet Discourse." *The Conservative Theological Journal* 1:1 (April 1997): 47–60.

Ryrie, C. C. "Mystery in Ephesians 3." *BSac* 123 (1966): 24–31.

Saucy, R. L. *The Church in God's Program*. Chicago: Moody, 1972.

———. "The Church as the Mystery of God." In *Dispensationalism, Israel, and the Church*. Ed. C. A. Blaising and D. L. Bock, 127–55. Grand Rapids: Zondervan, 1984.

———. "Dispensationalism and the Salvation of the Kingdom." *TSF Bulletin* 7 (May–June 1984): 6–7.

———. "The Locus of the Church." *Criswell Theological Review* 1 (spring 1987): 387–99.

———. "The Presence of the Kingdom in the Life of the Church." *BSac* 145 (1988): 33–46.

———. "A Rationale for the Future of Israel." *Journal of the Evangelical Theological Society* 28 (1985): 433–42.

Thomas, R. L. "The Mission of Israel and of the Messiah in the Plan of God." *The Master's Seminary Journal* 8 (fall 1997): 191–210.

Toussaint, S. D. "The Church and Israel." *Conservative Theological Journal* 2 (December 1998): 350–74.

———. "The Contingency of the Coming of the Kingdom. In *Integrity of Heart, Skillfulness of Hands*. Ed. C. H. Dyer and R. B. Zuck, 222–237. Grand Rapids: Baker, 1994.

Walvoord, J. "Does the Church Fulfill Israel's Program?" *BSac* 137 (1980): 17–31, 118–24, 212–22.

Ware, B. A. "Is the Church in View in Matthew 24–25?" *BSac* 138 (1981): 158–72.

Williams, M. "Where's the Church? The Church as the Unfinished Business of Dispensational Theology." *Grace Theological Journal* 10 (1989): 165–82.

Zuck, Roy B. "Periodical Reviews: 'The Church and Israel,'" Stanley Toussaint, *Conservative Theological Journal* 2 (December 1998): 350–74." *BSac* 156 (April–June, 1999): 233–34.

Scripture Index

Author Index

Subject Index

341

messianic
  hope 112, 115, 172, 217–18, 266,
    312, 314
  ideal 217–18
  kingdom 15, 29–31, 56, 76, 87–89,
    91, 112, 230–49, 313–15
midrash texts 41–42
millennium 93, 115, 223, 228–32,
  250–58, 264, 272–73, 289–91, 296,
  300
millennialism. *See by type.*
Moody Bible Institute 44
morning star 197
Mosaic law 93, 287
multiple meaning 91, 101, 105
mystery 81, 117, 214
  church as 249, 252, 285, 292,
  kingdom in 25, 29, 31, 144, 231,
    241, 272, 313–15
  parables, 237

New Scofield Reference Bible. *See*
  Scofield Reference Bible.
New Testament Priority School 38–
  39, 58
Niagara Bible and Prophecy Confer-
  ence 43–44
normative dispensationalism 48
Northfield Conferences 46

Palestinian covenant 211
Parousia 245, 253, 281
peace, hymn of 197
pesher texts 41–42
Philadelphia College of Bible 34, 44
premillennialism 56
  covenant in 110, 115
  developments in 21–43, 44, 46,
    52–53
  historic, 75, 155, 164, 296–97,
    309–10
principial-traditional approach 86–
  89, 101–2
  as label 310
progressive dispensationalism 15, 23,
  48, 109, 117–18, 203, 241–43, 249,
  259, 290, 307–16

covenants in 30, 34, 169–223
  hermeneutics of 56, 59, 86, 89, 94,
    98, 101, 114, 147, 165, 171, 230–
    31, 273
  Israel in, 173
  kingdom in 135–36, 230–31
  practical theology and 116
promise, covenants of. *See* covenants,
  promissory.
promise, land of 83, 138, 141, 176–77,
  182, 184, 211, 214–15. *See also*
  covenants, promissory.
prophecy
  First Advent 149–50, 154–55,
    255–56
  fulfillment of 118, 204, 216, 322
  history of 21–22, 25, 27–34
  Holy Spirit and 148, 151
  problems of 49, 57, 87–88, 300–301
  Second Advent 21, 204, 207, 216–
    17, 231

reign
  God's 53, 218
  millennial 22–23, 25, 155, 204,
    239, 248, 255, 313
  on David's throne 87–88, 103–4,
    127–28, 143, 183, 202, 207, 222,
    230, 244–45
remnant 297–98, 300
revelation, progressive 40–41, 66–67,
  74–76, 96–98, 122–24
revised dispensationalism 23, 27, 30,
  34, 70, 82–83, 118, 230–31, 309
royal priesthood 131, 159, 160, 247,
  286–87, 303

sacrifice of Christ 200
salvation, image of 201–2
Scofield Reference Bible 21–22, 24–
  34, 42, 44, 50–51, 54, 297
Scripture
  authority of 15, 26
  meaning of 59, 322
Second Advent 255
seed 81
  of Abraham 68–69, 72–73, 77–79,